Barangay

Barangay

Sixteenth-Century
Philippine Culture and Society

William Henry Scott

 ATENEO DE MANILA UNIVERSITY PRESS

ATENEO DE MANILA UNIVERSITY PRESS
Bellarmine Hall, Katipunan Avenue
Loyola Heights, Quezon City
P.O. Box 154, 1099 Manila, Philippines
Tel.: (632) 426–59–84 / Fax: (632) 426–59–09
E-mail: unipress@admu.edu.ph
Website: www.ateneopress.com

Cover design by Fidel Rillo

Earlier versions of certain chapters have been published in Philippine journals: chapter 2 in *Philippine Quarterly of Culture and Society* (Scott 1990a); chapter 4 in *Philippiniana Sacra* (Scott 1990b); and part of chapter 5, in *Kinaadman* (Scott 1992b).

The illustrations from the Boxer Codex reproduced in this book are taken from the article on the Codex by Carlos Quirino and Mauro Garcia in the *Philippine Journal of Science* 87 (1958): 325–453. For the cover illustration taken from the Boxer Codex, a color slide was provided by the Lilly Library of the University of Indiana, which gave permission for its reproduction.

National Library Cataloging-in-Publication Data

Recommended entry:

Scott, William Henry.
    Barangay : sixteenth-century
Philippine culture and society /
by William Henry Scott. – Quezon City
ADMU Press, c1994. – 1 v

    1. Ethnology – Philippines.
I. Title.

GN308.3P5 305.8009'599 1994 P944000012
ISBN 971–550–135–4 (pbk.)

Contents

PART 1 *The Visayas*

PART 2 *Mindanao and Luzon*

Foreword

William Henry Scott (1921-1993), distinguished historian and eminent scholar, puts us in considerable debt with the publication of *Barangay: Sixteenth-Century Philippine Culture and Society*. By bringing to the fore the native inhabitants of the archipelago who in colonial documents and sadly even in historical writing are relegated to the background, Scott fills an egregious lack. The book is an ethnography of sixteenth-century Philippine communities that answers the question: What did the Spaniards actually say about the Filipino people when they first met them?

Scott derived his information to answer the question from an extensive bibliographic base. A major cluster of his sources is the historical documents published in five collections. The first three are the *colecciones de documentos inéditos* (collections of unpublished documents, cited in this volume as CDIA, CDIU, and CVD), published by the Spanish government beginning in 1825 with Martín Fernández Navarrete's five volumes and totaling sixty volumes by 1932. The fourth collection is Blair and Robertson's *The Philippine Islands, 1493–1898* (BR), fifty-five volumes of translations into English. The fifth collection is the ongoing *Historia de la Provincia Agustiniana del Smo. Nombre de Jesús de Filipinas* (HPAF) by Isacio Rodríguez with volume 20 being the most recent. In addition to these published collections is a wide array of such other published and unpublished sources as chronicles, travel accounts, navigational logs, letters. sermon books, catechisms, reports, and dictionaries.

Dictionaries figure importantly in this book. In the sixteenth century, there were about a million and a half natives and only a small number of missionaries. Aware of the acute imbalance between their number and that of the native population and the enormous challenge in teaching the natives the Spanish language, the Spanish missionaries decided to communicate in the local languages. They calculated that it was more efficient for them to learn the local languages than to teach Spanish to the entire native population. A consequence of the decision was serious efforts toward the production of tools in aid of teaching missionaries the local languages. Among these tools were Spanish-vernacular, vernacular-Spanish dictionaries. Some comprising more than seven hundred printed pages, these dictionaries not only list hundreds of local words but also provide in the glosses samples of actual usage of the words. In a way not possible for most other sources, these dictionaries open for us a window to how things were perceived in local categories. The Sánchez Samareño dictionary gives the phases of the moon for every day of the month; the Lisboa Bikolano dictionary defines the parts of the backstrap loom; the Méntrida Hiligaynon dictionary contains the most extensive glossary of seafaring terms. And the San Buenaventura Tagalog dictionary includes ethnographic data found in none of the accounts—details of technology and industry, commercial contracts and interest rates, head taking and puberty rites, mortuary rituals and sexual mores.

This ethnography of sixteenth-century Philippines covers a wide geographical terrain. Due to the spread of available sources and the chronology of Spanish activities in the early years of colonization, the chapters on the Visayan islands comprise the most substantial portion of the book. Luzon and Mindanao, however, also get proportionate attention: the second half of the book provides a survey of areas outside of the Visayas— the island of Mindanao, the Cagayan Valley, the Bikol peninsula, and the territory of Tagalog, Pampanga, Pangasinan communities. Scott had notes for a chapter on the Ilocos, but his passing away prevented its completion.

An impressive range of topics is treated in the book. The section on the Visayas, for instance, discusses physical appearance, food and farming, trades and commerce, religion, literature and entertainment, natural science, social organization, and warfare. Even more impressive than the range of topics is the degree of detail in which the topics are explored. Under the heading of Visayan physical appearance, the book describes and analyzes decorative dentistry, skull moulding, penis pins, circumcision, ear-piercing, hair, clothing, jewelry, and tattooing. The treatment of each item goes as far as the documents allow. In the case of tattooing, for example, Scott examines various aspects of the custom such as who wore tattoos; how, when, and on which parts of the body they were applied; who actually applied them; what were their regional variations; what risks to health they posed. Most important of all, the author explains what tattoos meant in society.

If the information Scott gathered together in his book is representative of what the Spaniards said about the natives, it is clear that they said quite a lot — at least, quite a lot more than is normally supposed. A case can be made that the Spaniards carefully took note of details in the native world so as to destroy or transform native culture the more thoroughly. But prescinding from their motives, the Spaniards collected data that now allow us to attempt a description of the native world.

Spanish documentary sources were products of the colonial machinery. They were written by Spaniards, for Spanish purposes such as trading, evangelization, tribute-taking. But as he shows in *Cracks in the parchment curtain and other essays in Philippine history*, Scott had found a way of catching "fleeting glimpses of Filipinos and their reactions to Spanish domination . . . unintentional and merely incidental to the purpose of the documents." And particularly in this book, Scott took seriously all available texts in the local languages which, despite their Spanish provenance, are indigenous in the most basic sense. In them, the natives are the objects of study and of colonial intervention. Yet, they remain subjects as well, since it is they who in the first instance spoke the language the missionaries used. The documents conserve the native languaging of the native world.

Scott ventured to answer the question: What did the Spaniards actually say about the Filipino people when they first met them? Using a wide array of sources and a method conducive to gleaning information on native inhabitants, Scott lays out an answer to the question in a manner that reveals an intensely committed scholarship and an unfailing affection for his adopted people.

— JOSE M. CRUZ, S.J.

Introduction

    This book presents a sixteenth-century Philippine ethnography based on contemporaneous sources. It does not attempt to reconstruct that society by consideration of present Philippine societies, or of features believed to be common to all Austronesian peoples. Nor does it seek similarities with neighboring cultures in Southeast Asia, though the raw data presented should be of use to scholars who might wish to do so. Rather it seeks to answer the question: What did the Spaniards actually say about the Filipino people when they first met them? It is hoped that the answer to that question will permit Filipino readers today to pay a vicarious visit to the land of their ancestors four centuries ago.

    History texts in use in the Philippine school system generally include a chapter on pre-Hispanic society and culture derived from five main sources available in English in the monumental Blair and Robertson compendium of translations, *The Philippine Islands 1493–1898:* these are Antonio Pigafetta's account of the Magellan voyage, Miguel de Loarca's 1582 *Relación,* Juan Plasencia's 1589 treatises on custom law and religious practices, Pedro Chirino's 1604 *Relación,* and chapter 8 of Antonio de Morga's 1609 *Sucesos.* Unfortunately, they also make use of two twentieth-century forgeries attributed to sixteenth-century Diego Povedano and nineteenth-century José

María Pavón, and misrepresent Pedro A. Monteclaro's 1907 *Maragtas* as a pre-Hispanic document.[1]

To the authentic documents may be added four other eyewitness accounts of the Magellan voyage, and a dozen from the other early Spanish expeditions. The 1526 Loaysa expedition touched on the east coast of Mindanao, and Álvaro de Saavedra visited Sarangani Island three times in 1528. Four accounts, one of them running to a hundred pages, have survived from the Ruy López de Villalobos expedition, which spent eighteen months in Sarangani, Mindanao, Leyte, and Samar in 1542–1543, and circumnavigated both Mindanao and Samar. From the Miguel López de Legazpi 1565 expedition which established the Spanish colony, come a detailed sixteen-month journal, separate reports of local products and customs, and a ream of missionary and conquistador correspondence. And from the next century comes Francisco Alcina's unpublished four-volume *Historia de las islas e Indios de Bisayas,* which is invaluable both for its author's descriptions of material culture and his attempt to reconstruct pre-Hispanic Visayan society by interviewing the oldest residents.

Much information can also be gleaned through what I have called "cracks in the parchment curtain" in an earlier essay—"chinks, so to speak, through which fleeting glimpses of Filipinos and their reactions to Spanish dominion may be seen . . . unintentional and merely incidental to the purpose of the documents" (Scott 1982, 1). A peace pact between Magellan's survivors and a ruler in Palawan, for example, indicates that it was translated by a Spanish-speaking Makassarese slave seized from a royal Luzon vessel in Borneo. Court proceedings against backsliding Manila converts include a description of a Muslim burial, and notarized testimonies by Filipino chiefs reveal that few of them could sign their names. Tagalog sermons by friar missionaries mention deities otherwise unknown, refer to the number of days a slave is expected to work for his master, and inveigh against the vanity of tooth filing and eyebrow shaving.

But by far the richest sources of information on Filipino ethnography are the early seventeenth-century Spanish dictionaries of Philippine languages. By their very nature, dictionaries contain more information than any other sort of literature or documentation. Moreover, since those in the Spanish colony were compiled by missionaries for the use of other missionaries, their definitions may be incorrect but they would not be deliberately dissembling. The Sánchez Samareño dictionary gives the phases of the moon for every day of the month; the Lisboa Bikolano dictionary defines the parts of the backstrap loom; the Méntrida Hiligaynon dictionary contains the most extensive glossary of seafaring terms. And the San

Buenaventura Tagalog dictionary includes ethnographic data found in none of the accounts—details of technology and industry, commercial contracts and interest rates, head taking and puberty rites, jar burial and sexual mores.

Naturally, these sources must be used critically. Dictionary definitions are often tantalizingly brief, and the absence of a particular term may reflect the lexicographer's limitations rather than the nonexistence of the concept. Comments on Filipino ethics and morality are hopelessly skewed by Spanish ethnocentricity and the reactions of aliens caught in the grip of culture shock. On the other hand, missionary reports intended for European audiences are often distorted by the desire to prevent converts from appearing like naked savages. Reports to the king on products and industries suitable for colonial exploitation are obviously more reliable than those recounting Filipino belligerence and treachery which might excuse conquistador brutality. Information on native religion is especially problematic. Direct questions about God, creation, the Flood, the human soul, heaven and hell, regularly produced obliging answers contrary to actual cult practices. In this ethnography, therefore, all descriptions will be based on a synthesis of all the sources available; no data will be presented unless they accord with that synthesis. Moreover, with few exceptions, they will be derived from primary sources in their original languages, not secondary sources or translations.

Regrettably, these sources contain two significant lacunae—lack of statistics and failure to cover the whole archipelago. Vital statistics are completely wanting, as well as figures on production and distribution which would permit an estimate of Filipino living standards before the imposition of colonial burdens. Tagalog and Visayan culture can be reconstructed from documents and dictionaries, but there is little information on the peoples of northern Luzon, and none at all on the Mindanao and Sulu sultanates, which the Spaniards did not visit in the sixteenth century except for military attacks.

It should also be noted that the Philippines was neither isolated nor unchanged during the century. A Malaccan prince founded a new sultanate in Maguindanao, Brunei established commercial and political ties with Manila, and Filipinos themselves traveled as far as Burma and Timor as merchants or mercenaries. But the many Spanish and Chinese innovations of the last two decades of the century cannot be considered part of traditional Philippine culture, though they quickly became regarded as such. Camote and corn, for example, rice mills and draft animals, were all introduced during a single lifetime.

Among surviving sixteenth-century sources, there happen to be more voluminous data on Visayan culture than on the rest of the Philippines combined. The Spaniards were in the Visayas fifty years before they reached Luzon, and they recorded their observations with the enthusiasm of new discoveries. Loarca's *Relación* was written in Iloilo, and Alcina's *Historia* in Leyte and Samar. Mateo Sánchez's Visayan dictionary written in Dagami, Leyte, is the best of the early Spanish lexicons, and can be supplemented by the contemporary Panay dictionary of Alonso Méntrida. However, this documentary concentration may be seen as a fortuitous accident for our purposes. Visayan culture and languages are the most widely dispersed in the archipelago, and Leyte and Samar are the islands farthest removed from direct Asian contact. It is therefore possible to regard the civilization portrayed in these sources as a kind of basic Philippine society and culture.

This uneven distribution of data has suggested the plan of this book. Part 1 describes Visayan culture in eight chapters on physical appearance, food and farming, trades and commerce, religion, literature and entertainment, natural science, social organization, and warfare. Part 2 surveys the rest of the archipelago from south to north—Mindanao, Bikol, Tagalog, Pampanga, Pangasinan, Ilocos, Igorot, and Cagayan. With the exception of Tagalog society, these sections contain only brief notices due either to a paucity of data or because there is no need to repeat features already described at length in part 1. An afterword has been added to examine the survival of sixteenth-century minorities. And a bibliographic essay locates and describes the book's sources.

The Word "Barangay"

Barangay, or *balangay*, was one of the first native words the Spaniards learned in the Philippines. When Antonio Pigafetta, Magellan's Italian expeditionary ethnographer, went ashore to parley with the ruler of Limasawa, they sat together in a boat drawn up on shore which Pigafetta (1524b, 118) called a *balangai*. This word appears as either *balangay* or *barangay*, with the same meaning, in all the major languages of the Philippines, and the earliest Spanish dictionaries make it clear that it was pronounced "ba-la-ngay," not "ba-lang-gay." It is also worth noting that Pigafetta recorded the word both as *balangai* and as *balanghai*, which, of course, he would have pronounced the same since Italian had no *h*–sound. Unfortunately, this orthographic oddity gave birth in 1976, with the archaeological discovery of an ancient boat in Butuan, to a bastardized Philippine term, "balanghay," which has gained popular currency though no such word is known in any Philippine language.

When the Spaniards reached Luzon, they found this word for boat also being used for the smallest political unit of Tagalog society. Franciscan friar Juan de Plasencia (1589a, 23v) described it as follows:

> These [datus] were chiefs of but few people, as many as a hundred houses and even less than thirty; and this they call in Tagalog, barangay. And what was inferred from this name is that their being called this was because, since these are known from their language to be Malayos, when they came to this land, the head of barangay was taken for a datu, and even today it is still ascertained that one whole barangay was originally one family of parents and children, slaves and relatives.[2]

No doubt, the ancestors of the Tagalogs reached the archipelago in boats, but it is hardly likely that Tagalog communities could have maintained their discrete boatload identities across centuries and millennia. But the choice of the term, and the explanation for it, would have reinforced the perception of each community as historically distinct from all others, and legitimized its captain's claim to personal allegiance.

These two meanings of the word *barangay* call attention to two important characteristics of the sixteenth-century Philippines not characteristic of the twentieth—dependence on boats and highly localized government. "Barangay" is therefore not an inappropriate title for a book about Philippine society and culture in the sixteenth century.

With the exception of sparse populations inhabiting the interior mountain ranges, all sixteenth-century Filipinos lived on the seacoast or the banks of navigable lakes and streams. Their only means of transportation were boats: there is no evidence of wheeled vehicles or draft animals. Traders and raiders, friends and foes crossed from one side of a river to the other by boat, from island to island, and between distant ports on the same island. Communities were connected, not separated, by water: it was by water that they exchanged foodstuffs, manufactured wares, and foreign imports. The eventual clearing off of interior forests and the opening of new land to the plow and population expansion may be seen as an emancipation from the limitations of the older boat culture. But the new economy was dependent, and still is, on an overland road system periodically interrupted by the destruction of bridges across waterways that were once the arteries of Filipino culture, channels for the movement of people, goods, and ideas, not obstacles to it.

A Tagalog barangay was a group of people ruled over by one datu. It was to him they owed allegiance, not to a municipal, provincial, tribal, or national government, though datus often joined their barangays in common communities, reckoning precedence and making alliances among themselves. This was true even in the Muslim sultanates in the south: the sultan ruled his datus but they in turn ruled their own communities. After Manila became the seat of colonial government, the word spread with its Tagalog meaning to other parts of the archipelago where it meant a boat in the local languages.

The Spaniards retained both the term and the institution as a convenient means of collecting tribute through barangay heads. It should be noted, however, that the word continued to mean the people, not the place. Up to the end of the Spanish regime, baptismal registers identified nonelite parents not by their place of residence but as belonging to the barangay of Don So-and-so, some member of the local gentry. Of course, members of the same barangay usually lived in the same place, but not necessarily: they sometimes res ifferent barrios and occasioned jurisdictional disputes between tribute collectors. Recently the term has been revived by the Philippine government to replace the colonial term *barrio,* despite the irony of the native word's original meaning—a political unit loyal to a local boss.

The Word "Filipino"

When Spanish expeditionary commander Ruy López de Villalobos reached the Philippines in 1542, he named the islands of Leyte and Samar *Filipinas* after the young prince who would become King Philip II, from which the later colony would be called *Las Islas Filipinas.* The Spaniards called the natives of the archipelago *indios,* compounding Christopher Columbus's well-known error of thinking he had reached the Orient—that is, the Indies—in the Caribbean. But when it was necessary to distinguish the indios of the Philippines from those of the Americas, they were called Filipinos. So Pedro Chirino's 1604 *Relación* has a chapter on "The food and terms of courtesy and good manners of the Filipinos" (Chirino 1604, 38), and Juan Francisco de San Antonio devotes a chapter of his 1738 *Crónicas* to "The letters, languages, and politeness of the Philipinos" (San Antonio 1738, 140), while Francisco Antolín argues in 1789 that "the ancient wealth of the Philipinos is much like that which the Igorots have at present" (Antolín 1789, 279). In short, the people of the Philippines were called

Filipinos when they were practicing their own culture—or, to put it another way, before they became indios.

In the nineteenth century, Spaniards born in the colony began to be called *Españoles filipinos* to distinguish them from Spaniards born in Spain, a designation which was logically contracted to *Filipinos* when speaking of Spaniards. Philippine-born Spaniards, however, often resented being called Filipinos by *peninsulares*, preferring the term *hijos del país*—children of the land. Sinibaldo de Mas (1843, 138) in his 1842 population estimates more neutrally divides Spaniards and Filipinos into the following categories— Filipinos (indios), Españoles filipinos, and *Españoles europeos*. "Indio filipino" was just how Francisco Suárez signed himself a century before when he engraved a portrait of Philip V for Pedro Murillo Velarde's 1743 *Cursus Juris Canonici* (frontispiece), and native Filipinos were still using the term in the next century. As Jose Rizal (1887, 111) said of the Philippine community in Madrid, "Creoles, Mestizos and Malays, we simply call ourselves Filipinos." Finally, with the growth of a national consciousness, Filipino patriots began to project the term anachronistically into past centuries. Thus, they identified all Spanish bishops born in the Philippines as native Filipinos, however surprised those bishops would have been to hear themselves referred to as such.

When the Americans seized the Spanish colony as spoils of the Spanish-American War, they called its inhabitants Filipinos, and so today citizens of the Republic of the Philippines are recognized in international law as Filipinos. Common parlance, however, has tended to exclude people whose ancestors were never acculturated into the Spanish colony, even though they vote in national elections and travel abroad on Philippine passports. Carlos P. Romulo was once burned in effigy by Baguio collegians for stating that Igorots were not Filipinos, and many Muslims reject the term as a colonial imposition by a foreign power their ancestors resisted. Nor does the confusion end there. In 1955, Agnes Newton Keith incorporated a popular perception in her *Bare Feet in the Palace:* "In the nineteenth century, by Spanish edict, the native born in the Islands was known as an 'indio' and not called Filipino" (Keith 1955, 74). But no such edict is known to serious history, though nonhistorians have not infrequently referred to such a restriction.[3]

Despite this somewhat checkered career, the term *Filipino* will be used in this work to refer to those ancestors of the present Filipino citizens, who resided in the archipelago in the sixteenth century, and who spoke Philippine languages.

7

The Filipino People

According to the latest historical study of Philippine populations, there were between one and two million inhabitants in the archipelago at the time of Spanish advent.[4] The Spaniards recognized them as one race of medium stature, black hair, and dark skin—though those dark enough to be called *kayumanggi* (brown) in Tagalog were exceptions rather than the norm. Individual friars sometimes referred to Filipinos in a particular island as being taller, lighter, braver, or more muscular than others, but these were subjective comments which reflected value judgments and the fact that Spaniards themselves varied greatly in complexion and stature. As an early Tagalog dictionary says of the word *cayomangi*, "There are some they call this . . . like Father Domingo de Nieva, and Father Fray Antonio they call *maitim sa cayomangi* [almost black]" (Blancas de San José 1610, *moreno*). Otherwise, they distinguished Filipinos by their languages, the Visayans by their tattoos, and highlanders as primitive. And they did not include those they called *negros* or *negrillos* (blacks or "little blacks," that is, Negritos) under the rubric of *indio* at all.

Negritos obviously belonged to a different race from the rest of the Filipino people, though observed variations in pigmentation and stature suggested considerable intermarriage with non-Negritos. Spaniards were also inclined to refer to Muslim Filipinos—Moros—as a separate race, an unfortunate equation of race, language, and religion which persists in popular prejudice even today. Christian Filipinos frequently refer to a nonexistent "Moro language," and the Taosug Muslims in Sulu fondly recall their ancestors as Arabs rather than Filipino converts. The king of Spain, however, knew better. Philip II ordered that his indio subjects who were converts to Islam should not be enslaved like Moro invaders and preachers from outside the colony.

The Spaniards also recognized the Chinese as another race—like the political refugees they found settled on the Tondo waterfront and Manila environs. Spanish failure to mention any Chinese trading colonies, except for one dubious reference to Chinese men and women in Vigan, comes as a surprise, considering their sanguine interest in China as a commercial and missionary target. Of course, they would have been unable to recognize any descendants of Chinese who dressed like indios and spoke Philippine languages. For this same reason, the Chinese will be used in this work only to mean people who spoke Chinese and practiced Chinese customs.

It has often been averred that the Spaniards found highland and lowland Filipinos in a state of traditional enmity when they arrived. But the examples cited always involve independent tribes on the one hand, and subjugated Filipinos on the other. What the Spaniards did report on their arrival was that armed conflict and raiding were commonplace, if not endemic, in precolonial Philippine society. No doubt this included highland-lowland warfare, but was not limited to it. A well-known passage from Miguel de Loarca's 1582 *Relación* indicates that enmity did not preclude mutual trade:

> There are two kinds of men in this land [Panay] who, though they are all one, behave somewhat differently and are almost always enemies—the one, those who live on the seacoast, and the other, those who live in the mountains, and if they have some peace between them it is because of the necessity they have of one another to sustain human life, because those of the mountains cannot live without the fish and salt and other things and jars and plates which come from other parts, nor can those on the coast live without the rice and cotton which the mountaineers have (Loarca 1582, 120).

Scholarly friars also speculated on the origins of the Filipino people. They had no doubt that the Negritos were the aboriginal inhabitants of the land, but were unable to account for the highlanders in the interior. Perhaps—they speculated—they were also aborigines who withdrew in the face of later migrations; or they may have been a mixture of civilized and uncivilized tribes, or even the descendants of shipwrecked Chinese or Japanese seafarers. But they were agreed that the lowland population came from Malay-speaking islands to the south, and they accounted for the variety of Philippine languages accordingly—for example, Tagalogs from Borneo, Kapampangans from Sumatra, or Visayans from Makassar. These Malay origins were based on observed similarities between Malay and Philippine languages, similarities arising from the fact that both Malay and all Philippine languages are members of the great Austronesian family of languages.

Malay was the trade language of Southeast Asia at the time, and took its name from the Sumatran port of Melayu (now Djambi), once the seat of expansive political power. Speakers of this language could be found in all the trading ports in the Philippines from Sarangani to Manila, either professional interpreters or members of the ruling families. When Magellan's Sumatran slave spoke to the ruler of Limasawa, himself a native of the trading center of Butuan, "the king understood him," Pigafetta (1524b, 114) said, "because in those parts the kings know more languages than the other people." And because of Manila's Bornean connections, Tagalog today has more Malay loan words than any of the other major Philippine languages. Indeed, it seems that the Manila elite were speaking Malay as a prestigious second language in the sixteenth century. That is no doubt why Tagalog was long considered to be a derivative of Malay, if not an actual dialect of that language.

The word *Malay* was also used to mean people of the same physical type as Malay speakers, even if they did not speak that language themselves. So Austrian Filipinist Ferdinand Blumentritt used it in a famous essay in 1882 in which he derived the Filipino people from three waves of Malay migration into the archipelago. The first wave, he theorized, displaced the Negritos they found on the coast, but married their women; the second wave drove the first into interior mountains, and became the progenitors of the present lowland population; and the third wave introduced Islam. Blumentritt was not the only modern ethnologist who proposed a series of racially discrete migrations to account for the island populations of Southeast Asia, nor would he be the last. In the twentieth century, H. Otley Beyer may well be said to have surpassed them all with the grandeur of a wave migration theory which is known to every literate Filipino today.[5]

The Beyer Wave Migration Theory

The well-known theory was produced by Beyer, then head of the Anthropology Department of the University of the Philippines, for the 1916 Census, to explain the physical and cultural variations among the Filipino people. The physical differences he attributed to genetic commingling among a series of migrating peoples of unlike racial type, and cultural differences presumed to be precolonial—like tools and weapons, food crops and agriculture—he assigned to these different waves. At the time, no archaeological fieldwork had been done in the archipelago: it was Beyer himself who would pioneer that field in 1921 with the discovery of Stone Age sites in Novaliches. During the next twenty years, he assigned every bone and artifact recovered to one of the waves, and placed the waves themselves in a chronological sequence from primitive to advanced. And since he considered any similarity between Philippine finds and those made elsewhere in Asia to be evidence of migrations rather than culture contacts, the number of waves steadily multiplied. By 1953 they had reached their final count. In Beyer's own terminology, they were as follows:

First came the Java Man, and then the "little people"—Australoid Sakai, Negritos, and Proto-Malays—followed by two waves of Indonesians—Type A and Type B—with a smaller wave of Papuans, who were succeeded in turn by separate Northern and Southern Malay waves, and finally the Jar Burial

People. To these were added two peoples from nineteenth-century folk-lore—the Orang Dampuan in Sulu, and the Ten Datus of Borneo said to have purchased Panay Island from native Negritos. Each of these waves was provided with a point of origin, credited with distinct cultural traits, and described in physical detail. Migrants of the first waves walked dry-shod into the archipelago together with Pleistocene mammals over land bridges since submerged, but later ones came from China, Vietnam, Borneo, and the Celebes in dugout canoes or plank-built boats. The Proto-Malays carried blowguns, bows and arrows; the Northern Malays introduced bronze and rice terraces; and the Southern Malays were blacksmiths, weavers, and potters. Java Man was powerfully muscled and hairy; Type A Indonesians, tall, light-skinned, and thin-lipped; and Southern Malays were tattooed. All in all, it was an imaginative and comprehensive synthesis. But it was also flawed by little evidence, dubious methodology, and simple fantasy.

Since Beyer's day, forty years of additional research have cast doubt on this synthesis. Geologists question the existence of the land bridges; archaeologists cannot fit lithic finds into his categories; anthropologists demand skeletal remains to determine human stature; prehistorians are persuaded of the antiquity of trade contacts in Southeast Asia; and linguists believe that people speaking Philippine languages were living in the archipelago thousands of years ago. Probably none of them would accept Beyer's assumption that by examining living populations you can determine what kind of tools their ancestors used, or that by examining tools you can determine the race of the men who made them. Beyer also gave little consideration to the fact that cultures are dynamic, not static, that they survive through change, adjustment, innovation, development, and borrowing. Thus the fact that Filipinos in Manila eat McDonald's hamburgers but those in Bontoc do not does not require one more wave migration to explain it. It is probably safe to say that no anthropologist accepts the Beyer Wave Migration Theory today.[6]

Most prehistorians today only postulate two movements of people into the islands of Southeast Asia and the Pacific to account for the present populations. The first they call Australoid, people whose surviving representatives are generally characterized by very dark pigmentation. Philippine Negritos are considered to be a specialized physical variation of this stock. The second movement is thought to have begun some five or six thousand years ago, and to have largely displaced or absorbed the earlier population, though whether it reached the Philippines from the north or south is a question still being debated with some heat. These people are known to anthropologists as Southern Mongoloid and to laymen as the brown race, but are also called Austronesian because their descendants speak languages belonging to that family. The physical types which an earlier generation of anthropologists provided with a long list of racial and subracial names are now regarded as genetic specializations within the normal range of variations of the larger movement. Moreover, many of these people have continued to move from island to island up into historic times, not as migration waves but as small groups of settlers, traders, or castaways. All of them would have contributed to local gene pools, but those new genes would not have carried language skills or tool-making techniques.[7]

It is important to note that these migrating populations are not considered to have been physically homogeneous. This means that Austronesian settlers arrived in the Philippines with considerable variations in stature, pigmentation, and facial features, though it is not now possible to identify these differences. Settlement and intermarriage in small communities would cause such genetic traits, as well as those of any strangers marrying in from outside, to be shared by an increasing portion of the population in each generation. Thus inhabitants of a whole valley might come to exhibit a kind of family resemblance, and even to be regarded by outsiders as a separate race. Conversely, many such differences are not genetically significant: It is a common observation that with improved diet and hygiene, younger generations are taller than their parents. In the same vein, elderly Igorots often develop enlarged first toes, and so do Tagalog boatmen who pole barges walking barefoot along bamboo runways, but their children are not born with this deformity.[8]

Philippine Languages

Philippine languages belong to the Austronesian language family, a huge group of more than six hundred languages spread from Madagascar off the coast of Africa in the west to Easter Island off the coast of South America in the east. All these languages, like the cultures of which they are a part, are dynamic, not static; their vocabularies, grammar, and pronunciations are constantly changing. When two speech communities diverge until they are recognizably different but can still understand each other, they are said to speak two dialects of the same language; but if they diverge to such an extent that they cannot understand each other, they constitute two separate languages. Thus, for example, Banaue and Kiangan are two dialects of Ifugao, but Ifugao and Tagalog are two different languages, mutually unintelligible. In time, the mother tongue from which daughter dialects and languages are derived will disappear, but linguists can theoretically reconstruct such extinct protolanguages by comparing the similarities between the living languages which are descended from them.

These similarities are accounted for in two ways—outright borrowing from other languages, or inheritance from a common ancestral stock. Terms are often borrowed to accompany new cultural introductions—like Malay *kuda* for horse in Manobo and T'boli, or Spanish *caballo* (that is, *kabayo*) in Tagalog, Ilocano, and Visayan. Or they may reflect the prestige in which the donor language is held. So Malay *binibini* (female) was taken for "princess" in Tagalog, while *daddy* and *papa* have replaced *ama* (father) in many Philippine households today. But there would be little need to borrow a word like *mata* (eye) which appears in many Austronesian languages. Linguists seeking the relationship of sister languages therefore compare a basic vocabulary of concepts like sun and moon, nose and hair, and up and down, which would presumably be common to any human society. From this exercise, they are able to construct a family tree which shows the relationship of the languages belonging to the family as a kind of genealogy.

On an Austronesian language tree produced by this method, Philippine languages are found on the lowest branches, meaning to say that Austronesian languages were being spoken in the archipelago earlier than in places like the Malay Peninsula or the Pacific Islands. By the time of Spanish advent, Austronesian speakers had occupied the whole archipelago, absorbing or displacing the sparse populations already present, as their original tongue diversified into three main branches: A northern branch included Luzon languages like Ilocano, Ibanag, and those on the Cordillera. A southern branch included almost all the languages spoken in Mindanao. A central branch had proliferated most widely; it included not only Visayan but all the languages between Pampanga and Butuan, as well as Taosug in Sulu. In addition, a non-Philippine Austronesian language had entered with a boat people the Spaniards called Lutaw or Lutaya, and diversified into the Sama-Badjaw languages. With this exception, however, all Philippine languages have more in common with one another than any one of them does with a language outside the Philippines. This means that the Filipinos the Spaniards met in the sixteenth century were speaking languages produced within the archipelago, not introduced by separate migrations from abroad.[9]

A Word about Orthography

Spanish orthography confuses *b* and *v*, and non-Castilians confuse *s* and *z*, so the same place in the Philippines appears both as *Bisaya* and as *Vizaya;* so, too, *Bigan* was written *Vigan*, and Legazpi's name was often spelled "Legaspi." The Spanish alphabet had no *w* or *ng* (so Father Chirino omitted these letters from his Philippine alphabet); thus Dr. Morga spelled *timawa*, "timagua"; and since *n* and *g* were pronounced as separate consonants, Pangasinan (land of salt) came to be pronounced "Pang-ga-si-nan." Indeed, many of these Spanish mispronunciations have been accepted in modern Philippine languages. Wawa (in Pampanga) is now spelled and pronounced "Guagua," while *barangay*, which was always spelled "balangay" in Tagalog dictionaries, is now pronounced "ba-rang-gay."

In citing Philippine terms from Spanish dictionaries, I have respelled them in accordance with normal Philippine usage. Thus I have changed *c* and *qu* to *k* as appropriate, and *gui* to *gi*, replaced *u* with *w* and *i* with *y* before or after vowels, and doubled the *g* of *ng* where necessary—as in *kayumanggi* for *cayomangi*. But I have been unable to solve the problems of *u* and *o*, and *e* and *i* being used inconsistently even in the same lexicon, or the fact that some dialects have *l* where others have *r*, and that *r* is sometimes a variant of *d*. For Tagalog, however, I have simply adopted the conventional modern spelling.

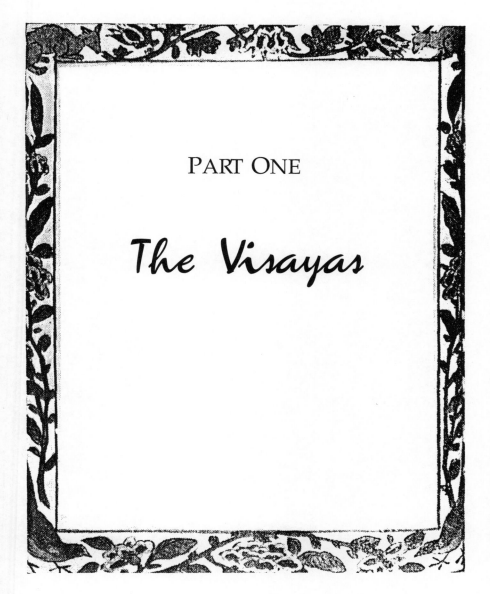

PART ONE

The Visayas

CHAPTER 1

Physical Appearance

Descriptions of the color of Filipinos by Spaniards in the sixteenth century were often contradictory. For example, the first Filipinos the Spaniards observed were Visayans from Homonhon, Limasawa, and Butuan, and were described by the visitors as being of medium stature and dark-skinned. As for Pigafetta, he called them *olivastri* (in Italian), meaning olive-skinned or tanned, and English corsair Thomas Cavendish called Capul Islanders tawny. But the most frequent designation was "the color of cooked quince" (Pretty 1588, 42).

On the other hand, Father Alcina said he did not think they were really that dark, though almost, and that the natives of Leyte and Samar were lighter than those of Davao. Méntrida, however, defined Visayan *mailum* as a color a bit darker than that natural to the Visayans, though not black like the Ate (Negroes or Negritos). From Cebu, Juan de la Isla reported that the natives were darker than the *indios* of Mexico, but a contemporaneous account written in Mexico said they were lighter.

The subjectivity of these descriptions is indicated not only by their contradictions but also by the fact that sympathetic accounts regularly refer to Filipinos as light-skinned. Thus the natives of Leyte in whose homes a dozen shipwrecked Spaniards spent seven months in 1544 were referred to as white. It is also significant that in such accounts this color is coupled with other approving adjectives: Loarca said the Visayans were well-built, good-looking, and not very dark. Chirino said the same thing, and in the case of the Boholanos, said they were not only lighter and more handsome than other Visayans, but braver and more spirited.

Women were generally lighter than men due to occupations like weaving which kept them less exposed to the sun. In particular, the secluded daughters of ranking datus were said to be as light as European ladies, and so were the slave girls who danced naked to entertain royal visitors. Children were also light at birth, and when men stripped, they revealed a pale area under their G-strings.

Of course to begin with, Filipinos were not all the same shade nor were they all necessarily darker than Spaniards. In any event, before the development of a colonial consciousness, Visayans themselves were unimpressed by these color differences. Their Iberian invaders were perceived not as *maputi*, white, but as *mapuraw*, natural or undyed—that is, untattooed. And to the Visayans the most distinctive feature of these foreigners was their plain white teeth, a feature shared with monkeys, dogs, and pigs. As the Visayans said of the smiles of persons who exposed a mouthful of undecorated teeth, these were "baga napkangnan huligid [like a chaw of coconut meat]" (Sánchez 1617, 254v).[10]

Decorative Dentistry

The idea that only wild animals had white teeth was widespread in southeastern Asia: English businessman Ralph Fitch noted it in Burma in 1591. Human beings were thought to be distinguished by cosmetic refinements like filed and stained teeth.

The Visayans called tooth filing *sangka*, leveling, and it was done by an expert with a slender stone file, who sometimes removed half the tooth in the process. Variations included opening the space between teeth, or grinding them to saw-toothed points, but the desired effect was always to render them even and symmetrical. This involved correcting or obviating natural misalignment, and the reduction of those eye teeth so suggestive of fangs or tusks.

Once filed, the teeth were colored in different ways. Regular chewing of *anipay* root made them black, or the application of a tar-based coating called *tapul* gave them the appearance of polished ebony, and probably had a preservative effect. Red *lakha* ant eggs were used to color teeth—and *kaso* flowers, both teeth and fingernails—a deep red, an effect heightened and preserved by habitual betel nut chewing.

The most impressive examples of Visayan dentistry were its goldwork. Gold-pegged incisors were noted by Pigafetta in Limasawa and by Urdaneta in Lianga Bay, and plenty of beautiful specimens have been recovered from archaeological digs. *Pusad* was the general term for teeth goldwork, whether they were inlays, crowns, or plating. The *mananusad* was the dental worker, a professional who got paid for his services. As the Sánchez dictionary (1617, 434v) puts it, "Pilay sohol ko nga papamusad ako dimo [How much will you charge me for gold teeth]?"

Halop, covering, included both plating held on by little gold rivets run through the tooth, and actual caps extending beyond the gum line, also secured by pegs. *Bansil* were gold pegs inserted in holes drilled with an awl called *ulok,* usually in a thumbnail-shaped field that had been filed into the surface of the incisors beforehand. If they were simple pegs without heads they looked like gold dots on ivory dice when filed flush with the surface of the tooth. (Si Awi, king of Butuan, had three in each tooth.) But if the pegs were tack-shaped, their flat heads overlapped like golden fish scales; or if round-headed, they could be worked into intricate filigreelike designs similar to beadwork. Of course, this goldwork was considered all the more effective if displayed on teeth polished bright red or jet black.

Such dentistry figures in the epic literature of Mindanao: a common image is the flash of golden brilliance when the hero opens his mouth to speak or smile. A lyrical passage in the Manobo Ulahingan describes how it is highlighted by the blood red of a chew of betel nut:

> He then picked up
> The ready-made *mema'an* [quid].
> Tenderly he pushed this through
> His teeth artistically designed,
> Gently he pressed it in between
> His molars with lovely pattern.
> There is nothing you can see
> Except the flashing of crimson . . .
> No need to be surprised!
> Because what is sparkling
> Are his shining gold-crowned teeth,
> What is glittering all over
> Are the shining *empenetek* [caps] (Maquiso 1977, 183).

Tattooing

The Spaniards called the Visayans "Pintados" because they were "painted"—that is, tattooed. *Batuk* was the general term for tattoos—or *patik* in some places—and it also meant the marking of snakes or lizards, or any design printed or stamped on. These tattoos were symbols of male valor: they were applied only after a man had performed in battle with fitting courage and, like modern military decorations, they accumulated with additional feats. Any applied on one who had not killed or captured an enemy were scorned as counterfeit. Moreover, a tattooed man who was considered cowardly was compared to a *halo* lizard, a large black and yellow reptile "tattooed" all over but extremely timid.

Warfare itself was seen as a kind of initiation rite into manhood: *tigma* was a youth's first taste of war or sex, and *tiklad* was his first conquest either in battle or love. Tattoos were therefore required for public esteem by either sex. Celibate transvestites, however, were socially acceptable mapuraw, natural-colored. Not surprisingly, the Visayan vocabulary included terms like *kulmat,* to strut around showing off new tattoos, and *hundawas,* stripped to the waist for bravado.

Tattooing itself was painful enough to serve as a test of manhood. For this reason, some men who were qualified as warriors postponed the operation until shamed into it. On the other hand, there were those who showed more macho mettle by adding *labong* scars on their arms with burning moxa, pellets of wooly fibers used in medical cautery. Still more rugged were those who submitted to facial tattooing. Indeed, those with tattoos right up to the eyelids constituted a Spartan elite. Such countenances were truly terrifying and no doubt intimidated enemies in battle as well as townmates at home. Men would be slow to challenge or antagonize a tough with such visible signs of physical fortitude.

Tattoo work was done by a skillful artist who was well paid for his services. He began by tracing the designs on the body with an ink made from pitch soot, then pricked them into the skin with a small tool set with a number of short needles like the teeth of a comb, and then rubbed soot into the fresh wounds. *Biro* was both the soot and the ink, and the Spaniards mistakenly thought the reason tattoos were permanent was because the biro mixed with the blood. (Not a few of them also believed tattoos were burned on with a hot iron.) The operation was not performed all in one sitting but in installments, but even so, often caused a high fever and occasionally infection and death. *Baug* or *binogok* was the healing period when the wounds were still swollen, and if infection caused the designs to be muddied, they were called just that—mud *(lusak).*

The first tattoos a person received were applied to the legs beginning at the ankles and ending at the waist. Chest tattoos which looked like breast-plates—less frequently, tattoos on the abdomen—only came after further action in battle; and still later, those on the whole back, widest field for the tattooer's artistry. Facial tattoos from ear to chin to eye were restricted to the boldest and toughest warriors. If the illustrations in the late sixteenth-century Boxer Codex accurately portray Visayan tattoos, these were characterized by bold lines up legs and back, and matching geometric floral designs on both pectorals and buttocks (see fig.1).

Different regions were no doubt distinguished by different patterns, but a few generalizations can be made. *Labid* were the distinctive inch-wide lines, both the straight ones and those which, in Father Sánchez's (1617, 283) words, "go snaking or zigzagging up the leg to the waist." *Ablay* were those on the shoulder; *dubdub,* those on the chest up to the throat; and *daya-daya*—or *tagur* in Panay—on the arms. *Bangut* (a muzzle or halter) were the ones that made of the face such a frightening mask, also called *langi,* "gaping" like a crocodile's jaws or the beak of a bird of prey. *Hinawak*—from *hawak,* a tight, lean waist—were men tattooed below the waist, and *lipong* were heroes tattooed all over (except under the G-string) like the fancy *linipong* porcelain jars from China. Women, however, only tattooed their hands, one or both, and the lines were exceedingly fine and had the appearance of damask or embroidery.

Early Spanish descriptions give the impression that Visayan men wore long robes which covered them from neck to ankle. It is true that such garments existed, sometimes cut from expensive textile imported from mainland Asia, but it is hard to believe any pre-Hispanic dress code would have dictated the hiding of those prestigious decorations so painfully acquired. Of course, Filipinos quickly learned to adjust to colonial requirements—the Boxer Codex shows a Tagalog wearing *pantalones* instead of a G-string—but missionaries addressing European audiences also wished to avoid the impression that their converts were naked savages. For example, in his *Relación* published in Rome in 1604, Jesuit Pedro Chirino (1604, 18) quickly added to his description of Visayan tattooing, "Not for this do they go around naked . . . but are always and in all places very circumspect and careful to cover their persons with extreme modesty and decency." However, in a later manuscript which his order never published, he said,

> The principal clothing of the Cebuanos and all the Visayans is the tattooing of which we have already spoken, with which a naked man appears to be dressed in a kind of handsome armor engraved with very fine work, a dress so esteemed by them they take it for their proudest attire, covering their bodies neither more nor less than a

21

Christ crucified, so that although for solemn occasions they have the *marlotas* [smock] we mentioned, their dress at home and in the barrio is their tattoos and a bahag, as they call that cloth they wrap around their waist, which is the sort the ancient actors and gladiators used in Rome for decency's sake (Colín 1900, intro. 120:1).

Skull Moulding

As mothers and midwives are well aware, the skulls of newborn infants are so soft that if they are continuously laid in the same position, their heads become flat on one side. Many cultures have taken advantage of this phenomenon to give their children a skull shape which conforms to the local canons of beauty. In non-Muslim parts of Sumatra, women used to bind babies' heads to produce flat foreheads and noses; the Melanau of Sarawak wanted their children to grow up "moon-faced"; and the Minahasa of Celebes formerly restricted binding with a forehead board to the nobility. So too, ancient Visayans considered broad faces with receding foreheads and flat noses handsome, and compressed their babies' skulls to achieve them.

Dozens of skulls of this sort have been recovered from burial sites in Albay, Marinduque, Samar, Cebu, Bohol, Surigao, and Davao. The Aga Khan Museum in Marawi displays two complete skeletons just as they were discovered in a Butuan grave: with reshaped skulls with black teeth filed to points. A scientific study of twenty-two Philippine specimens revealed considerable variation according to the amount and location of the pressure, whether between the forehead and the upper or lower part of the occiput. Thus some had normally arched foreheads but were flat behind, others were flattened at both front and back, and a few were asymmetrical because of uneven pressure. However, all were short and broad: one even rated a cephalic index of 100—meaning it was of equal length and width, or isocephalic.

Visayan skull moulding was done with a device called *tangad*, a comblike set of thin rods bound to a baby's forehead by bandages fastened at some point behind. (The Bikolanos used a kind of little plate or tablet called *sipit*, or a padded one called *saop*.) This prevented the forward growth of the frontal bone and directed it backward so that the head grew higher at the rear. Adults with the desired tangad profile were called *tinangad*, but flatness of the back of the head was called *puyak*. The opposite of tangad was *ondo*: as Father Sánchez (1617, 378) commented, "just as there are *puraw* and *binatakan* [tattooed], so there are *tinangad* and *ondo*." The word *ondo* is itself a comment on the Visayan attitude toward unmoulded skulls: it meant tight-packed or overstuffed—like a hunchback's hump.

Fig.1. Tattooed Visayans
(From the Boxer Codex)

Penis Pins

Visayan men wore a pin through their penis for the greater stimulation of their sex partners. The custom startled Spanish, Portuguese, Italian, and English observers alike, and scandalized missionary clergy of all orders. Most of them thought it was literally satanic—"Certainly a device no man could have invented," Juan Martínez (1567, 461) said, "were it not by revelation of the Devil, the inhumanity of the pain being so great which the youths suffer in the piercing."

The pin was called *tugbuk* and was inserted in childhood: Cavendish removed one from the ten-year-old son of a Capul chieftain. Tugbuk examined by Pigafetta—and he asked to examine many in order to dispel his disbelief—penetrated the urinary canal and therefore had a hole to facilitate urination. They were small bars of brass, gold, ivory, or lead, or a little tube of tin driven across the head of the penis to protrude on both sides far enough to receive decorations which ranged in size from simple rivets to hold them in place, to rosettes as large as the rowel of a horseman's spur. But generally they served to anchor a kind of ring or cogwheel with blunt teeth called *sakra*. In the case of the rings, one or more were pressed on, like finger rings, behind the pin; but the penis wheels had opposed holes to accommodate the tugbuk. One dug up in Dumangas (Iloilo), which is now in the Rajah Tupas Collection in Capiz, has eight knobby protrusions with a diameter of 5 centimeters; but some were reported in the sixteenth century to have been 7 centimeters across with a weight of 230 grams.[11]

But, in use, these ornaments required manipulation by the woman herself to insert, and could not be withdrawn until the male organ was completely relaxed, a condition Visayans referred to as *kinamakawing* whether in humans or canines. Although there were twenty or thirty different kinds to cater to a lady's choice, men preferred to leave the pin in place after the original operation, both to prevent the hole from growing shut and to avoid the discomfort of replacing it, though running the risk of calculous formations. (Urdaneta was told in Lianga Bay that virgins were always deflowered by slaves not fitted with tugbuk and sakra.)

Aside from tugbuk and sakra, Martínez reported in Cebu, that "not far from here they say others make use of another device." He was perhaps referring to the pellets implanted beneath the skin by men in Surigao or by Tagalog mountaineers east of Laguna de Bay.

Of course, these devices were of sufficient bulk to produce pain and draw blood, and could cause crippling complications for both partners.

Foreign observers, including chronicler Juan de Medina (1630, 58), therefore attributed their use to an inordinate sexual appetite,

> so much so that women considered it a compliment and were proud of it, and in their songs during their drunken feast were wont to man a *karakoa* [warship] with those who had been their lovers; and as further evidence of this, they would not let a man approach them who did not have a *sakra,* which is a little spiked wheel like a Catherine Wheel, with the point blunted, which was fastened with a bronze pin through it, for since childhood they had their male organs pierced through, with which they did it with women like dogs.

Circumcision

The practice of circumcision was widespread in the Visayas. It was called *tuli* and was technically supercision rather than circumcision—that is, cut lengthwise above rather than cut around. (If the prepuce was actually removed, the act was called *girlo,* the same term used for the cutting off a piece of a pig's ear for identification purposes.) The uncircumcised were called *pisot,* an unripe fruit or green youth, a term which was also a polite euphemism for the female parts. The operation was performed informally with no particular ceremony, and was thought to serve hygienic purposes.

Spanish missionaries were quick to conclude that the custom had been introduced by their Muslim competitors, as it probably had been in some areas, but Visayans claimed that their custom was of indigenous origin predating any contact with Islam—and so did circumcised natives of Guam. Certainly circumcision is too universal a practice to require any Semitic origin: it was practiced by the ancient Aztecs in Mexico, and still figures in male initiation rites among African tribes and native Australians. In the seventeenth century, however, the word *islam* came to be used in Visayan for circumcision according to the Muslim rite, and *magislam* meant to perform the ceremony.

Pierced Ears

Both men and women wore earrings. They had their ears pierced—men with one or two holes per lobe, while women with three or four—to accommodate a variety of ornaments.

Earrings with or without pendants were held by thin gold pins run through the ear and fastened behind, but earplugs required holes as wide as two fingers, or lobes distended into loops through which a person could stick his fist. The holes were made in the cartilage, one above the other, and women wore jewelry in all of them. The most common style for men, however, were single rings worn in the bottom holes. These rings were thick as a finger, some hollow and others of solid gold heavy enough to pull the earlobe down until the ring actually touched the shoulder. The swinging motion of these huge gold rings, like that of the glittering spangles dangling from the ladies' earrings, was part of their attractiveness. Among ceramic heads found in the Initao burial cave in Lekak (Cotabato), one was modeled with holes through elongated earlobes for free-moving rings.

The holes—*hogar* or *tosok*—were made with a copper needle. The first holes in the earlobes were made soon after birth, while the rest of the holes, before the second year. A thick cotton thread was looped through the hole to keep it from closing. After the wound had healed, the thread was replaced with a series of gradually thicker bamboo or hardwood splints until the hole was as large as the circumference of the little finger. It was then slowly extended to the desired size by inserting leaves tightly rolled up, springlike, to exert steady gentle pressure outward.

If the distended lobes tore out, the ends could be trimmed and the raw edges sutured together to heal whole again. This operation was called *kulot* or *sisip,* and was most frequently requested by women because when two of them got in a fight, they would go for each other's ears first.

Persons without pierced ears were called *bingbing.* Those whose earlobes were naturally too short for successful piercing and distending were *bibit.*

Hair

Hairstyles usually differed between one community and another and could go in and out of fashion quickly. In the 1520s, Visayans in Homonhon had hair down to their waist, while the king of Butuan wore his at shoulder length, and men on the coast of Surigao pulled theirs back into a knot at the nape of the neck. In the 1560s, Cebuanos were gathering it up in a headcloth; twenty years later, a knot or chignon either on top of the head or at the back was the style all over the Visayas. But they all had long hair: to cut it was a sign of deepest mourning, or a punishment.

Only where Spanish influence was greatest did Filipinos cut their hair short, a change Father Alcina (1668a, 1:39) considered part of "taming their ancient ferocity with the gentleness of the Gospel." Manila Muslims also had short hair, so Visayans considered them *alot,* shorn, and a rough curse to exclaim at a Tagalog was "Inalotan ka [You close-cropped, you]!" (Méntrida 1637a, 18).

However, facial hair—and in some places body hair, too—was removed with tweezers or a pair of clam shells. Both men and women had their eyebrows shaved into thin arcs likened to a crescent moon.

Women took pride in a great mass of hair, gathering up ankle-length tresses into a chignon as large as the head itself, with curls over the forehead, together with additional switches called *panta* or *talabhok* which were considered their crowning glory. For a man to touch such a hairdo was a terrible offense, but they were a handy target for other women: *sampolong* meant to grab somebody by the locks, especially the chignon. Flowers were worked in for fragrance, as well as sesame seed oil—also believed to encourage luxuriant growth—or a perfumed ointment called *bulat,* compounded of many ingredients. Datus, however, preferred the bolder scent of mammal excretions like ambergris, civet, or musk. A Panay epic waxes lyrical about Humadapnon's perfumed grooming:

> Lubricated and oiled
> With oil sweet-scented,
> The scent permeates;
> Add the sweet body scent,
> Increase the permeating scent,
> Scent so breathtakingly strong,
> Odor so sweet,
> Flowing along brooks and streams,
> Drifting along the rivers (Barte 1987, lines 323–31).

Spanish observers were impressed with the amount of time and care Visayans gave their hair, a preoccupation which is still echoed in oral literature. Datung Sumanga, the hero of a lost Visayan epic, only manages to overcome stubborn Princess Bubung Humasanun of Bohol by threatening to come and personally tear off her panta. In the Manuvu cycle of the Cotabato-Davao border region, Tuwaang's wife combs her warrior husband's long hair before he sets out on his adventures, braiding it into several kinds of knots. In the Suban-on epics, a hero's locks are oiled by his sister and wound into tight coils which should not come undone except in the hands of his sweetheart, and Chief Sandayo of Tubig Liyasan goes forth to battle, armed with two victory charms plaited into his hair—one for the enemy and the other for the ladies.

Clothing

Visayan clothing varied according to cost and current fashions and so indicated social standing. The basic garments were the G-string and tube skirt—what the Maranaw call *malong*—or a light blanket wrapped around instead. But more prestigious clothes, *lihin-lihin*, were added for public appearances and especially on formal occasions—blouses and tunics, loose smocks with sleeves, capes, or ankle-length robes. The textiles of which they were made were similarly varied. In ascending order of value, they were abaca, abaca decorated with colored cotton thread, cotton, cotton decorated with silk thread, silk, imported printstuffs, and an elegant abaca woven of selected fibers almost as thin as silk. In addition, Pigafetta mentioned both G-strings and skirts of bark cloth.

The G-string *(bahag)* was a piece of cloth 4 or 5 meters long and something less than a meter wide: it was therefore much larger than those worn in Zambales and the Cagayan Valley, or by Cordillera mountaineers today. The ends hanging down were called *wayaway*—*ampis* in front and *pakawar* behind—and were usually decorated. *Binkisi* was an expensive one with fancywork called *gowat*, and if it had a fringe of three-strand *lubid* cords, it was *lubitan*. G-strings were of the natural color of the cloth. However, in the case of men who had personally killed an enemy, they were qualified to wear deep red ones.

To put the G-string on, one end was held against the chest while the other was passed between the legs, pulled up between the buttocks and wrapped around the waist several times, thereby binding the front flap which was then allowed to hang down as ampis; the other end was then knotted behind and let fall as pakawar. Care was taken to see that one of the wayaway was longer than the other: wearing both of equal length was considered ludicrous. The word *watid* was for a G-string dragging on the ground, a deliberate sign of mourning.

Because its size permitted the bahag to be spread out to cover the entire hip, many observers thought it was a kind of kilt from the waist to the knees. And because of its bulk, men removed it in the privacy of their home: Sánchez (1617, 45) illustrated with the sentence, "Magbahag kita ay magatubang sa Padre [Let's put on our G-strings in front of the Father]."

Men also wore a blanket or another length of cloth as clothing. *Singal* was to put one on like a G-string; and *tampi* was simply to wrap it around the hips, tied with a knot in front, and not passed between the legs. *Alampay* meant to wrap anything around the shoulders or over the head like a cape, including G-strings which were then given fewer turns around the waist to allow it to extend over the shoulder or head. To lend greater dignity to a formal occasion, an ankle-length garment called *saob-saob* was worn, with or without sleeves but open down the front like a cloak. Rajah Humabon put on a silk one at Magellan's request to take his oath of vassalage to the Spanish king.

There seems to have been no Visayan term for the long-sleeved gowns depicted in the Boxer Codex, with fine Pintado ankles just peeping out at the bottom (see fig. 2)—nor for those tight-sleeved tunics the Tagalogs called *baro*. Perhaps this can be explained by the fact that these pictures were painted twenty-five years after Spanish advent. However, though references from whatever source were and have been made to such clothes, these togalike garb could not have been the ordinary Visayan costume. All royal datus who had dealings with early Spanish commanders were clothed only in tattoos and G-strings—Kolambu of Limasawa, Awi of Butuan, Katuna of Bohol, and Tupas of Cebu. Bare-chested exposure to the elements was a matter of masculine pride, and even a century later, men's jackets had still not caught on. Writing in 1668, Father Alcina said,

> They rarely used these tunics, or baros; what was common for going out and for working was the bahag only, except for old men who would cover up with these baros against the cold or extreme heat, or the flies and mosquitoes that bit them (Alcina 1668a, 1:49).

The tube skirt was described by Juan de la Isla in Cebu in 1565 as follows:

> The clothes which they wear are a piece of material closed like a sack or sleeve with two very wide mouths, and they make many pleats of the extra width on the left side, and, making a knot of the cloth itself, let the folds fall on the left, and although it does not go above their waist, with a tight blouse most of the body and legs are clothed (Isla 1565, 235).

This was the *lambong*, and because it could also be fastened under the armpits or over the shoulder, or even around the head, the Spaniards called it a *sayo* (smock or coat) rather than *saya* (skirt). The same term was extended to include any garment tailored to the body, like the *sinulog* (i.e., Sulu-style) or *sinina* (Chinese), a short jacket which exposed the midriff—and more, Father Sánchez observed, when they raised their arms. This sinina could have originated in Indonesia or Malaysia, since the Visayans called all foreigners *Sina* before the coming of the Europeans.

Untailored clothes, however, had no particular names. *Pandong*, a lady's cloak, simply meant any natural covering, like the growth on banana trunks or a natal caul. In Panay, the word *kurong*, meaning curly hair, was applied to any short skirt or blouse; and some better ones made of imported chintz or calico were simply called by the name of the cloth itself, *tabas*. So, too,

Fig. 2. Visayans in long-sleeved gowns and fine *pintado* ankles
(From the Boxer Codex)

the wraparound skirt the Tagalogs called *tapis* was hardly considered a skirt at all: Visayans just called it *habul* (woven stuff) or *halong* (abaca) or even *hulun* (sash). Father Sánchez (1617, 54v) shared their assessment: he defined *balikuskus* as

> the knot which women make in their blanket when they wrap it around instead of a real skirt like those they more decently wear in these parts; if it is from Panay, Pampanga or the Tagalogs, it is really indecent.

Open gowns or cloaks were closed in front by cords or gold *gansing*, a kind of hook-and-eye or button, at the throat; or a hulun sash, whence the waist or private parts were called *ginhunlan*. Imported textiles included fine white *kayo* from China and a thin red cotton from Borneo called *kalasumba*. High-quality local abaca or cotton was woven with alternating colored stripes *(liray)*, sometimes of silk, or in squares *(sokat)* like *alemaniscos* (German stuff). Humabon's queen walked in procession all in black and white, with a gold-striped silk scarf over her head, hat, and shoulders.

Good lambong, blankets, or other clothes had decorative strips added to the edges and ends. *Salukap* was a checkered design, and *potak,* little rosettes, while *luray* were separately woven strips that looked like a banister of many colors. Datus and their ladies were distinguished by exquisite luray on all four sides called *libot,* a circuit, such as that which the sun appears to make around the earth, *kalibutan.*

The usual male headdress was the *pudong,* turban, though in Panay both men and women also wore a headcloth or bandana called *potlong* or *saplung.* Commoners wore pudong of rough abaca cloth wrapped around only a few turns so that it was more of a headband than a turban and was therefore called *pudong-pudong*—as the crowns and diadems on Christian images were also later called. A red pudong was called *magalong,* and was the insignia of braves who had killed an enemy. The most prestigious kind of pudong, limited to the most valiant, was, like their G-strings, made of *pinayusan,* a gauze-thin abaca of fibers selected for their whiteness, tie-dyed a deep scarlet in patterns as fine as embroidery, and burnished to a silky sheen. Such pudong were lengthened with each additional feat of valor: real heroes therefore let one end hang loose with affected carelessness.

Women generally wore a kerchief, called *tubatub* if it was pulled tight over the whole head; but they also had a broad-brimmed hat called *sayap* or *tarindak,* woven of sago-palm leaves. Some were evidently signs of rank: when Humabon's queen went to hear mass during Magellan's visit, she was preceded by three girls each carrying one of her hats. A headdress from Cebu with a deep crown, used by both sexes for travel on foot or by boat, was called *sarok,* which actually meant to go for water.

Jewelry

Both Visayan men and women wore earrings and earplugs, necklaces and collars of beads or gold chain, bracelets, wristlets, anklets, and finger rings, as well as brooches, clasps, and gold sequins on their clothes, besides which men wore arm- and legbands. These ornaments were made of tortoise shell, mother-of-pearl, precious stones, giant clam shells (which the Spaniards mistook for marble), and gold. Vegetable fibers and seeds were also used by the poor for everyday wear, and as part of male mourning ritual. But most of this jewelry was gold.

From the day Magellan first saw gold earrings, armbands, and spear decorations in Homonhon, Spaniards kept reporting gold jewelry in truly astonishing quantities. They were struck not only by its amount and wide distribution, but by the fact that it appeared to be part of the normal attire of persons otherwise almost naked. A Samar datu by the name of Iberein was rowed out to a Spanish vessel anchored in his harbor in 1543 by oarsmen collared in gold; while wearing on his own person earrings and chains, which Bernardo de la Torre estimated to be worth more than a thousand pesos, and little else. The impact of this display is reflected in the illustrations of the well-appointed Filipinos in the Boxer Codex (see fig. 3): it is the only known manuscript from the Philippines to make use of gold leaf.

Such jewelry was part of the *bahandi* heirloom wealth buried with ranking datus. As soon as Spanish soldiers discovered this fact, Legazpi found it necessary to issue orders that Filipino graves must not be opened except in the presence of His Majesty's own officers—that is, to make sure that the king got his due fifth. More professional grave robbers have since recovered much of this buried treasure, including pieces which certainly rank among the world's most exquisite. Goldwork which remained above ground, however, rapidly disappeared as upper-class families liquidated ancestral property to meet new colonial demands, if not through outright robbery. Nonetheless, Father Alcina a century later officiated the wedding of a twelve-year-old Visayan girl he thought was wearing no less than 25 pounds of gold.

Visayan jewelry came in a bewildering variety of forms and styles. Among ear ornaments, for example, these were *panika,* the general term for rings and plugs worn in the lower hole *(panikaan)*. Panika were often decorated with *burit* granules of filigree. In particular, panika was also the term for those finger-thick gold rings which were split on top to be fastened to the earlobe "like a letter *O*," Father Alcina (1668a, 1:41) said, "without being

Fig. 3. Wealthy Filipinos
(From the Boxer Codex)

able to see the opening once they were inserted." *Pamarang* or *barat* were large gold plugs, sometimes wheel-shaped with a gem set in the middle, while *dalin-dalin* were simple loops. *Palbad* were more delicate rosettes worn by ladies in the uppermost hole; *dinalopang*, if shaped like a yellow *dalopang* blossom. *Kayong-kayong* was any pendant dangling from an earring, while *sangi* was a single ring worn in one ear only.

Necklaces, in the form of strands, chokers, and collars, ranged from dried seeds to precious stones and gold beads. *Tigbi* were a kind of fruit and *karopi*, any fruits strung like beads. Carnelians were the most popular precious stones, meat-colored beads that varied in hue from the deep red *panggi* and *tarlip* to the bright *aki* and *lasayon*, or the more lustrous *bair*. Garnets and other gems from China were called *taklay* and, like other jewels, were often strung in between gold beads. These gold beads included the four-sided *matambukaw*, long hollow *tinaklum*, and fancy *pinoro* finials with granules added to their surface like tiny gold islands (*poro*). Others were shaped like little fruits—*arlay* like Job's-tears, *tinigbi* like *tigbi* fruit, or *bongan buyo* like betel nuts.

Rings worn around the neck, wrists, or ankles, including the gold bands on men's biceps and above the calves of their legs, were called *kasikas* in general. Kasikas included *binukaw* bracelets of gold or silver, bracelets made of *onat* vines, as well as those of rattan *pikit* which men tied around their neck, wrist, or ankle with an oath not to remove these until they had avenged some loved one's death. *Dalak* and *karamkam* were either bracelets or wristlets—that is, actual cuffs—and *galis* were shell bracelets so snug in fit that the hand was greased to slip them on or off. Ladies generally wore bracelets in sufficient number to attract attention with their jangling—and loose: *makalululu* was the hour of the day when one's bracelets slid down one's arm if one pointed at the sun.

The most spectacular item in this Visayan inventory was the *kamagi*, a heavy gold chain of such tightly interlocked links it hardly looked like a chain at all, but rather as solid and sinuous as a golden serpent. These included both what are now called "gear-bead" necklaces and multiple "loop-in-loop" chains. They were also the most socially significant, an absolute essential for community standing, not simply by their possession but by the number and quality a family could display. The individual loops were called *goar*. When woven in their simplest form, they were called *sinoyot;* but if square, *pinarogmok;* or if octagonal and with large round finials called t*ontonan*, they were called *siniwalo*. A single large kamagi strand was called.*saay*, but the long thin *barbar* could reach 4 meters and so swing grandly to the ground even when doubled or tripled.[12]

CHAPTER 2

Food and Farming

The staple crops of the Visayans were rice, millet, taro, yams, and bananas grown in swiddens *(kaingin)*, wild yams and sago. Rice was grown everywhere and was the preferred food. But since only in a few places could a year's supply of rice be produced, root crops were therefore the most common food for part of the year, or all of the year for part of the people. This dearth in rice supply was later even more characteristic of the Spanish colony because tribute was collected in rice from the very beginning. As Father Alcina (1668a, 8:101–2) observed a century later, "the rice usually does not last them longer than the time it takes to harvest it, since the rest they pay in tribute or sell to get the cash to pay it."

Spaniards made much of the fact that Visayans did not produce a year's supply of rice, and that even datus with many slaves ate root crops in certain seasons. Apparently, neither were the Spaniards aware that low-intensity farmers wished to distribute to several different crops the risks of bad weather or infestation by locusts and other pests, nor did they consider that the Filipinos might not have found such annual variation in diet a particular hardship in the first place. Adverse conditions did, of course, cause food shortages, or even famines so severe that parents would sell children for food that was brought in from as far away as Borneo. Such painful exchanges enabled them to provide for other children, while those they lost would be nourished to adulthood either as slaves or foster children. Indeed, cases were not unknown of such children returning years later, married and prosperous.

The fact that Visayans lived in permanent settlements is evidence that their swiddening techniques were not destructive—meaning that a favorable balance between their numbers and the land available to them permitted new swiddens to be made in the secondary growth on abandoned swiddens without cutting into virgin woodland each time. The late twentieth–century observer familiar with the denuded, eroded Visayan terrain can hardly imagine the lushness of its sixteenth-century flora and fauna. Forest plants and honey were part of normal diet in season, wild game was so plentiful swiddens needed fences like little stockades, and pigs gorging on fallen fruit grew so fat they were easy prey for hunting dogs. Spanish accounts speak of the fertility of a soil that produced larger and better corn, cacao, and sweet potatoes than the original specimens introduced from Mexico. In short, it was an environment which was able to carry a sparse Visayan population that burned off a small portion of its cover every year.

Rice Farming

In the sixteenth century, Visayans called rice *humay, tipasi,* or *paray,* but did not grow much of it irrigated—that is, in pond fields with standing water. The early dictionaries include dozens of terms for rice cultivation and many more for different varieties, but not a word about wet rice—or, more accurately, just *one* word about wet rice, and that was *gani,* a seedbed for rice to be transplanted to swampland or the floodplain of rivers, where it was all too frequently drowned. Instead, they planted dry rice in hillside swiddens with natural drainage. This often resulted in a symbiotic relationship between uplanders and lowlanders on the coast, the former exchanging rice for seafood, salt, and pottery from the latter. From Cebu, Legazpi sent soldiers to look for rice "in the mountains and highlands of the other islands around" (Paes Soto Mayor, et al. 1597, 157) and eventually transferred to Panay where "there is a great quantity of rice, and from the sea [the Portuguese] cannot stop it from coming down the river from the hills." (ibid., 20)

Swidden farming called for close attention to the weather: fields had to be dry to burn but sprouting rice needed moisture. Visayans were aware of the changing seasons from the appearance of stars, the shifting direction of winds, the flowering of plants, and the songs of birds. Because of varying exposure to monsoon winds, the best time for beginning the agricultural cycle was not the same on all islands and coasts. Magellan was asked for help by Rajah Kolambu of Limasawa in a harvest in late March; Bernardo de la Torre harvested some Filipinos' rice under arms on the southern coast of Mindanao in October; and Legazpi reported that Panayanos were harvesting in October and November. Perhaps crops were grown twice a year in Iloilo: Miguel de Loarca gave a four-month schedule for preparing swiddens beginning in June—that is, when the Pleiades first appeared— which would presumably have been planted in September.

Available swidden land was, for all practical purposes, unlimited: a century after Spanish advent, Alcina (1668a, 3:75) could still write, "Regarding land, here there is no difference between mine and thine . . . because it is so great, so extensive, and in almost all places so good." Farmers simply drove a stake in the ground or cut some branches off a tree to establish their claim. This claim did not include ownership of the land, however, but only of the crops grown on it. But not only crops could be harvested, traded, or sold. So could a full field of standing grain—for example, "Iyo ako daganihan sining akun taba-taba [Help me harvest this rice I have bought]" (Sánchez 1617, 24v). Two farmers might work a field in common *(tobong)*, and all fields were worked by exchange labor *(alayon)*, planting or harvesting each one's field in turn, the owner feeding all the workers.

Most swiddens were made in secondary growth where earlier ones had been fallowed *(bunglayan* or *habohabun)*, or even last year's field with the dried stalks still standing *(dinagamian)*. *Balasubas, kalasokas, kanat,* and *higabon* all meant the process of clearing off the undergrowth, including *guro,* to slash through bamboo or vines, and *harabay* or *haras,* to hack off shrubs and small plants at the root.

Hadhad was to chop down full-grown trees. But not all trees were cut down to clear a swidden. Some were left standing with their branches removed: small ones to serve as poles for climbing vegetables, large ones because they were too laborious to fell—and *hilay* or *hiklay* was to cut those branches along the edges of a swidden that would shade the crops. All this debris *(dorok* or *dopok)* was gathered into large piles called *tapong* for burning when dry, though pieces of wood large enough to be useful were dragged off to be saved. The climax came with the actual firing *(dobdob)* and the swidden was then a kaingin, ready to be planted and cultivated as a field, *uma* (or *baul* in Cebu).

All this work would be stopped if it was discovered that there was a mound of a termites' nest *(posgo)*, or some evil portent like a *balinkokogo* snail, which the Visayans considered unnatural because, they said, it made a squeaking sound. Once the field was ready for planting, omens were taken to determine if it would be fruitful, and sacrifices offered in the middle of the field at a bamboo post called *bunglan* or *timbaya;* only then could planting begin *(pugas)*. A row of men strode across the field punching thumb-sized holes with a heavy wooden pole *(hasuk* or *bakol)* as thick as their arm and pointed at the bottom. They were immediately followed by a row of women who dropped five or six seeds into each hole and covered them over with their toes, all with a speed and accuracy which elicited wonder from foreign observers for three centuries. Some fields were deliberately planted later than others to stagger the time of reaping and distribute the risk of bad crops. Taro and millet were often planted along the edges of the field depending on the type of soil, and weeding was required two or three times during the season *(dalos, gunit,* or *hilamon)*.

Once planted, swiddens had to be protected from birds, wild boar, and deer—though little protection could be taken against a swarm of locusts. Sturdy fences were constructed all around: either *tarluk* with fence posts as thick as a hasuk dibble stick with thinner ones lashed in between close enough together to obstruct a pig's snout; or *saruk,* a double row of posts with brush and branches piled in between and woven tight to make a veritable stockade as high as a man's chest. Even so, field huts called *bugawan* or *hulayag* had to be manned daily, and reinforced when the grain ripened, to drive off birds by beating large pieces of bamboo *(kalakopak)*, or pulling cords which jerked dangling scarecrows or wooden noisemakers at the edge of the field for wild animals, or simply by shouting, clapping, or stomping.

Harvesting was accompanied by strict religious tabus. For three days before, harvesters had to remain continent and keep away from fire. Neither could outsiders enter the house: otherwise, they believed, the rice would be all straw with very few grains. In some places they even camped in the field all during harvest, lest the rice decrease—as they said—by running away angry because the house had not been left to it alone. Harvesting was usually done by women, and men could not join them even if the crop would be lost for want of reapers. Even where it was the custom for men to join in, the harvest had to be begun by a woman ritually cutting a prescribed amount at a specific hour of the day. And once the harvest was finished, more tabus were enforced for seven days—for example, houses were closed to outsiders, and cooking fires had to be rekindled each time.

Rice was reaped panicle by panicle, leaving the stalks standing, with a sickle called *salat* or any kind of knife—for example, *sipol,* a little paring knife women ordinarily carried around with them, or *bisong*, an even smaller one for cutting threads or betel nuts. Green ears were separated to be pounded and toasted as *pilipig*, and the rest were sunned and stored unthreshed in field granaries called *kurob*, or *olog* if standing on a tree stump, or under the house in *tambobong*, a kind of huge basket of woven reed mats. It was threshed as needed by being trampled underfoot, *gilyuk;* scraped against a seashell, *kagur;* or pulled through with the hands, *humo*, a term which also meant to rub ripe grains loose from a growing plant in time of hunger, leaving the others to mature. After threshing, it was winnowed, milled with a mortar and pestle, then winnowed again. If especially white rice was wanted, it was pounded again *(hashas)*. (It was this plain white rice cooked without condiments or seasoning which the Spaniards came to call *morisqueta*—because, as Father Colín said, "it was no better than a Moro meal" [Alcina 1668a, 1:82].) It could also be pounded as fine as flour *(binokbok)*, and mixed with ingredients like honey and grated coconut to prepare confections, or fermented into yeast cakes *(tapay)* for brewing—whence, *tinapay:* leavened bread.

Second only to rice in importance and esteem was millet *(dawa)*, which in some islands was the main crop, with rice not being grown at all. It was sown by broadcasting *(sabuag);* and unlike rice, could grow in poorer soil, yielded more bountifully, and ripened sooner. But it had the great disadvantage of having seeds so hard they were tiresome to mill by pounding. Sorghum *(batar)* was also planted and eaten as a cereal but was less common, though it was regularly mentioned in Cebu. The grainlike Job's-tears *(arlay)* was also eaten in place of rice. It grew wild, and had large seeds so hard they could be drilled through and strung as necklaces. But whether rice or millet was the preferred food, root crops were actually the most common Visayan staple.

Root Crops

Among their many root crops, or tubers, the one the Visayans considered most nutritious was taro *(Colocasia)*, which required moist soil, even mud or standing water, and had large shield-shaped leaves. It was called *gabi, lagway, gaway,* or *soli* in various places, but one called *biga* was not *Colocasia* at all, but *Alocasia*. There were may varieties: Alcina (1668a, 8:103) said he counted seventy-eight, including *humnaw*, "a kind of yellowish gabi so soft and mellow it might have been mixed with butter." Taro's prominent place in Visayan life was reflected by extensive vocabulary for its parts, uses, and stages of growth. *Apay* were the leaves wrapped around other food for roasting, *laon* were edible leaves cooked on coals, and *dagmay* was an old leaf. *Hungay* was gabi too young to harvest, so they said of little children, "Hungay man an tao," meaning, "Let him play, he's still growing" (Sánchez 1617, 257).[13]

Yams *(Dioscores)* were the most widespread root crop, growing both wild and domestic in four or five different species with dozens of varieties. The most common was *ubi (D. alata);* while *abobo* was *D. bulbifera,* a species so called from the fruitlike little bulbs which grew on the stem and were cooked and eaten rather than the root itself. But *ubi,* like the English word *yam,* was also applied loosely to any bulky edible root. Sánchez (1617, 540v) glossed many Samareño terms with "a root, a kind of ubi," and defined ubi itself simply as "an edible root." Méntrida (1637a, 422) called it "a camote, a certain common species" in Hiligaynon, just as Americans often call sweet potatoes "yams."

The domestic varieties were planted in hard soil too poor for rice and too dry for taro, in holes opened with a stout planting stick; a pole was driven into the ground alongside each plant for the stem to climb. Just as important as any domestic variety was the wild yam called *korot* or *kobong,* which, when not well cured, was caustic to the taste, intoxicating, or even poisonous. It had to be treated by being cut in slices, pounded or scaled, soaked preferably in salt water in a wooden tub, and squeezed out by fistfulls. *Butwa* was the stage in this process when it could be eaten even though still wet, or *pinalagdang,* half dry; but if it was kept until it became hard, it was *buggus*—and so was a stubborn man who insisted on having his own way.

Sago

Another starchy staple food was a kind of flour made from the inner trunk of the sago palm *(lumbia),* or of a number of other palms like nipa or buri—for example, *ambolong, pugahan,* or *sakol.* The trunk was stripped, cut into pieces (measured by the ax handle if for sale), pulverized in mortars, and then washed, dissolved, and allowed to settle in tubs of water. A reddish sediment *(unaw)* collected on the bottoms, leaving the lighter bran *(olabot)* floating on the surface to be skimmed off and discarded. The flour *(arasip* or *natuk)* was boiled into a paste which could be sunned, dried, and stored in granaries called *sonson* or *olog.* In Mindanao and islands to the south, it was the main staple, where it was pressed into moulds to make little

40

cakes *(landan)* which dried as hard as bricks but became soft and palatable on boiling—like macaroni from Sicily, Alcina said. These were commercial products imported into the Philippines from Makassar packaged in leaves: Magellan's survivors intercepted a boat loaded with them just off Basilan.

Bananas

A number of different bananas and plantains (cooking bananas), boiled like rice or yams when still unripe, were also a staple food crop. Spaniards regularly praised the flavor and variety of Visayan bananas. Juan Martínez (1567, 456) rhapsodized over their Latin name, *musa*, "There can be no doubt that they are the very fruit which Jupiter's nine sisters [that is, the Muses] used to eat in their day, because they gave them the name of *musas*." Like Spaniards, Visayans ate ripe ones as fruit or between-meal snacks, especially the fragrant little ones called *todlong binokot*, "ladyfingers"— though, unlike them, probably not sprinkled with cinnamon or doused with wine. But the reason they were cultivated so widely was that before ripening, their sugar content was all starch, and so provided a valuable staple of diet.

Visayan Farming Terms

Sixteenth-century Visayan farmers knew neither the plow nor the carabao—and the rather puny plows which became available in the next century would have been of little use in swiddens anyway, because of snagging on roots. Farming tools and techniques other than those for clearing swiddens included those in the listing below.

Bakar	To till the soil by any method
Bunyag	To water plants by sprinkling
Damus or *napon*	A field of root crops
Gibo	A crude broom for sweeping a field
Habuk	To cultivate the soil for planting with a bolo
Kahig	A rake or harrow
Koyog	To plant trees, vines, bananas, or camotes in rows
Lalong	To transfer a whole plant, including the roots with soil attached
Pusok	To plant a whole field to one crop or one kind of tree
Sandol	A *paganito* (religious rite) for rain in time of drought
Sun-ad or *sunag*	A transplanted tuber
Tagbung or *hamugdas*	To plant something whole, like a coconut

41

Camote

The camote, or sweet potato *(Ipomoea batatas)*, was native to tropical America, and is not to be confused with the common potato, S*olanum tuberosum.* It had spread to the islands of Polynesia, and as far south as New Zealand under the name *kumara,* before the arrival of the Europeans—but not to Asia. The Spaniards brought it to the Philippines, at a date which cannot be determined because of a confusion of terms—that is, because sixteenth-century Spaniards called all Philippine root crops "camotes."

The problem was that when the Iberians started their maritime expeditions in the fifteenth century, they had no word for such tubers. The only root crops they knew were vegetables like radishes and turnips—indeed, the Spanish word for turnip, *nabo,* was used for roots in general. The Portuguese, in turn, did not know what to call the yams they found the Africans of Senegal eating, and so they called them *inyamis,* the local word for "eat." Because of this, later on Columbus himself called the sweet potatoes he found in Santo Domingo "ñames." However, explorers who came after him soon learned the native Taino word, *batata,* and later in Mexico, the Aztec word *kamoti,* which was Hispanized as *camote.* Both words subsequently became a convenient way to refer to root crops for which there were no equivalent in Spanish.

Pigafetta reported "batatas" in Guam and Palawan, for instance, but used this same word in Tidore to refer to *gumbili,* a kind of yam. The Legazpi expedition received "two or three batatas or ñames" in Guam, and recorded the same combination, "batatas and ñames," like a refrain all along the coast of Samar, Leyte, and Bohol, even interchanging the two words in the same sentence (Anon. 1565, 434–51). Loarca (1582, 236) said Visayans ate "some roots like the Santo Domingo batatas they call camotes."[14] And Juan de la Isla (1565, 236) referred to "some roots almost like the patatas they call oropisa, ñames and camotes." "Oropisa" is presumably Oropesa, the old Bolivian province of Cochabamba in the Andes, where potatoes, not sweet potatoes, are still grown.

During the next fifty years of Spanish arrivals from Acapulco, The Caribbean word *batata* gave way to its Mexican equivalent, *camote.* The first dictionaries of Philippine languages, dating from the early seventeenth century, always used *camote* as a Spanish word, not as a Bikolano, Tagalog, or Visayan one. Sánchez defined *halagbung* as "a certain kind of edible root or camote," and Méntrida (1637a, 62) defined *biga* as "large camotes with wide leaves." In Bikol, Marcos de Lisboa (1628, 28) called ubi "big brown camotes," and *apare* "little white camotes like testicles." The San Buenaventura Spanish-Tagalog dictionary equates camotes with gabi, *nami, tugi,* and ubi, and the unpublished manuscript dictionary of Francisco Blancas de San José defines *baging* as "some wild camotes," and *butil* as "the bud of the camote they call gabi." The historian therefore cannot tell whether early Spanish explorers—Dasmariñas in Nueva Vizcaya in 1591, for example, or Quirante in Benguet in 1623—reporting "camotes" were referring to sweet potatoes or some other root crops.

On the assumption that the "batatas" and "camotes" reported in 1565 were actually New World sweet potatoes, it has sometimes been suggested that they must have been brought over by the Villalobos expedition of 1543. It is well known that Villalobos's starving crewmen tried to grow food on Sarangani Island, but what they planted was corn, not camotes—and it did not grow. What is more likely is that camotes were introduced like corn and cacao as new crops for the benefit of the colony only after Manila was established as its capital. A reference by English corsair Thomas Cavendish in 1588 is suggestive in this connection. He said that while anchored off Capul Island (he was hoping to intercept the Manila galleon), "one of the chief Casiques . . . brought us patato rootes, which they call camotas" (Pretty 1588, 40). These were probably real camotes, since it seems u nlikely that the Filipino chieftain would have applied the alien name to a native crop.

In any event, whenever and however they were introduced, both the word and·the plant were widespread in the Visayas in Alcina's day. He probably gave what was the last word about camotes in 1668:

> The camotes which were brought here from Nueva España [Mexico] and keep the name, are really what they call batatas in Spain, but these here differ in size, being generally much larger. There are red ones and white. The camote is the refuge of the poor. These roots are rather sweet but of little sustenance and good only for wind (Alcina 1668a, 8:106).

Hunting

Visayans hunted with dogs and nets. The dogs were called *ayam*, the hunters *mangangayam*, and those who could predict whether the dog would be a good hunter by examining the teats at birth were *inayam*. Good dogs were highly valued, and had to be guarded against poison or witchcraft. When their mother or a sibling of the same litter died, a rattan collar was put around their neck, like a man in mourning, until they took their next prey. Some were raised in the house, where they were pampered and fondled: their masters rubbed noses with them—the local equivalent of kissing—and carried them out to the forest on their shoulders. To file their teeth slightly was thought to increase their bravery. (Also thought to make dogs bolder was a crocodile tooth or a boar's tusk grown in a full circle, which was carried by the hunter.) Visayan dogs were small but fearless— quick enough to avoid a boar's tusks and fierce enough to grab one three times their size by the ankle and hang on until the hunter arrived to spear it. Dogs either took a boar in the chase or drove it into a strong net *(batung)* with mesh wide enough for little shoats to pass through but catching large ones *(hababatung)*.

Large animals were also caught in pits *(awang)* or deadfall traps *(atub)*, while smaller animals were caught with snares—*balolong* in general, *balyug* for iguanas, *gawa* for monkeys, *anihas* for wild chickens, and *alikubkub, barang,* or *bitik* for birds. The most dangerous trap was the *balatik*, an automatic crossbow or ballista which, when triggered by a line stretched across an animal run, could drive a shaft clean through a pig's body. Thirty or forty of these crossbows might be set in a line at different heights. Aside from the regular ones, there were also small balatik for rats.

The balatik was a rather sophisticated machine. Standing on two stout poles driven into the ground in the form of an *X*, it had a long stock with a slot to hold the shaft, a powerful bow or spring to propel it, and a catch to hold the string and release it when triggered. It even had a safety lock *(goom)* to prevent it from firing accidentally: thus, of somebody who was restrained from acting they said, "Ginogoom kun balatik." And of a man who was all set and "rarin' to go," they said, "Bingat kun balatik [Cocked like a crossbow]" (Sánchez 1617, 52–52v).

Hunters stayed out many days, sleeping in huts called *hokdung* and opening trails in the brush to lead the game into the nets. During their absence their wives could not perform labor like weaving or pounding rice.

Part of the hunter's first catch was offered up on a tree-stump altar to Banwanun, the mountain-dwelling spirit. The rest was carried home slung on the hunter's back by a tumpline over his forehead, and later shared with others. It was never sold or preserved, though it might be exchanged informally. All animals whose flesh was considered fit for human consumption—for example, deer or civet cat—were referred to as *babuy*, pig.

Fishing

In the sixteenth century, Visayan waters literally teemed with fish. Fish swam upstream to spawn in inland streams, inhabited swamps and thick muddy waters, rose to the surface to breathe, and even climbed up onto the roots of mangrove trees. Large ones competed with fishermen by attacking their nets, and more voracious ones like barracuda actually endangered the fishermen themselves. Fish were caught in nets, traps, and corrals at the mouth of rivers or dammed-up streams, snared with hook and line, or speared with harpoons.

Most fishing was done close inshore, so there was little incentive for deep-sea fishing or for the use of nets large enough to require organized parties. It was often done at night, because schools of fish could be seen shimmering in the moonlight, or because they could be attracted to torches in the boats.

There was a variety of nets. *Paggiyod* were dragnets used in shallow water, fastened to the small of the fishermen's back by a leather brace *(paholan)* like the belt the weaver uses with a backstrap loom. *Laya* was a casting net: Sánchez thought it was a recent introduction in his day, though there was a similar net *(holos)* in use, except that it was lighter and had no lead sinkers. Some were 5 meters across and so required considerable dexterity to cast: datus were as proud of such skill as they were of their hunting skills. *Baring* were nets woven like loose cloth; fine ones were for catching tiny *hipon* shrimp in the surf; while *howar* were nets with the widest mesh and were used in swamps. *Pansag* was what is nowadays called a *salambaw*—a large four-cornered net lowered by a simple derrick mounted on a raft. *Pagbiday* was to set nets upright along the edge of thirty or forty boats strung out along the shore, which caught fish leaping into the air to escape fishermen wading alongside. It was a raucous activity accompanied by much hilarity as fish fell all over those fishermen who were in the boats, sometimes even wounding them.

There was quite a variety of ways of catching fish. Rivers were dammed to lead fish into nets or traps; for this, weirs or corrals *(bakod)* were constructed as long as 250 meters. The roots, bark, or berries of more than a dozen different trees, called *tubli* in general, were squeezed into the water to stun the fish. Rattan basket traps *(bobo)* were set in creeks. A hook and line called *rombos* was also used, as well as harpoons made in different styles—*kalawit* or *isi* (also used for hunting) which were barbed like an arrowhead; *sikap*, a two-pronged fork; *sarapang*, a real trident with three or more points; and *bontal,* a heavier one for catching *duyong,* the manatee or seacow. These harpoons were thrown with a line attached to the boat, and a powerful fish could pull one out to sea if the line was not quickly cut.

Domestic Animals

Seafood was the main source of protein in the Visayan diet; but pigs and chickens were also raised—not just for consumption but also for sacrificial offerings. Since deer and wild hogs were also called babuy, domestic pigs were distinguished as *sohong.* Different islands had their own breeds, some of which yielded 120 liters of lard or 240 kilos of pork on butchering. They foraged between village houses and kept the ground clean of offal, or were pastured in nearby woodlands with their ears clipped for identification.

A pig was often raised in the house, where it was reported to be cleaner than a dog, and was called "princess" *(binokot)* like the secluded daughters of upper-class datus because—like them—it never set foot on the ground. There was also a cat in every house to keep it free of rats, and if a civet cat could be caught young enough to tame, it made an even better mouser. Household dogs were provided with a special ladder to come and go as they pleased, and pet monkeys also acted as watchdogs to give noisy warning of approaching strangers.

Goats were rare: Spanish explorers observed only a few on the coast of Samar and in Cebu. But they were common in Mindanao and areas in contact with Muslims in the south—for example, they were raised for trade in the Semirara Islands between Panay and Mindoro, which the Spaniards called Islas de Cabras (Goat Islands) because they were populated with goats that had been turned loose to breed wild.

Horned cattle—that is, cows—were only introduced late in the century from China and Mexico, with a few bulls brought from Spain to improve the stock.[15]

The absence of the carabao is noteworthy. That it was not used as a draft animal is not surprising, but that colonial reports listing natural resources do not mention buffalo meat, hide, or horns, is. Mention was made of small horn containers for perfume and of one shaman wearing a horn headdress, but no mention made of buffalo horn armor or battle trumpets. The beast was found wild, or feral, in Luzon from Bikol to the Ilocos, in all of which places it was called *nowang* or *anowang,* but in the Visayas it was *karabaw*—that is, Malay *kerbau.* But whether it roamed the Visayan hills or not, the

Visayans evidently did not hunt it in sufficient quantity to attract Spanish attention.

Cooking

Visayan cooking was done on a clay *kalan* stove, or three stones *(sugang)* in an open hearth. Besides flint-and-steel, there were three other traditional methods of *bag-id,* making fire by friction: by pulling a band of rattan back and forth around a split stick driven upright in the ground holding the tinder; by rubbing a knife-shaped piece of bamboo along another stuffed with tinder and held horizontal with the foot; or by rotating a wooden rod between the palms, drill-like, against a wooden board. The tinder was either fine wood shavings or the lintlike fuzz of various palms.

Staple foods were boiled; though tubers, bananas, and fleshy leaves or leaf stems were also roasted in hot coals. Viands were frequently fried in coconut oil, and both meat and fish were barbecued or smoked as *tapa.* Steamed in sections of bamboo were all kinds of food—*paylaw* in general; *sakol,* if rice flour with grated coconut; and *lotlot,* if broken out afterwards to retain their cylindrical shape. Grain was also parched in dry pots; likewise dried were seeds and fruit pits intended to be pulverized to mix with rice to stretch a limited supply: *lamur* was any such mixing with millet, sorghum, beans, or nuts. Pili seeds were collected for this purpose, having been picked from under the trees where they had been dropped by *kalaw* birds after digesting the flesh.

Seafood—not only fish but eels, snails, squid, crabs, mollusks, turtles, and turtle eggs—were the main source of Visayan protein and was preferred to meat. Wild game was considered a typical masculine food and little preferred by women. All meat was forbidden pregnant women—and so was shark flesh because baby sharks were believed to swim in and out of their mother's womb during her pregnancy. Fish were preserved and marketed as sun-dried *daing,* or split open and salted before sunning as *barol. Lasi* was fermented fish paste or meat brine; *dayok, danglusi,* and *ginamus* were high-flavored *adobo*-like dishes of minced meat or fish. *Yaman* or *panakot* were any kind of spices and seasonings—all pungent and sour foods fit to supplement a bland starchy diet.

Honey was also an important food, as indicated by the frequent mention of activities connected with it. Seasons were designated by the flowering of trees and plants whose nectar fed the bees—like Katparasan from January to March when the *paraasan* rattan was in bloom. Wind and rain could

47

destroy the blossoms, and typhoons the bees themselves, so the weather was a subject of constant speculation. Conversely, it was believed that for bees to swarm low in the trees was a sign of a bad year to come. Similarly, *kagas*, a dry honeycomb, was the euphemism for any vain undertaking or unrewarded labor. In a good year, men could expect to find as many as fifty hives in one expedition, during which they would sleep in the forest, drive the bees off with smouldering torches, and boil the honey to prevent its souring before they got back with it. Honey was eaten as a food together with the white grubs it contained, or made into confections and sauces, used as a preservative for meat and fruit, or brewed into the meadlike *kabarawan*.

Rice cakes boiled in a little wrapper of coconut leaves were called *puso* after the banana flower, and were prepared in a number of different sizes and shapes—for example, *linalaki*, masculine; *binuwaya*, crocodilelike; or *kumol sin datu*, "datu's fistful." (The normal way to eat rice was to squeeze a fistful into a lump—*kumol*.) *Tambol* were made with rice flour, *kombo* with rice flour and coconut milk, *linanggang* with rice and grated coconut, and *handab* were deep-fried.

Though Visayans did not make cane sugar, they obtained an unrefined brown sugar called *kalamay*—or *chancaca* in Spanish—from palm sap, and peddled it in little square packets of palm leaves called *parak*, ten parak being tied together and sold as one *dankay*. *Sara-sara* was rice mixed with such sugar, one of a number of snacks or tidbits called *doom*.

Salt was served in rock-hard lumps to be given a few sharp blows over the food, or stirred a few turns in liquids. It was made by pouring a lye, which had been drained off burnt wood earlier soaked in salt water, into moulds shaped like a little boat *(baloto)*, whence the lump was called *binaloto*.

Meals were served on low tables about 20 centimeters high (nicely carved in the case of those of datus) or directly on the house floor on large leaves. Tubers and rice—saffron-yellow for feasts—were boiled unseasoned; so salt, ginger, and other condiments were served for diners to choose their own seasoning. *Dolot* was one serving—whence *dolotan* was a medium-sized plate. *Gakas* was the food a guest carried home; and *bahaw* was cold food left over from a meal, the usual breakfast. In the case of feeding workers in exchange for group labor, the meat and fish were piled in mounds called *bongdo* (literally, anthills) by families or neighborhoods. In real feasts and drinkfests, however, food was taken casually and in small quantities to leave time for talk and wine (invitations said "drink," not "eat"), and it was considered good form to place a mouthful of already-chewed food in a guest's mouth.

Betel Nut

Betel nut is the fruit of the areca palm, and is chewed together with a leaf of the betel piper vine, from which it has borrowed its name. The nut is cut into segments, sprinkled with lime made from shells, wrapped in a leaf, and chewed into a quid which produces a blood-red spittle. In Visayan, the nut was called *bonga* (literally "fruit"); the betel vine was called *buyo,* and so was a prepared quid; to chew it was *mama,* whence the quid was also called *mamun.*

The preparation, exchange, and serving of betel nut was the most important social act among Visayans. Men carried the necessary ingredients with them in little baskets or pouches, ready to share segments of the same nut, *kulo,* and thus become *kakulo* with another, an essential relationship before beginning any discussion or business. For a householder to fail to offer betel nut to anyone who entered his house was an insult inviting enmity. On formal visits, the quids were prepared and served in valuable metal trays or boxes by females of the household—slaves, daughters, or the lady herself, depending on the social standing of the guest. (The Panay epic of Humadapnon climaxes with a sixty-two-line description of betel nut being prepared and served by binokot maidens.) A special honor was to add a touch of musk or a slice of cinnamon bark, or some other aromatic flavoring. Betel nut also figured in romance and courtship: to offer a quid partially chewed *(upa)* was an act of flirtation; to send one in response to a man's clandestine request was an acceptance of his advances; to send it unbidden, an open invitation.

Bonga palms were extensively cultivated, often with a buyo vine planted at their base. However, inferior nuts from wild palms were used when necessary—such as *sarwang,* which was not an areca palm at all.

Youths chewing for the first time usually suffered giddiness like that produced by alcohol or korot root, and even a young lady's first chew was a kind of puberty rite. In a Suban-on epic, when the hero Sandayo appears before Datu Daugbulawan so young that "the sword at his waist scraped the floor," he is told, "Bata, k'na ginapog: po dapa no p'nlebon [Child, no lime for you: you know not woman]" (Resma 1982, 291).

Distilling and Drinking

One of the first things the Spaniards learned about the Visayans was that they were good drinkers. Magellan had no sooner landed on Homonhon, when people from nearby Suluan presented him with a jarful of what Pigafetta recorded as *uraca*—that is, *arak,* the Malay-Arabic word for distilled liquors. In Limasawa, Pigafetta drank from the same cup as Rajah Kolambu, and his translator, Enrique de Malacca, got so drunk he was not much use; and a few days later, the local harvest was delayed while Kolambu and his brother Awi slept off a hangover. In Cebu, Pigafetta drank palm wine, *tuba nga nipa,* straight from the jar with reed straws together with Rajah Humabon, but in Quipit he excused himself after one draught when Rajah Kalanaw and his companions finished off a whole jar without eating anything.

The Spaniards therefore called Visayan social occasions *bacanales,* drinkfests. Loarca (1582, 116) commented, however, "It's good they rarely get angry when drunk," and Father Chirino (1604, 79) left a well-known tribute to the Boholanos' ability to carry their liquor:

> It is proverbial among us that none of them who leaves a party completely drunk in the middle of the night fails to find his way home; and if they happen to be buying or selling something, not only do they not become confused in the business but when they have to weigh out gold or silver for the price ... they do it with such delicate touch that neither does their hand tremble nor do they err in accuracy.

There were basically five kinds of Visayan alcoholic beverages—*tuba,* kabarawan, *intus or kilang, pangasi,* and *alak.* Tuba was the sap of palms which fermented naturally in a few hours and soured quickly. Kabarawan was honey fermented with a kind of boiled bark. Intus or kilang was sugarcane wine, which improved with aging. Pangasi was rice wine or beer (that is, toddy), fermented with yeast, but could also be brewed from other grains like millet, all called *pitarrilla* by Spaniards. And alak was any of these beverages distilled into hard liquor. Alak was drunk from cups, but the others with reed straws from the porcelain jars in which they were brewed or stored. Pangasi was required for all formal or ceremonial occasions.

Tuba. Nipa tuba *(paog)* was made from the sap of wild trees, and was usually strengthened—and given a red color—by the addition of ground *tungug* or *lawaan* bark. But tuba made from coconut palms was considered better and was therefore a profitable item of trade. Distilled into alak, it could be transported as far as the oil, vinegar, or nuts themselves, but brought a much better price.

Tuba tappers rented the trees or were hired to tend them, and where the soil was favorable, whole islands became coconut plantations with trees spreading by natural propagation to the exclusion of all other vegetation. Suluan was one such island: Pigafetta got the impression that a family of ten could live off two trees there. That is no doubt why Magellan threatened Lapulapu that he would "burn their land and the palm groves off which they supported themselves" (Anon. n.d.a, 11).

Kabarawan. Kabarawan (from *baraw*, to temper or mediate) was the wood whose bark was decocted to produce the beverage. The decoction was further boiled to half its volume, mixed with an equal volume of fresh honey, and left to ferment naturally to become a smooth, strong liquor— "muy regalado y fuerte," Father Sánchez said. Unlike more ceremonial drinks like pangasi, it was consumed by men gathered around the jar, all sipping through straws until the bottom of the jar was visible. Since honey was an important item in the Visayan diet, kabarawan was produced in sufficient quantity to market—and its production and consumption were no doubt increased by Spanish tribute demands for candle wax.

Intus. Sugarcane juice was extracted with a simple one-man press. A long springy pole was pivoted over a tree stump and kept bouncing up and down with one hand and a foot pedal, while with the other hand, the cane was inserted to be squeezed near the fulcrum. The juice was boiled, preferably in a cast-iron *baong* that held as much as 15 liters, to half its volume. (For Spanish consumption, it was boiled down to a thick syrup.) It was then *sinubaw*, and a small bundle of kabarawan bark was added as seasoning. When cool, it was stored in Chinese porcelains if available and left to ferment and age as intus or kilang.

Visayans did not make sugar itself. Even after the introduction of the Chinese sugar mill—the one with two rollers geared together and turned by a carabao—when sugar was for sale to those who could afford it, intus remained the main use for sugarcane. The juice was also drunk as a tonic, and served as a substitute for mother's milk when necessary. Varieties of cane less suitable for pressing were eaten as food or snacks, and invariably offered to visitors upon arrival. *Sagaw*, for instance, was the sweetest variety, but was too hard and fibrous for the Visayan press—though these same characteristics were desirable when inserting it between the rollers of the Chinese mill.

Pangasi. *Basi* was the mash of cooked rice, already leavened with tapay, which was placed in the jar to produce the liquid pangasi. It was let stand until it became strong and sour, and was drunk with the addition of water and, as the jar was drained, the addition of more basi. It was drunk through reed straws called *tayuk* or *halasam,* or drawn from the jar with a *poot,* a node of thin bamboo open at the bottom and with a finger hole near the top, which was submerged in the pangasi until it filled, and then withdrawn with the finger hole closed to create a vacuum to retain its contents. The mash left in the drained jar was called *borohu.*

Pangasi drinking began with formality and ceremony. The jars were placed in a long row down the middle of the room. Then the master of ceremonies, after invoking the *diwata* (deity) to drink first, invited the guests to drink in turn, indicating which guest and which jar. Constantly checking the contents of the jars as the drinking went on (a procedure called "nesting," *pugad),* he would call on drinkers to add a certain amount of water. They were then required to drink as much pangasi as the water they added. These selections were made amid increasing banter and challenges, and finally the singing of *daihuan,* a kind of song in which one man would be victimized by rough teasing—but, as Loarca noted, was expected to show no resentment. In the end, some of the pangasi might be "bought"— that is, the host compensated by filling an emptied jar with raw rice.

Alak. Alak or *alaksiw* was anything made with a still—for example, *alak sa sampaga,* sampaguita perfume—and *makialak* was a confirmed drunkard. The still *(alakan)* was made of a hollow tree trunk *(toong)* and two Chinese vats *(baong, kawa,* or *karahay).* The toong was caulked onto the top of the vat containing the tuba or intus to be boiled, and the other vat in turn placed on top of the toong. The steam condensed on the upper vat's round bottom and dripped off its lowest point into a shallow wooden plate suspended in the middle of the toong, whence the liquid flowed out through a bamboo tube *(tadluyan)* run through the side.

The first liter or two were the strongest and best, and, in the case of intus, had the qualities of brandy. This was called *dalisay,* pure or first-class, a term of high esteem for both wine and gold. (A Tagalog dictionary [1613, 601] says, "Metaphorically, 24 karats strong, . . . burns without fire.")

Pangasi was not used as a base for alak, though Pigafetta thought he tasted distilled rice wine in Palawan. *Lambug* was to mix, dilute, or adulterate any of these liquors, and was a common practice. Watered wine was thus called *linambugan,* and so was the child of a mixed marriage or adulterous union.

Drinking Etiquette

Except for outright alcoholics who suffered poor health and early demise, Visayans did not drink alone, nor appear drunk in public. Drinking was done in small groups or in social gatherings where men and women sat on opposite sides of the room, and any passerby was welcome to join in. Women drank more moderately than men, and were expected to stretch their menfolk out, to sleep off any resulting stupor. But men were proud of their capacity. Father Alcina had a Samareño parishioner whom "neither Spaniards on a bet nor Filipinos with the same intent" could make drunk, no matter how much they gave him, and a famous Bohol datu enjoyed the reputation of downing three liters fresh from the still with one breath. Prudent drinkers, however, prepared beforehand by "lining the belly with food," like lining the cooking pot with banana leaves *(banig)*—"hinanigan an ginhawa sin kanun" (Sánchez 1617, 62v).

Drinking etiquette began with *agda*, exhorting some person, or diwata, to take the first drink. *Gasa* was to propose a toast to somebody's health, usually of the opposite sex, and *salabat* was a toast in which the cup itself was offered, even carried from one house to another for this purpose. *Itib* were milk brothers, and *naga itib* was for two to drink together from the same jar, like two babies nursing at the same breast. *Abong* was an honor a datu might pay one of his *timawa* vassals by presenting his own cup after he had taken a few sips himself. *Sumsum* was any food taken with the wine (that is, *pulotan*), like the plate of pork Rajah Kolambu shared with Pigafetta (1524b, 118), who reported, "We took a cup with every mouthful." And had Pigafetta been a Visayan, he would have murmured politely with each piece, "Tabi-tabi dinyo [By your leave, sir]."

Drinking was commonly called *pagampang*, conversation; and neither business deals, family affairs, nor community decisions were discussed without it. For this reason, Spaniards often attributed Filipino attempts to subvert their occupation to an overindulgence in wine. But Alcina (1668a, 3:325) assessed the custom more realistically:

> When practical matters come up, whether for public projects, orders from the King or his officials, or any other work, and they discuss among themselves the best, quickest and most equitable way to carry it out, if they meet dry and without a little wine first to enliven their interest, they talk little, discourse poorly and slowly, and decide worse; but after drinking something, he who proposes does it with eloquence, those who respond, with discretion, those who decide, with attention, and all with fairness.

CHAPTER 3

Trades and Commerce

Visayans who practiced trades like blacksmithy, boat building, or pot making were professionals in the sense of being compensated for specialized skills, but not necessarily in the sense of supporting themselves by their professions. Markets for their wares and services were limited; most men did their own carpentry and their wives wove their own cloth. It appears that all either farmed or belonged to a farming family, including fishermen, even members of the datu class. But there were clearly those who practiced their crafts full time—experts like shipwrights or goldsmiths, for example, or the producers of export textiles who were the slaves, dependents, or employees of datu capitalists. Traders, too, were full-time professionals—peddlers and itinerant merchants, especially those who owned their own vessels, rented out cargo space, and traveled long distances from island to island carrying goods in both directions.

Ironworking

Blacksmiths were *panday*—or, more accurately, *panday sa puthaw*, workers in iron, to distinguish them from other craftsmen like goldsmiths, master carpenters, and boat builders, all of whom were called panday. Smithing was considered the noblest profession, probably because only the wealthiest datus had the means to import the raw material. If they were indeed the ultimate source of all metal tools, including the swidden farmers' bolos, they would have exercised effective control over Visayan means of production. As Father Alcina (1668a, 3:105) said, "it is certain that no profession among the Visayans is more profitable than this, and so it is the most honored and esteemed among them, since the greatest chiefs are the best iron-workers."

Iron itself had actually been produced in the Philippines in ancient times. Iron slag has been recovered in considerable quantities from archaeological sites, including Visayan graves, and slag is normally a waste product of iron smelting and refining. But to extract the metal from the ore by primitive methods is very difficult, and so is the transportation of the ore. Thus it is generally more economical to trade local forest products for malleable cast iron if available, and it was available at least by the thirteenth century. Bornean refineries were then producing it in large quantities in Santubong (Sarawak), and Song traders were delivering big Chinese cauldrons and pig iron direct. By the sixteenth century, iron was also being produced in Sulawesi, but was still so rare and valuable that when the *Santa María del Parral* ran aground in Sangir in 1526, the natives burned her to recover the nails. In the Visayas, those Chinese cauldrons remained the major source: they were deliberately broken up to supply local forges.

The bellows of the forge *(hasohas)* were two upright cylinders *(tayhop)* about a meter high, hollowed out of small tree trunks, with pistons *(tamborok)* ringed with chicken feathers set so as to collapse on the return stroke. They were alternately raised and lowered by the blacksmith's apprentice *(masaop)* to produce a steady draft. Both cylinders had a bamboo outlet near the bottom which led to a common stone receptacle *(lilong)* which concentrated their draft into a charcoal fire. The anvil *(landasan)* was a piece of iron set in a heavy wooden block, and the smith's tools were a two-handed stone maul *(palo)*, a stone hammer *(palo-palo)*, a pair of tongs *(kipit)*, and an assortment of ordinary bolos for cutting the red-hot metal.

The most important tool manufactured, repaired, or retempered by the blacksmith was the bolo. *Dohong* or *dayopak* was the ordinary one; *tuwad*, a heavier one for woodcutting; *bako* or *bantok*, one with a curved blade for weeding or cultivating; and *pisaw*, one with a short blade and long handle to be pressed under the arm or against the ground with the foot to leave both hands free for stripping rattan. The blade had a tang for hafting into the wooden handle, and was held firm with resinous sap and a ring of rattan or metal. The head of the ax *(wasay)* was also hafted into the handle; it was only about two fingers wide and could be rotated a quarter turn to be used as an adze.

More specialized tools included those in the list below.

Abluwang	Drill, awl
Batakan	A blade for slicing *korot*
Barit	A rough piece of iron for whetting tools or striking with flint for fire
Binkong	Curved adze
Bisong	Small knife for preparing betel nut
Dallag	Straight adze
Garol	Spurs for fighting cocks
Kalob	Spoon bit
Sabit or *sared*	Billhook or hoe
Salat	Sickle
Sipol	Paring knife
Sanggut	Tuba tapper's knife for "gelding" the buds
Tigib	Chisel
Tirlos	Lancet for bleeding
Ulok	Dentist's awl

Two carpenter's tools which later became common were apparently missing from the sixteenth-century Visayan tool kit—the saw *(lagari)* and the plane *(saiyo)*.

Woodworking

Carpenters cut their own timber, carefully observing accepted nature lore in selecting it. Different species were felled during different phases of the moon; some were believed to be more solid on the eastern side, and "male" trees were always stronger than "females" of the same species. The trees were cut with an ax and bolo, split down the middle with wedges, and each half adzed into a single plank, squared with the same tool. All carpentry and house construction were done by skillful joinery without saws or nails.

Boards were fitted together with mortise-and-tenons, joined end to end with scarf joints, or rabbeted into grooves. Lugs called *tambuko* were carved out of the surface of planks to receive other pieces lashed to them; and pegs and tenons were glued in place with a resin so sticky these broke off before coming loose. Large wooden houses stood on hardwood posts *(harigi)* chosen for their incorruptibility, with huge pegs set into them to carry the floor beams, and wooden walls were fitted into channels chiseled into sills above and below. Plates, bowls, spoons, and ladles, urns called *bohon*, coffins and chests of all sizes were hewn from single blocks of wood, and often decorated with fine carvings. Rough leaves of the *hagopit* tree or *biri* palm were used as sandpaper or wood rasps, and the tough tail of the *bisol* ray fish or hide of the *dahonan* served to smooth even the hardest woods.

Architecture

The Visayan word for house was *balay;* whence *kabalayan* was a settlement; *magkabalay,* a man and wife; and *minalay* meant married. There were basically three types—permanent wooden structures that might be called town houses, cottages built of light materials near the fields, and tree houses. The first were occupied by datus, the second by ordinary people, and the third only in time of war. Houses were elevated off the ground on posts and dominated by steep roofs, both features appropriate to a tropical environment characterized by heavy rains. The prominence of the roof was reflected in Pigafetta's symbol for houses on his maps—a triangle standing on legs: 🔺 . In addition, there was a variety of huts *(balay-balay)* and temporary shelters for hunters, farmers, and travelers.

The large town houses were supported on tall hardwood pillars (harigi, or *togbong* if supporting the ridgepole, *toko* if only reaching floor level). There were five to ten on a side, planted deep in the ground with some valuable *(sanag)* buried under the first one, so sturdy and incorruptible that some were known to survive decay and typhoon for two or three generations. The upper ends were set into a girder *(sablayan)* which carried the main rafters *(saragunting,* so called because they crossed at the ridgepole like *gunting,* shears, to extend beyond the ridge), and joined to the opposite harigi by a tie beam *(ubung-ubung)*. A lower girder *(sasagangan)* which carried the floor joists *(batangan)* and the sills *(bakalan)* into which the wallboards *(dingding)* were rabbeted, was supported on big pegs *(tanor)* driven into the harigis, or directly on shorter toko. (See fig. 4.)

The floor *(salog)* was divided into two sections *(puta)*, one slightly higher than the other, by a squared beam *(puthanan)* running lengthwise, and was made of bamboo, rattan, or cane strips lashed together on top of a wooden grill. Both the grill and the rattan strips were called *buklag*, and were loose enough to permit liquids to run through—and noisy enough to keep respectful house members off it while the datu was sleeping. The roof

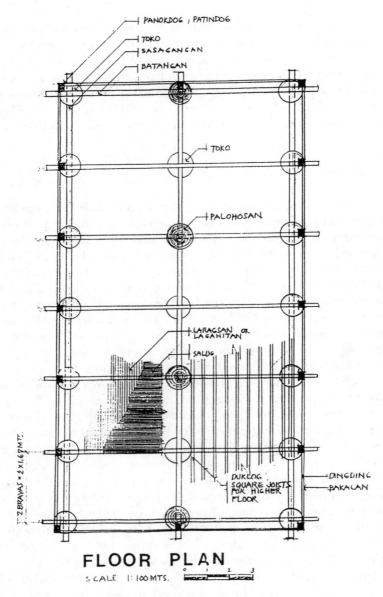

FLOOR PLAN

SCALE 1:100 MTS.

Fig. 4. A sixteenth-century Visayan "balay"
(Artist's representation by architect Rosario Encarnacion-Tan,
under the supervision of W. H. Scott)

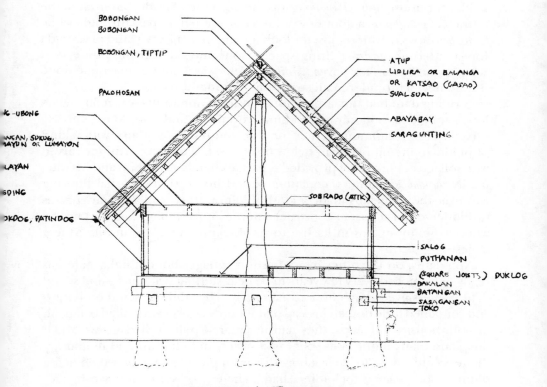

BOBONGAN
BOBONGAN

BOBONGAN, TIPTIP

PALOHOSAN

IG -UBONG

INGAN, SUKUG,
MAYUN OR LUMAYON

LAYAN

SDING

OKDOG, PATINDOG

ATUP
LIDLIRA OR BALANGA
OR KATSAO (GASAO)
SUAL SUAL

ABAYABAY
SARAGUNTING

SOBRADO (ATTIK)

SALOG
PUTHANAN
(SQUARE JOISTS) DUKLOG
BAKALAN
BATANGAN
SASAGANGAN
TOKO

CROSS SECTION

SCALE   1:100 MTS.   0   1   2   3 MTS.

(atup) was bamboo or palm leaf shingles lashed to parallel strips of heavy rattan *(katsaw),* rising to the ridgepole *(bobongan,* from *bobong,* the ridge and its covering)—or, actually to three ridgepoles in the case of large buildings, one above the other with one protruding beyond the ends of the house like horns, or *sayong* (see fig. 4).

Finer details of Visayan architecture are revealed by their special terms. *Hagdan,* for example, was a house ladder or stairway; *balitang,* one rung or step; and *alantaga,* a landing; but *lugdog* was a single bamboo used as a ladder with stubs of branches left on; and *salugsog* was a split-bamboo ladder for house dogs. *Pamulong* was the decorated facade; *pasngawan,* the entrance; *ganghaan,* a door or window large enough to pass through; while *tarambowan* was a window just for looking out. *Batalan* was a kind of veranda for laundering; *saramde,* living spaces along the sides of the house; and *sibay,* a small room for slaves *(isinibay). Pusor* was a kind of macramé done in rattan which rendered all structural bindings artistic.

A ruling datu had the largest house in the community—even 30 meters long—and it was not only his dwelling, workplace, and storehouse, but also served as the community center for civic and religious affairs, with a kind of public lounging platform below or in front. Wooden partitions carved with foliage in high relief provided separate chambers for him and his wife, family, *binokot* daughters, concubines, and house slaves. Partial flooring laid over the tie beams made a kind of loft or attic. Similar grandeur was forbidden other datus: to construct a house large enough to entertain the whole community was in itself a form of competition amounting to lese majesty.

Non-datus, on the other hand, lived in cottages built of light materials ready to be moved every few years to be near shifting swiddens—and so did datu farmers live in such houses seasonally. They did not stand on harigis and contained little timber: instead of the sturdy crossbeams called batangan in both houses and ships, they had unsquared poles called *sagbat.* Much time, and many nights, was spent in a variety of field huts and temporary shelters convenient to their labor—for example, the *ogsoran,* which had a sliding roof to serve for either shade, shelter, or sunning. (See fig. 5.) Travelers, farmers, hunters, and fishers, even seamen beaching their boats for the night, put up so many of them that they could usually be found already standing along well-traveled roads or river fords.

Tree houses were occupied only in time of war, built either in actual trees 15 or more meters above the ground, or on tall posts. If they were intended only for male warriors, they were reached simply by a vine which could be pulled up; but if a whole family occupied them, they were full-

Fig. 5. Visayan houses
(From Alcina's *Historia de las islas e indios de Bisayas*)

scale dwellings with a platform midway up reached by a removable ladder, with a second ladder up to the house itself. (See fig. 5.) They all disappeared after Spanish pacification, and so did those datu mansions, as their public functions were taken over by government buildings and churches.

Boat Building

Visayan boat builders preferred *lawaan* because it grew large enough for a baroto 120 centimeters wide to be hewn out of a single trunk. The panday adzed the outer form of the hull to shape first—sharp at the bottom like a keel, pointed and V-shaped at both ends, with sides no thicker than a thin board. He hollowed out the interior, leaving the necessary tambuko projecting to seat thwarts called *agar*. To check the thickness of the thinning process as he worked, he kept boring holes through the sides, to be plugged up watertight later. A good panday could make such a canoe 9 meters long and 1.5 meters wide, working by himself in just ten days.

Although a baroto could have boards added to increase its freeboard, real ships intended for cargo capacity or seagoing raids were built on squared keels with stems at both ends. As long as 25 meters, they had five or six planks to a side, each carved to the desired curve beforehand, preferably in one continuous stroke. Since it was their flare and curvature which determined the contour of the hull and consequently the speed of the vessel, the skill to produce them was the hallmark of the master panday. The planks were edge-pegged together, with thin wooden nails run through each peg in place, plank and all, and the chinks between the planks caulked tight. The whole shell was then tightened by placing logs across the gunwales, running heavy ropes under the hull fastened to the log on each side, and driving wedges into the ends of the logs to expand them enough to draw the ropes taut. Only then were the ribs added: flexible branches forced down in an arc and lashed to the tambukos that they crossed to induce prestressed tension in a hull that was strong and light but not rigid.[16]

A baroto was basically what the Spaniards called a *canoa*—a dugout canoe. If it was simply a single piece, it was called *damlog*, or *balasiyan* if small enough for a man to pick up, but if it had bark washboards added for increased freeboard, it was *bilos*, and if wooden planks were added, *tilimbaw* or *yahit*. The well-known *barangay* was an edge-pegged, plank-built boat constructed on a keel: large ones for carrying cargo were *bidok*, *biroko*, *biray*, or *lapid*.

Flat, open boats were *daya* or *paya* (literally, a half coconut shell), but by the end of the century they were being called *champan* from Chinese *sampan* ("three boards"), a term eighteenth-century Europeans would extend to any Chinese vessel, even huge seagoing junks. All foreign vessels with high freeboard were called *adyong*—that is, Malay *jong*. But the most celebrated Visayan vessel was the warship called *karakoa* —a sleek, double-ended cruiser with an elevated fighting deck amidships, and catwalks mounted on the outrigger supports to seat as many as six banks of paddlers (see fig. 6). They displayed tall staffs of brilliant plumage fore and aft as a sign of victory, called *sombol* on the prow, *tongol* on the stern.

All these vessels were designed for coastal seas full of reefs and rocks, and interisland passages with treacherous currents. They therefore drew little water, had low freeboard, had outriggers on both sides and steering oars instead of center-line rudders, and their flexible hulls could absorb underwater blows that would have stayed in the sides of a more rigid vessel. They had one or more tripod masts that carried matting sails woven of palm fibers—though ironically, the Manila galleons would later be sailing under Philippine canvas woven on backstrap looms. Their sails were wider than high and had a yard both top and bottom, a type of lug sail the Spaniards called Lutaw after a seafaring people (*lutaw* meant floating) in Mindanao and Sulu. Paddles, a meter or 120 centimeters long *(bugsay)* and with a leaf-shaped blade, were carved of a single piece of wood. Oars *(gaor)*, however, had a blade shaped like a dinner plate. The karakoa could mount forty of them on a side, and its speed was proverbial. As Father Combés (1667, 70) said, "The care and technique with which they build them makes their ships sail like birds, while ours are like lead in comparison."

Pottery

The Visayan potter's craft was *dihoon,* and it was practiced by female potters using not a potter's wheel but the paddle-and-anvil technique. The *maninihon* gathered the clay herself *(kalot),* kneaded it *(luyang),* and then made a lump for each pot shaped like half a coconut husk. She placed this over one hand holding inside it a smooth round stone—the anvil *(igsosool).* She then thinned and enlarged the lump of clay into pot shape by giving it light blows on the outside with a paddle *(dokol* or *dapi).* (From the slapping sound, *pakpak* or *pikpik,* she was also called *mamarakpak* or *mamirikpik.*) Sticking the soft pot on a board or basin for easy rotating, she widened and smoothed the lip with a wet cloth *(igigihit),* and then left the

63

Fig. 6. Classic Philippine *karakoa*
(Artist's reconstruction by Raoul Castro, under the supervision
of W. H. Scott; from *Philippine Studies* vol.30, 3d quarter)

finished pot to dry in the sun. It was then fired *(pagba)* without a kiln, while still "green" *(lunhaw);* and it was strictly tabu to make any clicking sounds with the mouth within earshot, lest the pot make the same sound by cracking. (If it cracked later from long use, however, it might be mended with *bayog* bark.)

The common cooking pot was *daba* or *koron,* or *anglet* or *tanuk* in Panay. *Bogoy* was one with an especially wide mouth; and *balanga,* a flat pan suitable for frying. The *banga* water jar was shaped like the porcelains preferred for brewing and drinking *pangasi. Dulang,* a large plate with a foot, had a wooden counterpart by the same name. This is a limited inventory, obviously of ordinary household crockery.

Conspicuously absent from lexicons compiled by the Spaniards are names of the elegant ceramics which appeared in ancient Philippine graves—all those decorated jars and jarlets, delicate little goblets, bowls standing on three or four legs, and plates raised up on perforated stands like serving dishes in a modern Cantonese restaurant. These were evidently ceremonial or funerary items which ultimately could not compete with the trade porcelains introduced from China and Thailand by the tens of thousands. By the sixteenth century, even dinner plates were mainly chinaware—whether *pingan lasa,* large ones, *lampay,* small ones, or *siwit,* little ones like sauce dishes.

Fine porcelain, along with gold jewelry and bronze gongs, constituted that heirloom wealth which Visayans called *bahandi*— "property [hacienda] to be distinguished from *ginamikun,*" Sánchez (1617, 45v) said, "which is ordinary jewelry, plates, pots, etc." Thus, when the people of Sarangani evacuated under Spanish attack in 1543, they carried their plates, gongs, and gold with them and buried them in the hills. (Villalobos had them dug up to send home, but had to trade them off for food in Samar instead.) The Visayans called large porcelain items—say, 12 or 15 liters—*tadyaw.* Thus anything valued at that price was *tinadyaw;* and when a man was enslaved for inability to pay a fine, it might be calculated in *tinaradyaw.*

Naturally there was also a long list of names for specific types of porcelain ware. Ordinary Chinese jars were *ang-ang.* The ones used for pangasi were *gining. Abdan* and *lumbang* were large ones. *Linoping* were the big Zheiiang wares with "ears" (handles) the Portuguese called *martabanas;* they were called "linoping" because they were decorated all over like *loping,* men tattooed all over. *Hinalasan* were dragon jars, so called from the "snake" *(halas)* done in high relief on their sides; they were also called *basingun* because they were worth 1 *basing,* a gold tael. *Tinampilak* was a large black jar; *tuytuy,* a small black one; and *kabo,* a Ming blue and white jarlet.

Plates had even more names according to their size, shape, and color, but all the big deep ones were called *kawkawun* from *kawkaw,* to swish the fingers from side to side; and some were valued at more than 2 taels. Status symbols all, both jars and plates were displayed in a kind of wickerwork holders on the house beams.

Goldworking

Gold is mentioned in early Spanish accounts more often than any other one substance, evidence not only of their interest in it but of the fact that they found it everywhere they went. They seem never to have seen a Visayan without gold on his person, and said that all of them could tell where any gold came from just by looking at it. But the Spanish were surprised at the low intensity of Visayan mining operations: the Visayans only went to get it as needed. "They would rather keep it below the ground than in cash-boxes," Juan Martínez (1567, 463) said, "because since they have wars, they can steal it in the house but not in the ground." The "wars," of course, included Spanish tribute collecting and looting, and moved Filipinos to curtail or even cease local production.

Most of this mining was placer mining—gold panning in streams or riverbeds. Placers were called *dulangan* from *dulang,* the wooden pan used; the activity, *pamiling,* meaning sifting; and a wooden trough or tub, *bilingan.* There were streams that could be worked in most islands, and Bohol was said to have one in Kabularan where as much as 1 *mas* (2.4 grams) a day could be recovered. *Kotkot* or *kali* was to mine by actual excavation, whence the mine was called *kalian,* and *sabod* was a rich vein—like those found 5 or 6 meters deep in Masbate. Masbate attracted miners from neighboring islands and supplied the famous itinerant goldsmiths of Bikol, and a Spanish assay in 1567 gave 6 ounces per hundredweight of 15-karat quality. Many deposits went unworked for lack of tools and technique, and some in Butuan and Surigao were leased by the month instead to outsiders who came and went by sea.

The Visáyans called gold *bulawan* and fine gold *himulawan,* presumably from *bulaw,* red or rosy, a color they often produced artificially with *porog,* ochre. Though they had touchstones *(sanitran)* to test its quality, most men could estimate its content on sight, and they carried little scales and weights around with them in a special pouch to make spot purchases. (So the

Cebuanos weighed out the 20 pesos in gold which they paid Magellan for 6 kilos of iron.) The weights were various kinds of seeds or beans, based on a little red one called *bangati*, but convertible to standard Southeast Asian weights of the time—the mas, the *kupang* (0.25 mas), and the tael or *tahil* (16 mas), which was *basing* in Visayan. The Visayans, however, reckoned three different kinds of basing according to the quality of its gold content—*labingsiam* worth 12 Spanish reals, *labingwalo* worth 10 or 11, and *labingpito*, only 9.

Gold is a supremely workable metal, especially when pure, and *panday sa bulawan* took advantage of its properties in a number of ways. Solid lumps they carved, modeled, and hammered into shape, beat out into sheets as thin as onionskin to be cut with shears into silhouettes or wrapped into beads or sheathing, or drawn out into thin wires to be used in filigree work or "woven" into thick ropes. Or they soldered tiny granules together, several hundred to the square centimeter, a technique in which ancient Filipino goldsmiths have never been surpassed.

The local custom of interring such goldwork with the deceased, and the universal custom of robbing graves, have provided representative samples for examination in modern museums and collections. Many are of stunning beauty and incredible complexity—like those bahandi necklaces called *kamagi* which contain hundreds of links and rods and wires. Such jewelry was obviously not going to be replaced once it disappeared— together with the skills to produce it—in the first few generations of colonial occupation. As Alcina said a century later, "one who knows how to make them today is hard to find."

Alcina arrived in the Visayas in 1634, and at that time noted that the number of local jewelers had increased but that the quality of their goldwork had declined. He believed what accounted for this change was the disappearance of Philippine gold and the introduction of Mexican silver. Nevertheless, he had no doubts about the quality of ancient Visayan goldwork:

> The many different kinds of large and small beads, all of what they call filigree work here . . . is clear evidence that they did careful, delicate and beautiful work even better in their antiquity than now, since all the ancient goldwork is of higher gold content and craftsmanship than what is being made now . . . [like the kamagi], a piece of jewelry of greater value and curiosity than could be expected of a people apparently so crude and uncivilized (Alcina 1668a, 3:121).

Alcina would not be the last person to see a contrast between the level of Visayan culture and the perfection of their goldwork. As more and more elegant goldwork would later be unearthed, the opinion came to be expressed that the low level of pre-Hispanic Philippine technology would have prevented Filipinos from producing such sophisticated jewelry. But the logic is dubious at best: many nomadic barbarians have produced very fine jewelry. On the other hand, jeweler Ramon Villegas, leading authority on Philippine gold, argues persuasively that many motifs and techniques of Philippine goldwork which have origins or similarities elsewhere, are here combined and developed in ways not found outside the archipelago. Until such examples are found elsewhere, therefore, the easiest way to account for the vast hordes of unique goldwork that have been uncovered is to assume that it was crafted by Filipinos of Philippine gold in the Philippines.

Weaving

The Visayan word for cloth, blanket, or skirt was *habul,* which was woven on a backstrap loom by women or male transvestites. The backstrap loom was so called because the warp threads were supported, not in a permanent framework, but in one continuous loop around a loom bar held in the weaver's lap by a strap behind her back, and another one suspended from a house beam or tree branch as convenient. These two bars were tradition-ally about 4 meters apart, and so produced a textile twice that length and a meter wide: the standard measure was one *birang,* half of what came from the loom, *lakdug.*[17]

The front loom bar was called *os-osan* and it was coated with a sticky black wax to keep the threads from slipping. *Gikos* were the cords fastening the os-osan to a leather or wooden backstrap *(paholan).* The back loom bar was *sablayan.* Riding on the warp was the reed or comb *(salangtan),* made of two parallel rattan rods *(tangkup)* about three fingers apart, grooved to hold the teeth *(salisi)* by wrapping a thread around it and in between them; the reed could thus be opened by removing the thread in order to insert it, comblike, over the upper set of warp threads. Beyond the reed, these warp threads passed alternately over and under a bamboo shed rod *(bukug),* forming a shed to pass the weft threads through. The alternate shed, for passing them in the opposite direction, was formed by pulling up a heddle *(koghon)*—a heddle stick *(borboran)* with a thread wrapped loosely around it to pick up every other warp thread. And beyond this, each warp thread was wrapped once around a cross rod called *sankad*—technically a coil rod—to keep them taut and evenly spaced.

The weaving process required a hardwood batten *(barila)* shaped like a dull sword as long as the fabric was wide. The weaver would insert it flat into the shed, turn it on edge to widen the opening, run the shuttle through in front of the reed, then lay it flat again to strike the reed and beat the weft tight *(hulug* or *pogawa)*. The shuttle *(sikwan* or *bosali)* was a thin cane the same length as the barila, forked at both ends to hold the weft thread wrapped lengthwise. And to begin, a temporary lease rod *(pugi)* was inserted in front of the weaver to provide an edge for the first weft threads, and removed after a few centimeters of cloth was woven. This equipment was sufficient for weaving plain or striped fabric, but to produce designs, additional koghon heddles were needed, and for fancy border strips which looked like embroidery, one or more pointed rods like oversized knitting needles *(koging* or *kohit)* were used to separate a few warp threads at a time.

Since the weaver obviously could not reach the back loom bar when seated behind the front one, she had to prepare the warp beforehand. She did this by wrapping it back and forth around a series of upright stakes, including the sankad coil rod to keep the threads in order when transferring them to the two loom bars. The transfer *(han-ay)* was made by inserting the os-osan and sablayan inside the loops of the last two stakes, and lifting the warp out on them, ready to be set up *(hinan-ay* or *tindug)*. Once the weaver and warp were in position, she maintained her seating by pushing against a footrest *(puran* or *sikaran)*. And she could interrupt her work simply by rolling up the warp on the front loom bar—heddles, batten, and all—taking down the back bar, and putting it all under her arm to carry off and set aside until ready to continue.

Weaving was a normal part of housekeeping, and women supplied all their menfolk's clothing: *ladok* was either a bachelor or a shabbily dressed married man. In epic literature, this is the pastime of even royal ladies, and heroes departing on amorous adventures are ritually clothed with magical garments by their mothers or sisters. Both cotton and abaca were pre-Hispanic exports: the Chinese called Mindoro abaca *yu-da*, jute, in the thirteenth century. The wives of householding slaves were required to spin cotton which their masters supplied them in the boll, and paid workers *(moo)* were employed as domestic weavers. The Spaniards quickly demanded cotton as tribute for sailcloth or export to Mexico, and a year after Legazpi seized Manila, two galleons sailed for Acapulco with 22,600 pesos worth of cloth and 3,800 kilos of thread.

Textiles

Habul was generally taken to mean abaca cloth—what the Spaniards called *medriñaque*. The cleaned fibers were *lanot*—*lanote* to Spaniards collecting them as tribute for cordage—and were graded according to quality. *Gamay* fiber was the finest and produced a light fabric called *sandulan; lapnis* was for heavy cloth; and *bikil* made a canvas like horsehide and also strong thread for heddles. Tying these fibers together with fine knots to produce thread was the first task little girls learned to perform. More than a dozen varieties of abaca were grown, but wild abaca and other hemplike fibers, including buri leaves, were also woven into cloth.

Cotton was *gapas*—or *bunang* or *tingkal* when spun into thread with a distaff and spindle *(tingkalan)*. *Kupang* was one skein, composed of ten *boko,* each of which was ten *kawol,* and a kawol was ten threads *(lugas);* and a *baye* was half a kupang. Cotton cloth was called *lompot,* both the textile and standard piece or blanket—as in *usa ka lompot.* The standard measure was *gintas,* 3 meters. Cloth straight from the loom *(kobal),* both cotton and abaca, was ordinarily soaked in lime, sometimes with dye added, and then cudgeled to soften it. Dyestuffs were red *sibukaw* brazilwood made more intense with *nino* wood; *tagum,* indigo; *dulaw,* a yellow gingerlike root; *kasuba,* a kind of saffron; and an impermanent dye of black soil called *tina.*

Dyed thread was used less to weave colored cloth than to insert colored stripes *(liray)* in plain cloth, including imported silk threads or even threads of gold. When a cloth was fully covered in alternate stripes, it was called by a variety of terms which implied such repetition—for example, *imong-imong, buruk-buruk,* or *solot-solot.*

The most elegant textile, considered a monopoly of Visayan weavers, was the *pinayusan* which was the strict prerogative of men who had personally killed an enemy. It was woven of abaca fibers hand-selected for their whiteness and hair-thin texture, and then tie-dyed by binding little pinches of cloth *(puyos)* to leave a fine flowered pattern in natural color on a field of deep red. It made gauze-thin pudong whose loose ends heroes let carelessly fall over their shoulders to flap in the breeze.

Domestic Trade

The day after Magellan made his first Philippine landing on Homonhon Island off the southern tip of Samar, some fishermen appeared from nearby Suluan to trade fish, coconuts, and arrack. Suluan is one of the most remote bits of land in the archipelago, and the alacrity with which its inhabitants initiated trade with unknown foreigners reflected a common feature of Visayan life—all communities exchanged foodstuffs. Moreover, the fact that these Suluanon were tattooed indicates that trade and warfare in the pre-Hispanic Visayas, as in the rest of the world, were not mutually exclusive activities. Indeed, Loarca (1582, 140) listed the betrayal of such intercourse as a major cause for war—"if they go to trade in other towns as friends and they offend or maltreat them there and commit treachery against them under cover of friendship."

Staple food crops were items of daily trade, due to both need and preference. When Sebastián de Puerto was captured on the Surigao coast in 1526, his master took him along to sell rice in Cebu. In 1565 Legazpi noticed large boats loading rice and tubers in Cabalian (Leyte) and a week later, encountered a boatload of rice and yams off Bohol which had come from Sugod (Leyte). When he anchored in Loay, boats came alongside to barter fish, wax, and goatmeat—which Legazpi suspected was dogmeat— "haggling four hours over a trifle" (Anon. 1565, 476). Few Visayan islands produced a surplus of rice, so it was traded for long distances: when Cebuanos tried to starve the Spaniards out, Muslim merchants supplied them with rice from Luzon and Panay. Wild roots were also traded: *korot* was sold, stripped and ready for curing, by the "ax handle." Coconuts were almost a cash crop: they were grown in plantations, shipped by boatloads or processed as oil, and tuba tappers rented the trees or were hired to tend them. Wax and honey were traded by men with professional skill in locating the hives, even following the flight of bees through the forest. Wild fruits and nuts, garden vegetables and medicinal herbs, as well as packaged foods like palm sugar (*kalamay*), were exchanged in local markets.

Salt derived from seawater was such an essential item of trade it served as a medium of exchange. One *gantang* was a cake 5 to 6 centimeters square, worth a ganta of rice (3 liters). Thus, *usa ka gantang* of cloth—about 80 centimeters—was the length for which a weaver was paid such a piece of salt.

Next to foodstuffs, the most common domestic trade goods were thread, cloth, and clothing. Spinning, weaving, and sewing were all women's work, sometimes for hire, and so was the marketing of their products. The laborious task of stripping, cleaning, bleaching, and dyeing abaca was also done by women, usually working in groups, except for especially tough varieties which were carded by men. Cotton thread was sold by the skein (kupang), and cloth by the "blanket" (lompot). Cleaned abaca fibers (lanot), however, were sold by the skein or bundle which could be encompassed by the thumb and forefinger (*kumo*). Although they could be purchased as such, tying them into thread was a normal part of housework.

Pottery was also a female craft, from gathering the clay to paddling the finished products, but whether they were distributed to other islands by merchants or the potters themselves is not clear. Blacksmiths, however, practiced their profession from town to town with an apprentice carrying the anvil and bellows, repairing and retempering tools and forging new ones out of used iron.

In the Visayan marketplace, heavy items were weighed with a steelyard called *sinanta* (Spaniards reckoned one *chinanta* at half an *arroba*, or 6.3 kilos), but gold was weighed against little seeds in a pair of balances small enough to be carried on the person. Rice was itself a medium of exchange: pots were sold for the amount they could hold, and a gantang was the value of a ganta of unhusked rice. Expensive items like boats, slaves, or good hunting dogs were priced in gold tahil (38.4 grams), or, conversely, in bahandi items themselves valued in tahil—for example, *pakaagungon*, to price in gongs *(agung)*, or *hinalasan,* the value of an imported dragon jar.

Calculations were made with little wooden counters *(kukot)*, every tenth one being of different size. But there are no reports of pre-European coinage, even though the square-holed Chinese *caz* was in wide circulation in islands to the south. (Martín de Islares brought some back from the Loaysa expedition minted early in the fifteenth century.) Cebuanos would not accept copper, silver, or gold coins from Magellan in 1521, but twenty years later, Diego de Bustos bought a piece of silk in Abuyo (Leyte) for 2 pesos, and in 1565, Luzon and Borneo merchants would accept nothing but silver. That this change was due to the Portuguese presence in Malacca is suggested by the fact that the Visayan word for silver coin, *salapi,* meant half a peso—that is, a Portuguese *toston.* Indeed, Visayans always calculated Spanish currency in terms of a 4–real toston rather than an 8–real peso— for example, *si kiwalo* (0.5 real), an eighth of a toston; or *sikapat* (1 real), a quarter-toston; and the *kahati* (2–real coin), meaning half a toston.

To appreciate the vigor and scope of Visayan trade, it is only necessary to review its specialized vocabulary.

Visayan Trade Terms

Alig-ig	To buy a little at a time
Ankat-angkayan	To take merchandise on credit
Abang	To rent a house or boat
Alang or *botong*	To deal in expensive or luxury goods, like boats, slaves, bahandi jars, or gongs
Bakal or *palit*	To deal in ordinary goods
Bakas	A business partner
Baligiya, balidiya	To carry rice, pigs, chickens, or foodstuffs by sea to sell
Biniyaga	To sell notions to women
Botong	The price of alang goods

Dagiya	A gathering of people for trade
Dalawat	To deal in grain; to buy at harvesttime
Doong	For a foreign vessel to anchor
Gaga	To prevent a merchantman from making port or engaging in business before paying anchorage fees
Gamit	To buy on credit
Gasa	A discount
Himongkog	Gratuity given a boat's officers
Hinikayan	Freightage or passage by boat *(sakayan)*
Hokot	To buy hunting dogs
Hoyot	Lowland-highland barter, usually fish for fruit or rice
Karakal	A traveling merchant
Laba; hilaba	Profit or illicit gain
Lito	To sell secondhand goods
Lokap	To be overcharged, deceived
Sahul	Anything sold without profit or at a loss
Samuhan	For two or more to form a business partnership
Sibo	To barter one for one; for example, a ganta of rice for a ganta of wine
Talagidyut	Small items of bahandi
Tamhangan	Marketplace
Tangway	To deal in wine; *tarangwayan:* tavern or wineshop
Tarauta	To make change, including small things for large
Tongtong	An overcharge or illicit commission
Tunay	To buy for cash

The Chinese Enigma

The presence of Chinese trade goods in the sixteenth-century Visayas is a well-attested fact, but the presence of the Chinese themselves is more problematic. Early Spanish explorers were told in Lianga Bay that Chinese junks came to Cebu and Mindanao every year. In Cebu they were told that eight survivors of the Magellan expedition had been sold to Chinese traders; in Sarangani, that Chinese traded in Cotabato; and in Abuyo, that Chinese traders actually resided in Sugod. In June 1544, a Bornean in Limasawa reported that two junks were then anchored in Butuan. But the Spaniards never saw either these Chinese or their ships: not until 1569 when Legazpi moved to Capiz did they capture a Chinese vessel and its crew—that is, on the far western littoral of the islands. (One of those Chinese taught his language to Fray Martín de Rada, and twenty years later was the head of the Chinese community in Manila—Don Francisco Zanco.) The problem is that non-Chinese traders who sold Chinese goods were often called Chinese.

74

When Legazpi captured a *parao* owned by Antón Maletis, a Portuguese resident of Borneo, carrying cargo belonging to the sultan of Brunei, its chief pilot was interviewed.

> This Moro told the General that two junks from Luzon were in Butuan bartering gold, wax and slaves, and that everything they carried is almost the same as the Borneans', and it's all goods from China, and that since what they carry is goods from China, they call Bornean boats and those from Luzon Chinese junks in these islands, and they themselves are called Chinese among these islanders, but in truth Chinese junks do not come here because they are very large and not fit for sailing between these islands (Anon. 1565, 467).

This testimony appears to be corroborated by the fact that Visayans called "foreign nations like the Borneans and Sangleyes [Chinese], *Sina*," and that Chinese sailing directions published in 1617 avoided inland Visayan waters by passing from Mindoro to Oton (Iloilo) to Dapitan. Moreover, the word *junk (junco)* of early Spanish accounts was actually Malay *jong,* a ship of Southeast Asian build, not Chinese—whence Visayan *adyong,* "a ship of high freeboard."

International Commerce

At the time Magellan reached the Philippines, a friend of his was captain general to the sultan of Ternate, a Luzon businessman was governor of the Muslims in Portuguese Malacca, the sultan of Brunei's Manila son-in-law had a Makassarese slave who could speak Spanish, and the Butuanon ruler of Limasawa understood a Malay-speaking merchant from Ciama (Champa?).[18] This is impressive evidence of an international commerce which extended literally from the Atlantic to the Pacific. By the middle of the sixteenth century, the Visayan end was being serviced by traders from Borneo, Sulu, and Luzon, and possibly Sangils settled on Davao Bay. Chinese goods were delivered to Manila and Borneo in large seagoing junks—sometimes taken in piratical action off Mindoro, too—and redistributed for local retail, preferably in exchange for gold and slaves. That all these traders were Muslims, including the Ciama merchant, suggests a kind of cultural bonding like that enjoyed by Chinese businessmen. But there were also local trading networks sealed with marriage alliances, as illustrated by Rajah Kolambu of Butuan personally guiding Magellan from Limasawa to Cebu.

The greatest bulk of Chinese trade goods was in porcelain, stoneware, and unglazed crockery; prior to the galleon trade, silk was limited to thinner, cheaper varieties or thread. Common white or black-and-white blankets, sarsaparilla (chinaroot), incense, glass beads, tin, and brassware also came from China. Most important, however, were ironware and the cast-iron pans which were the major source for Visayan blacksmiths—"a kind of iron," the Bornean pilot remarked with only slight exaggeration, "as easy to break as glass with any blow they give it" (Anon. 1565, 466).

But Chinese brass (or copper?) gongs were considered inferior to bronze ones from Borneo and Sangir. Hardware also came from Borneo—for example, small knives and spearheads—and fine steel blades, though the best krises and kampilans came from Sangir, and Japanese swords also reached the Visayas through Manila. Bornean imports included camphor, fine-woven mats, sago cakes, expensive red cloth and elegant G-strings, and tropical perfumes and drugs, as well as products from farther west like Indian chintzes and Javanese batik stuffs, or precious red stones like carnelians, garnets, and rubies. Sulu trade was reflected in a style of short jacket called *sinulog*.

Whatever profit foreign merchants may have made on slaves and gold, the bulk of Visayan exports were forest and marine products—wax, civet, musk, ambergris, cinnamon, dyewood, and aromatic hardwood, "dragon's blood" (that is, red resin), and red ants for coloring Chinese ink. Cowry shells were used as currency in Cambodia, Siam, and Patani (Sumatra), and both abaca and cotton cloth, as well as cotton thread and cottonseed, had a steady market in China. But the popular picture of a Chinese junk anchored in some Visayan port with natives scrambling aboard to barter beeswax for porcelain is rather a caricature of what was actually a sophisticated commerce. In little emporia like Cebu, Filipino and foreign vessels registered, paid harbor fees, and loaded merchandise which did not originate in Cebu. Pearls, coral, and tortoise shell came from islands to the south, while deerskins, antlers, and caged civet cats destined for Japan came from Mindanao, and so did carabao horns from China. Conversely, cheap cotton blankets were available from China, where they may well have been woven of Visayan cotton, just as their fragrant little boxes may have been carved of Visayan sandalwood which had been included among logs transported to Manila and which had served as ballast on homebound Fujian junk. As for Chinese jars that arrived in Manila filled with wine or preserved fruits they were widely resold empty.

CHAPTER 4

Religion

Visayans worshiped nature spirits, gods of particular localities or activities, and their own ancestors. Religious practitioners were male or female mediums who contacted spirit patrons in a state of trance to determine the cause and cure of illness. Sacrifices included foodstuffs, beverages, and live fowl, hogs or human beings; and ancestors, spirits, and deities were invoked at feasts in which these things were offered up. Ancestors were also invited to partake of any meal or drinking, and their well-being in the next world depended on sacrifices offered by their descendants both before and after their death and burial.

Nature Spirits

Natural forces like celestial bodies or flowing waters were personified for reverence or worship. Chief among them were the sun and moon, especially the new moon whose regular waxing from a thin silver to full brilliance so strongly suggested prosperity and fertility. Stars and constellations connected with the agricultural cycle were invoked for good crops. To the winds themselves were addressed prayers for fair weather and favorable winds. There were river gods, both in general and as resident in particular streams, and important gods and spirits of the sea which received all these waters. Part of ordinary river traffic were little rafts—or, in the case of community sacrifices, large ones—headed downstream bearing the offerings and paraphernalia of ceremonies celebrated along their banks. As for spirits dwelling in the mountains, hunters were sure to offer their first catch to them.

Crocodiles were held in special veneration because of their obvious danger: they were addressed as Grandfather, and were offered symbolic foodstuffs by the prudent when crossing rivers or even on entering boats. Pahali, the spirit of the strangler fig, or balete tree, was also given offerings in recognition of its sinister powers: as Father Chirino (1604, 53) said, "there is no ancient tree to whom they do not attribute divinity, and it was a sacrilege to think of cutting one under any circumstances." Dangerous cliffs or strange rock formations were also invoked for safe passage: many porcelain plates that had contained offerings were to be found on a rocky promontory on Potol Point, the northwestern headland of Panay, and so, too, a natural formation along the Araut River that looked like a man paddling a canoe was venerated as epic hero Labaw Donggon.

The Unseen World

Visayans considered themselves vastly outnumbered by a variety of invisible beings, spirits, and deities. Gods and goddesses were called *diwata* and ancestor spirits, *umalagad,* both words still in use among Visayans living in the remote mountains of Panay. These were generally benevolent or neutral and could be approached ritually for good crops, health, and fortune, but they also caused illness or misfortune if not given due respect. They thus functioned to sanction approved social behavior.

Naturally malevolent beings, on the other hand, had to be avoided or kept off by precautionary acts, and ranged from the mischievous to the ghoulish, the most common and fearful being those who ate away the livers of living persons. They had no single name as a class—Spanish lexicographers simply called them witches, *brujas* or *hechiceros*—a lack which has been supplied in modern Visayan by Spanish *duende,* meaning hobgoblin, or *encanto,* enchanted.

Diwata is a Malay-Sanskrit term for gods or godhead, and Visayan *maniwata* or *magdiwata* meant to invoke or deify them, and *diya* was a Panay synonym. They had individual personalities and names, which differed from place to

78

place: as Juan de la Isla (1565, 233) said, "in every town they have their god, all called Diwata in general, but as a personal name, that of their town." Their number must have been legion considering that individual shamans during seances named different ones with whom they were in communication or who took possession of them.

Some gods constituted a genuine pantheon, a hierarchy with specific roles to play, particularly in connection with birth, longevity, death, and the afterlife. Others were the patrons of specific human conditions: Dalikmata, a diwata with many eyes, was invoked in the case of eye ailments, while Makabosog moved men to gluttony. Cebuanos referred to the image of the Holy Child which Magellan gave Humabon's wife as "the Spaniards' diwata," and supposedly rendered it homage after Magellan's death, and were said to have taken it down to the shore and immersed it in time of drought.

Our earliest list of Visayan deities was recorded by Miguel de Loarca in Panay in 1582: Si Dapa was a diwata who marked out one's mortal lifespan on a tree trunk on Mount Madyaas at the time of birth; Magwayen ferried the souls of the deceased across to a kind of Inferno, and Pandaki rescued the deserving for a more pleasant fate. Lalahon was the fire-breathing goddess of Mount Canlaon who could be invoked for good crops but who sent out swarms of locusts if angered, while Mayong was the diwata of the volcano in Ibalon (Albay) which bears her name. Inaginid and Malanduk were invoked for success in battle and plunder, and Nagined, Arapayan, and Makbarubak could be appealed to when concocting a poisonous oil. A few were actually hostile to mankind—Makaptan, for example, who lived in the highest heavens and so had never tasted human food or drink and, presumably for this reason, capriciously caused them death and disease.

One of the first questions Spanish explorers always asked Filipinos was what their religion was. When Magellan asked Rajah Kolambu whether they were Muslims or pagans, what they believed in, he was told that they "did not worship anything but raised their face and clasped hands to heaven, and called their god Abba" (Pigafetta 1524b, 126). This was an understandable confusion. Magellan's interpreter was a Malay-speaking Sumatran and *aba* was a Malay-Arabic word for father, while in Visayan *Aba!* was a common expression of wonder or admiration—like "Hail!" in the Ave Maria. Five years later, Sebastián de Puerto reported from the Surigao coast that the natives sacrificed to a god called Amito—that is, *anito*, the ordinary Visayan term for sacrifice or religious offering.

Father Chirino (1604, 53), on the other hand, stated that of the multitude of Filipino gods, "they make one the principal and superior of all, whom the Tagalogs called *Bathala Mei-Capal,* which means the creator god or maker, and the Bisayans, *Laon,* which denotes antiquity." The Tagalog Bathala was well known in Chirino's day, but he was the first to mention a Visayan equivalent, and his statement was repeated verbatim by Jesuits of the next generation such as Diego de Bobdilla and Francisco Colín. But not by Father Alcina: rather, he devoted one whole chapter to the thesis that Malaon was simply one of many names which Visayans applied to the True Godhead of which they had some hazy knowledge. Thus he equated Malaon—whom the Samareños thought was a female—with the Ancient of Days, Makapatag (to level or seize) with the Old Testament God of Vengeance, and Makaobus (to finish) with the Alpha and Omega, attributing these coincidences to some long-forgotten contact with Jews in China or India.

Raom (Laon) appears as a Bohol idol in the Jesuit annual letter of 1609, but none of Chirino's contemporaries mentioned a creator god by this or any other name, least of all when recording origin myths. Neither did the early dictionaries. *Laon* was not said of persons but of things: it meant aged or dried out like root crops or grain left from last year's harvest, or a barren domestic animal. But *Manlaon* appears as the name of a mountain peak. Thus Laon may well have been the goddess of Mount Canlaon in Negros— Loarca's Lalahon—but it is unlikely that the Visayans had a supreme deity by that name.

The soul or élan vital was *kalag:* when people set new rice aside for the deceased, they would say, "Himulaw, himulaw, manga kalag: ayaw kami pagsuli [Eat, souls, eat: let it not be bad for us]" (Alcina 1668a, 3:218), and a spirited, forceful man was called *kalagan na tao.* The kalag might separate from the body during dreams, illness, or insanity, or be carried off by a diwata for envy or desire, especially those who were *bugus,* that is, perfect, handsome, or otherwise enviable. *Daay* was the diwata's desire for such a person, a beautiful woman for himself, a powerful man for a son. Women were therefore advised, "Dika mag bukas sang paño sa olo mo kay daayon ka [Do not uncover your head lest you be desired]" (Méntrida 1637a, 116). The loss of kalag might also result in a kind of enchanted death—*linahos inkamatay*—of which Sánchez said (1617, 291v), "There are those among the Visayans who remain like dead for two or three days, and afterwards revive and recount visions."

Ancestor spirits specifically were called *umalagad,* from *alagad,* a follower or voluntary assistant, and they were venerated as personal guardians or companions. They were invoked on leaving the house and during agricultural rites in the field, and were considered essential shipmates on any sea raid, sometimes going on board in the form of a python. Indeed, some were said to have been born as snake twins from the same womb as the persons they were destined to protect. It was these umalagad and kalag, rather than the diwata, who were the main objects of Visayan adoration, receiving not only formal worship conducted by priests and priestesses, but domestic offerings and routinary acts of reverence on the part of laymen.

The Spirit Underworld

Visayans also believed in a demimonde of monsters and ghouls who had the characteristics modern medicine assigns to germs—invisible, ubiquitous, harmful, avoidable by simple health precautions and home remedies, but requiring professional diagnosis, prescription, and treatment in the event of serious infections. Twentieth-century folklore considers them invisible creatures who sometimes permit themselves to be seen in their true shape or in the form of human beings, but sixteenth-century Spaniards thought they were really human beings who could assume such monstrous forms, witches whose abnormal behavior and powers were the result of demon possession or pacts with the devil. But in either case, if Visayans became convinced that a death had been caused by one of their townmates who was such a creature, he or she was put to death—along with their whole families if the victim had been a datu.

The most common but most feared were the *aswang,* flesh eaters who devoured the liver like a slow cancer. At the least liverish symptom, people said, "Kinibtan ang atay [Liver's being chipped away]," and conducted a *tingalok* omen-seeking rite to discover the progress of the disease. If it appeared that the organ was completely consumed, emergency appeal had to be made promptly to some diwata to restore it. Aswang also ate the flesh of corpses, disinterring them if not well guarded, or actually causing them to disappear in the plain sight of mourners at a wake. Their presence was often revealed by level spots of ground they had trampled down during their witches' dance at night, or their singing, which sounded like the cackling of a hen—*nangangakak.* But like all other evil creatures, they were afraid of noise and so could be kept at bay by pounding on bamboo-slat floors.

Spanish lexicons listed *alok, balbal, kakag, oko, onglo,* and *wakwak* as synonyms of *aswang,* but *tiktik* as one that flew around at night, and *tanggal* one that left the lower half of the body behind, or even the whole body with only the head flying off by itself. *Mantiw* were ghosts or apparitions, and

81

landung were any imaginary visions or phantoms. *Yawa* was a general term for demons which came to be adopted for non-Christians—for example, "Yawa ka pa [Are you still pagan]?" (Sánchez 1617, 264). *Ogima* were man-shaped demons with the hind quarters of a beast and were therefore called satyrs or fauns by Father Méntrida (1637a, 274), who soberly reported, "Plenty of them were seen in Aklan and Ibahay in 1600 and before 1599." *Baliw* was to change—that is, from one thing into another, like Lot's wife into a pillar of salt—and a demon by this name had to be kept away from the sick. *Binaliw* was a witch who had become invisible, but also anyone suffering a change attributed to divine retribution, like crossed eyes or a withered limb, so that "Binaliw ka!" was one of the worst possible curses.

Omens and Divination

Visayans also believed that supernatural forces filled the natural world with signs and portents that it would be unwise to ignore. These were indicated by the behavior of birds and reptiles, or could be elicited by casting lots or by omen-seeking ceremonies conducted by *babaylan* or other diviners. Spanish missionaries and commanders often had to cancel their plans because Filipino guides refused to continue on after hearing the cry of some bird.

Any snake or lizard crossing the path, even a common house lizard that "spoke to" somebody descending the house steps, was a warning to turn back. A sneeze was also enough to interrupt any activity, including business transactions that were going badly. If somebody happened to ask them about their plans, hunters turned around because their quarry would then have been forewarned and hide. A monitor lizard under the house was a sure sign of impending death or disaster; though if it was killed, enshrouded, and buried like a human being, its life might be accepted as a substitute for the householder's. But the most famous of these omens was the *limokon*, a kind of turtledove with striking green and white plumage and red feet and beak, also called *koro-koro* from its call. In a Suban-on epic, as Taake sinks into the depths of the sea, he laments, "Had the limokon sounded, I would not have come" (Ochotorena 1981, 420).

Fortunetelling by palmistry was *himalad,* from *palad,* the lines in the palm of the hand. (Old folks were said to be "broken" because they had as many cracks in their palm as an old pot.) *Luknit* was to cast lots by four crocodile teeth or boar's tusks, and *tali* was a stone or egg which the diviner made stand upright on a plate. The most popular method of divination was to ask the diwata to answer questions by causing some inanimate object to move: *Abiyog* was to swing, like a bolo suspended from a cord, and *kibang* was to move or wiggle, like a winnowing tray or a shield laid convex-side down. *Mangayaw* raiders before putting to sea were sure to board a small *baroto* without outriggers and, sitting perfectly still on the center line, ask the diwata to rock the boat if it was propitious to proceed with the expedition. If they received a favorable response, they asked who it was who had rocked the boat, naming a list of possibilities, and then offered a predeparture sacrifice to the one who had favored them.

Sorcerers were believed to derive their secret knowledge of black magic— spells and charms—from unnatural forces. *Habit* was a spell and *ginhabit*, the one bewitched by it: *bakwit* was a spell by which women detained their lovers; *lumay*, a love potion; and *buringot*, the opposite. Buringot also made its possessor fearless in the face of danger. *Mentala* were incantations and verbal formulas—for example, to request crocodiles not to bite or hot iron not to burn. *Awug* was a spell put on coconut palms to make a thief's stomach swell up; *tiwtiw* made fish follow the fisherman to shore or wild boar follow the hunter out of the woods; and *oropok* caused rats to multiply in somebody else's field. *Tagosilangan* were persons with a charm which enabled them to see hidden things, and *tagarlum* was a charmed herb that rendered its owner invisible.

A powerful datu's power was enhanced by popular fear of his arcane knowledge of black magic, sometimes reputed to be handed down from one generation to another. *Ropok* was a charm which caused the one who received it to obey like a slave. *Panlus* was a spear or G-string which caused leg pains or swelling in the victim as soon as he stepped over it. *Bosong* caused intestinal swelling in those who crossed the datu. *Hokhok* was to kill simply with a breath or the touch of a hand, and *kaykay* was to pierce somebody through just by pointing a finger at him from a distance. A reputation for such powers no doubt both facilitated a datu's effective control over his subjects, and arose from it.

Worship

Anito was a sacrifice, a formal act of worship conducted by a babaylan. This same word was reported from Luzon as meaning an idol, ancestor spirit, or deity—that is, an object of worship—but although Visayan missionaries sometimes used the word in this sense, their dictionary definitions are unambiguous. *Anito* was the root of the words *paganito* and

83

maganito, which both mean an act of sacrifice, *paga anito*, to perform that act, and *iganito*, the things being sacrificed. But the idol, diwata, or umalagad being worshiped, Father Sánchez said, was *paganitohan*.

Paganito were basically seances—that is, ceremonies in which a medium established audible communication with spirits. They were conducted for fertility of crops, newlyweds, or domestic animals, for rain or fair weather, for victory in war or plunder in raids, recovery from illness or the control of epidemics, or the placating of the souls of the deceased. Minor paganito, however, could be performed by any householder. When drought threatened, for instance, *pagobo* was offered—a wild hen and a bird-shaped rice cake together with leaves or sprouts from the crops threatened—to the diwata of the family hearth. When a hunting dog's poor performance was attributed to witchcraft, *pabto* was conducted: a node of hot bamboo was struck on the ground to explode in front of the dog while the hunter said, "Palas na an palhi [Out with all spells and curses]!" (Sánchez 1617, 387v). But solemn paganito had to be conducted by a babaylan.

Babaylan were shamans or spirit mediums, given to seizures and trances in which they spoke with the voice of diwata or other spirits and acted out conflicts in the spirit world, brandishing spears, foaming at the mouth, and often becoming violent enough to require restraint. They were also called *daitan*, befriended, in recognition of their patronage by a particular diwata. They could be either male or female, or male transvestites called *asog*, but were most commonly women. They came to their calling through attacks of illness or insanity which could only be cured by accepting the call, and then attached themselves as *alabay*, apprentices, to some older babaylan, frequently a relative. Their remuneration was a designated share of the offerings, usually choice cuts of the hog or the head. But in full-scale paganito sponsored by prominent datus, they went home with heirloom valuables like porcelain plates or gold ornaments. There were also outright charlatans. One Bohol babaylan attracted a crowd of worshipers to make sacrifices on the seashore with the promise that their ancestors would appear in a golden boat.

This worship took place in private homes or fields; at grave sites or sacred spots outside the community; or along beaches or streams where little rafts could be launched, aboard which were disease and bad luck, or live pests like locusts or rats. There were no temples, though there were little platforms or sheds at the entrance to the village where offerings were made. Some paganito were for the benefit of individuals or kindred, some were by nature seasonal, and some sought relief from a public crisis like drought or pestilence.

A solemn paganito in Cebu was described in the sixteenth century as follows: The site was adorned with green branches, palm-leaf cloths, and colorful blankets; and the offerings—red blossoms, roasted fish, rice and millet cakes wrapped in leaves, and a piece of imported Cambay cloth—were set out on large plates. A live large hog, raised and fattened for this end, lay bound on a grass mat, and cacophonous music was provided by gongs, drums, and resonant porcelain plates. The babaylan was an old woman wearing a headdress topped by a pair of horns and accompanied by a second medium, both of them carrying bamboo trumpets which they either played or spoke through. They both proceeded to dance around the hog with scarfs in their hand, acting out a dialogue between the spirits possessing them, drinking wine on their behalf, and sprinkling some of it on the hog.

Finally, a spear was given the presiding babaylan, and with it she began a series of feints at the hog as the tempo of her movements increased to a frenzy, and then, with a sudden thrust, ran the victim through the heart with unerring aim. The foreheads of the main beneficiaries of the ceremony were marked with the blood of the victim, whose wounds were then stanched; and the mat that had been bloodied during the sacrifice was carefully burned. The babaylan was then divested of her accoutrements and awakened from her trance, while the hog was singed, butchered, and cooked. The feasting then began, everybody receiving a share, though the flesh touched by the spear was reserved for the babaylan. Some of the meat was taken down to an altar on the seashore or riverbank where, after prayers, it was placed on a little raft together with the altar and all other paraphernalia, and set adrift. This brought the ritual to a close though the celebrating continued.

Naturally these ceremonies had their own vocabulary. *Ginayaw* were offerings of spherical yellow-rice cakes; *tinorlok* was the hog reserved for sacrifice; and *bani* was the tabu requiring the mat to be burned. *Taruk* was the babaylan's dance; *bodyong,* her bamboo trumpet; and *banay,* a fan or fly whisk with which she kept time. *Hola, hulak,* or *tagdug* all meant spirit possession, with *saob* including even animals. *Tabo* was the wheezing sound when the diwata spoke. The little houses or altars on the riverbank were *latangan,* or *magdantang* if large enough for major community sacrifices.

The babaylan's healing prowess was described in dramatic terms: *agaw,* to carry off by force, was to snatch a pain from the sufferer; *tawag,* to call someone out, was to summon the spirit that had kidnapped the soul; and *bawi,* to rescue, was to free the invalid from the grip of the afflicting spirit.

Paglehe or *magrehe* were religious restrictions or tabus, like mourning restrictions following a datu's death, or a seven-day thanksgiving period following harvest during which rice could not be pounded nor outsiders enter the house. Ordinary activities which involved risk or doubt were always accompanied by prescribed tabus—planting, setting traps, starting dogs on the hunt, the swarming of locusts, or the arrival of alien datus, who were considered naturally hostile if not actually bent on mischief. Missionaries adopted the word *lehe* for Lenten abstinences and restriction on eating meat on Fridays, and also accepted the pre-Christian term *harang* or *halad* for offering. So, too, Christians continued *darangin*, a perfunctory invocation of ancestor spirits when leaving the house, only they were supposed to murmur "Jesus" instead of "Apo-Apo."

Idols

Visayans kept small idols in their homes called *tao-tao, bata-bata,* or *larawan,* guardians of family welfare and the first recourse in the case of sickness or trouble. Tao-tao meant a manikin or little *tao* (human being); bata-bata was a little *bata* (great-grandparent); and *ladaw* or larawan was an image, mould, or model.

Idols of individual diwata with their names and properties, however, did not figure prominently enough in Visayan worship to attract Spanish attention. Nor were they anointed, perfumed, or decked with gold and jewels as they were in the lake district of Manila. Thus members of the Legazpi expedition, fresh from Mexico with its monumental Aztec imagery, reported that Cebuanos had neither temples nor idols. But the household idols were common enough and visible enough to attract Magellan's disapproving attention. Why were they not all burned? he demanded after the mass baptisms he instigated.

Hernando de la Torre (1528, 280) reported that the natives of Surigao worshiped idols of wood—"and they paint them as well as they can, as we do Santos." Pigafetta (1524b, 166) left the following description of one in Cebu:

> These idols are made of wood, and are hollow, and lack the back parts. Their arms are open and their feet turned up under them with legs open. They have a large face with four huge tusks like those of the wild boar, and are painted all over.

But if these were really the sort of household idols which Humabon's queen gave up in favor of Magellan's Santo Niño, it seems strange that Visayans would represent their ancestral spirits in such monstrous form.

Further confusion is added to the picture of Visayan idol worship by the fact that the English word *idol* inevitably suggests an actual carved figure. But Spanish *idolo* means not only a graven image, but anything worshiped, idolized, or deified—like an ancestor or a balete tree. Father Méntrida (1637a, 132) defines *diwata* as "God, idol of the pagans, not images because they worship the Demon in the spirit." Thus modern English translations obscure the fact that the "idols" invoked by a babaylan during a solemn paganito were not wooden statues, but invisible spirits.

Origin Myths

In the beginning there was only sea and sky—so says a Visayan myth well known to Spanish chroniclers. The following is the account attributed to Legazpi himself in 1567:

> In the beginning of the world there was nothing more than sky and water, and between the two, a hawk was flying which, getting angry at finding no place to alight or rest, turned the water against the sky, which was offended and so scattered the water with islands and then the hawk had some place to nest. And when it was on one of them along the seashore, the current threw up a piece of bamboo at its feet, which the hawk grabbed and opened by pecking, and from the two sections of the bamboo, a man came out of the one and a woman from the other. These, they say, married with the approval of Linog, which is the earthquake, and in time they had many children, who fled when their parents got angry and wanted to drive them out of the house and began to hit them with sticks. Some got in the inner room of the house, and from these the grandees or nobles are descended; others went down the steps and from these the *timawa* are descended, who are the plebeian people; and from the children who remained hidden in the kitchen, they say the slaves are descended (San Agustín 1698, 293–94).

With local variations, the myth was known all over the Visayas. In a Panay version, the bamboo itself was produced by a marriage between the sea breeze and the land breeze—probably the primordial pair of deities, Kaptan and Magwayen—but in Leyte and Samar, the first man and woman issued from two young coconuts floating on the water and pecked open by the bird. The highlanders of Panay listed two other categories of fleeing children—those who hid in the kitchen ash box and became the ancestors of the blacks, and those who fled to the open sea, the progenitors of the Spaniards. The most detailed account was recorded by Loarca from the coastal people of Panay, probably in Oton (Iloilo) where he was operating a Spanish shipyard.

In this version, the man and woman who came forth from the bamboo were Si Kalak (that is, *laki,* male) and Si Kabai (female), and they had three children—two sons, Sibo and Pandagwan, and a daughter, Samar. Samar and Sibo married and had a daughter named Lupluban, who married her uncle Pandagwan, the inventor of the fishnet, and they, in turn, had a son named Anoranor, whose son Panas was the inventor of war. Pandagwan's first catch was a shark which died when he took it out of the water, the first death in the world; grieved, he mourned its death and blamed the gods Kaptan and Magwayen, who, angered, killed him with a thunderbolt. But thirty days later they revived him from the underworld and restored him to the land of the living. But during his absence his wife had been won over by Marakoyrun with a stolen pig and would not now return to him. So he went back to the land of the dead, setting the pattern of mortality for all mankind.

The Visayan origin myth thus describes the creation of man and woman, accounts for the introduction of death, theft, concubinage, war, and class and race differences into the world, and provides a human genealogy with divine roots. But it does not contain any creator god. Christians, however, called the Creator "The Potter," Mamarikpik, from *pikpik,* the slaps the potter gives the clay in the paddle-and-anvil technique. Father Sánchez (1617, 388v) quoted an educated Cebuano as saying, "Kanino pikpik inin kalibutan, dile kanan Dios [Who made this world if not God]?"

Death and Burial

When all healing paganito failed to revive the moribund, one last desperate rite was performed to call back the departed soul—the *Paguli.* A coconut shell of water was placed on the stomach of the inert invalid and rotated to chants of "Uli, uli, kalag [Come back, soul, come back]" (Alcina 1668a, 3:220). In the care of a datu, some of his slaves were sacrificed in the hope they would be accepted in his stead by the ancestor spirit who was calling him away. Or an *itatanun* expedition would be sent to take captives in some other community.

These captives were sacrificed in a variety of brutal ways, though after first being intoxicated. In Cebu they were speared on the edge of the house porch to drop into graves already dug for them. In Carigara, a boat was rolled over their prostrate bodies. In Butuan, they were bound to a cross, tortured all day with bamboo spikes, and finally run through with a spear and cast into the river at dawn—"cross and all," pioneer missionary Martín de Rada wrote. This violence indicates the conviction that a datu was the ordinary target for vengeful spirits of men he had vanquished, and that fitting retribution was therefore required to satisfy his own ancestors.

The cadaver was usually anointed and groomed as in life, though in Cebu subjected to a ritual haircut: Pigafetta attended a funeral in which the widow lay on the body, mouth to mouth, while this mournful ritual was performed. So as to be assured of a ready reception in the next life, the deceased were bedecked with the jewelry they were accustomed to wearing on festive occasions, and as much gold as possible, some even being placed in their mouth and between the layers of as many as ten blankets with which they were shrouded. Aromatics like camphor were applied for embalming effect, and the house was meanwhile fumigated with burning incense in porcelain jars.

During a wake which lasted as long as the bereaved family could supply food and drink for guests, the widow or widower, together with first-degree kin, were secluded behind tattered white hangings—actually, *mapuraw,* undyed, not *maputi,* white. Professional mourners, generally old women, sang dirges which emphasized the grief of the survivors (who responded with keening wails), and eulogized the qualities of the deceased—the bravery and generosity of men, the beauty and industry of women, and the sexual fulfillment of either. These eulogies were addressed directly to the deceased and included prayers of petition: they were therefore a form of ancestor worship, one of such vigor that Spanish missionaries were never able to eradicate it.

Poor Visayans were buried wrapped in a banana leaf in simple caskets of thin boards or even bamboo, but the standard Visayan coffin was made of a hardwood like ipil, incorruptible enough to outlast its contents. It was hewn from a single tree trunk with a lid cut from the same piece, fitted, pegged, and caulked airtight with resin. (This hermetic seal was an essential feature since coffins were often kept unburied in the house.) These were called *longon,* a term Visayans did not apply to the sort of casket introduced by the missionary fathers. All datus or prominent persons wanted to be buried in a traditional longon, decorated with fanciful carvings often executed by the future occupant himself during his lifetime.

The corpse was placed in the coffin with all body cavities filled with buyo sap, together with its finery and such heirloom valuables as porcelain jars or plates and saucers placed under the head like a pillow or over the face and breasts. Some wore actual masks and mouthpieces of beaten gold, or were provided with bejeweled side arms. Aside from these, an ax handle was placed in the coffin of a *bingil,* a woman who had known no man other than her husband—just as the hole in the ax handle fit only the axhead made for it. Naturally, all this gold and porcelain attracted grave robbers in the sixteenth century just as it does in the twentieth: Father Alcina sent a gold earring to Spain which he purchased from this source. (*Langab* meant to bury a coffin in a secret location in hopes of protecting its contents.)

Infants and newborn or aborted babies were buried in crocks or jars, sometimes Chinese porcelains with matching lids; but no Spanish observer seems to have witnessed an adult jar burial. Alcina (1668a, 3:237), however, was aware of the practice. He said that Visayans buried not only in longon, "but in large jars, glazed and strong, in which they placed the bodies seated, and all the wealth they had when alive." He received this information from Boholano workmen who had dug into a burial site full of them when excavating for the Jesuit chapel in Baklongan earlier in the century, a discovery which attracted Spaniards from Cebu to do some digging of their own. Some of these must have been secondary burials since the "dragon jars" mentioned—what Visayans called *ihalasan* from *ihas,* snake—would have been too small to accommodate an adult body, even with the knees drawn up under the chin.

There was considerable local variation in Visayan grave sites. There were graveyards outside village limits, frequently dug into the banks of upstream rivers or the seacoast, where they were often exposed by natural erosion; more than a kilometer of them were revealed along the Mandawi water-front in Cebu. Caves were also used where available, or small islands reserved for this purpose: the reason Homonhon was uninhabited when Magellan landed there was that Visayans considered it haunted. But sha-mans and members of the datu class were never buried in these public graveyards: their caskets were kept in or under their houses or, in the case of babaylan, exposed to the elements in the branches of the balete trees where they had established spirit contact.

Renowned sea raiders sometimes left instructions for their burial. One in Leyte directed that his longon be placed in a shrine on the seacoast between Abuyog and Dulag, where his kalag could serve as patron for followers in his tradition. Many were interred in actual boats: the most celebrated case was that of Bohol chieftain who was buried a few years before Legazpi's arrival in a karakoa with seventy slaves, a full complement of oarsmen.

A slave called *dayo* might be stationed at a datu's tomb for the rest of his life to guard it against robbers or aswang, with the right to feed himself off anybody's field, a security considered enviable in a subsistence economy:

men with permanent positions said, "Baga dayo na kita dinhi [We are like dayo here]" (Alcina 1668a, 3:244). Slaves were also sacrificed at a datu's death, even being killed in the same manner in which he had died—for example, by drowning. These slaves were usually foreign captives, but occasionally a lifelong personal attendant–*atubang*—who expected to follow his master to the grave.

Most prestigious, and regarded as especially respectful and affectionate, was secondary burial—that is, the reburial of bones exhumed from a primary burial after the body has decomposed. For one year, the coffin was kept in the house suspended from the rafters, or in a small chamber extended to one side, or in a shed underneath, or in a field. If it was hung in the house, putrefied matter was drained off as necessary by caulking a bamboo tube into a small hole in the bottom which was resealed afterwards. If it was removed from the house, it was not taken out the door—lest the spirits of the living follow it—but through a temporary opening in the wall. A year or so later, the bones were removed, given a ritual cleansing by a babaylan, and placed in a small chest: here they were permanently preserved, venerated, and carried along if the family moved.

The most dramatic expression of grief for a departed parent was to dismantle or burn the house in which he died, or cut down trees he had planted. All these things, like a slave sacrificed to accompany him, were called *onong,* something which shares the same fate. When placing heirloom wealth—bahandi like gold or porcelain—in the grave, his children would say, "Iyonong ta inin bahandi kan ama [May this bahandi accompany our father]"; and when men swore by the sun, they said, "May I share the sun's fate [nahaonong ako sa arlaw] if I am not telling the truth"—that is, disappear at sunset (Sánchez 1617, 379v). Not surprisingly, missionaries applied the term to the Christian sacrifice: "An atun ginoo Yesu Christo napahaonong dakwa [Our Lord Jesus Christ took on our fate]" (Sánchez 1617, 379v).

Mourning

Both widows and widowers observed three days of fasting and silence during which they neither bathed nor combed, and might even shave their hair and eyebrows as a special sign of grief; and until the full mourning period was ended, they did not eat cooked food. Family members draped undyed cloth over their heads when they went out, men let their G-strings drag in the dust, and widowers did not don their red pudong or G-strings again until they had contracted another marriage. The house was fenced off, all seeds were taken out and planted lest they be contaminated with death, and all fires were extinguished and rekindled for each new use.

In the case of the death of a datu, or of one of his wives or children, the whole community was placed under strict mourning interdict, *pumaraw*. Nobody could wear colored clothes, climb palm trees, or fish in certain streams; and spears were carried point down and side arms blade up. A mournful silence was to be maintained, and families are said to have been enslaved as a punishment for breaking the tabu when their dogs barked or cocks crowed. The mourning period only ended with the taking of human life.

This same requirement pertained to any death by violence, drowning, or suspected sorcery, though when the cause was not certain, a wild boar or deer could be speared instead. Men charged with responsibility for family honor would tie rings of irritating vines around their arms or neck, and swear not to remove them or partake of certain food or drink until they had completed this duty. Once the requirement was satisfied, the end of the mourning period was announced by the ranking lady of the household presenting gifts of wine to allied communities, being rowed there by three respected warriors singing victory chants and boasting of their exploits. The oaths were called *balata* or *lalaw*, while *awut* was the promised fasting or abstinence. The fact that these same terms were applied to a pact two men would make when one of them was leaving on a trip, swearing to observe awut until they met again, suggests the insecurity of travel outside one's own community in the sixteenth-century Visayas.

The Afterlife

The departing Visayan soul was delivered to the land of the dead, Saad or Sulad, by boat. On the other shore, the kalag would be met by relatives who had predeceased him, but they accepted him only if he was well ornamented with gold jewelry. If rejected, he remained permanently in Sulad unless reprieved by the god Pandaki in response to rich paganito offered by his survivors. In Panay, Magwayen was the boatman; the lords of the underworld were Mural and Ginarugan; and Sumpos, the one who rescued the souls on Pandaki's behalf and gave them to Siburanen who, in turn, brought them to where they would live out their afterlife—Mount Madyaas for the Kiniray-a, or Borneo for the Cebuanos and Boholanos.

In the afterlife, married couples were reunited to continue accustomed activities like farming, fishing, raiding, spinning, and weaving, but did not bear children. (Babies, who had never engaged in adult activities, did not have an afterlife.) In this way, they spent their days for nine lifetimes, being reborn each time smaller than the last, until in their final reincarnation, they were buried in a coffin the size of a grain of rice. The souls of those who drowned, however, remained in the sea; indeed, drowning was such a common cause of death that Samareños figuratively used the terms meaning drowning for any death. Those who died in war, who were murdered, or killed by crocodiles, traveled up the rainbow to the sky; in the Panay epic Labaw Donggon, the rainbow itself is formed by their blood falling to earth. In the sky world they became gods who, deprived of the company of their kin, were presumably ready to lend their aid to survivors who undertook to avenge their deaths.

Sulad was therefore not a hell where evildoers as judged by European mores were punished, though, as Father Méntrida (1637a, 350) said, "because they have no knowledge of the Inferno, they call the Inferno, Solar [that is, Sulad], and those who dwell in the Inferno, *solanun*." These solanun, of course, were simply those who went to the grave without sufficient gold and whose relatives could not afford the paganito to rescue them. There was also a common belief that there was a deep cave called Lalangban which was an entrance to the underworld, and that from it a loud noise like the slamming of a door could be heard prior to a ranking datu's death.

Nor was the sky a heaven where the good were rewarded. It was the abode of Makaptan, that deity who killed the first man with a thunderbolt and visited disease and death on his descendants. "They did not realize," Father Alcina (1668a, 3:175) complained, "that the sky served as God's own house and the abode of the blessed." Indeed, the Visayans long resisted the Christian dogma of a heavenly paradise. Juan de la Isla (1565, 234) wrote, "They believe that their souls go down below and say that this is better because they are cooler there than up above where it is very hot." A century later, a wise old Visayan told Alcina (1668a, 182–83):

> Father, we do not doubt that there will be a heaven for the Castilians, but not for the Visayans, because God created us in this part of the world so very different from you; and since, as we see, the Spaniards will not even let us sit down in their houses here, nor show us any respect, how much less there where, as you say, all is grandeur, majesty and glory without end?

CHAPTER 5

Literature and Entertainment

Literacy came late to the Visayans. Both Colín and Alcina thought in the 1660s that it had been received from the Tagalog only a few years before their conversion to Christianity. Antonio Pigafetta said that Rajah Kolambu of Limasawa was amazed to see writing for the first time in 1521; Loarca said the "Pintados" had no writing at all in 1582; and when Legazpi's royal notary took the sworn testimony of a number of Visayans and Borneans in Bohol in 1565—including the famous Si Katuna—none of them were able to sign their names. But by 1597, Jesuits had found their catechumens in Ormuc (Leyte) literate enough to copy down their lesson on bamboo slips to take home to study. Furthermore, a report attributed to Legazpi in 1567 states,

> They have their letters and characters like those of the Malays, from whom they learned them; they write them on bamboo, bark and palm leaves with a pointed tool, but never is any ancient writing found among them nor word of their origin and arrival in these islands, their customs and rites being preserved by traditions handed down from father to son without any other record (San Agustín 1698, 292).

Legazpi presumably got this information from those Muslim merchants from Borneo and Luzon from whom he bought rice, and through whom he sent word to the "King of Luzon" that he would like to open trading relations with him. In Alcina's day it was assumed that Philippine literacy was ultimately derived from non-Filipino Muslims because the first literate Filipinos the Spaniards encountered were Muslims in Manila. Indeed, the Visayans referred to the Philippine script as "Moro writing," as they referred to many Manila imports as "Moro" (for example, granulated salt).

The Alphabet

The only specimens of Visayan penmanship known today are the signatures of Bernardino Dimabasa and Maria Mutia of Bantay Island which appear in their divorce proceedings of 1647. In addition, four missionary fathers recorded the letters the Visayans were using in their day. Alcina included them in his 1668 *Historia,* but unfortunately they survive only in a late eighteenth-century copy made in Seville by somebody who naturally was unfamiliar with them. Those recorded in the *Arte de la lengua Visaya* of Alcina's vice-provincial, Domingo Ezguerra, contain what are probably engraver's errors—for example, the use of a marginal check mark normal to Spanish usage of the time, to represent two different letters of the alphabet. And those which appeared in the manuscript *Arte Bisaya-Cebuano* of Father Francisco Encina (who died in 1760) are known only from an 1895 copy made in Manila by Cipriano Marcilla y Martín.

Father Méntrida (1637a, 248) made the following comment on Visayan script in his 1663 *Arte de lengua Bisaya hiliguaina de la Isla de Panay:*

> It is to be noted that our Bisayans have some letters with different shapes, which I place here; but even they themselves do not agree on the shapes of their letters; for this reason, and because we are limited by the types available, I have shown the characters according to the Tagalogs.

The 1818 edition of the Méntrida *Arte,* however, presents a curious alphabet obviously not based on any Tagalog type font. Father Juan Delgado (1752, 331), for his part, said in his 1751 *Historia sacro-profana,* "As a curiosity I will place here the Visayan characters, which differ little from the Tagalog." But when the book was published in Manila for the first time in 1892, it made use of the same plate as appeared in the 1890 edition of Chirino's *Relación,* which shows characters very different from the "Letras de los Filipinos" of Chirino's original Rome edition of 1604.

It has been a popular belief that Visayans used a different alphabet from the Tagalogs, but our sources give little support to such a theory. These sources themselves are limited to the genuine signatures of two individuals—which are indistinguishable from Tagalog signatures preserved in local and foreign archives—and an alphabet drawn up or copied by five different persons who did not use it themselves. None exhibit greater differences than could be expected of seven different hands in three different centuries.

Alcina (1668a, 3:35–37) described the system in considerable detail:

> We will end this chapter with the characters of these natives, or, better said, those that have been in use for a few years in these parts, an art which was communicated to them from the Tagalogs, and the latter learned it from the Borneans who came from the great island of Borneo to Manila, with whom they had considerable traffic . . . . From these Borneans the Tagalogs learned their characters, and from them the Visayans, so they call them Moro characters or letters because the Moros taught them; and although the accursed sect did not reach the Visayas, or they did not accept it, they learned their letters, which many use today, and the women much more than the men, which they write and read more readily than the latter.
>
> Their letters, then, are these: *a. e. b. c. d. g. h. l. m. n. p. r. s. t. nga.* All these characters or letters without any dot are pronounced with *a*—e.g., *ba, da, ga,* etc.—and with a dot over them, with *i* or *e*, and if it is put below, they are pronounced with *o* or *u*—e.g., *ba. be. bu. ca. ci. co.*—so that they do not have letters for vowels in their writing except when two vowels come together or a word begins with a vowel, nor letters for consonants when intermediate or final, either, so when there are two consonants—except for the letter *nga*—the one that is missing is supplied, and the same with all finals. Thus it can be said that their reading is more guessing than pronouncing what's written, so those who are not skillful in supplying the consonants, which some, and most women, read with dexterity and without stumbling, mumble what they read, guessing and even erring more often than not. So for this reason, although it is easy to learn their method of writing, reading is more difficult because, as we have said, it is mostly supplying what's missing. For greater clarity and to make reading easier, they usually place two lines ‖ after each word to separate them—though some write without them—since if they were all continuous without these divisions, they would be even more confused. In the past, these Indios used to write like the Chinese and Japanese up and down, beginning the opposite from the right hand upwards, and then their lines from bottom up until they finished on the left hand where we begin. But nowadays they begin like us and make their lines in our way from left to right, for the whole page.

Literature

Spanish accounts are unanimous in saying that Filipinos did not use their alphabet for literary compositions or record keeping: the Boxer Codex states unambiguously that they used their script only for letters and messages. Visayan literature therefore was oral literature, and as such, was not recorded by friar chroniclers or ethnographers who would have considered the idea of oral literature a contradiction in terms. But it was well developed, sophisticated, and presented by artists rewarded for their skills. This is amply shown by Alcina's (1668a, 3:20) chapter, "Concerning the alphabet and manner of writing of the Bisayans [and] the various and particular types of poetry in which they take pride," which includes the full summary of what must have been an actual epic.

There is no evidence of any prose literature, but ordinary Visayan speech was itself rich with metaphor and colorful imagery, and their poetry must have been even more so. A high proportion of the dictionary terms have both a literal and a figurative meaning, and a wide selection of pejorative terms to apply to common objects when angry. Men, women, and children are referred to by the names of birds and animals they resemble in appearance or behavior, or trees and baskets whose shapes they share. Somebody who is articulate and talkative is likened to luxuriant foliage, while one who speaks ill of his own relatives is like a big bat—because these creatures are believed to defecate in their own face while hanging upside-down. The red-faced are like *dapdap* blossoms; an untattooed man is called plain white; undecorated teeth, a chaw of coconut meat; and foreheads not sufficiently flattened as a baby, bulging or overstuffed. When irritated, a tired oarsman calls his oar a *kabkab*—the heart-shaped leaf of the *malu-iban* vine—and a cat is called *musankag* or *mosaraw* in such sentences as, "Damned cat stole my food again!"

Naturally, formal poetry had a special vocabulary of its own. *Handoy*, for instance, was the poetic term for damsel, and slaves were called *guhay* in epics and eulogies. But the essence of Visayan poetic skill lay not so much in a command of vocabulary as in the ability to use words figuratively to create subtle images. Alcina (1668a, 3:28–29) said,

> In their poetry, even if not with the variety of rhyme scheme and meters of ours though they do have their own rhymes somewhat different from ours, they no doubt excel us, for the language they use in their poems, even most of the words, is very different from what they use in common everyday speech, so much so that there are very few Europeans who understand their poems or rhymes when they hear them, even if they are very good linguists and know a lot of Visayan, because, besides the words and meaning which they use in verse being so different, even when using the ordinary words they sometimes apply to their courtesies, what they say in verse is so figurative that everything is the subtlest metaphor, and for one who doesn't know and understand them, it is impossible to understand them in it.

To this may be added that less sophisticated Visayans were also unable to follow "deep" poetry, and that when two lovers sang to each other, their words became mere symbols that were understood by nobody but the two of them.

All this poetry was generally sung or chanted rather than recited, so our sources include songs in the same category as poems. Even real songs—that is, melodies with lyrics—were poetic rather than musical compositions: the singer set his words to common tunes known to all. For community respect, a man must have been able to participate in the spontaneous versifying that accompanied social gatherings; and for peer acceptance, youths had to compete in amatory jousts. The really skillful were practically professionals: they were eagerly sought after for weddings and prestige feasts and were rewarded not only with ample food, drink, and public acclaim, but with a payment called *bayakaw*. Many were said to be more articulate in verse than in ordinary conversation, and all were able to perform for hours at a time, even whole days or nights, "without dropping a syllable or fumbling a word," Alcina (1668a, 3:30) said. Funerals, on the other hand, called for female eulogists able to improvise dirges which combined grief and laud.

The simplest form of verse, popular among children and adults of both sexes, was the *ambahan,* which used the ordinary vocabulary though often figuratively. It consisted of an unrhymed seven-syllable couplet which had to contain a complete thought—like a Greek distich—whose two lines could be interchanged and still make sense. Some people composed their own words, others repeated well-known verses, and listeners could join in by repeating the couplet, either as sung or inverted.

The ambahan was also used in the *balak,* a poetic debate between a man and a woman on the subject of love. They might also accompany themselves with musical instruments—the woman on the *korlong,* the man on the *kudyapi*—but in either case they used many subtleties of speech which not everybody understood. The *bikal* was another kind of contest which used the ambahan form, a poetic joust between two men or two women in which they satirized each other's physical or moral shortcomings, but were expected to harbor no hard feelings afterwards. They could continue for an hour or two, encouraged by raucous laughter and occasional help from the sidelines. Since the ambahan was a verse form almost as demanding as a Japanese haiku, its wide currency suggests an extremely poetic populace.

The noblest literary form was the *siday* or *kandu.* This was the most difficult of all—long, sustained, repetitious, and heavy with metaphor and allusion. A single one might take six hours to sing or the whole night through, or even be continued the next night, during which rapt audiences neither yawned nor nodded, though the frequent repetition of long lines with only the variation of a few words struck Spanish listeners as tiresome.

Subject matter was the heroic exploits of ancestors, the valor of warriors, or the beauty of women, or even the exaltation of heroes still living. Alcina (1668a, 4:257–59) recorded the summary of one or two of them with tantalizing brevity, like the following from the Pacific coast of Samar he knew as Ibabao:

Kabungaw and Bubung Ginbuna

On the coast of Ibabao were two celebrated lovers, the man called Kabungaw and the woman Bubung Ginbuna. Before they were married, these two had been in love for a long time, and once when he had to go on a certain rather long voyage, in company with others who were setting out on a *pangayaw* raid, he left instructions with his sweetheart that she should go straight to his parents' house to get whatever she needed for comfort. (He only had a mother or sister since his father had already died.) She went one time when she had to get a little abaca to weave clothes for her lover, but was so ill received by her swain's mother and his sister, who was called Halinai, that after abusing her by word, they did not give her what she had come to get, so she went back displeased and determined not to return there or even be seen by her lover again. He learned this as soon as he returned and asked if she had requested anything, and the bad sendoff she had been given instead, so after much brooding, he refused to go up into his house until he learned where and with whom his lady was living.

He did many things and particular deeds (which I am not putting down so as not to be too long-winded) until he learned that she was on a little island where she had fled with her slaves. He was almost drowned the times he went in search of her and escaped only by means of supernatural aid, until on the third attempt he reached there, and pretended to be dead near the house where she was living, until he was recognized by a slave who reported it to his lady. She went down drawn by love, and in her presence he recovered the life he pretended to have lost in her absence, and both rejoicing, they were married. They remained there as lords of that little island, which they called Natunawan in allusion to the love they had felt on first sight, because *natunawan* means that they melted together with happiness, or Nawadan, which means "lost footsteps." There, they say, not only men followed them from the mainland, but even plants, attracted by the goodness of the land and the good reception from those settlers.

The reason why the story of Kabungaw and Ginbuna is so badly truncated is that it appears in a chapter entitled, "Of the troubles which some famous princesses had in their antiquity to get married [and] the efforts of men to abduct others" (Alcina 1668a, 4:245). Thus the whole meat of what must have been an epic-length tale has been excised as being of no service to Alcina's purpose—all those adventures which form the flesh of Philippine epics that he did not put down so as not to be too long-winded: those heroic deeds, shipwrecks, and drownings, the intervention of deities, and the flight to distant lands to live happily ever after. Moreover, the incident of Kabungaw's pretending to be dead sounds suspiciously like a moderni-zation in Alcina's own day, since the magical revival of dead heroes by their wives or sweethearts is a common climax to Mindanao epics.

Epics

The siday or kandu must have been what Philippine folklorists nowadays call a folk epic. The epic as a literary form is thought to have originated in the stories of Indo-European tribal bards regaling a band of warriors gathered around a campfire with tales that glorified approved standards of male conduct. These warriors historically fought hand-to-hand in cattle raids which were eventually recast as the rescue of abducted wives in great epics like the Iliad and Mahabharata. In the societies that produced Phil-ippine epics, however, power and prestige were not based on the owner-ship of herds of cattle but on the control of slave labor. Thus Visayan heroes who were celebrated as *karanduun*—that is, worthy of kandu acclaim—would have won their reputations in real life on pangayaw slave raids. As one kandu says of its heroine, "You raid with your eyes and capture many, and with only a glance you take more prisoners than raiders do with their pangayaw" (Alcina 1668a, 4:178).

Alcina concluded his chapters on the courtship patterns among Visayan aristocrats by telling the kandu of Datung Sumanga and Bugbung Humasanun, that princess who captured men with her eyes. He said he was presenting it in a faithful translation, but what he presented was obviously a mere summary or scenario. A fleeting glimpse of one line, however, is incidentally preserved in his chapter on warfare—"The captives he took on land were 70, and 50 of those who were as weak and delicate as women so they led them by the hand, and those taken at sea were 100, so that they were 220 in all, not counting the rest of the booty and prizes" (Alcina 1668a, 4:178). But even in its abbreviated outline, it is possible to recognize stylistic features common to well-known Mindanao epics like the Darangan, Ulahingon, or Agyu, and therefore get some sense of what the original must have sounded like. Only the ending seems to be deviant: the hero sets out to storm heaven itself, fails to do so, comes home empty-handed, but then claims his bride, a dénouement told in Alcina's version with inappro-priate irony.

These epics are characterized by highly repetitious plots: battle follows battle with only minor variations, and voyage after voyage by sea or air in search of a kidnapped princess or some hidden treasure. In Alcina's résumé, Datung Sumanga's six forays are given only a sentence or two apiece, but if this kandu took all night to sing, they must have included details like the hero's flashing gold teeth and magic sword or gong obtained from deities in a many-layered heaven, and the magnificent plumage at prow and stern of ships miraculously propelled by guardian spirits rather than oars or sails.

Another characteristic of Philippine epics is the amount of space given to betel nut. The datu's followers turn the ground as bloody as a battlefield with their spittle, demigods chew *bonga* of pure gold, ladies make their appearance preparing quids for their menfolk and serving them ceremoniously, and lovers seal their commitment by exchanging them partially masticated. Heroines are royal princesses secluded as inaccessible *binokot* in their chambers, where they are found spinning, weaving, or embroidering their princes' clothes. They are esteemed for such skills as well as for their beauty crowned with a great mass of hair embellished with artificial switches which it is a great offense for a man even to touch. And a good epic ends with a colorful description of the lavish wedding feast in which its protagonists join to display their wealth and magnanimity.

Datung Sumanga and Bugbung Humasanun

There was, so says the singer, a princess in the island of Bohol of great repute and fame called Bugbung Humasanun, the most renowned among all the beauties and of the greatest fame for her talent among all the damsels, so secluded and enclosed in her chamber that nobody ever saw her except by sheerest chance. Her visage was like the sun when it spreads its first rays over the world or like a sudden flash of lightning, the one causing fear and respect, the other, joy and delight. A great chief desirous of marrying her called Datung Sumanga one day arrived below her house and, giving a salute, asked for the said princess without going up by calling out her name and surname and the other names which she had been given for her beauty. Irritated by his call, and either angry at his boldness or pretending to be, she sent a maid to ask who he was, and learning his name, acted angrier still that the courtesy had not been shown according to their custom, and replied, why had he come in person? Had he no negroes to command or slaves to send, perhaps not even someone he esteemed like a son whom he trusted as faithful and could send as a friend? So, without replying or speaking a single word, the chief had to go right off rebuffed.

So, selecting a negro slave, he ordered him to go as intermediary and ask that princess for buyos, and told him not to come back without them. The negro go-between went with his message and asked for the buyos in his master's name, repeating the words of courtesy and praise which were customarily most polite. To this she responded with the same courtesy, saying that she had neither bongas to put in the buyos nor leaves to make them, for the bongas which she used came from where the sun rose and the leaves which she added from where it set. And she said nothing more.

When her reply was received by the suitor chief, he immediately ordered his slaves to embark to go and search, some to the east for the bongas, and others to the west for the leaves, just as the princess had asked for them. This they did at once, and the same one who had brought the message was sent back with them, and handed them over and asked her to make the buyos for his lord. To this the lady replied that she could not make them because she had no lime, since her lime was only found in a certain distant and isolated island. With only this reply he returned. So the datu immediately ordered ships launched at sea and sent them flying to find the lime in the place indicated. This the slaves carried out promptly, and returned with all speed and delivered the lime, which the same experienced messenger took at once and gave to the lady on behalf of his master, asking her for those buyos. Her response was that she was not about to make them until his master went in person to Tandag town on the coast of Caraga and made a mangayaw raid there and brought her those he captured.

So he started out at once, and with his *joangas,* or barangays, armed with all his warriors, embarked for the said Caraga, made his attack, and took 120 persons in all, whom, before even disembarking or going to his house, he sent to be handed over to that binokot by the same messenger with the necessary guards, who did so immediately and asked for the buyos in return for his lord who was exhausted from the battle.

But still not content with this, she sent back to say she could not make the buyos until he did the same thing he had done in Tandag in the islands of Yambig and Camiguin, which the chief set out to do at once. Reinforcing his fleet and taking only a few days, he brought his ships back full of captives, some 220 persons of all kinds, whom he immediately sent to his lady, asking again for those buyos by means of that slave, to which, stubborn as ever, she added that he had to perform the same deed with the people of the island of Siquihor and the town of Dapitan.

This he did at once and sent her all the captives, who were no fewer than on the past occasions, though still not enough to win her consent or for her to give the buyos which the gallant was asking of her. Instead, she sent to tell him that he had to do the same thing with the towns subject to Mindanao and those of the island of Jolo. So, undaunted by even this challenge, for a lover, unless he is mad, fears as little as those who are, he started out on the fourth expedition. He weighed anchor with his fleet and went to Mindanao and Jolo, where he fought valiantly and took many more captives than on the other occasions, and sent them all to her, once more asking for his buyos, since for these he was giving her she must surely say yes and set the wedding for certain.

But not even this time was she willing to give in, but rather, sent him another demand by the fuming go-between, who told him, "Sire, what the princess said is that she esteems your favors and admires your valor, but that in order to demonstrate you really love her and so your prowess may be better known, she has heard that not very far from these islands is the great kingdom of China, a people very rich and opulent who chirp like birds with a singsong voice and nobody understands them, and she said no more."

When her lover heard this, he fitted out his ships with stronger rigging, added more vessels, men, and arms, and undertook the fifth voyage for Grand China, at which coast he arrived safely, made his assaults on towns little prepared, captured enough to fill the ships, and made the return voyage to his land with great speed, laden with captives and spoils, which he immediately sent to his lady with the oft-repeated plea for the buyos.

But the lady was not won over by even all of this, but rather, setting her contract still higher, asked for the impossible, for the reply which she gave was to say (and here the poet speaks in the hyperboles which the Visayans use with much elegance) that in due time and without fail she would make the buyos if he performed one more task first, which was that he should bring her something from heaven as important as what he had brought her from earth.

On this reply, seeing that she was asking for the impossible, he said, "Come then, let's get started: we will try to conquer heaven. Prepare the ships," he said, "and we'll go there. We'll make an attack on the sky; we'll unhinge a piece of it; we'll unfold part of one of its eight layers or levels, and we'll seize one of its greatest thunder claps; we'll rob the moon of a bit of its splendor, or if nothing else, at least one ray of those that are forged in its workshops. Come then, we're off, we're off!"

So he embarked, but in vain, and so he sailed, but without end, for of all the receding horizons, he neither reached one nor could he cover them all, so he returned satisfied, and sent word to her that he had done what she had ordered but that could only dedicate, not give, the thunder and lightning to her, for throughout the many regions he had coursed, many were heard but few were found. He added that unless she sent him the buyos immediately which had cost him so much and had so tired him out, he would come and personally remove her hairpiece and make a *sombol-*plume of it for his ship.

On receiving this message, she began to cry and moan, terrified in her heart lest he dishonor her, and so she decided to make the buyos so many times denied. When they were made, she put them in a little casket of marble fashioned with much art, and this inside another little case like those in which ladies keep their jewels, and sent them with the negro go-between who had so many times come and gone with messages. But when he told his lord that he had them, he was unwilling to see or receive them and sent them back instead, saying he would not accept them whole but only chewed, and that she should send one in a perfumed box of gold, all of which was a sign of her consent and pledge of their intended wedding celebrations, which they performed afterwards with the pomp and ostentation fit for their class and wealth (Alcina 1668a, 4:248–56).

Folklore

Visayan folklore is scattered all through Alcina's *Historia*. In the volume devoted to botany, he tells the origin myth of the first man and woman, and remarks that the *makapaag* flower was believed to blossom well indoors because it was originally a man whom the gods changed into a plant. Under zoology, he recounts monkey lore that are still popularly believed—that they fish for crabs by using their tails as bait, for example, or form living chain bridges by grabbing each other's tails to cross crocodile-infested rivers—as well as the story of the Monkey and the Tortoise which was later given literary dignity by Jose Rizal. Describing birds, he mentions in passing a moralizing song about a man who kept three in his house—a *tabilalang*, which is always in flight and never known to sleep, a *tarinting*, which keeps nervously turning its head in all directions, and a *gitgit*, which, like a sentry, never stops giving its call. (The moral is that a householder who intends to protect his wealth and honor must be vigilant.) Speculating about the existence of giants, he encapsulates the legend of Pusung of Magtaon, and in discussing *daragangan*, folk heroes, he cites a folk song about fleet-footed Parapat. But unfortunately, his collection of 600 riddles *(titigoon)* has not survived.

The First Man and Woman

After the world was made and the coconut palms had borne fruit, two coconuts, well ripened, happened to fall into the sea on whose shore their palm tree was growing, whose waters received them and carried them on its waves for many days wherever the wind and current wanted, until one day when the sea was raging, it threw them with violence against some rocks. Ready to hatch—as if they were eggs—they broke open with the blow and—as if preordained—there came forth from the larger a man, who was the first one, whom they call Laki, and from the smaller a woman, whom they call Baye. And from these two as the first parents of the human race, all people are descended (Alcina 1668a, 1:178).

Why the Bat Is Called Stupid

We will add a Bisayan fable here which gives [these bats] their name and the reason they go out at night. This is, that after their creation (the Bisayans in their antiquity did not know who created them, though they had some inkling), all the birds got together for each one to choose his food, and so that they would not be taking each others', each would choose according to his desire and taste. When this big bat's turn came, he chose for his kind the fruit of a tree which is called *tabigi* here, which is beautiful to the eye, as big as a medium melon and, seen from a distance, not dissimilar to the big oranges from China. They all made fun of him because this fruit, although of nice appearance outside, inside has nothing more than a few seeds as large as eggs, although of different shapes to fill the shell; they are very hard, bitter and tasteless (although very good for curing loose stool, most especially bloody stool, though the birds did not know this quality). From this incident, he was given the name of Kabug, which means dunce *[bobo]* in this language, or one who has little sense. They also have a saying which serves very appropriately for no few occasions, and it is that when somebody selects what pleases the eye without checking its quality—like a beautiful woman but foolish, or a handsome man but stupid, and fruit of good color but rotten, etc.—they say of him, *"Daw napili sin tabigi,"* which means that, like the Kabug, he chose the tabigi fruit, good to look at but for nothing else (Alcina 1668a, 2:233–34).

The Tortoise and the Monkey

From the sayings which are common among these natives about this animal [the tortoise] we can deduce its characteristics. In one of them they say of it what we say of doctors over there [in Spain], "He doesn't want it [even as a gift]," because they tell a story and it is this.

This Tortoise and the Monkey found by chance a bud or sprout of a banana plant, which we have already said is called *sahan*. They fought over who would take the best part, and in order to deceive the Monkey, the Tortoise asked for the part which had the leaves, which thus seemed best to the monkey and he kept it, giving him the part with the root, which is what the latter wanted because it is what sprouts, grows and bears fruit, and so he gave signs of wanting the opposite so they would let him have what he wanted and was more profitable.

So to say of somebody that he is a man of intrigues and plots, they say he is like this animal's intestines because they have many twists and turns, and even though small, it knows a lot since it was able to trick the Monkey, which is so much larger and wiser than it; and also when they give somebody the worst part, they say they treated him like the Tortoise.

So to continue the story begun above, we say that when the piece of stalk or root which the Monkey had given him sprouted, grew and bore fruit, the Tortoise, since he could not climb, went to find the Monkey to climb up and get the fruit, which he did gladly, and seated above, began to gather the ripe bananas and to eat them, throwing down all the rinds or skins on the Tortoise who was down below, with which he tricked him, or revenged the first trick. And from this fable they get the said proverbs (Alcina 1668a, 2:202–3).

Pusong of Magtaon

I will tell of one brave whose memory was still very fresh because it happened not many years before the Spaniards arrived here. This one was an Indio of gigantic stature called Pusong, a native of the town of Magtaon in the interior of the island of Samar and Ibabao, who used to make frequent invasions of the towns of Calbiga and Libunao which are on the Samar side, but not so much around Borongan because those on that coast were much more feared. Those he had killed were many when they stood up to him, and even more those who had been captured in repeated times because he was a great raider, or *magahat* as they call them, until near the town of Calbiga they set a trap for him in which he was killed.

This trap was that in a stream he had to cross, which was all flat stones with very high banks of rock, one of the more daring hid below it on the side he usually came from, and the other waited for him on the opposite side, with arms ready, though not trusting so much in them as in the treachery and trap they had set for him. This one challenged him from the side where he was, with the stream in between, and when the one from Magtaon jumped over, the one who was hidden below the bank threw his spear with such great force that it passed through his body, with which he fell. And the one who had challenged him came down and they killed him—since "a dead Moro gets many blows"—in the very place where he had fallen with the first wound, and since this was of very wide flat stones, as I saw when I went there just to see what traces remained on that rock where, stretched out in the same position, they had traced and carved out with a chisel the whole body in the very posture in which he had died.

I have seen these lines or carving which still survive today, and they show that he was a remarkable man and husky because although he wore a *barote* [padded breastplate], the rest of his body was naked except for his bahag, and from the lines which traced his thighs, legs, arms, head, and body (he had one arm caught underneath and one leg twisted or bent), it is clear that he was a giant of a man, of greater stature and build than the tallest ordinarily are (Alcina 1668a, 4:167–69).

[But] what a Calbigan told me, an intelligent chief more knowledgeable about their affairs than the ordinary (he was incumbent governor of his town when he told me, as he had been several times before) . . . was that they were pygmies they call Bongan in their language who killed him, and they were so small that they didn't exceed half a good-sized man's forearm. The way they did it, they say, was that they covered the streambed with nipa leaves, and since these were on top of the slick stones, when he crossed the said stream and stepped on those leaves, both feet shot out from under him and threw him down on the stones, and immediately many of the said Bongan, or pygmies, rushed up—like ants that drag things which weigh ten times more than all of them together—and with their little spears and other arms, they killed him (Alcina 1668a, 277–78).

Parapat

I will tell an unusual tale which I have heard many times and have repeated not a few, both because of the oddity of the subject and the nice language of the wording. It says, then, that there was an Indio called—if I remember right—Parapat, who was so swift when running along the beach—which over here are of very fine clean sand— he left no trace or footprint by which it could be known that he had run across it, and the same song also adds that only on top of the rocks would some grains of sand be discovered which had stuck to the soles of his feet or between his toes, by which those who knew his speed and that he was accustomed to pass that way, knew he had passed by (Alcina 1668a, 4:181).

Bingi of Lawan

There lived in this place a chief called Karagrag, who was its lord and ruler. He was married to a lady of his rank called Bingi, a name which had been bestowed on her because of her chastity, as we shall see. (I was not able to find out if she came from the same town; most probably she was from upstream on the Catubig River, where she was the daughter of the chief there.) This lady, according to what they recount, was endowed with many fine virtues and greatly celebrated for her beauty among these natives, so much so that, moved by the fame of her beauty, the Datu, or ruler, of Albay got ready a hundred ships. This chief was called Dumaraug, which means the victor, and with all those ships he weighed anchor in his land, and within a short time came in view of the [Lawan Island] town of Makarato.

His unexpected arrival excited the town, but since it was well-fortified by its natural location and it was the season of the Vendavales (the best time for going there from

106

Albay) when the force of the sea and its waves were strong and turbulent, he did not venture to go straight in but took shelter instead near the beach which Rawis Point makes with very fine sand and free of shoals, where, because of an islet across the entrance from the sea, the surf is less obstructive and the sea milder and calm. From there he sent a small boat with a sign of peace to announce the purpose of his coming, which was simply to carry Bingi away as his wife, the fame of whose beauty alone had left him lovestruck and with only this would he then return to his land without making any attack and always afterward remain their friend and protector, since being more powerful than they, he could do it to their advantage.

Karagrag, rather than making reply, showed them how well prepared he was by entertaining them, and when his wife was informed of Dumaraug's intentions, she responded at once that she was greatly surprised that for something of such little worth he had made such a demonstration and launched so many ships, that she was content with the husband she had and did not care to exchange him for any other, even one much more powerful, and that so long as he was alive, she could not think of leaving him; and if it should be her unlucky fate to fall into his hands captive, he should understand that though he might carry her off and command her as his slave, that to make her his wife, she would never consent and was ready to give her life first.

Encouraged by so bold a response, her husband Karagrag simply added that he was there waiting with his men deployed, and that although they were not many, they were very good men, and that the place where they were was very secure, and if he came to try his arms in battle, they would do their duty; and if he should defeat them, he would be lord of his wife and property, but if not, he would return to his land empty-handed, if indeed he escaped from there with his life.

With this reply, and in view of the strength and impregnability of the place for them, with no more arms than spears and shields or at most some arrows, the chief reconsidered and hesitated a bit but not for long, and without attempting anything more and risking his men, he returned home just as he had come, leaving both the chief and his wife Bingi happy.

This happened a few years before the Spaniards came, and is still fresh in the memory of the natives of the Lawan town, who today are their descendants. Not many years ago, I buried a chief of the said island, who was more than seventy years old, whose parent had been alive when this raid took place; and a son of his who had heard it many times, related it to me with all the aforesaid details (Alcina 1668a, 4:20–23).

A *bingi* or *bingil* was a virgin or a woman who had been faithful to one man all her life. It must therefore have been bestowed on the heroine of this romance sometime after the Albay raid, the first step in an historic event's becoming a legend. The quotation of her and her husband's noble words indicates that the poetic process had already had its effect by the time Father Alcina heard the story. Perhaps with retelling over the centuries and the accumulation of apocryphal embellishments, the tale might have grown into a full-fledged kandu. Indeed, had ancient Visayan culture not succumbed to colonial acculturation, some Waray bard might now be singing the Epic of Bingi.

Musical Instruments

There were basically eight kinds of Visayan musical instruments. Four were very quiet instruments and so were played indoors at nighttime: a small lute, bamboo zither, nose flute, and reed Jew's harp. The other four were very loud, and therefore suitable for war, dancing, and public gatherings: bamboo or seashell bugle, metal gongs, skin-headed drums, and bamboo resonators.

The kudyapi was a kind of small lute carved out of a single piece of wood with a belly of half a coconut shell added for resonance, with two or three wire strings plucked with a quill plectrum, and three or four frets, often of metal.[19] The body was called *sungar-sungar* or *burbuwaya;* the neck, *burubunkun;* the strings, *dulos;* the fretboard, *pidya;* and the tuning pegs, *birik-birik.* The scroll was called *apil-apil* or *sayong,* the same as the hornlike protrusions at the ends of the ridgepole of a house. The kudyapi was only played by men, mainly to accompany their own love songs. The female equivalent was the korlong, a kind of zither made of a single node of bamboo with strings cut from the skin of the bamboo itself, each raised and tuned on two little bridges, and played with both hands like a harp. A variant form had a row of thinner canes with a string cut from each one.

Tolali or *lantuy* was a nose flute with three or four finger holes, and was played in imitation of a mournful human voice with shakes and trills thought appropriate to wakes and funerals. *Subing* was a Jew's harp—a twanging reed plucked between the lips or teeth with the open mouth as a variable resonating chamber, and since its sound could be shaped into a kind of code words understood only by the player and his sweetheart, it was considered the courting instrument par excellence. *Bodyong* was a conch shell or section of bamboo played against the lips like a bugle, used as a signal in war or as part of a babaylan's paraphernalia during a *paganito.* Babaylan also kept time with tambourines called *kalatong,* a term which included war drums *(gadang* or *gimbal),* with the huge ones that were carried on mangayaw cruisers being fashioned out of hollow tree trunks with a deerskin head. *Tibongbong* was a node of bamboo pounded on the floor as a rhythm instrument.

The most important instrument was the *agong,* a bronze gong Spanish explorers encountered wherever they went ashore. Pigafetta noted an ensemble in Cebu—a pair suspended and struck alternately, another large one, and two small ones played like cymbals—and in Quipit, three different sizes hanging in the queen's quarters. The natives of Sarangani buried theirs in a vain attempt to avoid looting by Villalobos; and thirty Samareños boarded Legazpi's flagship in Oras Bay and danced to the rhythm of one, after his blood compact with their chief. Mindanao epics provide a few details of their use. Agong were played either on the edge or on the navel (that is, the center boss or knob), slowly to announce bad news, faster (by the ruling datu himself) to summon the people. Warships approached the enemy with all gongs sounding.

Gongs were given a larger vocabulary than any other instrument. Alcina (1668a, 4:129) considered it an evidence of the elegance of the Visayan language that there were special terms "even for the cord with which they fasten and hang it, which it would be improper to apply to anything else." *Mungmungan* was the boss or teat. A flat gong, or one from which the boss had been worn off by long use, was *panas*, including the platelike Chinese ones *(mangmang)*. The largest one in an ensemble was *ganding*. *Hototok* was to play them on the edge with a simple stick, or *sarawisaw* if more than one player alternated strokes. *Pagdanaw* or *pagbasal* was to strike them on the boss with a padded drumstick called *basal*. (A governor or chief was also called basal, presumably because of his prerogative of sounding a gong to assemble his people.) Actual bells from Spain or Asia were *linganay,* and little jingle bells—like those the epic hero Bantungan had on the handle of his kampilan—were *golong-golong.*

Chinese gongs were little valued: ones from Sangir were worth three or four times as much, and those from Borneo three or four times that—4 or 5 pesos in 1616. Huge ones said to reach a meter and a half in diameter could fetch one or two slaves. The Bornean gong was a standard of value when bargaining for expensive goods—for example, "Pakaagongonta ining katana [Let's price this Japanese sword]" (Sánchez 1617, 9v). Indeed, assessments like *pinipito* or *pinakapito* (both referring to the number seven) were understood by themselves to mean seven gongs.

Gongs were one of four items—along with gold; porcelain, and slaves— required for any datu-class dowry, or bride-price, and men mortgaged themselves to borrow one for this purpose. The bargaining between the two families was done with little wooden counters placed on top of a gong turned boss-up on the floor, and the gong itself became the property of the mediating go-between upon the conclusion of a successful settlement.

Vocal Music

Visayans were said to be always singing except when they were sick or asleep. Singing meant the extemporaneous composition of verses to common tunes, not the performance of set pieces composed by musical special-ists. There was no separate poetic art: all poems were sung or chanted, including full-fledged epics or public declamations. Singing was unaccom-panied except in the case of love songs, in which either male or female singers accompanied themselves on their respective instruments, kudyapi or korlong. Well-bred ladies were called upon to perform with the korlong during social gatherings, and all adults were expected to participate in group singing on any occasion.

Awit was the general term for singing and a *paraawit* was an expert "considered a professional singer," Sánchez (1617, 38) said, "like a leader whom the others follow." *Biyaw* was to sing solo, while a *mamaratbat* was the precentor who set the tune and beat by singing a couplet, to which the others *(mananabat)* responded in chorus, *batbat* meaning to beat metal flat. *Bagaw* or *dagaw* was for two or more singers to reinforce or complement each other in male drinkfests, during which might be sung *daihuan*—songs in which drinkers made fun of one of their fellows. The narrative content of these songs was called *biriyawan*—tales or fables—or *karanduun* if it was of epic length and loftiness. *Hiya* or *hele* was the shout of men putting their shoulders to a common task like dragging a log or rowing a boat, whence sea chanteys were called *otohele.*

When distinguishing different types of song, however, *awit* was used as a specific term for sea chanteys, which were called *hilimbanganon* in Panay. The cantor, himself pulling an oar—a paddle, actually—would lead off with an unrhymed couplet and the whole crew would respond in a heavy beat with a refrain *(hotlo)* like "Hód-lo, hé-le, hí-ya, hé-le!" A good paraawit or parahele had a wide repertoire of tunes with different tempos, some of them handed down from generation to generation by fathers teaching their sons. The content of these sea chanteys, if not their actual wording, was also handed down from ancestral times and so perpetuated and prom-ulgated Visayan traditions and values. More than one Spanish observer, commenting on the lack of written records, said that Filipino history and beliefs were preserved in the songs they heard while rowing boats.

Sabi was the general term for poetry or song in Panay, especially that with a chorus responding to a precentor, but might also refer specifically to *handum* or *bat-ar.* Handum was to recall somebody departed with affection-ate praise—"like a good minister or alcalde mayor," Father Méntrida remarked rather fondly—and bat-ar was a dirge or eulogy addressed to the deceased at a wake. Dirges in Leyte and Samar were called *haya* (from *tihaya,* to be face-up like a corpse or a canoe carried on the shoulder), and female parahaya were hired to sing mournful tunes which evoked shrieks of grief from the widowed and relatives present. Haya were also called *anogon* or *kanogon* ("Alas! Woe is me!"), and since they not only praised the dead but petitioned them directly for supernatural favor, the missionary fathers took a dim view of their performance. As Father Sánchez (1617, 127) said, "*Kanogon* is also to bewail the deceased and is like paying him an honor, or better said, to sing something which should be prohibited because in the singing they invoke the deceased and the *diwata.*"

Dancing

With the exception of funerals, all Visayan feasts sponsored by datus were accompanied by dancing and gong playing—weddings, birth of children, planting and harvesting of crops, preparations for war, and victory celebrations afterwards. *Sayaw* or *sabay* was the general term—*magsalabay* for men, *magkigal* for women, *magbabanug* for a pair of dancers, and *magsisibay* for group dancing in two opposed lines.

Sabay suggested birdlike motions with the arms—for men, one arm pointing down and the other up, to be reversed while opening and closing the fists; for ladies, extended with slow deliberate finger motions. *Taruk* referred to the delicate foot movements characteristic of dancing by women—including babaylan around the pig or wine jar during paganito—often only slightly lifting either the heels or toes. *Patad-patad* was stomping to a light tread by either sex. In the Kigal, a lady held a kerchief in both hands, waving it to one side and then the other, placing it around her neck from time to time. (*Kigal* meant to hold hands: perhaps she and her partner joined hands to end the dance, since otherwise men and women never touched each other in Visayan dances.) *Salabay* was actually a war dance in which two men armed with shields and spears performed a ritualized but energetic duel with feints and lunges accompanied by gong beat. They sometimes became so enthusiastic they had to be separated lest intentional or unintentional body contact lead to a real fight.

Games and Gambling

Spanish lexicographers gave little space to toys, mentioning only little girls' dolls *(bata-bata* or *kulasot)* and a children's game called *kunggit* played with *kigay* or *buskay* seashells—probably modern *sungka.* But youths—for that matter, men of all ages—spun tops, which was the most popular form of gambling. Good top throwing required both skill and muscle, and the action was accompanied by much laughter, shouting, and stomping. Made of hardwood, the top was thrown with a strong soft cord of maguey *(gamowan)* wound around its head *(ulo)*, with the object of striking another top with its point *(tagad)* to splinter or split—or at least knock over—that other top. When a top was spun so that it appeared motionless—or "sleeping," as they said in Spanish—it was called *tuyong* or *urok*. The top itself was called *kasing*, and its shape was so commonly known that the human heart was called *kasing-kasing*.

Betting during a game of tops varied according to different rules of play which included twenty or thirty specific terms—*nagbibigay, nagigoway, nagdaugay*, for example, "and many other names," Father Sánchez (1617, 132) said, "not used in the pulpit or confessional."

Cockfighting was observed by Pigafetta in Palawan in 1521. Philippine historians would later conclude that the custom had been introduced by the Spaniards themselves, but the practice was already widespread and important in Southeast Asian cultures at that time. In pre-Islamic Java, cockfights had religious significance in public ceremonies, and they were carved in stone in the temple friezes of Angkor Wat in Cambodia in the twelfth century. Kings sometimes identified so personally with their favorites that Sultan Iskander Muda of Ache could order a courtier castrated whose bird had defeated his own.

The Visayan word *bulang* was applied in Malay not only to tying the blade to the cock's spur, but a weapon to a man's wrist. Similarly, Visayan *magbubulang* meant not only for cocks to fight but also men who had challenged one another. (The razorlike blade itself [*garol*] was also called bulang.)

Cockfighters raised their birds in the house, crossbred them with wild ones, imported others from Jolo with a reputation for bravery, and assessed their abilities by the color of their feathers—for example, black ones fought best in the afternoon, white ones in the morning. The winner took the defeated bird—"Binulang ako niya sing tolo kaharangsar [He took three cocks from me]"—unless the owner wished to ransom it for healing with the milky sap of the *gatas-gatas* plant (Sánchez 1637a, 80). Whatever the size of spectator betting may have been before the Spanish advent, it was greatly increased by the introduction of the colonizers' coinage. Once, when a galleon ran aground in Borongan in 1655, private salvage operations flooded the Samar coast with so much Mexican silver that the price of a fighting cock rose to 20 pesos and bets to 500 pesos and 1,000 pesos.

CHAPTER 6

Natural Science

Visayan society knew no schools or classrooms: children became functioning adults through informal instruction within the family. In the field of morals, most communities recognized some wise and persuasive elder as a kind of pastor, *parawali*—probably from Malay-Arabic *wali,* "saint"—who gave advice in household gatherings. But knowledge of the physical environment was learned from parents—the movement of heavenly bodies and change of seasons, the direction of winds and recognition of storm signals, the nature and habits of different species in the animal kingdom. All such knowledge might be called natural science.

Environment

The Visayans called their natural environment *banwa,* a word which meant mountain, countryside, terrain, climate, and homeland. (In colonial times, it was extended to mean town—for example, Hiligaynon "Naga binanwa kami pag pakaon sa Hokom [We supply the alcalde with food, town by town in turn]" [Méntrida 1637a, 53].) *Banwaan* meant overgrown and *napabanwa* gone to the hills; *binmanwa* was a man who could take care of himself in the wilds, and *banwaanun* or *tagubanwa* were mountain-dwelling spirits.

The banwa covered every island from sea to sea, even into the sea with mangroves growing in salt water; Spanish explorers were often unable to see coastal villages for the trees. A small Visayan population cut its settlements rather precariously out of this banwa but neither destroyed nor tamed it: its voracious vegetation was always ready to reclaim their fields and gardens as its crocodiles and pythons were ready to prey on their children and livestock.

The Visayan child probably first learned the names and characteristics of wildlife from comparisons with human behavior. People who affected gaudy clothes were said to be like the brilliant big *kakanog* butterflies, evil omens that brought swiddening activities to a halt and the abandonment of the site. Men who strutted around in blood-red *pudong* were red-headed *piyak* woodpeckers who pecked any branch they happened to light on, and those with an extra turn in their G-strings were like *piyas,* a baby monkey, because monkeys supposedly tied their young to their breasts with rattan. Women who were not good mothers to their babies were like *tabon* birds or sea turtles which did not hatch their own eggs but buried them in the sand to be incubated by the sun. A promising youth who died young was like the *balitnung* tree whose leathery bark was easily removed; a boastful man who promised much but delivered little was like a *biribog* crab that moved backwards; and if a man said he was like a giant tridacna clam in a certain place, he meant he would never move. And both the greedy or voracious, and the powerful who "swallowed up everything" were naturally called crocodiles *(buwaya).*

Later lessons included the information that all albinos—like a deer or turtle—were *pangasa,* bad luck, since their unnatural color must mean they were bewitched, and a person could be transformed into a beast just by looking at an albino, or even by entering the house of somebody else who had seen one. It was taught too that a crocodile's age could be determined from the number of pebbles found in its craw since it swallowed one a year as ballast, and that they never hurt villagers on the same stream where they lived. Nevertheless, the actual danger of crocodiles was an everyday fact of village life: Sánchez (1617, 448) illustrated *salaw,* parental care or concern, with the example, "Like when counseling a son who's going traveling, they warn him there's a buwaya in a certain place." In unusual cases—for example, a woman swallowed whole while weaving, loomsticks and all—the beast was explained as a kind of divine sheriff punishing an infraction of some religious tabu. (Missionaries were not wanting who made the same prediction for converts who sneaked off to bathe during mass.)

114

Many of these phenomena which would be rejected by modern science were accepted by well-educated missionaries in their day. Father Alcina, for example, did not doubt that the *ipo* tree was so venomous that it killed any who passed through its shade or downwind, and that the tree was therefore surrounded by the bones of wild animals poisoned in this manner. Neither did he doubt that one of his own parishioners had given birth to a crocodile twin. She was the wife of Pakotolini of Tubig, who had been raised in a Jesuit house as a church boy, and the little creature was delivered together with a normal child. The parents moved away to get rid of it, but it not only followed them but regularly brought them a wild hog or deer, or large fish. Father Alcina heard the story from the parents themselves and did not doubt it because, as he said, they were both exemplary Christians and therefore trustworthy.

Like all peoples in the sixteenth century, Visayans believed in an extensive menagerie of fabulous beasts, or ordinary beasts with fabulous qualities. Below is a sampling.

A Visayan Bestiary

Bangot or *sikop*	Hawks in whose nests a root or herb could be found, which contained the secret of their fishing ability (This root or herb could be sold to fishermen for a good price, or to weavers because it made their arms light and tireless.)
Barangitaw	A species of small crocodiles friendly to human beings (It drew near to listen to their conversations, and allowed them to step on its back to cross water.)
Basol	A caterpillar whose hairs caused dangerous infection when accidentally touched, but were harmless if it was seen before touching
Bukaw	An owl which was a sure sign of death if it perched on a rooftop (It always flew in pairs with its mate, and children were told they were witches come to eat them.)
Dumorogmon	A black snake that made bark-leaf nests, and cured wounded snakes of its kind by applying medicinal herbs
Kolago or *kagwang*	A kind of flying squirrel whose loud clear cry at dawn meant there would be no rain that day
Mago	A tarsier that lived on charcoal
Magpopo	A small viper with a crest and that crowed like a rooster
Miro	A civet cat which charmed roosting hens with its eyes so that they fell from the branch
Taligatos	A snake which was always accompanied by 100 others which would rush up if it was killed, so nobody dared to touch it
Tigi	A snake whose bite was not fatal if the victim called for help and somebody responded, who would then suffer the effects of the poison instead

115

Tila	Clams which screeched with a loud voice if left exposed by receding tides
Walo-walo	A snake which spent eight days on land and eight at sea, alternately

Health and Hygiene

A feature of Filipino life which always attracted Spanish attention was their personal cleanliness, especially the frequency with which they took a bath. Dr. Antonio Morga (1609, 174) considered it noteworthy that they immersed the whole body, "without considering that it could do them harm at any time"; Father Colín thought that the reason Filipinos settled along streams and riverbanks was their fondness for bathing. An attractive description by Father Chirino (1604, 21–22), which has been repeated by many other authors, is worth quoting at length.

> From the time these islanders are born, they grow up in the water, so both men and women swim like fish even when young, and to cross rivers have no need of bridges. They bathe at any hour without distinction, for pleasure or cleanliness, and not even a woman just delivered refrains from bathing, nor is there a newborn infant which is not immediately bathed in the river itself or springs of cold water. And on coming out of the bath, they anoint their hair with sesame oil mixed with civet. . . . They bathe squatting down almost sitting, with the water up to their neck, taking the greatest care not to be visible even if there is nobody who could see them. The most common or general hour for bathing is at sunset, because as soon as they quit work then, they go to bathe in the river to relax and cool off, and on their way back take along a jar of water for household use. For in each house they have a water jar at the door and whoever goes up, whether from the household or an outsider, takes water from there to wash his feet before entering, especially in the muddy season. This they do with great facility, rubbing one foot against the other, and the water runs through the house floor, which is all bamboo like a very tight grating.

Upper-class Visayans wanted to have a pleasing body odor. They therefore scrubbed their bodies with pumice when bathing, perfuming and oiling them afterwards: Pigafetta detected the scent of benzoin and storax on the persons of the two Butuan rajahs. Clothes were laundered with citrus not only because of its effectiveness in removing stains, but because of the fresh odor it left in them. The civet which Father Chirino said was mixed with sesame oil was used in making perfume, not because of its own pungent odor but because of its property of fixing the fragrance of the flowers that were added.

They were also careful of personal hygiene. *Kulkug* or *kilikug* was to clean out the ears with a feather or swab, and *silat* was a kind of toothbrush made of vegetable husk for cleaning and polishing the teeth, *sipan* being fancy ones of betel nut bark which ladies often gave their lovers. *Bobho* was a tree whose scrapings were used as a shampoo to get rid of dandruff, and *puno* was a fine comb for removing head lice or ringworm scales. But any reference to dirt in the ears *(atole)*, under the nails *(atinglig)*, or the private parts *(buras)* was an extreme offense, *burason* being an insult so serious it required revenge or satisfaction.

Ailments

Despite their attention to personal cleanliness, Visayans suffered skin diseases as one of their most common complaints. Some of these were simple discomforts connected with ordinary activities—*nugas* blisters from poisonous plants, *aripunga* sores between the toes, or chafing from loads or clothing—*buyook* on the throat, *bulok* or *buyok* on the groin. More serious were *alatay* or *kalamayo*, defined by Méntrida as *erysipela*—that is, an intense inflammation accompanied by streptococcus infection. Pocks in general were called *buti*, with *pinarurkan* being distinguished as "the virulent kind"—that is, smallpox. More widespread were *bangtas, tabahak,* or *tabukaw* ulcers, and *bulog* glandular swelling, all of which the Spaniards called *bubas*, indiscriminately. *Iri* was to separate somebody outside the village who was offensively *buboso,* covered with sores.

The classic meaning of bubas was the lymphatic swellings symptomatic of bubonic plague, but following Columbus's return from the New World, it became the common term for syphilis, a disease no doubt confused with yaws in the tropics. Spanish lexicographers in the Visayas, however, used it to mean any pustules or ulcers, though Loarca (1582, 66) must have been referring to an actual contagious disease when he wrote,

> In this island of Panay, the natives say that none of them ever had bubas until the Boholanos (who, as was said above, abandoned Bohol because of the Moluccans) came to settle here, since when some natives have caught it.

Saint Lazarus's disease—leprosy—was called *karanga, kagirkit,* or *tuyug,* with *amomotol* especially suggesting the loss of fingers or toes. *Goor* or *god-on* was the stage when the ravages of the disease were still not visible externally; *butog,* the thickening of the skin; *bangag,* the loss of the nose; and *binokbok,* wounds so deep they seemed to be eaten by *bokbok* wood borers. This specialized vocabulary, however, probably does not reflect the incidence of the disease so much as the emotional reaction which it elicits in human societies.

117

Ailments localized in internal organs include those related to *bagu*, the spleen and *sulok-sulok*, stomach; *pantog* was bladder or scrotal rupture; while any complaints pertaining to the liver *(atay)* was attributed to the appetite of witches, so that "Ginitay ka!" was in itself a curse invoking such a result. *Wati* or *bituk* were intestinal worms; *otol*, bloody stool; *botbot*, protruding hemorrhoids; *tibak* was gout; *tiyan*, dropsy or edema (that is, swelling caused by retention of body fluids, which was usually considered the result of a spell cast by a datu against one who had deceived him). *Piyol* were joint pains; and scrofulous swellings or goiter were called *bonga* after the betel nut fruit. *Uyangas* was an ingrown nail or an infection that caused a nail to drop off; *atolay*, any infected scratch or abrasion; and *tayum* was toothache or gum infection. *Malhit* and *mila-mila* were eye ailments, and *puling* was any defect in vision: thus the price the tuba seller asked for his wares was *himoling* because of their expected effect. It is noteworthy that recognizable symptoms of tuberculosis like coughing blood are not listed: perhaps they were subsumed under respiratory complaints like *hukab*, *hubaw*, or *ubo*–cough, asthma, or hoarseness—or perhaps even *bugtas*, an infirmity attributed to hunger or overwork.

Treatment

There were five general categories of Visayan treatment of disease—massage, fumigating or sweating, prescription of medicine, countersorcery, and propitiation of supernatural beings. The first three were indicated for recognizable physical symptoms, the latter two for ailments requiring diagnosis and treatment by religious specialists.

Massage was applied for injured or dislocated muscles, or pressure put on nerve centers by physical experts called *hilot*, and their reputation was sufficient for Father Sánchez (1617, 56v) to use *hilotar* as a Spanish verb—that is to say, "*Balokar:* hilotar or to massage a woman's abdomen to cause a miscarriage and abortion." *Mamarokpok* was a masseur who simply pummeled the back and spine and was usually a datu's husky slave.

Abortions were a common form of family planning, practiced by ranking ladies to limit their lineage and preserve their heritage, or by others because of poverty or poor prospects for their children. They were induced by massage, strong herbal medicines, or probing with a stick. Furthermore, Visayans had a custom of abandoning babies born with debilitating defects, which led many observers to conclude that Visayans were never born blind or crippled.

Surgery was limited to suturing or cauterizing wounds and to cosmetic surgery to repair torn earlobes. S*isip* or *kulot* was to trim the edges of ragged lobes so the raw surfaces could be sutured together. For flat areas like the stomach or scalp where stitches were difficult to make with a straight needle—it was said—red *animitas* ants were used, a species as large as wasps which had the characteristic of leaving its head behind with jaws clamped in its vicious bite. *Tiyun* was "button cautery"—that is, igniting a pellet of moxa, the wooly lint of certain plants, to smoulder on a small wound.

Atolob was sweat induced by smoke, steam, or rubbing with hot stones or ashes, and was the most popular specific against skin diseases. *Toob* was to fumigate by covering the patient with mats and blankets to concentrate the smoke of medicinal fuels, and *oslob* was a steam bath in which the patient lay enclosed on a rack over containers of water into which hot stones were dropped. The woods used for this purpose were called *bulung*, meaning medicine—China wood (sarsaparilla), *obat*, was the most effective—from which was derived the terms *burulngan* or *bulnganan* for the little enclosed sheds. So, too, hospitals came to be called *pamulngagan* when they were introduced by Spanish missionaries.[20]

Tambal were all plants, roots, leaves, or bark with medicinal properties, for which reason the Spaniards called the *tambalan* an *herbolario*, "one who has knowledge of plants *[hierbas]*, their powers and properties." (They were not to be confused with practitioners of sleight-of-hand who pretended to extract a bone or stone from some part of the patient's body—*naga botbot*.) Tambal were taken internally or externally, with plasters or poultices distinguished as haklup or tampus. Below is a sampling of Visayan materia medica.

Agoho	A tree whose leaves were a specific against muscle cramps (The leaves were applied to the affected part or used for a bath.)
Agusip	A tree whose bark was a specific for intestinal pains (The bark was chewed, or decocted for drinking.)
Argaw	A very medicinal plant (Its shoots were boiled and the decoction drunk for stomach ache, its leaves used as a plaster for headache; it was also used in baths to bring down fevers.)
Bangati	A vine used as a preventative for epilepsy
Hagonoy	A plant prescribed for bladder stones or other urinary complaints
Halilitan	A plant whose leaves were chewed mixed with lime, or mixed with oil and hot sulfur as an antidote for poison
Hangapitan	A tree whose toasted leaves were boiled as an antiseptic for bathing wounds

119

Kalampisaw	A plant whose root and leaves were applied to open sores
Kalaring	An antiseptic composed of citrus juice and iron filings, for drying up small sores
Lagtang	A potent vine whose root was an antidote for poison and when sliced, cleared vision (Its fruit was poisonous; its juice filtered, a laxative.)
Lampuyang	A plant with an offensive odor applied to swellings
Lumaka or *hanono*	A tree whose leaves were masticated, sprinkled with salt, heated, then wrapped in another leaf for application to wounds
Pili	A large tree whose resin was used as a healing balm or ointment
Salimbagat	A plant whose cooked broth was a specific for bloody stool
Tangan-tangan	Very peppery seeds from which a medicinal oil was made, and whose leaves were good for swellings, chills, and sores
Tigaw	A small tree whose leaves, smoked like tobacco or decoction drunk, were good for coughs

There were also medicines of animal or mineral origin. The soil of abandoned termite mounds was good for fumigating; calculous stones found in a shark's head were a cure for similar stones in the human bladder or kidney; and powdered *duyong* bones were almost a panacea, good for bloody stool, diarrhea, colds, and fevers. A kind of jet-black coral was not only taken internally, pulverized, but worn on the wrist as jewelry as a preventative for rheumatic pains. Antidotes for poison often had properties more magical than medical—for example, the marginals *(bontok)* of turtle shells were said to crack in contact with any poison. As for a tincture of python bile, of it Alcina (1668a, 3:347) remarked, "I tried it once, but frankly, only by an innate desire to preserve life could such a medicine be taken."

Illnesses attributed to sorcery had to be relieved either by the sorcerers themselves, by discovering their secret, or by employing the services of another sorcerer. By sorcery we mean spells or incantations cast by a normal human being—that is, not a witch through the use of acquired arcane knowledge. Some sorcerers were believed to be so powerful they could kill with a breath or the touch of a hand *(hokhok)*. *Panlus* was either a spear, G-string, or some other personal possession which caused leg pains or swelling in the victim when he stepped over it. Indeed, *bosong*, swelling of the stomach, was immediately suspected of having been caused by an evil spell worked by a datu.

Diseases with no visible symptoms or those which stubbornly resisted treatment, as well as chronic or lingering illnesses, were attributed to spirits, ancestral or otherwise, who had been wittingly or unwittingly offended by the behavior of the person afflicted. These required diagnosis and prescription by *babaylan* or *daetan,* shamans or mediums able to contact the spirit world in a state of trance to learn the nature of the offense and what was required for satisfaction. In the case of witches, or naturally malignant spirits, monsters, or ghouls who could not be reached by this technique, the babaylan sought to enlist the intervention of a personal patron spirit. Prescriptions were the performance of a specific *paganito* involving the sacrifice of a live animal or other food offerings. Omens were taken during both diagnosis and treatment to facilitate prognosis, and were the last resort in preparing the moribund and their families for the inevitable.

Timekeeping

The Visayans divided the daylight hours into a dozen or more specific times according to the position of the sun. Between dawn and noon, they reckoned *nasirakna,* shining, and *nabahadna,* climbing, and then *iguritlogna,* time for hens to lay, and *makalululu,* when your bracelets slid down your raised arm if you pointed at the sun. High noon was o*dto na an adlaw;* followed by two points of descent in the afternoon, *palisna* and *ligasna;* until midway to setting, *tungana. Natupongna sa lubi* was when the sun sank to the height of the palm trees seen against the horizon; and sunset was *apuna;* or *natorna,* when the sun finally disappeared. Day ended with *igsirinto,* when it was too dark to recognize other people.

Beyond the day, however, they distinguished no time period shorter than one month. This means they did not recognize either the Eurasian seven-day or Javanese five-day week, neither of which, as a matter of fact, was based on any celestial cycle. But they reckoned the days of the month precisely—that is, the days from one new moon to the next. Just as they divided the hours of the day by the movement of the sun, so they identified the days of the month by the appearance of the moon in the night sky.

The new moon was *subang* the first night it could be seen, or more colorfully, *kilat-kilat,* a little lightning flash. When it appeared as a full crescent the next night or two, it seemed to have opened its eyes *(gimata)* or, alternately, closed its mouth *(ungut)*—like a baby's on a mother's breast. Then came a "three-day moon" or high new moon, *hitaas na an subang,* followed by *balirig,* the fourth or fifth night, and next it was "near the zenith" *(odto).* When it appeared as an exact half disk—what western calendars call the first quarter moon—it was directly overhead at sunset,

121

and therefore *odto na an bulan*. Then as it continued to wax, it "passed the barrier" *(lakad)*, and when it was lopsided both before and after full moon, it looked like a crab shell *(maalimangona)*.

The full moon was greeted with a variety of names—*paghipono, takdul, ugsar*—but most significantly as *dayaw*, perfect or praiseworthy, fit recognition of its spectacular shape and sunset-to-sunrise brilliance. And as it began to wane—that is, darken *(madulumdulum)*—a night or two later, it set on the western horizon just before dawn and so was called *banolor*, to exchange or take by mistake—like a man who dies just before a son or grandson is born. The fifth or sixth night of waning was *parik*, to level or flatten, because it then rose so late the witches had many hours of darkness in which to beat down the earth by the stomping of their feet during their dances. *Katin* was the third quarter, so it had crossed this second barrier *(lakad na an magsag-uli)* by the twenty-fourth or twenty-fifth night, and then got ready for new moon again *(malasumbang)* about the twenty-ninth. This was the dark of the moon, or what the Spaniards called *conjunción* (meaning the conjunction of the sun and the moon) when the moon disappeared for a night or two. To the Visayans, it was then dead, lost, or gone hunting.

These phases of the moon were common time markers known to all. They would say, for example, "Duldulman an bulan [The moon begins to wane today]" or "Paodtononta an bulan [Let's wait for the quarter moon]" (Sánchez 1617, 37, 188). And *nasubang nga tao* was a newcomer or upstart. But the Visayan month was a lunar month—29–and-a-half days and 43 minutes, to be exact—so twelve of them did not add up to a year, but only 354 days. They were therefore not the equivalent of months in the western calendar, which are arbitrary divisions unrelated to the moon, approximately one-twelfth of a solar year of 365 days. Thus, unschooled Visayans—*plebe imperita*, as Father Alcina said—calculated months in the Christian calendar as beginning with a new moon, and observers familiar with the twelve-month year, both sixteenth-century Spaniards and twentieth-century Filipinos, tend to equate the two: the use of a moon-based calendar with lack of education. But Miguel de Loarca (1582, 164, 166) wrote more carefully in 1582,

> They divide the year into twelve months though they do not name more than seven, and these are lunar months because they count them by the moons. The first month is when the Little Goats [Pleiades] appear, which they call Ulalen. The next month they call Dagankahuy, which is when they clear off the trees to plant. The next they call Daganenan Bulan, which is when they pile up this wood in the fields. The next they call Elkilin, which is when they burn the field. The next they call Inabuyan, which is

the time of the *bonanzas* [fair winds when the monsoon is changing]. The next they call Kaway, which is when they weed the fields. The next [that is, another] is called Irarapun, which is when they begin to harvest the rice. The next they call Manululsul, which is when the harvest is finished. The other months they take no account of because they have nothing to do in the fields then.

What Loarca called months were seasonal events connected with swidden farming: they do not appear in early Visayan dictionaries as the names of months, nor do any other names. Rather, the year is defined as the time between one harvest and the next, a time which naturally varies according to whether the monsoon rains come early or late and in what quantity. Alcina (1668a, 3:40) explained the word *tuig*, year, as follows:

> [It is a word] with which they also counted the years, but without computing or numbering the months, which from harvest to harvest they would count as eleven or twelve distinct and past, and which they called *tuig*, and although they now confuse it with the year, it was not a single year but an indefinite time because that word means to them the same as "time" does to us.

There were three Visayan words for year—*taon, tuig,* and *dag-on. Taon* actually meant harvest—"Taon na didto dile [It's already harvest in their place]"—and was used for calculating age: old folks were those who had seen many harvests (Sánchez 1617, 504v). *Tuig* was both harvest (for example, *tinutuigan,* what is ready for harvest) and any recurring period of time, not necessarily annual. *Tinuig na siya* was said of a menstruating woman, and *panuigan sang olan sang habagat* was the coming of the rains either from the south or *sang amihan,* from the north. *Dag-on* was used in the same way: *panog-on sa manga kakahuyan* was when everything was in bloom. Indeed, it was the flowering of trees and plants which indicated the rotation of the seasons. *Katparasan* (January–March), *kattaloto* (March–May), *katlawaan* (June–August), and *katkisiw* (October–December) were the months during which trees of these names blossomed. The seasonal behavior of birds was another indicator: when the *kahaw* bird gave its "kahaw" call in the morning, it was time to plant.

The agricultural cycle began, as Loarca noted, with the appearance of certain stars. Most often these were the Pleiades in the constellation of Taurus which can first be seen in June, locally called Moroporo, meaning either "the boiling lights" or a flock of birds. Swiddens were prepared at that time, and seeds were sown in September when they were directly overhead at sunset, though the exact time depended on local climatic conditions. Indeed, because the rainy season varied from island to island, in some places farmers made use of the Big Dipper (Ursa Major), which

123

they called Losong (rice mortar) or Balatik (ballista), though in Panay Balatik was what they called the two bright stars in Gemini. Still others planted when the Southern Cross was upright at sunset, a constellation that looked to the Visayans it looked like a coconut palm, Lubi, or blowfish, Butete. Similarly, the constellation Aries, the Ram, they called Alimango, the Crab.

Visayans also believed that just as the moon times the human menstrual cycle, so its phases controlled all biological growth. Starfish were said to increase and decrease in size as the moon waxed and waned; crab shells hardened and softened to the same rhythm; yellow turtles only grew at nighttime when there was a moon, black ones during the dark of the moon, and white ones during the daytime. So too, coconut trees were thought to produce one new sprout each new moon; the silklike fibers of the *ulango* palm had to be gathered at quarter moon; and stems of boats made from *dao* roots could be expected to outlast the vessel but only if cut during the waning moon. Furthermore, Visayans had a prescription for which phase of the moon was best for gathering any of a dozen varieties of abaca, though the most commonly planted variety was one that could be cut at any time.

The dark of the moon was considered sinister because it was the favorite of witches and *aswang*, who fled at the first sight of the crescent moon showing its horns. Fieldwork and weaving were accordingly forbidden the following day as a precaution against illness during the coming month, and a one- to three-day holiday was taken to celebrate the full moon because the *diwata* came to earth at that time. Nobody doubted that an eclipse *(bakunawa)* was caused by a huge *sawa*, python, trying to swallow the moon, and that it had to be frightened away by noisy pounding on mortars and house floors, followed by another holiday. They treated the sun in the same manner during a solar eclipse, but otherwise rendered it no such public veneration, nor even recognized the point of its rising as a cardinal compass bearing called East.

Winds and Weather

Visayans called the northeast monsoon *amihan* and the southwest monsoon *habagat*, what the Spaniards called the *brisas* and *vendavales*. Another major airstream, the northeast trade wind, brought fair weather, but due to the rotation of the earth, it veered in a clockwise direction as it moved south, and so struck the archipelago not only from the northeast, but from the east, southeast, and south as well, or even from the southwest. The Visayans called it *timog*, which Sánchez (1617, 515) defined accurately as "wind that blows between Brisa and Mediodía"—that is, between north-east and due south.[21]

Leyte-Samareños called all cool winds blowing in off the Pacific amihan in general, and they considered habagat a west wind. Habagat lasted from April to September, amihan from December to April. In between, came a chill north wind, *kanaway*—or northwest wind, *ipo*—regularly causing respitory ills. Timog was always considered a relief from the monsoons—blowing in from the east in July–September, the south in May–June—but the south wind itself was properly called *salatan* or *iphag* ("the other side"), winds issued from caverns deep in the earth that were opened and closed to control them. Visayans, however, did not recognize these winds as the Four Winds of western navigators, so Spanish lexicographers selected four Visayan terms and applied these to the Four Winds: Kanawayan, Amihan, Salatanan, and Habagatan.

Some old men were renowned for the accuracy of their weather fore-casts. They predicted storms, their severity, and the flooding that would follow, three or four days in advance, or even a week, by judging from cloud formations and the color of the skies, sun, and moon. Dark clouds meant a squally storm *(onos)*, but leaden skies meant a real typhoon *(bagyo)*. The new moon of October was considered the most likely time for a typhoon; conversely, typhoons were said to be rare during the waning of the same moon. These men believed, too, that unless a typhoon ended with winds from the south, it was sure to be followed by another one. They also prophesied whether the coming year would be wet or dry, supposedly by observing the position of stars and constellations.

Seamanship

Visayans spent a lot of time on the water because boats were their only form of transportation. Heavy loads like ships' hulls or tree trunks could be moved on land with log rollers, but neither wheeled vehicles nor draft animals are mentioned in any early account or dictionary. So in the seventeenth century, the word for a sheave or pulley *(galingan)* was extended to the wheels of Spanish *carros* (carts) and *carrozas* (carriages).

Except for reasons of defense, settlements were built on the coast or riverbanks, and nobody lived more than 40 kilometers from salt water. Orientation was taken, not from the direction of the sun, but of the sea—*ilawod*, downstream, or *iraya*, upstream. Everybody and everything moved by boat, from *basura* to fertilize fields to guests to attend weddings. Farmers from Bantayan Island went to till fields on the Cebu coast by boat, and miners from the Camarines to work gold deposits in Masbate, and youths learned their people's traditions listening to sea chanteys while rowing boats. Interisland waters were therefore the means of connecting, not separating, Visayan society, the avenues by which Philippine culture spread.

Men were as handy with a paddle as a bolo: they carved their own, and made pony-sized models for their sons as soon as they were big enough to hold one. Good paddling required both skill and stamina, and *karakoa* speed required the coordination to get a hundred paddles in the water at the same instant. The sound of such swift, well-timed paddling was called r*agabrab,* but *bunkalis* was splashing and *hagdol* was striking the hull. *Kabig* was to move a boat broadside-to, and *sowal* was the opposite. Paddling against the wind was called *bulsa-bulsa,* from *bulos,* to take revenge or pay back in kind. Paddlers were also ready to work in the water. If the boat took on too much water, they went over the side and rocked it to slosh the water out, and for emergency bursts of speed, they sat on the outrigger floats. Outriggers not only enabled boatmen, working up to the waist in the water, to bring a swamped vessel to port; outriggers were also the handles by which the vessel was picked up for launching or beaching high and dry when not in use. (People living on the coast showed their orientation by calling the Milky Way, Binugsay, "paddled," because it looked like a ship's wake across the sky.)

Sailors in Visayan waters never had to sail out of sight of land in fair weather, and so set their courses by piloting rather than by celestial navigation—that is, by sighting landmarks and knowing the waters. Their seamanship thus required an intimate knowledge of depths and types of bottom, the configuration of reefs and rocks, and the position of shoals and sandbanks which shifted after storms, as well as the ability to interpret the color and surface appearance of the waters themselves. Most important was familiarity with the strong currents typical of both the Pacific coast and narrow interisland channels. A 5–knot current flowing down the coast of Mindanao could only be avoided by northbound vessels by hugging the shore, and San Bernardino Strait between Sorsogon and Samar was characterized by whirlpools in which unwary boats could be caught for days at a time until broken up. The local technique for getting boats across this treacherous passage was to abandon them to the current with paddles held firmly against the hull like leeboards, until catching the stream running in the opposite direction. Thus, though Visayans coined a term for the mariner's compass when it was introduced in the next century—*padaluman,* "thing with a needle"—they made little use of it because it did not tell them anything they did not know already.

hunting dogs and were proud of their dexterity in handling casting nets, and among them were skillful blacksmiths working imported metal. They owned cargo vessels and war cruisers, and all maritime expeditions whether for raid or trade were captained by datus with the necessary seafaring skill and experience. Their ladies wove the elegant textiles with ornate borders which were the distinctive marks of their class. Butuanon King Awi's silk kerchief was no doubt a Chinese import, but his cotton G-string decorated with silk thread was probably produced in his own household.

Timawa

Spanish dictionaries always define timawa as freemen *(libres)* or freedmen *(libertos)*. They were originally the offspring or descendants of a datu's commoner wives or slave concubines, and they were technically free because their progenitor had granted it. But slaves could also be freed *(matitimawa)*, so Loarca, in describing this social class, found it necessary to call them "true" or "recognized" timawa. All persons liberated by their own master were called *ginoo,* and might be chided, "Dika magpadayaw, kay akun ka ginoo [Don't put on airs, I'm the one who made you ginoo]" (Sánchez 1617, 204).[22] In English, "freedmen" has little meaning today: in modern societies, all citizens are free. But when Isla referred to timawa as "citizens," he meant a privileged class, not ordinary people. In sixteenth-century Spain, citizens *(ciudadanos)* were the nonslave residents of chartered cities *(ciudades)* who enjoyed its special laws and exemptions. They were not peasants, peons, serfs, tenants, or farmhands—all of whom would have been called oripun in the Visayas.

Timawa paid tribute called *buhis* or *handug* and, in theory at least, were free to transfer their allegiance to some other datu. But those attached to their lord as personal vassals paid no tribute and rendered no agricultural labor: thus the Boxer Codex called them "knights and hidalgos." They won their tattoos beside him in battle, rowed and manned his warship, received his favors, and shared in the public accolade for his victories. Their datu was obligated to defend or avenge them at the risk of his own person if need be, and to share booty and captives with them. They attended his feasts as retainers and familiars, acting as his wine tasters, and were sometimes honored by receiving a cup from his own hand from which he had already taken a sip. They were sent as his emissaries to open marriage negotiations for his sons, and at the time of his death, acted as bailiffs to enforce his mourning tabus, and three of the most renowned among them would accompany his grieving womenfolk on a ritual voyage in which they boasted of their personal conquests and bravery.

Timawa were therefore men of consequence in the community. But they were not often men of substance: if they were wealthy enough to behave like a datu, they were belittled as *timindok,* a big banana. They had no right to booty beyond what their datu gave them, and they were held accountable for wounding or killing any captives. Though they could lend and borrow money, enter business partnerships, and acquire slaves of their own, their children inherited only at their datu's pleasure.[23] As Loarca (1582, 158) said when speaking of weddings, "the timaguas do not perform these ceremonies because they have no estate." This right to restrict timawa—or oripun—inheritance enabled a datu to reward and indebt his favorites, and leave others under threat of the sort of economic reversal which set downward social mobility in motion. A 12–peso debt could plunge a man into the depths of domestic slavery, with the high probability of transmitting that status to his offspring because any children born during his bondage became the property of his master.

These warrior roles of both datu and timawa were destined to disappear under colonial pacification, of course. Fray Rodrigo de Aganduru Móriz (1623, 452) described the changes that had taken place by 1623 as follows:

> The indios of the Bisayas say that before they gave obedience to the King our Lord, and became Christians, not only did the Mindanaons not make raids in their territory, but that, on the contrary, they would go to Mindanao where they took many captives, and terrified them; and now it is the opposite, because since they are Christians and it is not licit for them to make those raids, and they are disarmed, they are paying for what they did then.

These changes meant that datus no longer had need of their timawas' Viking-like services or means of rewarding them, nor a fresh supply of captives for their own use or sale. Worse, timawa were now paying tribute to the colonial government just like datus. These were conditions which no doubt gave added incentive for reducing timawa to slave status by usurious loans or arbitrary fines. Father Sánchez (1617, 334) said, "For anything at all, the datus would fine the timawa heavily . . . and if they had no bahandi to give, make them slaves." By the seventeenth century, timawa were being referred to as commoners *(plebeyos)* or *tungan tawo,* "people in-between," and in Alcina's day, the pre-Hispanic timawa were being fondly recalled as a "third rank of nobility." And even that memory was fading. "Today they call everybody timawa who are not slaves," Alcina (1668a, 4:59) said, a practice which ultimately led to the modern Visayan word which means "poor, destitute."

Oripun

The word *oripun* appears to be a transitive form of an archaic root *udip* (to live) meaning "to let live"—for example, to spare life on the field of battle, to ransom a captive, or to redeem a debt equivalent to a man's price. The market for these exchanges was provided by a shortage of labor for exploiting a rich natural environment; and debt slavery was prevalent because agriculture was undeveloped, goods limited, and interest rates high, so debtors had little collateral except their own persons. The oripun produced by these conditions were legally slaves: they could be bought and sold. But that was all they had in common. Some were foreign captives or purchases who served as victims for human sacrifice; some were members of their master's household and suckled at the same breast as his own children; some were householders who gave their masters or creditors a portion of their crops or labor; and some were hardly distinguishable from freemen. Sociologically, therefore, they constituted the class which in contemporary European society would have been called commoners.

Individual status within the oripun class depended on birthright, inherited or acquired debt, commuted penal sentence, or victimization by the more powerful. Outright captives were *bihag,* and they were marketed by dealers in *along* or *botong* as expensive merchandise like bahandi porcelain and gongs, or ships and houses. Oripun who lived in their master's house were *hayohay* or *ayuey,* and those with their own house and field were *tuhay* or *mamahay.* Like datus and timawa, they bore children of their same class; or in the case of mixed marriages, their children became half- or quarter-slaves who served their masters half time or quarter time. Half-slaves were called *bulan* (month) if their owners divided their time by the month. Debt slaves, too, only served their creditors part time in proportion to their debt. Their owners often paid such partial slaves the balance to take full possession of them. As for householding oripun, they supported themselves, giving their masters only a share of their labor or crops. With opportunity and enterprise, they could earn enough to decrease their debt or even pay it off in full.

Hayohay were at the bottom of the oripun social scale—those "most enslaved," as Loarca (1582, 142) put it, "the ones they mostly sell to the Spaniards." They were domestics who lived in their master's house, received their food and clothing from him, but were given one day out of four to work for themselves. Their children born or raised in his house were *gintubo,* who might become favorites called *sibin* or *ginogatan,* treated like his own children and set free on his death. If both parents were house-born slaves like themselves, or actual purchases, they were *ginlubos,* and if of the fourth generation of their kind, *lubos nga oripun.* But if only one of their parents was hayohay, they were half-slaves *(bulan* or *pikas),* or if three of their grandparents were nonslaves, they were quarter-slaves *(tilor* or *sagipat).* Hayohay married off from their master's house assumed householding tuhay status, owing him only two days out of five. He still had claim to their children, however, though his raising them was often seen as a favor rather than an imposition: a grown gintubo, Sánchez (1617, 529v) said, "is like a freedman who lives on his own." It was normal for offspring of slaves to take over their parents' obligations, who could then move into some more favorable status like *tumaranpok.*

Debt slavery ranged from outright sale to contractual mortgage. In time of famine, men sold themselves or their children, or attached themselves to a datu as *kabalangay* ("crewman"?) for a loan. Datus themselves went into bondage for the loan of bahandi to use as bride-price, or became their father-in-law's legal dependent. Debt was commonplace as evidenced by the fact that rice was loaned at 100 percent interest compounded annually, and crimes were punished by fines.

A man became *tinubos* (redeemed or ransomed) to any creditor who underwrote his debt, and could be transferred from one to another for profit, and his obligations varied with the value of the bond. In Iloilo, a *tumataban* slave could be bonded for 6 pesos in the 1580s, his creditor then enjoying five days of his labor per month, while a *tumaranpok* was valued at 12 pesos, for which he rendered four days' labor out of seven. Both occupied their own houses with their families but their wives were also obliged to perform services, namely, spinning cotton their master supplied them in the boll. However, either could commute these obligations to payment in palay—15 cavans a harvest for the former, 30 for the latter.

Some oripun were hardly distinguishable from timawa. *Horohan* performed lower-echelon military services as *mangayaw* oarsmen or *magahat* warriors, and, as the author of the Boxer Codex (1590b, 362) remarked with some surprise, "they were taken into their [datu's] houses when they give some feast or drunken revel to be received just like guests." Other tuhay or mamahay might also participate in raids, though receiving a smaller portion of the booty than timawa. Indeed, if they distinguished themselves regularly enough by bravery in action, they might attract a following of their own and actually become datus. Although they were obliged to come at their datu's summons for communal work like house building, they paid a vassalage fee called *dagupan* instead of field labor. But, like the timawa above them and the hayohay below, their children could inherit their property only at the pleasure of their datus.

These variations in oripun status and opportunity for upward social mobility no doubt reflect local differences in economic conditions—crops, markets, demand on labor, and the size of the datu-tumao-timawa population. They also suggest that the majority of Visayans prior to Spanish advent were oripun.

Debt and Dependence

Visayan social fabric was thus woven of debt and dependence-that is, relationships in which one person was dependent on the decisions of another, the one exercising choice, the other not. The slave did not choose to work for his master, but his master might choose to grant him a favor— for example, *tagolaling* were the days given a slave to work for himself. Parents chose their children's mates as a normal act of social order, just as datus had the right to choose the booty their timawa comrades received. One's position in the social scale was therefore measurable by the amount of control he exercised over his own time and labor—the hayohay at one extreme and the timawa or tumao at the other, where they could transfer their whole service to another person. Among oripun, such dependence was expressed in frank terms of debt.

The high interest rates which created these debts were based on the natural increase of crops or livestock. *Sulit* meant a debt without interest, a sale without profit, or a crop without increase; the loan of an inanimate object like a knife or boat was *huram* and did not incur *utang* (debt). A debtor's children were born in debt, his first-degree kin were also liable, and any favor received incurred debt. Captured timawa rescued by their datu became his personal debtors—unlike the Spaniards ransomed or purchased from Filipino captors by Saavedra in 1528 or Torre in 1544. In convictions for grand larceny, a whole family could be enslaved: Alcina had oripun parishioners whose ancestor's crime had been to break a borrowed bahandi gong. *Gaon* was a kind of involuntary collateral seized until the debt was paid, and *tokod,* "to make sure," was to collect a debt from somebody other than the debtor, who thus effectively acquired a new creditor who then had to collect as best he could.

Community

A datu's following was his *haop* or *dolohan,* Visayan terms to which Tagalog *barangay* was added after Manila became the colonial capital.

135

These terms all referred to the people themselves, not the place where they lived—for example, "Nahaop ako kan Koan [I belong to So-and-so's barangay]"—and they ranged in size from thirty to a hundred households (Sánchez 1617, 225v). *Haop* appears to be cognate with *sakop*, any inclusive group, but especially one supportive of a person on whom they were dependent, like children on their parents or slaves on their master. Alms called *palos* or *hinapot* were given by the community to one released from captivity, or to the poor by anybody selling food.

The villages and towns where one or more haop lived were *bongto* or *lungsod;* and hamlets or neighborhoods were *gamuro,* a cluster of houses within earshot. Community decisions affecting more than one haop required datu consensus, and so did alliances between settlements. But there were no formal confederations, for which reason Spanish explorers always made blood compacts with more than one chief, from chiefs of Samar hamlets too small to be seen from the coast to those of large communities like Cebu spread out for several kilometers.

Members of a haop were usually related—a *parentela,* or kindred. The Boxer manuscript (1590b, 357) says that datus were obeyed because "those in the settlement who are not [their slaves] are the relatives of the datus." Indeed, blood relationship, either real of fictive, was considered essential for personal security. Men became ritual brothers, *sandugo,* by imbibing a few drops of each other's blood in wine or betel nut, swearing to support and defend one another until death. They might also take a common name, like some ring they exchanged or banana they ate, to become *kasungar* or *katawagan,* or share the same clothes or sweetheart as *ubas,* comrades. And if they had to be separated from one another, they would swear a *balata* oath not to partake of a certain food or drink till they met again.

Proper community conduct reinforced social structure. Members of the datu class were privileged to wear garments with luxurious edging, and non-datus who affected gold teeth were mocked as being *yabyab,* spread out like a mat. Datus strode around with loose clothes flowing or with slow measured tread in processions, and their binokot daughters were carried on men's shoulders so as never to touch the ground. Competition from peers and relatives was discouraged by restrictions on the size and ostentation of their houses. Lower-class persons entered their presence with head bowed, twisting and wriggling their bodies, and addressed them in the third person while squatting down, and nobody dared to spit in their presence. (Belching and breaking wind were socially acceptable, however.) Women hung back before passing in front of them, and then gathered up

136

a fold of their skirt as if to assure that their private parts were doubly covered. And everybody addressed seniors or respected persons with polite *tabi* expressions like "Tabi sa iyo umagi ako [With your permission, I will pass]" (Méntrida 1637a, 365).

Kinship

Early Spanish dictionaries of Visayan languages often list Cebuano, Hiligaynon, or Samareño variants under a single entry. This is especially true of kinship terminology. Thus the word for father is given as *amahan, amay,* and *anduyon* without distinction, though with a Cebu variant of *amba* or *ambuyon;* and mother as *inahan, indayon,* and *iloy,* with a Kiniray-a variant, *inang. Ama* and *Ina* or *Inda* were terms of special respect used as proper nouns (for example, *si Ama*), and often extended to nonparents for that purpose, while "Mama" was what people called their own father. Fathers were also addressed affectionately as "Baba," thus *himaba* was a gift to a go-between by a suitor who wished to establish such a relationship with his prospective father-in-law.

Parents' brothers and sisters were also differentiated by sex: uncles were *yoyo, oyo-an,* or *bata,* and aunts were *iyaan* or *dada.* But sons and daughters were simply *anak,* offspring; and so, too, brothers, sisters, and cousins of either sex were *igkaanak, igsoon, igmanhod, igtotood,* or *otod.* (*Otod* was a piece cut off something; hence, *kaotoran,* relatives of one lineage.) Cousins could also be distinguished from siblings as *patod* or *ig-agaw,* and second cousins in Kiniray-a as *igkampor,* while *bogto* or *boggong tinay,* "gut brothers," meant children of the same parents—"like a piece of the same cord." But siblings related through only one parent were *mabaw,* and stepchildren or ones adopted were *hablus.*

Grandparents of either sex, together with their brothers and sisters and their spouses, were all *apuy, apohan,* or *owang,* or more respectfully, "Laki" or "Bai," sometimes with "Gurang" (mature) added. Great-grandparents were *apo,* or "Bata" with or without *laki, bai,* or *gurang* attached. A prudent person therefore muttered "Laki-laki" or "Apo-apo" when leaving the house in order to invoke his ancestors' protection against harm or accident—a custom continued by Christians, Father Méntrida said, "or they say, 'Jesus.'" Grandchildren were *apo,* and they and all their descendants were *kaapohan,* though a great-grandchild might be distinguished as *apo sa tohod* just as a great-grandparent was *apuy sa tohod*—*sa tohod* meaning literally "at the knee."

Husband and wife were both called *asawa* in Leyte and Samar, but in Cebu and Panay the term was restricted to the wife (the man was *bana*)— or, more accurately, the chief wife: any others were *sandil,* whether of slave, timawa, or datu stock. A son-in-law was *nugang* and his parents-in-law, *ugangan;* and *numigang* was for him to render bride-service to them prior to marriage. Both son- and daughter-in-law were *umagad,* a term which emphasized their role in uniting their two families into one: *agad* were the thwarts between the two sides of a boat, and *alagadun* was to adjust or conform. *Bayaw* was a brother-in-law, *hipag* was sister-in-law. If two men were married to sisters, they called each other *bilas,* while women married to brothers called each other *idas.* Parents who married their children off to one another's children were *balaye.*

With the exception of brothers- and sisters-in-law, therefore, and honorifics like *laki* and *bai,* Visayan kinship terms only distinguished sex in the parental generation. Conversely, there was no term for a parent of either sex; parents were simply *manyanak.* But within the family, there were courteous forms of address which made this distinction. Sisters called their brothers *oyo* or *titi;* brothers called their sisters *akay;* and older brothers were addressed as *magulang, ubo,* or *aso,* older sisters as *umbo.* (*Oyo* was really a polite term by which an older man addressed a younger, including a father his son or an uncle his nephew.) Parents, especially mothers, also addressed their daughters with terms of endearment like *owa, wawa,* or *paki;* in Cebu, mothers called their daughters *bubu* (actually, "madame") or *ipi* in Candaya, and *umboy, idi,* or *didi* in Samar, with *titi* being a local Giwan word. And between man and wife, *oto* or *otoy* was an affectionate name for the husband; while an only son was fondly called *boto* (penis).

Law

Laws were part of the customs and traditions handed down from one generation to another: they were not considered products of legislation but part of the natural order of things. *Kabtangan* were customs, but *kahimtang* was nature or condition, both words derived from *butang,* to put something in its place. The origin myths make it clear that class differences were just as natural as color of skin, and mestizos *(kalibugan)* were the children of a datu and timawa or of unmarried parents, as well as of a Spaniard and a Visayan. *Alagag* was the natural awe which juniors felt in the presence of seniors; *hilas* was ingrained reluctance to contradict parents or superiors; and *naga kahilas* was for an ancestor spirit to keep a disrespectful descendant awake with a guilty conscience. A synonym for *kabtangan* was *kagawiyan,* from *gawi,* to keep or preserve (for example, *paragawi,* a steward, or *gawiyunan,* propertied people.) But *batas* or *batasan* was a decree regulating commerce—for example, "Sino in nagbatas sining iyo ipapalit [Who assessed this merchandise of yours]?"—and *batas-batas* was tariff (Sánchez 1617, 70v).

A datu acted as judge *(hukom)* in both civil claims and criminal cases, sometimes in consultation with an expert in custom law, by hearing testimony of sworn witnesses. If the results were inconclusive, he might order the litigants to submit to trial by ordeal—for example, retrieving an object from a pot of boiling water with the least injury, or staying underwater longest. Recognized crimes were theft, defamation, murder, witchcraft, lese majesty (that is, offense to a datu's authority), and malicious vandalism like poisoning livestock.

Penalties were fines set in accord with the litigants' standing: crimes against upper-class persons were fined more heavily, and an oripun who murdered a datu was simply killed outright. Killings among high-ranking datus could not be settled until a blood feud had run its course, and wergeld (man-price) was argued as hotly as bride-price. All fines were imposed in terms of bahandi valuables, too high to be met by agricultural products or handicrafts.

In theory, nobody was condemned to slavery: they became slaves for inability to meet fines. There were no sentences like imprisonment or deportation which would take labor out of production; rather, punishments realigned labor forces within the community. The only exception was the death penalty for convicted witches or sorcerers.

The most common thefts were of foodstuffs—for example, *dangpas* was for theft of root crops; *ugnas* for fallen fruit; *sorok* for bananas, sugarcane, or coconuts—and sneak thieves crept into houses naked and oiled so as to be slippery if caught. The stealing of valuables, however, was associated with raiding and so was rare within the community and punished severely: first-generation missionaries were always struck by the absence of locked doors and coffers in the homes of the wealthy.

Any altercation that resulted in wounding had to be compensated with *hilugo,* blood-price, and insult was also valid grounds for litigation. The most serious was an accusation of witchcraft, but there were also violent curses like "Binaliw ka [Be changed]!" (that is, become crippled or deformed), "Ginanitan ka [Be flayed]!" (like an animal hide), or "Nahahaan tinay mo [Get your guts]!" (from *haha,* to remove marrow, or meat from shells). But insults reflecting on a man's virility required personal satisfaction. When a Leyteaño tried to change the price of something he was selling to a Spanish soldier in 1544, the soldier punched him and said, "You dog! Did I not give you what you asked? Why do you ask for more!"—and the soldier was stabbed to death that evening with his own dagger (Grijalva 1624, 56).

Adultery was not considered a crime but a personal offense, and was settled by the adulterer indemnifying the offended husband; the wife was not punished at all. Premarital sexual mores were lax: contacts between single men and women went unremarked unless the girl's relatives demanded *hingulaw,* a shame payment. Some liaisons were publicly known and long-lasting; that they were a substitute for marriage to avoid the formal expense is suggested by the term *kubot,* which meant for longtime lovers to marry. There appears to have been no specific term for virginity. *Dalaga* was a young woman of marriageable age whether virgin or not, but women were admired as *bugus,* complete, or *bingil,* chaste, both for virginity and for faithfulness to one man. However, women who gave their favors freely to many men were considered *kiral,* lewd or prostitutes, and compared to animals available to any male of the species. Thus the virginity of those secluded binokot, who were only glimpsed by men when surrounded by attendants, was part of their allure and mystery.

Marriage

Weddings between people without property to share by bequest were simple ceremonies in which the couple partook of the same cup or plate, and *hayohay* were simply married off by their masters and given a few pots. But the weddings of datus were the most important social events in a Visayan community. Since they were contracts between families rather than individuals, they were also political events creating new alliances. (They were often made when the man and woman concerned were still children, or even before their birth.) Their importance depended on the size and ritual settlement of a bride-price called *bugay*—"bride-price" rather than "dowry" because it was set by the girl's father, bargained down like goods in a marketplace, and was not conjugal property. Spanish dowry *(dote),* on the other hand, was property a bride brought into her marriage to be enjoyed by her husband. Visayan bugay was shared within the kin group that set the price and sealed the bargain, including the bride's brothers-in-law if she was a widow, and redistributed to meet their own future needs for bride-price. And since it had to be returned in case of divorce, it gave the wife's family a vested interest in the permanence of the union; indeed, a share called *kukod* went to the bride's brothers specifically to guarantee her return in the event she ran home after a marital squabble.

The engagement required a relative or friend of the suitor to obtain permission from the girl's father to open proceedings. The man's relatives then went to the girl's house with a respected timawa bearing his spear. There they were received with gongs sounding to assemble her relatives and give public notice, but not admitted until they bargained with the girl's grandmother to let down the house ladder. Then, with a fine Freudian gesture, the spear bearer drove the weapon into the house ladder and invoked the ancestors on both sides for fertility. They then entered, presented a gift, and fixed the date for negotiating the marriage contract. The father's acceptance of the gift was his pledge of his daughter's hand.

On the date set, the marriage contract was negotiated in the girl's house. The man's relatives were accompanied by two or three mediators *(kagon)*, who placed a porcelain plate in front of the father containing a number of little sticks—the ordinary counters used in Visayan calculations. The father tossed a betel nut quid in the bowl to signal the opening of the discussion. This began with painful formality, but became less inhibited as drinking continued, and often had to be broken off and resumed another day. As each item was agreed on—slave, porcelain, or gold—one counter was placed on top of a gong on the floor. As agreement was reached on the schedule of payment, the counters were moved from one side to the other. Part of the bugay had to be paid immediately as a kind of down payment, but the rest was deferred until later, and some even held in abeyance and only demanded in case of connubial conflict. Still another part of the bugay was really not intended to be paid in the first place: it was only agreed to for the sake of the lady's prestige. Conversely, the *hingusul,* a fine if either party withdrew, might be demanded in advance if the girl was of much higher rank than the man.

The girl's father usually asked for the same bugay as he had given for her mother; and if the father were a proud datu who refused to lower his demand, the match would be canceled unless the suitor agsreed to enter his father-in-law's household for a number of years or even a lifetime. (It was normal for a man to serve his father-in-law for one year before his wedding, a period of adjustment and trial, or actual training in the case of a young boy.) Once the contract was settled, the mother came forward to ask for *himaraw,* a compensation in gold for all the sleep she had lost while the bride was an infant.

During the wedding celebration, the bride and groom were seated beside one another—after her shyness was overcome with suitable gifts.

They were tied together by the hair for a short time, then served a plate of rice, from which they each took a handful and squeezed it into a ball. She tossed hers down the house ladder, the symbol of his coming and going to support his new family, and he threw his out the window to indicate that her place was in the home looking out. Then, as they drank together, an old man rose and made public announcement of the match, stated the conditions pertaining to the bride-price in the case either one went astray, and called on those present to act as witnesses. He then united their hands over a bowl of raw rice, which he then threw over the guests.

When the newlyweds finally retired to the bridal chamber—that is, the *bokot* where she had spent her days as binokot—her brother would bar the groom's entrance until he gave them something; slaves would ignite a smouldering fire underneath until receiving a gift; and others would enter the chamber with bright torches and had to be paid to leave. Meanwhile, the party went raucously on, and if the bridegroom's father was a man of sufficient rank and means, he presented gifts to all his new in-laws, perhaps even their slaves. Guests playfully snatched off one another's *pudong* to be returned only on payment, and slaves were permitted to keep anything they could grab from the bridegroom's party. These prestige feasts were public celebrations and might last as long as ten days.

When it came time to fetch the bride, she required another round of gifts—before crossing a river, climbing the house ladder, or entering a crowded room. Her father contributed *bantal* to the new household—a number of slaves equal to, or even double, the number included in the bugay, but only for the newlyweds' use, not their possession: they remained his own property. Any slaves the wife brought along remained her personal property just like her gold and jewelry, and if she and her husband quarreled, they might refuse to obey him. A wife's paramount housekeeping duty was to keep her husband well clothed by weaving, sewing, trade, or purchases—just as unmarried women were expected to clothe their lovers, as Bubung Ginbuna does for epic hero Kabungaw. As Alcina (1668a, 4:218) said, "Both husband and lovers are accustomed to leave their women if they do not do *dapi* or *darapi*, which is to give them the clothes they need."

Marriage was forbidden between first-degree kin, but a niece could marry her uncle. (In a Panay origin myth, Lupluban, granddaughter of the primordial pair, married her mother's brother, Pandagwan.) Spanish references to polygamy differ, perhaps because of confusion between secondary wives and concubines: Legazpi said Visayan men took two or three wives if they could afford it, but Chirino said the practice was very rare. Father

Chirino also said that husband and wife separated "for the least reason in the world"—actually, for incompatibility, neglect, or misconduct—and a man or woman who had been married only once was rather the exception than the rule. *Pangoli* was a gift to attract back a wife who had fled to her relatives, and legal divorce was often avoided only because of the difficulty of restoring a bride-price that had already been "spent." Moreover, if divorce was common, the premature death of one partner was by no means uncommon, so remarriages filled families with half-siblings and adopted nephews, nieces, or foundlings.

Inheritance

Children of both sexes inherited equally unless their parents specified some preference in a will *(bilin)*. Illegitimate children inherited only at the pleasure of the legal heirs. But heritage strictly followed bloodline: step-children inherited only from their actual parents, and spouses did not inherit from each other. A man and wife might bequeath to each other conjugal property which they had accumulated together, but not what they had inherited. It was a principle of which Spanish justices were often unaware when trying lawsuits over contested inheritance. Two cases recorded by Alcina will illustrate.

An unmarried girl died who was the only child of a widowed datu, leaving six slaves she had inherited from her deceased mother. Her father had no claim to those slaves, but some fifty of her mother's kin gathered around to claim their share. "Since there would not have been even a finger for each," as Father Alcina (1668a, 4:227) said, search had to be made for the "trunk" *(puno)*—that is, the ultimate source of the slaves. This proved to be the girl's maternal grandfather, who had had three children—her mother and two sons—each of whom had inherited an equal number of slaves, and all of whom were dead. Since the girl was the last in her mother's line, it was the descendants of her two uncles who had the best claim. These were more than twenty in all, so each was awarded a quarter-slave.

In the other case, a childless woman adopted the daughter of her brother, raised her as her own daughter, and eventually married her off in another town. She then took in a foundling that had been abandoned in the forest, whom she also raised as a daughter but could not legally adopt because the parents were unknown. When the woman was dying, the foundling obtained a certificate from the parish priest stating that she was the woman's heir. The legally adopted daughter had by this time died but

143

her son appeared to claim his grandmother's property, which included three slaves from her original bride-price. But because of the existence of the anomalous Spanish paper, the case dragged on for twelve years. It was finally settled in the son's favor, leaving the foundling only her foster mother's personal possessions, not what she had inherited, and even from this the son could claim his grandmother's expenses in raising the girl, a claim which he refrained from pressing only because of Father Alcina's intervention.

Property and Labor

The property mentioned in bride-price exchanges or inheritance disputes was always slaves and bahandi—imported porcelains and gongs and gold, especially ornate gold ornaments whose value greatly exceeded their gold content. Slaves were readily transferable, but bahandi was alienated only in case of dire family emergency (an inaccessibility which made it a particular target of raiders), though it was sometimes loaned out in exchange for servitude.

But all property of whatever value—houses and boats, household furnishings and livestock, even raw materials and the contents of granaries—must have been inheritable. Most houses were built of light materials, highly inflammable, and readily abandoned in case of enemy attack or an occupant's death, but they could be bought or rented. The stately dwelling of ranking datus, however, standing on tall hardwood pillars and walled with intricately carved planks, often survived from one generation to the next, but were surely never sold.

All products of human labor were alienable property which could be bought and sold, not excluding children. With the notable exception of fruit trees, most of them were movable: lumber or rice could be sold, even vegetables still in the ground or unharvested grain, but not the forest or fields which produced them. Cleared swiddens were also sold or rented—though the terms "sold" or "rented" are rather inappropriate because the land itself was not owned. Manufactured goods were often jointly owned: women might pool their efforts to strip abaca or weave textiles, for example. Trees in the forest could be blazed to ripen fruit or for beehives, but the claim was only good for one season.

All these natural resources were themselves public domain although subject to a datu's regulation. He could build fish dams, obstruct river traffic, claim a share of hunters' catch, or collect all turtle eggs in a restricted stretch of beach. Datus could also lease such resources to outsiders: Legazpi (1569b, 22n.63) reported of Visayan gold production in 1569,

> In some place where we know there are mines, the natives are not willing to work them and do not, but when foreign vessels come, in exchange for what they bring, they agree to let them work in the mines for the days or period contracted.

Labor, of course, was itself a commodity that could be bught and sold—or, in the case of bonded tinubos, rented. Indeed, it was the commodity in which creditors were investing when they underwrote somebody's debt: *lito* was resale, and *linilito pagtubos* was a person whose debt had been transferred many times from one speculator to another. Oripun were not bondservants working off their debt: *lowas* was the payment liquidating slavery, made either by the slave himself or somebody on his behalf, and *tubos* was a payment which transferred title to the one who paid it.

Namomoo was to work in somebody else's house, most frequently weaving. *Lihog* were hired hands compensated only with meals and with a feast when the project was completed. *Himakdul* was compensation given an agent or messenger for difficult service, and *hinguli* was a kind of hazardous duty pay on expeditions like those called *moro-moro* after the Spaniards introduced the concept.

In the practice of agriculture, terms distinguished the division of labor, not of property. *Lan-o* or *tagolaling* was the work a slave did for himself, and *tampok* (literally, "a precious stone") was what he did for his master; and if he made a *surabi* field for himself by stealth alongside his master's, what he was stealing was time, not land.

Householders had the right of usufruct to the land on which their houses and fruit trees stood, but it was not property held in fee simple. Under colonial law, however, such occupation eventually became the basis for legal title, while datus laid claim to unoccupied land where they had exercised jurisdiction. In Manila, land was being sold and mortgaged with Spanish title deeds as early as the 1590s. We do not know when this process began in colonial centers like Cebu and Iloilo, but in the rural Visayas it was just beginning a century after Legazpi's arrival. Alcina (1668a, 3:75–76) has left the following lucid description of indigenous land rights in his day:

> Regarding land, here there is no difference between mine and thine as in other parts, or the usual lawsuits in almost all of them over its dominion and possession; because it is so great, so extensive, and in almost all places so good, in all islands, that it is not only more than enough for all their inhabitants, but could be given to thousands of farmers of those in other parts who are begging for it and sometimes

145

cannot farm for lack of land, while here, on the contrary, there is more than enough and very extensive land but a shortage of those to cultivate it. And although it is true that every town or vicinity has its own boundaries and they are like their own lands and not those of other towns, nonetheless, to anybody who comes and settles among them, even if he was never seen before and is unknown, they give option to choose as he will, all and as much land as he wants without giving a penny for it or any contract, so long as it is uncultivated.

Regarding farming or cultivating it, the one who farms or cultivates it is the owner, and even more so if he planted coconuts or fruit trees, which are always his, without there ever having been disputes or lawsuits among them over it until now. God grant that this sincerity and good will might always endure among them, because these days it appears there have been some who wish to disrupt it somewhat, some who, by bringing in modern ideas *[ladinecer]*, are spoiling it with swindling. So the ancient good will and trust is being lost with which they used to live without grabbing from one another, but readily giving way to the one who made first choice, and much more so to the one who first planted coconuts, fruit trees, abaca or other things, to which they always had right and dominion, even if they only swear to it and then go live in another town.

CHAPTER 8

Weapons and War

Bladed weapons were an ordinary part of Visayan male costume, at least a dagger or spear. If bound with gold or set with gems, these constituted an essential part of a datu's personal jewelry. Daggers, knives, swords, spears and javelins, shields and body armor were found everywhere, but the bow and arrow had scattered distribution, and the blowgun was found only in Mindanao and Palawan. Stones, occasionally thrown with slings, and wooden darts were common missiles everywhere, but firearms were known only to Moros. Set in strategic locations were ballistas—that is, powerful crossbows which could drive a shaft through a wild boar's body "like a gourd" when triggered by a cord stretched across a path.

Swords and Daggers

The most intimate weapon was the *baladaw*. This was a short broad dagger with a single-edged leaf-shaped blade like a *songil* spearhead, and a cross-shaped hilt which was grasped with the blade protruding between the index and middle fingers. It was 20 to 25 centimeters long, with smaller ones made especially for youngsters since even a small boy felt naked without one. They were typically decorated with tassels made of silk or hairs from the bushy tail of the civet cat dyed red or, better, a lock of hair provided by one's own sweetheart. Like other bladed weapons, and even working bolos, they were strapped to the wrist for use, either by a cord or a tassel called *kulili*.

There were two kinds of swords—kris (Visayan *kalis*) and kampilan, both words of Malay origin. The kris was a long double-edged blade (modern specimens run to 60 or 70 centimeters), either straight or wavy but characterized by an asymmetrical hornlike flare at the hilt end, called *kalaw-kalaw* after the kalaw hornbill. The wavy kris was called *kiwo-kiwo*, and so was an astute, devious man whose movement could not be predicted. Hilts were carved of any solid material—hardwood, bone, antler, even shell—and great datu warriors had them of solid gold or encrusted with precious stones. Blades were forged from layers of different grades of steel, which gave them a veined or mottled surface—damascened or "watered." But even the best Visayan products were considered inferior to those from Mindanao or Sulu, and these in turn were less esteemed than imports from Makassar and Borneo. Alcina thought the best of them excelled Spanish blades.

The word *kampilan* came into Spanish during the Moluccan campaigns of the sixteenth century as "a heavy, pointed cutlass [*alfange*]"—inappropriately, however, since a cutlass had a curved blade weighted toward the tip for slashing blows, while the kampilan was straight. (Modern ones are two-handed weapons running to 90 centimeters.) It apparently was never manufactured by Visayan smiths but imported from parts of Mindanao, both Muslim and pagan, which had direct culture contact with the Moluccas. Like the kris, it was coated with poison before going into battle, and the fiction that the metal itself had been rendered poisonous by some arcane alchemy no doubt enhanced its market value. Fine ones were handed down from father to son, bore personal names known to the enemy, and could be recognized by the sound of little bells which formed part of their tasseled decoration. In the Maranaw epic Darangen, when Prince Bantugan leaves his beloved Bumburan for exile,

> He took his great kampilan, wrapped the strap
> Securely round his hand, and held his shield before him
> While he danced out the road and swung
> His bright kampilan round his head in such a wise
> Could be heard within the palace tower (Laubach 1930, 96).

148

Spears

The spear, *bankaw,* was the most important Visayan weapon. It was carried both for security and ceremony, and it figured not only in warfare but in religious functions and business transactions. *Pamankaw* was a spear the bridegroom's party gave the bride's grandmother to let down the house ladder. The part of the dowry that was held in abeyance and only demanded in case of a breach of connubial harmony was called *lantay*—to throw a spear at a distant target. Marriage negotiations actually began with a spear thrust: The man's father sent one of his *timawa* vassals bearing his son's spear to the girl's father. There, he drove it into the house steps and then, while he gripped it in his hand, the ancestral spirits of both families were invoked for fertility and prosperity.

The importance of the Visayan spear is indicated by the special vocabulary attached to it. The general term for it was *bankaw;* while a light spear was *barobankaw* or *bankaway,* or *piniris* if fitted with a short shaft. Men called their own spears by more intimate terms: *ipambuk* or *ipanonos* had the nuance of "my trusty blade"; and *bankaras* or *bankaraw,* something like "that damned spear of mine." The shaft, almost 2 meters long, was *duldug* or *ilhi,* and the spearhead was hafted into it by a tang, *tugod,* and held firm by a ring called *pitara* if it was metal, *bankorong* or *pikit* if rattan. The butt, *hele,* was strengthened by a pointed sheathing *(tikala)* of brass or even gold for 10 or 12 centimeters, which permitted it to serve as a staff for climbing, or to be conveniently driven into the ground to stand by itself when men met in friendly discussion.

Good spears were kept highly polished, and among them the most prestigious was the songil, a leaf-shaped blade 30 centimeters long and as wide as a man's hand, sharpened for as much as half its length, knifelike, on both edges. If it was *piniskan* or *pinamaskan,* it had elegant round or flamelike inlays of brass, copper, or silver, and could be valued at one slave. The *binalo* was similar in shape but cheaper, while the *budiak* was longer and wider but thinner. The *liparak* was short and broad, the *tumbak* medium-sized, and the *lanab* the longest and widest of all, while the *tinikol* was the shape of a *tikol* leaf. Some were thick and heavy: the *binusloran* was thick down the middle, and the *pinuso* was so called because of its similarity to the flower of a banana plant.

Missiles

These fine spears were thrown only where it was possible to retrieve them—in face-to-face combat, for instance, or from ambush. Even when

149

hunting wild boar, any expensive weapon was thrown with a cord attached to prevent the animal from running off with it. Normal for open combat were bamboo spears with fire-hardened wooden points, their last section loaded with sand for better balance, or, most common of all, the *sugob*, a length of sharpened *bagakay* bamboo. From the fighting decks of *karakoa* cruisers, 30–centimeter-long spikes or javelins of heavy hardwood pointed at both ends were thrown in large numbers with an accuracy which attracted the attention of all foreign observers. All these missiles were ordinarily poisoned with *bulit*, snake venom, preferably from a viper so deadly it was called *odto*, high noon, because its victims could not expect to survive more than half a day.

The small role assigned the bow and arrow in Visayan warfare is suggested by the poverty of its vocabulary. Bow was *busog*—which basically meant full, like a head of rice or a sail swollen with wind. *Odyong* was arrow; and *tanangan*, quiver. However, in Panay the arrow was called *pana*, presumably from Malay *panah*, bow. There appears to have been no special word for arrowhead. Arrowheads were made of wood and constituted one-third the length of cane arrows which were unfledged—that is, unfeathered, and therefore inaccurate in flight. Bows were generally short and weak, though Juan de la Isla reported some as long and strong as English bows. Archers were reported in most places but in small numbers, and their lack of skill was regularly contrasted with the expertise of mountain Negritos, or Sangil islanders who sent contingents of bowmen to reinforce their Mindanao allies when needed. But some Visayans used arrows to good effect in naval warfare, pouring volleys into enemy ships at close quarters, a use reflected in the expression, "Baga nauran nga odyong [Raining like arrows]."

The blowgun *(sumpit)* as found in Sarangani and Palawan was a rather sophisticated weapon. A natural tube of hollow cane, it projected a thick dart *(kalway* or *pangodyong)* about 20 centimeters long, with a butt of softwood to make an airtight plunger and a barbed head often made of fishbone—and poisoned. Its length permitted great accuracy, and it was also fitted with an iron spearhead for use after all ammunition had been spent. As for firearms, Legazpi in 1567 sent the king a Chinese arquebus, "some of which there are among these people." The Visayans called an arquebus or musket *luthang*, a Malay word of supposedly Chinese origin.

Defensive Arms

The Visayan equivalent of a cuirass, or chain mail, was *barote*, quilted or corded body armor, which the Spaniards called *escaupiles* after the cotton-

150

padded ones they found in the New World. The barote was woven of thick-braided abaca or bark cords, tight enough to be waterproof in good ones, and so intricately knotted that cuts did not spread. A piece similar to burlap *(habay-habay)* was worn next to the body under the barote itself. It extended to the elbow and knee, with an ankle-length variety with sleeves for manning defenseworks, though for greater agility in hand-to-hand combat, confident warriors preferred to fit without them. *Pakil* and *batung-batung* were breastplates or backplates made of bamboo, bark, hardwood like ebony, or, in Mindanao, carabao horn or elephant hide from Jolo. Shark-skin was used effectively for helmets or *moriones.*

The shield, *kalasag,* was made of a light, corky wood which was very fibrous so as to enmesh any spear or dagger which penetrated it, and it was generally considered sword-proof. It was strengthened and decorated with rattan binding coated with resinous pitch, and of sufficient size to give full body protection—about 50 by 150 centimeters. A small round buckler called *tamin* appears to have been copied from the Moluccans or the Spaniards themselves. The kalasag was typically painted red and decorated with shell sequins and hog bristles on top or, in the case of real braves, the hair of vanquished foes.

Warfare

Visayan life was sufficiently warlike to provide occasion for men to win the tattoos which caused the Spaniards to call them *pintados,* painted. The case of Limasawa is suggestive of this warlikeness. A small island of insignificant natural resources just off the southern tip of Leyte, it was a Butuan satellite. Its overlord, Rajah Kolambu, was the brother of Butuan ruler Rajah Awi, and his heir fled to Butuan following a devastating Ternatan-Portuguese raid in 1562. Kolambu himself did not reside on the island, but only went there when he and his brother wanted to meet and, as he told Magellan, "hunt." What attracted these Butuan rajahs to this tiny island? What were they hunting? An answer is suggested by its location: it was strategically positioned to control, or prey on, all shipping from the Pacific coast to the interior trade centers of Butuan and Cebu.[24]

A Spaniard, who observed Philippine society from within it as a captive slave, reported in 1528 that the people of Surigao lived off the sea "by raid and trade," and were enemies of those of Sarangani Island. Another Spaniard, Juan Flores, survived for twenty years in a Leyte village and finally disappeared on a raid together with thirty of his townmates. During Legazpi's first year in Cebu, he twice joined his reluctant vassal Tupas to avenge attacks by enemy villages on the same island, and twice provided escort against Panay enemies for datus come to sell rice from that island. Likewise, Spaniards happened to learn about the gold mines of Masbate when they went there to avenge a Leyte ally who had been attacked.

These enmities were generally the cause or result of raids which were seasonal in nature because sea raiders want the wind behind them when they attack. Kolambu told Magellan that he had two villages hostile to him but that it was not the time to go there then; and Loarca reported from Panay that maritime communities made their raids during the fair winds between the monsoon, but the uplanders after harvest. Father Martín de Rada wrote in 1577,

> Every year as soon as they harvest their fields, they man their ships to go to plunder wherever their luck leads them . . . and this is especially during October and November, and later in February and March and April, at which times a great number of corsairs go out, and still do today though not so many because of fear of the Spaniards (Rada 1577, 479).

In the next century, Alcina collected a wealth of data on Visayan warfare from both folklore and living memories. Favorite Samar targets were Albay and Catanduanes, with forays as far north as Casiguran; and marriage relations with Burias, Masbate, and Mindanao were the result of wife-seeking raids from those places. Datu Karagrag of Makarato on Lawan Island, and his beautiful wife Bingi, however, successfully resisted a kidnap attempt by Damaraug of Albay at the head of a fleet remembered by their descendants as numbering 100 vessels. Father Alcina had parishioners who were descendants of Luzon captives. Once, he resettled a Samareño chieftain named Kasilagan and his people in Catbalogan after their release from Caraga captivity in Davao Oriental. But not all such migration may have resulted from human raids: Leyte-speaking descendants of migrants whom Father Alcina met in Oton explained their presence with a curious story about their ancestors having been driven from their home in Ormuc Bay by an infestation of barracudalike garfish.

The men of eastern Samar, then called Ibabao, were still proud of their reputation as warriors in Alcina's day. "Ibabawkita!" they would tell each other on going into battle—"We are men of Ibabao!" Legend recounted the fame of a giant of a man from Magtaon called Pusong who used to raid Calbiga and Libunao on the west coast single-handed, and whose form chiseled into the rock where he finally fell was shown to Father Alcina. The warriors considered to be the bravest of all, however, were the Boholanos, men "who formerly would not permit any other nation to abuse them," Alcina (1668b, 396) commented of the Tamblot uprising. That Ternatan-Portuguese raid on Bohol and Limasawa so memorialized by Spanish chroniclers because it involved their colonial competitors, appears simply to have been the latest in an ongoing series of exchanges between Bohol and Ternate. A century later, outnumbered Boholanos successfully repulsed one more attack, sending the Ternatan karakoas home with colors struck.

Purpose and Causes of Wars

Visayan communities had small populations, low levels of production, and unlimited access to natural resources like sea and forest products. Their datus' ability to procure iron or prestigious imports depended on control of the manpower to exploit those resources. Wars were therefore fought to control people, not territory. They were waged by raids intended to seize slaves outright, to initiate or enforce alliances for trading networks, and to take booty to cover costs in any case. They were fought, not by standing armies or navies loyal to some superordinate political authority, but by citizen warriors owing personal allegiance to leaders who were physically present. Visayans were therefore willing to swear allegiance to Spanish raiders when it was to their advantage to do so, but were not prepared to resist foreign occupation and annexation of their territory.

Recognized causes for just war were direct raid or attack by another community, betrayal of blood pacts or alliances, treachery or abuse of traders in a friendly village, and murder or theft by an outsider. Slave raiding was the main motivation for unprovoked attack or, in special cases, the need for a sacrificial victim to complete mourning rites for some powerful datu. Retaliation for injuries received was not only a matter of revenge, but a punitive measure intended to discourage repetition of the offense. Failure to take revenge not only suggested a timidity which invited further enemy action, but ran the risk of supernatural punishment by the spirits of unavenged relatives.

Strategy and Tactics

Gubat was the general term for warfare, but actual engagements were distinguished as *gahat* by land and *mangayaw* by sea, or *salakay* for storming

153

a fortified position in distinction to *burhi,* to take by treachery. The preferred tactic on land was ambush—*habon, saghid, hoom,* or *poot*—either by lying in wait or by such strategies as exposing a few agile warriors to enemy view to lure them out into the trap. *Sayang* was to pass by hidden enemies unawares. To loot was *dahas* or *dampas, pangawat* being the one who took the lion's share. *Dugdug* was to rob on the trail like a highwayman; *lingo,* if it involved killing in an isolated spot. *Dakot* or *bakot* was a complete sacking of a community. *Taban* was anything taken by force, including wives and women; *sangbay* or *bansag,* any trophy, captive, or goods seized from an enemy; and *dangin* was both spoils of war and something set aside for a religious sacrifice.

Special roles connected with the conduct of war included *away,* enemy; *bantay,* sentinel; *bila,* allies; *kagon,* mediator; and *laway,* spy. *Asdang* was hand-to-hand combat. *Bulu* was a duel. *Hulaw* was a man known to be on the lookout for an enemy. *Angat* was to provoke or challenge—for example, "Pauli kita sa sulad [Let's both go to hell]!" (Méntrida 1637a, 350). *Pinaorihiyan* was for a fleeing warrior to turn and spear his pursuer; *naga kamatayan* was to fight to the death; and *mangin matay* was a desperate man determined to die on the field of battle. *Balita* was the bad news of death or captivity, but *hugyaw* or *ugyak* were the clamorous shouts or chants of returning victors.

Sea Raiding

The most celebrated form of Visayan warfare was sea raiding, *mangayaw,* a word which appeared in all the major languages of the Philippines. Its root appears to be *kayaw* (for example, Ilocano *kinayawan,* captive) though Spanish lexicographers extracted *ayaw, ngayaw,* and *agaw,* and it meant a raid to bring back slaves or heads. There is no record of Visayan headhunting—that is, warfare for the specific purpose of taking heads— but heads were cut off in the course of battle or murder. Pedro de Arana lost his head during the occupation of Cebu. *Luba, pogot, sumbali,* and *tongol* all meant to behead, and tongol was also the dress plumage displayed at the stern of a warship.

The sacrifice that was performed on launching a warship for a raid was called *pagdaga,* and it was considered most effective if the prow and keel were smeared with the blood of a victim from the target community. But karakoa cruisers were not designed simply for falling on undefended coastal communities: they were fitted with elevated fighting decks for ship-to-ship contact at sea. Such engagements were called *bangga,* and *bangal* was to pursue a fleeing enemy vessel. Ships traveling in company were *abay,* and a swift sailer sent out in advance of the fleet for scouting was *dulawan* ("visitor") or *lampitaw.*

Besides slaves, preferred spoils of war were the bronze gongs and Chinese porcelains which constituted *bahandi* wealth. Raids were also mounted to carry off choice ladies as brides, especially the daughters of men with whom it was advantageous to establish collateral ties. Ranking datus jealous of their lineage were often unable to obtain brides of their rank locally or to satisfy the requirements of families with prestigious pedigrees elsewhere, and so would resort to abduction. Raiders came from as far as Mindanao and Jolo for this purpose. (Alcina thought the similarity of certain Visayan and Mindanao languages was due to this cross-fertilization.) Once, to avenge one such raid, two Bantayan-Samar chiefs made a celebrated attack on Jolo, perhaps to settle bride-price and social precedence. Modern marketing jargon would have called this procedure a marry-now-pay-later plan, for the dowry expenses evaded at the time of abduction would be paid eventually when, after the birth of children and further exchange of eligible youths and ladies, the two parties would finally unite in amicable settlement.

Defense

The best defense against mangayaw attack was to intercept the enemy at sea, but most communities did not have the men-o'-war to do so. They would therefore abandon their homes to looting and the torch, and withdraw to the hills, returning when danger had passed to rebuild their houses of materials readily available. Indeed, settlements were often located in the interior precisely for security reasons. A native guide told García Descalante in 1544 that southeastern Mindanao was thickly populated with communities that had withdrawn from the coast because of war; and that Dawis, a large Bohol town opposite Panglao Island, was completely abandoned following the famous Ternatan raid, only to be resettled as Baclayon many years later.

Moog, ili, or *ilihan* was any tower, rocky outcropping, or natural pinnacle that could be fortified, to which evacuees retreated for defense. Spanish soldiers were regularly called upon by local allies to storm strongholds which must have been impregnable for less determined and more poorly armed invaders. Sometimes they were actual tree houses 15 or more meters above the ground, occupied only in time of war. If they were intended only for male warriors, they were reached simply by a vine which could be pulled up. *Balatik,* ordinarily used for large game, were set along the approaches; and the ground was planted with *suyak,* ankle-high poisoned spikes. Any fortification was called *tambangan,* but the Malay word *kota* seems only to have been applied to more permanent forts built by Moros.

Peace Pacts

Hostilities were suspended or avoided by *sandugo:* peace pacts in which the two parties drank a few drops of one another's blood in a draught of wine. All Spanish explorers from Magellan to Legazpi made such pacts with Visayan datus. It was a procedure by which two men, not necessarily enemies, became blood brothers, vowing to stick together through thick and thin, war and peace, and to observe mourning restriction whenever they were separated from one another. After the Spanish introduction of legal documentation, Filipinos were even known to dramatize their commitment by signing in blood—like the pious Visayan lady who appeared before Father Alcina (1668a, 4:275–75).

> Having brought a paper written in her own hand, in which she offered herself as a Slave of the Virgin for the rest of her life with a vow of absolute chastity (she had just been widowed a second time), she pulled out a needle and pierced herself with it over the heart, and with the blood that flowed out serving as ink, signed the document, with which act she showed she was making it irrevocable and enduring according to her custom.

These peace pacts were made between two datus, however, not between two nations or tribes, and so were binding on other members of the community only to the extent of the pact holder's effective authority, and in no case on other datus. For this reason, Spanish commanders usually drew blood with more than one chief when making treaties—Magellan in Cebu, Saavedra in Sarangani, Legazpi in Samar, Goiti in Leyte, Rodríguez in Negros. It is ironic that the blood compact between Legazpi and Si Katuna of Bohol memorialized in Juan Luna's famous 1883 *El Pacto de Sangre* was an exception to this practice of drawing blood with more than one chief.

Epic Heroes

Successful mangayaw raiders were regarded as popular heroes and enjoyed interisland reputations. They tattooed in proportion to their

156

prowess and were entitled to wear distinctive attire. Their exploits became the stuff of local legend, and the most famous among them were *karanduun,* worthy of being memorialized in those heroic epics called *kandu.* As a Suban-on epic says, "M'lat gosay dipaya datu di m'glayaglayag [It is not fitting that a datu ventures not]" (Resma 1982, 285).

The Spaniards, of course, considered any such venturing datus simple pirates, and defined mangayaw itself as piracy—armed robbery at sea. But it is a judgment which might be put in better perspective against sixteenth-century European concepts of international law on the high seas. Standard practice for dealing with unidentified ships at sea was to signal them to heave to and, if they did not, to open fire and take them "in fair fight," seizing everything on board including personnel. As Charles V (1519, 136) ordered Magellan,

> you will decide on those for ransom as best you can, and if there are persons whose value exceeds 500 *seráfines,* such will be held for us because of their value, and the others you will have evaluated or put up for auction, and it would be best if the people of that land wished to buy them, you selling them for the best price, to avoid the expense of feeding them.

Such was the Spanish king's concept of maritime law. Mangayaw was the Visayans'.

PART TWO

Mindanao And Luzon

CHAPTER 9

Mindanao

It is unfortunate that we have no early dictionaries of Mindanao languages like those that permitted a detailed description of classic Visayan culture. However, the northern and eastern coasts of Mindanao were part of the Visayan culture area: from Surigao in the east to Sindangan Bay in the west, missionaries were able to make themselves understood in Cebuano. Moreover, much that has been said of Visayan culture in part 1 is also applicable to the coastal populations of Mindanao, and even to many communities in the interior.

Rice was everywhere the preferred food, but recourse had to be made to root crops and sago in season. Houses stood on tall posts, men-o'-war were edge-pegged *karakoa*s, and weapons were the same as in the Visayas, with the addition of small artillery in Maguindanao and Sulu. Power and prominence depended on the control of slaves taken by debt and capture, and chiefs were respected for their warrior skills—but were not all tattooed. Ancestors and nature spirits were worshiped, and omens were taken from the *limokon* bird.

All these features were still to be observed in the seventeenth century. Father Francisco Combés described an ornate kris worn by Zamboanga

161

Chief Soksokan which was valued at ten slaves, and a spear in Jolo which killed Captain Gaspar de Morales by penetrating his steel-sheathed buckler. Traditional nuptial processions, pomp, and coquetry evidently survived conversion to Christianity: Father Combés (1667, 68) attended a two-week wedding celebration in which sixteen hundred gallons of wine and more than one thousand chickens were consumed and "the bride took a half hour to give her answer, and after having given it, another long half hour to reach the altar rail."

Caraga

It was on the Pacific coast in what is now Surigao del Sur and Davao Oriental that the Spaniards first learned the name "Vizaya." Dutch records also refer to southeastern Mindanao as Bisaya, and Villalobos in 1543 called Davao Gulf, Bisaya Bay. Like other Visayans, men on these shores were tattooed and wore penis pins, G-strings, and turbans or headbands, red in the case of those who had personally killed enemies, recognized insignia of the "nobility." They fought slave-raiding wars with long narrow shields, blowguns and in some places metal-tipped arrows, and the broad-bladed, single-edged *baladaw* but not the wavy kris or kampilan. They took omens with crocodile teeth, rocking boats, and the limokon bird, made use of charms and poisons, and were reputed to be able to kill with a breath. Half-slaves worked for their masters half time, shamans were either male or female *baylan*, and deified ancestor spirits were called *humalagar*. They had neither public idols nor temples—though more than one missionary thought that chiefs' large houses with family altars were the equivalent; and in Himologan (Cagayan de Oro), a kind of miniature house called *diwatahan* for offering sacrifices stood in the middle of a communal dwelling which housed the entire village. Little idols of wood or stone—which friar accounts always described as *diwata*, "black and ugly"—were small enough to be carried out to planting rituals. The dead were buried in coffins placed in caves with thin plates of gold over their mouth and eyes, after a mourning period during which people avoided all sites that had been frequented by the deceased.

The Spaniards later called the Pacific coast of Mindanao, Caraga, after a town of that name. Along this coast they got a generally hostile reception: their first three expeditions lost three boats, two ship's anchors, and dozens of lives. When one boatload was massacred near Bislig in 1526, deserter Sebastián de Puerto was captured by Chief Katunaw of Lianga Bay. Sebastián later described them as living off the sea by "raid and trade," a people who "weigh anchor like Arabs [pulling up stakes] since they move their towns from one place to another" (Granado 1529, 472). But they were also farmers who sold rice in Cebu (Sebastián himself was taken along on such a voyage), and wove a fine burlap out of tree bark. Katunaw had actually captured Sebastián while making a raid on his own enemies. He had a daughter married to a chief in Baganga Bay, where his Spanish slave finally escaped.

Early in the next century, the Spaniards tried to stop Caraga raids on their Leyte subjects by attacking them at Tandag, eventually freeing some fifteen hundred Christians, and building a permanent fort. Four years later, the Caragans surrounded and besieged it, a daring attack which no doubt contributed to a reputation they shared with Boholanos and Samareños as *valientes y tiránicos,* an expression of begrudging Spanish praise. A single chief by the name of Inuk was reputed to have captured two thousand slaves himself. He was said to have been feared and respected by datus all up and down the coast both before and after his submission to colonial authority. Whatever the true number of his slaves, they were presumably employed in extracting or producing his trade goods, for Fray Juan de la Madre de Dios said that at the time of Inuk's conversion, "he permitted trade between his countrymen and the Spaniards" (Jesús 1681, 33).

Father Alcina and the authors of the Visayan dictionaries always referred to slave raiding and human sacrifice in the past tense, but pioneer Recollect missionaries observed these practices in full vigor. Expeditions were launched in an apprehensive flurry of tabus, omens, and invocations: Octopus and squid were forbidden as food lest the raiders be blinded because these creatures discharge a cloud of blinding black ink. Fish caught by nets were likewise not eaten by raiders for fear of being caught themselves. Nor could a light be struck for cooking during the voyage. Meanwhile, villagers at home observed a seven-day holiday. Before departure, omens were carefully noted, prayers were addressed to war deities, and once under way, dangerous promontories were invoked with mournful chants.

Upon the victorious return of raiders, the best of the captives was sacrificed to the captain's humalagar, just as the first fruits of the field were offered up at harvest time. In some places, it was said, a second victim was dispatched in the victor's house by his wife. And men who had taken at least seven lives were qualified to wear distinctive turbans and G-strings of striped material.

163

Butuan

Butuan was a trading port with an illustrious past. It had direct contact with Champa in the tenth century. It was also the first Philippine "state" to establish diplomatic relations with China: On 3 October 1003, its envoys Liyihan and Jiaminan petitioned the Chinese emperor in Peking for tribute status—which simply meant ceremonial recognition of the emperor as the Supreme Ruler of the Universe, a requirement for legal trade. It was serviced from the south by a far-ranging boat people known as Sama or Samal, who were centered on Basilan Strait but had outposts as far north as Capul Island off Samar, where traces of their language survive to this day.

Butuanon themselves migrated south to settle in Sulu, where they became known as "people of the current"—Taosug—established a major exchange port on the Moluccan spice route, and were recognized by China in 1417. As late as 1600, the sultan of Sulu, Batara Shah Tengah, appears to have been an actual native of Butuan. But Butuan was gradually overshadowed by Borneo's commercial expansion into Mindoro and Luzon, and eventually became a Bornean dependency itself. By the time of Spanish advent, its former glory was too long forgotten for the Spaniards to learn about it.

Butuan stands at the mouth of the great Agusan River: behind it lies a well-watered valley, abundant wild game and forest products, and rich deposits of gold. Its reputation was still popular enough to attract the Spaniards on their arrival in 1565: Villalobos had been told that it was a port of call for Chinese junks. Legazpi meant to go there "since," as his chronicler wrote, "it is a trading town, it was impossible that it would not have somebody who understood Malay because that is the most common in these parts" (Anon. 1565, 461); however, he was blown off course to Bohol.

Limasawa was a Butuan satellite strategically placed to control passage between the Pacific coast and the central Visayas. Its ruler was the brother of the rajah of Butuan, and they were related to the royal family of Cebu. Limasawa had been devastated by a Ternatan-Portuguese raid in 1562, and when the Spaniards later met its ruler's heir in Butuan, he was still in mourning.

Butuan's reputation did not include "piracy," however: trading ports do not usually make slave raids even though they deal in slaves. This was also true of Cebu, Maguindanao, and Jolo—and, ironically, Spanish Manila, where Portuguese delivered thousands of African, Indian, and Moluccan

164

slaves in the seventeenth century for resale into Mexico. That is no doubt why Fray Luis de Jesús (1681, 34) said the Butuanon were "similar to the Caragans in their customs and rituals, but are not so difficult to deal with."

Dapitan

Mindanao Visayans farther west were mainly Boholanos who migrated there following the Moluccan raid. Eight Ternatan vessels with Portuguese allies aboard had anchored at Panglao-Dawis under guise of friendly trade, and then treacherously attacked, killing ruling datu Sarripada Dailisan, plundering and taking captives. They then proceeded to Limasawa for more of the same—where they lost four "white men with beards and strange clothes"—and on their way home, razed all the settlements on Camiguin, then stopped off in Maguindanao to sell Dailisan's lady for 90 gold taels.

Even allowing for exaggeration, the statistics suggest the size and wealth of the Bohol community—three hundred killed, including nine chiefs; five hundred men, women, and children captured; and three hundred taels of gold and two hundred gongs seized along with clothing and merchandise, leaving one thousand families to subsequently cross over to Dapitan. The fact that the Spaniards found Limasawa deserted three years later also illustrates the Visayan custom of abandoning sites associated with death and misfortune.

The exodus was led by Dailisan's brother, Pagbuaya, with five hundred slaves. He settled on an easily defended promontory which commanded the western entrance to the Bohol Sea, and from there he proceeded to subjugate the Suban-on population in both directions, enlisting the aid of Sama marines known as Lutaya or Lutaw ("to float") who had been dependents of Maguindanao or Sulu princes. He so quickly allied himself with the Spaniards on their arrival that his descendants always believed that it was he who had introduced Legazpi to his vassal Si Katuna of Bohol. He founded a line of encomenderos whose Lorenzo Kabiling in 1718 was still collecting 10 reales for every pagan Suban-on subjugated.

Like the Caragans, the valor and ferocity of the Boholanos of Dapitan became a Spanish legend once it was coopted on Spain's behalf. The great Jesuit authority on Mindanao, Francisco Combés (1667, 37), said that his contemporary, Pagbuaya's great-grandson Pedro, went to war at the age of seven and before he was thirty had personally killed in hand-to-hand combat more than two hundred "enemies of God and our king."

Thus, at the time of Spanish advent, the Suban-on were already subjects of maritime peoples, their chiefs being clients of Boholano overlords on the north of the Zamboanga Peninsula, and Sama Lutaw on the south. They were valued as suppliers of forest products like beeswax, cinnamon, civet, deerskin, dyewood, rattan, and resin—as well as live civet cats for export to Japan, caged.

On their own turf, however, Suban-on were a warlike people, giving precedence to red-turbaned chiefs who had killed other persons, often paying their wergeld afterwards. Taking their name from *suba* (river), they lived in small settlements scattered along the banks of streams: Pigafetta was rowed upstream from Quipit for more than two hours to reach Chief Kalanaw's house.

Sixteenth-century Spaniards learned little about them, and even less about the Maranaw on the shore of Lake Lanao, and nothing at all about the various Manobo tribes spread from Agusan to South Cotabato. The forbidding rain forests and Olympian heights of Mount Apo which they inhabited were always intimidating to coastal dwellers, and were peopled with ogres and monsters by lowland imagination. Pigafetta was told about a shaggy tribe called Benaian—perhaps *bayani*—who lived on human hearts, and Recollect friars described the *tekma*—tall, ugly forest denizens with feet turned backwards, so frightening that simply to glimpse one left a man permanently cross-eyed. In actual fact, however, these ancient Mindanao cultures as recalled by their own bards live on in an epic literature which has survived to be recorded by modern scholars.

Epic Culture

Mindanao epics are long narrative poems which celebrate the fabulous deeds of culture heroes in apocryphal wars between imaginary kingdoms, often for the purpose of rescuing or abducting beautiful women. They are an aristocratic form of literature, and so do not give a full picture of the cultures in which they were composed. Their protagonists are all members of the ruling class—datus or *timuay*—sometimes accompanied by lieutenants and always attended by slaves and servants, but there are no commoners or farmers. Like the Visayan *siday* or *kandu,* they are sung or chanted during public celebrations like important weddings, and last all night through.

Folklorists attribute great age to them, but whatever the age of the hero-tales themselves, the texts as recorded must have taken form in historic, or even modern, times. Muslims appear as *salip* or *sarip* (that is, Malay-Arabic *sharif*, noble); an alien datu is mentioned in Bukidnon who collects tribute *(buwis);* and there is a smattering of Spanish terms like *pandyo* (that is, *paño,* kerchief) in most. Moreover, in various versions of the Ulahingan, the action is set in motion by some hero killing an oppressive Moro or Spanish overlord—or even an American schoolteacher. The Darangan of the presently Muslim Maranaw, on the other hand, appears to be pre-Islamic, though it does refer to a sea people called Samar.

The epic hero has brilliant gold teeth and lips red from betel nut, but is not tattooed, and wears so many rings on his fingers that when he reaches for another quid, it seems as if "they were dipped in sea foam" (Manuel 1958, 328–29). His hair is tightly coiled into four or eight braids, and it is considered a great humiliation for them to come loose in a fight. He wears trousers—tight in the case of bachelors, loose for married men, and red for *managku* or *bahani* braves who have slain a specific number of foes—or, in some places, the *malong* tube skirt. The *monsala,* a kerchief almost a meter square and worked with designs of arcane meaning, is worn capelike over one shoulder. All this finery, together with padded armor or bamboo breastplates, is endowed with magical power when ritually donned before going into battle, especially the monsala which can even restore the dead to life. A man should be armed with a minimum of three weapons: one for slashing—the kris or kampilan—and two for piercing—the dagger and the spear. Like his shield, they are decorated with little hawk's bells to accompany his war dance, and are given the names of animals, hardwoods, or defeated enemies.

Musical instruments in the epics include the usual Visayan flutes, gongs, lutes, zithers, and Jew's harps, but also a long closed flute *(pondag)* with six holes (only four of which are fingered) and the *sigitan,* a bamboo zither closed at one end with a hole in the other which is stopped with one hand while the other strikes the strings with a stick instead of plucking them. The royal sport is *sipa,* a game in which a rattan ball is kept in the air by kicking with the side of the foot—only in the epics is the ball iron or, in the case of Prince Bantugan in the Darangan, a huge boulder. Large *torogan* houses serve as a datu's palace, administrative and ceremonial center, but may also house an entire community if the settlement contains only one barangay. Occupants sit under mosquito nets *(kolambo),* guests on a raised platform, and marriageable daughters are secluded in towers called *lamin* in Maranaw, *pintawan* in Suban-on—or *pinto-an,* a lower one for a younger daughter.

Much epic culture would have been familiar to any sixteenth-century Visayan. *Batara* is a title; *basal* is a drumstick for playing gongs; *bandi* are heirloom porcelain jars; and *kamahi* is a gold chain with *W*-shaped links. Swiddens are started on the appearance of certain constellations—like Molopolo (Ursa Minor). *Gasi* or *pangasi* is rice wine, sipped through straws, and heroes are expected to have heroic capacity for it—like Chief Sandayo who drains eight jars.

A sixteenth-century Visayan would also have understood the religion of the epics. Priests are *baylan,* shamans subject to spirit possession, and *diwata* are heavenly deities, spirits, or supernatural beings in general; but the word *humalagar* for deified ancestors does not appear. Rather, heroes themselves are apt to be demigods, offspring of a deity and a mortal. The sky has seven, eight, nine, or even ten levels, and the underworld is also of many layers, one of which is the land of the dead. *Anito* are more accessible spirits who can be invoked in case of illness, while *busaw* are frightening, malevolent demons. War deities are prominent among highlanders: there are Mandangan, the Manobo war god, and many other lesser Mandangans to take individual bahani under their protection. Gabon and Busung are guarantors of proper social behavior; so that *busungan* is to become bloated or wasted away for transgressing accepted norms. Plants, animals, and forces of nature with economic significance all have their protector spirits: thus, for example, hunters or honey gatherers place offerings at the foot of trees inhabited by the ones in charge of bees or wild game. Moreover, most Manobo groups consider one deity superior to all others—for example, Manama or Kerenen—though too remote to be approached directly or to require sacrifices.

The most extensive pantheon is found in the Ulahingan, and it is hierarchically structured. The six *katulusan* in charge of the terrestrial world, for instance, outrank the *imbayabay,* who are just above the lowest class, the *busaw.* There is also an additional paradise for the pure and righteous, *surugu*—no doubt Malay-Sanskrit *surga,* "abode of the blessed." Each of the four cardinal compass points has its own deity. Then there is the sea goddess Alimugkat who is a mermaid; and the diwata of law and justice whose name is Kakum—that is, Malay-Arabic *hukum* (judgment). One of the names given to the Supreme Being is Alataala, presumably from Arabic "Allah ta ala [Allah be exalted]." Like Allah, he is endowed with a list of names which describe his attributes: Midlimbag, the creator; Misuara, the giver of languages; or Mendayawi, the one who inspires right speech and conduct. These acculturative borrowings may be explained by the fact that the Ulahingan is the epic of the Manobo communities most exposed to prestigious, or even superordinate, Muslim cultures. Conversely, the absence of any such Supreme Being in the Maranaw epic suggests that the tales of the Darangan cycle antedate the coming of Islam.

A sociological feature of Philippine epics not found in Indo-European literature of the same genre is polygynous bilateral kinship. Aristocrats have more than one wife, and descent is reckoned in both male and female lines, producing a vast network of relationships. (In the Guman of Dumalinao, for example, a lady declines a gallant's offer to be her champion simply because they are not related.) The first wife ranks all the others: she is titled, and it is her marriage negotiations and wedding celebrations which are described in detail. (In the Tuwaang cycle, for instance, the bride's family prepares *savakan*, bundles of rice and chickens, which must be redeemed by the groom at a higher value in slaves and gongs.) Furthermore, it is the first wife's father who is the object of special deference: a man can become sick merely by treading on his father-in-law's mat. Moreover, genealogies indicate that most of the protagonists are related by blood or marriage, often including those in enemy kingdoms. So, too, in Nelendangan (paradise), all the immortals are related to one another.

Another characteristic of the epic aristocracy is a concern for proper precedence in interpersonal relations. People are not addressed by their names, but by polite terms which indicate rank. A man may address another as Laggi, or Bela if he is of the same or slightly higher rank, but as Bamga (Master) if clearly a superior. Datus and their wives are addressed as Aru or Apu, married women as Bai (Lady or Madame). Older siblings use terms of affection for younger siblings, who in turn call older brothers and sisters by terms of deference. Two friends, or even a man and wife, many take a common pet name—for example, a fruit or flower they both like, or an experience they shared.

In the courtly language of the Darangan, all the characters are referred to by poetic euphemisms: one Bembaran datu is called Dinaradiya, "Datu with a thunderous voice," and Princess Dalomabi Mindaya is known as Aya Paganay Bai, "First among all the ladies." No less courtly are these aristocrats' manners: they turn politely to one side when addressing each other, are seated according to rank, and arrive and depart with decorum. As a Suban-on epic says, "One is not a datu if he leaves abruptly, without permission" (Ochotorena 1981, 394). Indeed, the epic hero treats even slaves and underlings with courtesy: the first ruler of Bembaran instructs his daughter, "When visitors come, entertain them, even if they are slaves" (Coronel 1983, 29).

169

Sarangani Island

The Spaniards occupied Sarangani Island for seven months in 1543. When they arrived, they found almost a hundred boats along the shore, trading with men and women, and they themselves purchased coconuts, fruit, goats, hens, and pigs with tradewares. The largest vessels were traditional plank-built, edge-pegged karakoas with outriggers and quarter rudders, but with one slight variation in construction: the pegs were placed in sets of three about four fingers apart with 40 centimeters between each set. There was a protected anchorage where smaller vessels tied up, and local interpreters called *giribasa* were available to communicate directly with Malay speakers among the Spaniards. Coconut palms grew all along the shore and up the hills on both sides of town as far as the eye could see: when they finally abandoned the island, the Spaniards claimed to have cut more than thirty thousand for food. Under these trees all houses were built, both large and small standing on six to ten tall posts, with domestic animals and fowl penned underneath at night, and reached by ladders which could be drawn up for security. The large ones—like senior chief Lamorwata's which was located on a commanding crest—were solidly constructed, with living quarters divided into rooms and compartments, but "where houses in Spain have windows, these have doors" (Anon. n.d.c, 69).

The size of the town is not given, but the second largest settlement on the island, Tolula or Patuko on the northwest coast, was estimated to contain five hundred dwellings, not counting the outbuildings in the surrounding gardens and orchards. In both settlements the Spaniards found good provisions of rice, millet, and sago cakes.[25]

When the Spaniards attempted to land the morning after they arrived, they found that a stockade of palm tree trunks had been constructed along the beach, supplemented by boats drawn up on the shore and filled with sand. The Saranganis came out to battle to the sound of war drums of different sizes made of tree trunks—"sopranos, tenors and countertenors"—and gongs called *sino,* shouting and threatening in a kind of dance step with one leg raised, covered by body-length shields and brandishing swords overhead. (These sino were played while suspended by being struck on the boss with a padded drumstick.) They were armed with cutlasses and bows and arrows, and wore body armor of quilted cotton or wild boar hide, with wooden helmets covered with octopus skin. The shields and helmets had waving plumes on top, and both shields and armor were painted in bright colors. Their arrows had points of steel or fish bones which were poisoned, supposedly by having been stung by scorpions kept for that purpose, and could penetrate Spanish breastplates. The archers were good marksmen, and killed or wounded eight of the invaders. But Spanish firearms—which the Saranganis called *lutan*—soon turned the tide of battle, and the defenders were driven back into the hills and pursued, and eventually evacuated the whole island, fleeing to nearby Candigar (Balut Island) or the coast of Mindanao.[26]

The men wore large G-strings which hung down over their thighs, and short jackets which left their midriffs bare, with handsomely decorated sleeves. The ordinary textile was "woven palms"—probably abaca—but there was also cotton for those who could afford it. Lamorwata's son Babuti, a large man with powerful muscles, wore cotton, and his beautiful light-skinned wife was dressed in silk. The Spaniards looted gold beads, collars, bracelets, and diadems, as well as a piece of gold fabric woven like chain mail, all of which was a mere sampling of the wealth in gold and porcelain that was carried off by the manloads during the evacuation. None of this gold was mined on the island: it was all obtained through trade. So, too, a considerable array of aromatics like ambergris, benzoin, civet, musk, and storax came from Chinese traders calling at the port of Maguindanao (that is, Cotabato). But when evacuees returned to parley with the invaders and make blood compacts, they were careful to wear no more gold on their persons than some thin earrings.

The Saranganis worshiped natural objects like the sun or the first bird they saw in flight in the morning, and also their deceased parents, whose embalmed corpses they placed upright in a kind of niches. These were opened at the time of agricultural rites or when going to war or long sea voyages, with the burning of much incense and offerings of flowers and food. Saranganis also kept enemy heads hanging by the hair in their houses, their number determining a family's social standing and claims to nobility. These had generally been taken by young men who, when arranging their marriages, bound themselves to present a certain number to their father-in-law before being given their brides. It was a custom reminiscent of that of Visayan families, which made it necessary to settle, during bride-price negotiations, the number of lives to be taken as part of a father-in-law's future mourning requirements.

The people of Sarangani and Candigar had their origins in Sangir Island to the south, halfway between Mindanao and the Moluccas, whose language is still spoken in both islands. Father Combés in the seventeenth century even called Sarangani, Sangir. They occupied the strategic point where the northbound spice route veered westward to Sulu, Borneo, and Malacca, and had direct trade connections with Maguindanao. There

171

Candigar chiefs delivered a dozen small pieces of Spanish artillery, including one 450–kilo bronze cannon, which the Saranganis had managed to steal when they were taken ashore at Patuko to avoid typhoon loss. When the Spaniards mounted a rescue mission from Tidore the next year to recover crewmen stranded in Leyte and Samar, Descalante Alvarado was able to hire a guide in Candigar who was a Christian. The presence of a native Christian no doubt reflected Portuguese proselytizing efforts during the preceding decade, when two Morotai chiefs had been baptized and another two in Makassar, as well as six in Mindanao. "And in the same island," historian João de Barros (1628, 592) wrote, "the King of Butuano became Christian." (Some of their children were put in school in Ternate.)

The trade route along the north side of the Celebes Sea is nicely illustrated by the experience of Spaniards who were taken slaves in those waters. When the *Santa María del Parral* ran aground on Sangir in 1526, her survivors were all seized by the Sangirese, and five were sold to a boat from Maguindanao, where they were in turn purchased by traders from Luzon. Two others were ransomed off by Commander Saavedra two years later from some hard-bargaining chiefs on Sarangani. Yet another three were still in Maguindanao when the local ruler—probably the celebrated Kabungsuwan himself—notified them that the Portuguese in Malacca had requested the sultan of Brunei to intervene on their behalf and send them there, and that he would provide them transportation if they wished to go, as in fact he did.

When the Dutch reached the area early in the seventeenth century, the ranking Sarangani chief was Mangada of Candigar. He was the son of Datu Buisan of Davao, and was married into the royal family of Sangir. He was also related to the ruling family of Buayan, a chiefdom in the upper Pulangi Valley whose only free access to the sea was through Buayan Bay—known to the Spaniards as Buran or Berian, and now as Sarangani Bay. Mangada once acted as Buayan representative to the Dutch in Ternate, and three of his sons became Buayan datus. But in 1626 he was driven out of Sarangani by a devastating Maguindanao attack, transferring his seat to Cammarian on the opposite shore, and eventually to Sangir, where he was regarded by the Dutch as the Sangirese "King of Kandahar" (Candigar), and where he finally made peace by marrying one of his daughters to a Maguindanao sultan. The people of Sarangani had by this time embraced Islam: their second- and third-ranking chiefs were now being called by the Malay Muslim titles of Gugugu and Rajah Laut respectively. It was these officials to whom upper-class litigants appealed for justice, rather than to the two *hukum* (judges) who tried ordinary civil and criminal cases.

The cause of the Sarangani-Maguindanao conflict had been the struggle for control over the coastal peoples who supplied the forest products which were major items of both domestic and foreign trade, especially wax. They were also a source of rice, and the Spaniards had a chance to test both the fertility of their fields and the valor with which they defended them. For three months during the growing season of 1543, Villalobos's men occupied almost 40 hectares of rain-fed pond fields along the coast some 10 kilometers west of Sarangani Bay, under almost constant attack by the owners, who lived in villages on higher ground. By the time the Spaniards finally brought in the harvest, they had lost fifty lives to native bowmen who, as they said, "are good marksmen in the extreme" (Anon. n.d.b, 106). But already in the sixteenth century, these coast dwellers were withdrawing into the interior in the face of escalating slave raids, where many of their descendants today live on the slopes of Mount Apo.

Maguindanao

The Spaniards reported three Mindanao chiefdoms strong enough to dominate their neighbors in the middle of the sixteenth century—Maguindanao, Butuan, and Bisaya. Butuan was considered the wealthiest because of its gold, while Bisaya was considered the least of the three, though it is not clear where this Bisaya was. Earlier expeditions had called the east coast by this name (Vizaya), but Villalobos thought it was Davao Gulf—perhaps an ally or vassal of Buayan in the interior. In least, in the belief that it was one of the power centers, he avoided entering the gulf, hoping to meet less resistance on some smaller island like Sarangani. Maguindanao was the most powerful and best known: its name, in the form of Mindanao, was applied to the whole island by the Portuguese, Spanish, and Dutch alike, and was held in considerable respect in islands to the south. When the Spaniards invaded Cabiao near Sangir a month after they had been driven from the Maguindanao river mouth, its taunting defenders—"for greater insult"—told them to go to Saripara, that is, the lord of Maguindanao. (See fig. 7, an area map of Maguindanao.)

Maguindanao, from *danaw* (lake), meant "to be inundated," and referred to the low-lying delta of the Pulangi River with its two mouths, the location of the modern city of Cotabato. The valley's greatest natural resources, however, were to be found in the upstream region around Buayan—forest products as well as mountain tribes who could be impressed or enslaved to gather these, or themselves be seized and sold in

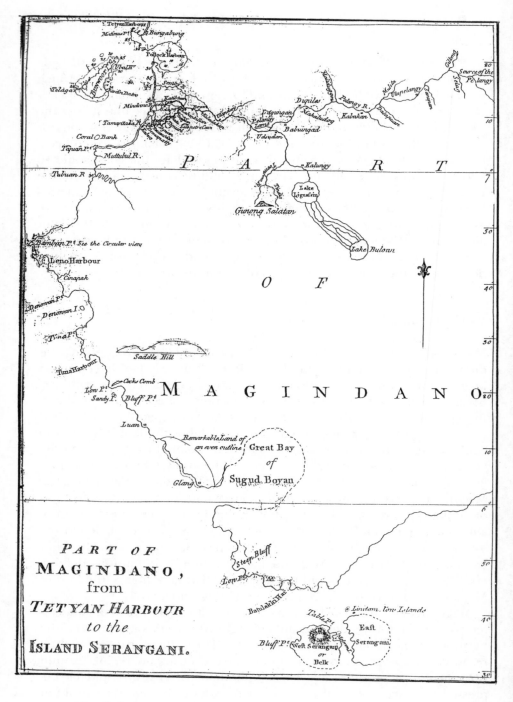

Fig. 7. A map of Maguindanao
(From Thomas Forrest's illustrated *Voyage to New Guinea and the Moluccas* [London: G. Scott: 1779])

slave markets. Competition between royal claimants in the upper and lower valley—*sa raya* and *sa ilud*—were endemic and fluctuated between open hostility and marriage alliances, with supporting chiefs shifting allegiance as political expediency recommended. At the end of the century, the Spaniards recognized Rajah Sirongan of Buayan as the paramount chief in the valley, and fifty years later still reckoned his followers as the majority population. But direct Buayan access to the sea could be inhibited by Maguindanao chiefs at the river mouth, and there the future Sultan Kudarat successfully expanded his base of support with alliances and conquests among coastal chiefs. These included Ilanun sea warriors along Illana Bay, who were kinsmen of the Maranaw on Lake Lanao, and far-ranging Samal Lutaya traders in contact with Malay cultural centers, as well as Samal boat-dwelling fishermen called Badjaw. In fact, Maguindanao supremacy depended on the support of these Samal seafarers. As Father Combés (1667, 31) wrote of them,

> he who can assemble the most from this nation is considered the most powerful and is most feared, for having the means to infest the seas and coasts, taking captives and robbing, and controlling the channels and passages necessary for commerce with the other islands.

Unlike the chiefdoms that the Spaniards encountered in the Visayas, Maguindanao had a centralized government modeled on Muslim states to the south. Its ruler was not merely the chiefest among a congeries of competing datus—*primus inter pares*—but a recognized sultan who inherited his position by direct descent in a royal bloodline, and as such could claim the allegiance of all other chiefs. But as in other Filipino chiefdoms, he directly governed only his own followers: others were governed by their local datus, chiefs who were themselves technically subordinate to him. Because of these separate foci of power, such a sultanate is sometimes called a segmentary state. However, only the sultan could declare war or give permission for others to do so, make decisions affecting the whole sultanate, or represent it in dealing with foreign states. Kudarat, for example, received trade missions from the Dutch and military aid from Ternate, and made a treaty with the Spanish, and an alliance with Sulu by marrying the daughter of Rajah Bongsu.

The sultan's court was convoked with ostentation and ceremony. He himself sat enthroned on a raised dais with his full entourage seated on the floor; foreign emissaries remained on their feet to present official communications in lacquered boxes. Small brass swivel guns *(lantaka)* were conspicuously displayed, not so much as weapons but as symbols of power and authority. Gold ornaments were restricted to the royalty and those whom the sultan favored with handsome gifts like kris with jeweled gold hilts and gold-encrusted sheaths.

Members of the royal family and the court were distinguished by a variety of honorific titles. The general designation for a prince of the blood was *katchil,* while the crown prince was called Rajah Muda (Young Lord); *gugu* was a prime minister; and Rajah Laut (Sea Lord) was the third-ranking dignitary—an office which would later be called Kapitan Laut after the arrival of Europeans. *Orangkaya* (rich people) formed a kind of nobility with the right and means to engage in trade, and *pandita* were wise men knowledgeable in Islamic law and customs. The sultan was also advised in his decisions—and often inhibited—by a council of elders called the Bichara Atas, who represented traditional customs and sources of power.

Maguindanao ruled over a great many pagan peoples, and even the celebrated Kudarat was reported to have sacrificed three of his household slaves during a terrifying volcanic eruption. But the Maguindanao court was clearly a Muslim court. It included members who could speak Arabic, and was frequent host to visiting pandita from abroad, and even slaves were permitted to chide royal masters who were inattentive to their personal prayers. The sultan himself was expected to be well versed in matters of the faith, an exemplar of its precepts, and scrupulous in observing its rites. They could all speak Malay (and Kudarat also knew the language of his Ternatan allies) and more than one was able to engage Spanish missionaries in religious debate.

They also behaved with the dignity and magnanimity befitting their position. Kudarat's father, Buisan, fed captured Jesuit Melchor Hurtado from his own board in 1603, and Sirongan of Buayan billeted him in a separate house with slaves to serve him, and his wife rendered him a thirteen-course farewell banquet when he was ransomed, with apologies for the lack of pork and wine.

According to traditional genealogies *(tarsila),* the Maguindanao sultanate was founded by a royal prince from Johore named Muhammad Kabungsuwan, whose father was an Arab sharif, that is, a descendant of the Prophet Muhammad. The sultanate of Johore was founded in 1527 by the son of the last sultan of Malacca, who had been driven out of that great Asian emporium by the Portuguese in 1511. Kabungsuwan would presumably have arrived between or after these dates, and it was his son Makaalang whom the Spaniards knew as Saripara. The royal families not only of

Maguindanao but also of Marawi and Buayan all claim descent from him.

If Maguindanao is the Mindolang of Chinese records, as seems likely, it was already a Chinese port of call in the fourteenth century. Later in 1420 a Chinese emissary established diplomatic and trade relations with nearby Kumalarang—that is, he attracted a local ruler to travel to Peking to formalize what the imperial court called tributary status. The Pulangi river port would therefore have offered commercial opportunities for the scion of a displaced Malaccan dynasty. Indeed, early in the Spanish regime, it was a regular port of call on a trade route that passed down the western littoral of the archipelago through Mindoro, Panay, Dapitan, and Sulu to the Moluccas.

Sulu

The island and archipelago of Sulu were not, of course, part of Mindanao, but they were subject to the same Malay Muslim influence which extended to the neighboring shores of that island. Like Maguindanao, Sulu had a centralized sultanate, and like Maguindanao, too, its access to overseas commerce depended on Sama Lutaw supporters. But the dominant people were the Taosug—"people of the current"—who, to judge from the similarity of languages, had their origin in Butuan. Indeed, Sultan Barafa Shah Tengah at the end of the sixteenth century was said to have been a Butuanon himself.

We have no sixteenth-century descriptions of Sulu culture. However, when Father Combés (1667, 44) visited the royal court in Jolo on a diplomatic mission in the seventeenth, he later described their rice cakes with scorn ("The durian sauce tastes like turpentine") and their unorthodox Islamic behavior at length: outside the capital, he said, they participated in drunken revels. He also wrote that they attributed miracles to the relics of their First Teacher, a Muslim pioneer whose venerated tomb made Jolo "the Mecca of this archipelago."

He reported that thievery was punished by amputation of fingers or hands, and sodomy or incest by drowning, and called the warlike people of the interior, Ximbanaos, from *gimba,* war drum. He also made the significant observation that overlords referred to their vassals as slaves, though they may well have been chiefs with their own followings. One of these, for example, refused to release a Christian captive for the ransom price agreed upon by the sultan and a Jesuit missionary. Combés even concluded that there were only two social classes—chiefs and slaves—not noting that the overlords *(tuam* or *orangkaya)* were of different ethnic groups from their vassals—for example, Joloanos (that is, Taosug) dominating Lutaw, or Lutaw dominating Suban-on and Manobo tribal chieftains.

The sultanate of Sulu was founded in the second half of the fifteenth century by an Arab sharif named Abu Bakr, whose tombstone gives his full titles as Paduka Maharasi Maulana al-Sultan Sharif ul-Hashim. He married into the local nobility, and his father-in-law was a Sumatran prince who had also married a Sulu princess. Sulu, however, had already been recognized as a Chinese tributary state when three Sulu rulers presented themselves at court in 1417, and one, Paduka Batara, was given an imperial jade seal recognizing him as senior to the other two. Such status was usually granted to petitioners who were perceived as potential sources of trade goods. That Sulu qualified is indicated by the non-Sulu products they were able to present during a second mission in 1421—brazilwood, black pepper, cubebs, tin, and more than one kind of camphor. Sulu's own pearls were legendary for their size and quality. Paduka Batara's younger brother, Paduka Suli, presented one recorded in Chinese annals as weighing 7 ounces; Father Combés (1667, 73) saw one in a sword hilt which he said was "the size of a musket ball"; Magellan's chronicler Pigafetta said that the sultan of Brunei had two of them—which he did not see—as big as hen's eggs.

Sulu and Borneo were rivals, their royal families were intermarried, and in the sixteenth century, Brunei was claiming sovereignty over Jolo. The famous Sultan Bulkeiah, who was known to Pigafetta as Saripara, was married to a Sulu princess named Putri Laila Men Chanei, and personally told the Italian chronicler that he had once attacked Sulu with 500 warships. That he may actually have ruled in Sulu is suggested by a Sulu tradition that marks him as their fourth sultan, Amir ul-Umara. When a Sulu ruler married the sultan's daughter in Brunei in 1535, a Portuguese officer who was present surmised that the bridegroom was the sultan's vassal. The seventh sultan of Sulu, Pangiran Buddiman, was married to Bulkeiah's granddaughter, the sister of Sultan Saif ur-Rejel; when Pangiran Buddiman joined Saif ur-Rejel in resisting a Spanish attack, the Spaniards thought that Buddiman was a Bornean himself. Brunei tradition identifies Bulkeiah as folk hero Nakhoda Ragam, believed to have conquered the Philippines in an expedition during which he gave the name of one island to each of a ganta of pepper seeds. In the popular Bornean epic, Sha'er Awang Semaun, these conquests are all made by head-taking hero Semaun, and produce tribute from Sulu and Manila in the form of Chinese porcelain.

CHAPTER 10

Bikolandia

Bikolandia—what the Spaniards called El Bicol—includes the modern provinces of Sorsogon, Albay, Camarines Sur, and Camarines Norte. The area was first reported as Ibalon from the old name of Sorsogon Bay. More particularly, the well-populated valley of the Bikol River in what is now Camarines Sur was reported as Camarines (Kamalignon), derived from Kamalig (now Naga City). *Camarines* was no doubt given popular currency by the fact that the Bikol *kamalig* (boat shed) was commonly called a *camarín* by the Spaniards. It was this fertile river valley which watered the fields of irrigated rice which were a distinctive feature of Bikol culture, and supported communities of four hundred to eight hundred households.[27]

The Bikolanos themselves were described as warriors, traders, goldsmiths, and almost the same as Visayans. They defended themselves with such spirit, Father Martín de Rada (1574, 181) said, "that more people have died in that land than in any other part which has been conquered." They traded by both land and sea, and their goldsmiths traveled from place to place, working gold mines in Paracale, Catanduanes, and Masbate. They tattooed in proportion to their performance in battle, and their general similarity to *pintado* Visayans can be seen from Fray Marcos de Lisboa's

179

1615(?) *Diccionario y vocabulario de el idioma Español y Bicol.* Though local variations are worth noting, it is clear that Bikolanos and Visayans shared a common culture.

Certainly Bikolanos looked like Visayans. Dutch Admiral Oliver Van Noort (1601, 93) met Albay chiefs in 1600 who were "very nicely, beautifully and artistically" tattooed. Elizabethan corsair Thomas Cavendish described one whose "skinne was carved and cut with sundry and many strakes and devices all over his body" (Pretty 1588, 41). Bikolanos filed their teeth, colored them red or black, and pegged them with gold; they moulded infants' skulls and flattened their noses by head binding.

Men were circumcised and wore penis pins—with real braves burning scars on their arms in addition to their tattoos—and wore G-strings, or simply a blanket wrapped around the waist. *Lakweg* were the dangling ends; *singal,* the part that passed between the legs; and *pintosan,* the bulge in front. A man who was sent back and forth to the same place many times might complain, "Nagbabahag na akon dalan, kyaning papapagbalik balika ako [I kept putting the road on like a G-string]" (Lisboa 1628a, 46). Women wore tube skirts or *tapis*—called *lawas* if worn high enough to cover the breasts—and both men and women used jackets and ankle-length tunics called *lambong* or *yambong,* and an artificial switch of hair to add to their own.

Bikolanos shared a common technology not only with Visayans but with most Filipinos from Mindanao to northern Luzon. They grew rice without plows, harvested it panicle by panicle, and milled it with mortar and pestle; extracted sugarcane juice by pressing the cane under a lever; and produced alcohol with a still made of a hollow tree trunk. Gold was mined both by excavating and by panning in streams; metal workers used a two-piston Malay forge; and women wove abaca and cotton cloth on backstrap looms, and made pots by hand without wheel or kiln. Carpenters constructed nailless houses by joinery, as well as built boats ranging from one-piece dugouts to plank-built men-o'-war and cargo vessels, products especially well known from Catanduanes, whence boat builders literally peddled their wares by sailing them to other islands.

Agriculture

Like the Visayans—and most other Filipinos—the Bikolanos grew both rice and root crops in hillside swiddens; but unlike them, they also grew rice under irrigation. The Bikol River basin appears to have been one of the most heavily inundated valleys in the archipelago. It was crisscrossed by smaller rivers and creeks which flowed into and out of one another seasonally, and every year the river itself spread as far as 15 kilometers from its banks. Deep water, whether in fields or streams, was called *salog*, and what the Spaniards called the Río Grande, Bikolanos simply called the Salog, with those living near it being Siminalog. Shifting depths and shallows made river navigation treacherous, and considerable hydraulic control was required to make even irrigated rice farming practicable. This extensive territory unsuitable for swidden farming no doubt inspired many innovations in agricultural techniques. A *masarawat* was a farmer who experimented with seeds by planting out of season, and *lataw* (to float) was a kind of platform or raft of intertwined weeds, covered with soil and planted to taro, which rose and fell with the water level.

Danawan were fields of standing water, especially those that required no artificial irrigation; and *layaw* or *kanaw-kanaw*, those with especially deep mud. *Atyan* meant to be left dry by receding waters. The general term for irrigating—that is, leading water into fields or from one field to another— was *pasakay*. *Sagop* was a dam; *sagobong*, a canal; and *tangharan*, the sign put on the irrigation ditches to indicate the division of water into different fields.

The additional importance of these fields as a source of protein is indicated by the special vocabulary pertaining to the presence of fish. *Sarang* was for fish to collect where the water was in motion; *aboab*, to burrow into the mud when chased; and *salakat*, to escape when the field overflowed after a heavy rain. It may be significant that fields were included along with palm trees and houses as *gatang*, alienable property.

Tarok was the general term for transplanting, but there were two methods of producing the seedlings. One method, *sabod*, was to sow seeds in a seedbed *(pimpin)* by broadcasting *(sabuag)*, with *dalogi* being the seedlings ready for transplanting *(hagidhid)* in the shallow water along the edges of a field. The second method was to wrap the seeds, already germinated by soaking, in wet leaves *(balanhig)* until they sprouted, whereupon they would be placed on inundated trays *(tabaw)* to put out roots. They would then be transplanted matted together *(tagbong)* on the edges of the field.

As said earlier, transplanting into the soil where seedlings were left to grow was tarok; however, a third transplanting *(talostos)* might be necessary to find deeper water. As for harvesting, a unique Bikol technique was the use of a conch shell in place of an iron blade, both called *gata*.

Other than wet rice farming, Bikol swiddening, hunting, fishing, and cooking were the same as Visayan. Millet, taro, and yams, both domestic

181

and wild, were eaten in place of rice or mixed with it, and sago flour was made from *Metroxylon* palms. Despite the abundance of rice in some places and for some people, the staple Bikol food was root crops: Lisboa (1628b, 17) glossed them with expressions like "It is the sustenance of these people" or "They eat it in times of hunger." And he called most of them *camotes*.

Both deer and wild boar were called *babuy* (domestic pigs were *orig*). As for wild carabao, their presence in the language is noteworthy: they were caught in pit traps *(atbong)*, and even their flayed hide *(bange)* was eaten. They were called *anuang* or *damulag*—or, more elegantly, *samayaw*—and ones mature enough to fight with their horns were *atandukan* (from *tanduk*, a piercing wound). But the word *karabaw* was only introduced in Father Lisboa's own time (he arrived in 1585).

Drinking

The production and consumption of alcoholic beverages was an important part of Bikol social life. *Tabang*, to help somebody out, also meant for two men to drink together; *silo* was to enter somebody's house with a token offering of fish or meat in hopes of getting a drink; and *tabad* was to return a favor by offering a drink—though tabad itself meant diluted wine. *Patulid* was a farewell drinkfest for somebody leaving for another town, and *patostos* was for a crowd to gather in a newly constructed house—"to test if the floor would carry the weight" (Lisboa 1628a, 285). To cause fellow drinkers to overindulge was a normal part of male play during drinkfests. *Alap* meant to toast somebody after drinking yourself; *padagmok* was to pass the cup to the same person again and again; *pintong*, to offer an especially large container; and *pisaw*, to pass the dipper itself. The standard bamboo cup was the half-pint *galong*. The drinks themselves were the same as those in the Visayas—*tuba, pangasi, intos,* and *alak*—but with certain refinements.

Tuba, fermented palm sap, was called *paog* or *lagoy,* and a confection called *labay* was made of it when still sweet by the addition of shredded young coconut flesh. *Solay* was a mixture of seasoning put in the jar where rice-wine pangasi was to be brewed—for example, *hilhilig*, toasted, gingered rice— and the mash itself was called *nasi*. *Base* was sugarcane juice squeezed out with a levered press, boiled to produce intos, and flavored with *pogod* bark. Intos was called *gabuyo* when young and low in alcoholic content, and *pinokate* if boiled down to a third its volume. A special liquor *(simbog)* was made by the admixture to sweet tuba of coconut milk or honey. The dregs or mash of any these beverages were also eaten, and presented as a special favor *(bayakaw)* to dancers at a feast. *Arak* was any hard liquor distilled in a wooden still.

Social Structure

Although sixteenth-century Spanish accounts make it possible to describe Visayan and Tagalog society in considerable detail, Franciscan missionaries in Bikol limited themselves to the comment that the natives had no form of government at all—*ni rey ni roque* (neither king nor castle). Fray Juan Pobre de Zamora (1595, 398) said, "He who has more gold or more people was able to subjugate those who had less, so that many of these became slaves," and Father Marcelo de Ribadeneira illustrated with the case of one who was so moved by a sermon on hellfire that he offered to restore all his ill-gotten wealth to those whom he had despoiled. Fray Juan felt that this lack of social order—"each one lives where and how he fancies"—made Bikolanos slow to accept Spanish concepts of law and polity (Zamora 1595, 398). Nonetheless, it appears that Bikolanos had a three-class social order like their Filipino neighbors to the north and south.

Lisboa defined both *datu* and *ginoo* as "rich and elite *(principal)*," and *maginoo* or *hiyangta* as one especially prominent among them. They were addressed as Kagoangnan (elder or senior), the equivalent of Lord and Lady, and men of distinguished lineage or accomplishment often assumed a flattering alias *(bansag)* which they passed on as a surname—like Makatikba, "Terrifier." But these were not political offices. The head of a community *(duluhan)* was called a *kagduluhan;* the ruler of a town (*banwaan*—or *longsod* in poetry) was a *namamanwa;* and one who was recognized by other chiefs as senior was a *pono* (first or foremost)—for example, *an pono sa banwaaan.* Kings or governors outside Bikolandia, or persons of similarly autocratic position, were called *hade.*

Timawa in Visayan and Tagalog culture were supporters of datus who accompanied them to war, but who were known after colonial pacification simply as freemen or freedmen. Thus, like other seventeenth-century lexicographers, Lisboa defined the term as "an ordinary person of the town who is neither chief nor slave, [or] a free man who was a slave." The form *natitimawa* reflects Bikol social mobility: "for a chief to become a timawa, or plebeian, by becoming poor, [or] for a slave to become free" (Lisboa 1628a, 393). These timawa would presumably have included the *dukha,* poor people, and *pido,* people of low estate. But the presence of another word for a "free man who is not a slave"—*batak (binabatak:* to be freed)—

suggests that the Bikol word *timawa* may have undergone the same shift in meaning as its Visayan-Tagalog equivalent (Lisboa 1628a, 61).

Slaves were called *oripun* in general, or *pandowan* in poetry, or pejoratively as *pongka* and *salpok*. *Gintobo* was a born slave or one inherited; *dayo* was one stationed at his master's tomb to protect the body against witches, and *sayat* was one sacrificed in mourning for a chief. These slaves came into their condition through capture, debt, or inheritance, and were bought and sold. *Bihag* was a captive; *sapod*, a person seized while lost. *Salew* was to deal in slaves, boats, or dogs. *Natubos* was for a captive to be ransomed or a debt redeemed; *hiwas*, to be freed from slavery or debt; and *hinalostos* was for a part owner to pay the remaining price to take full possession. *Kadangan* was one who lived alone with a slave, but slave concubinage with an upper-class owner was called *kalit, payat,* or *otay,* all words which implied deceit or fraud.

Religion

Juan Pobre de Zamora felt that the absence of Mexican-style temples and idolatry left the Bikol religious consciousness such a blank page–*tamquam tabula rasa*—that the very concepts of deity and worship had yet to be inscribed upon it. All they had, he said, were "superstitions, auguries, and some tricks the Devil played on them." In like vein, his Franciscan contemporary's dictionary reduces Bikol religion to the worship of ancestral spirits called *anito*. It gives the following definitions:

> *Anito:* [So] they called the souls of their ancestors, to whom they made figures of wood. . . . *Nagaanito:* to make a sacrifice, or drinkfest as a fiesta, to such anitos. . . . *Naatang:* to offer food to the anitos, as they did in ancient times, and afterwards they would eat it (Lisboa 1628a, 26).

Lisboa said that these figures, like the spirits themselves, were also called *diwata,* and thought that they included all idols or fetishes, large or small—*lagdong, pararangpan, tango, tatawo,* and *tinatawo*. He did not name any nature spirits or individual gods—nor any Supreme Deity—but listed a number of guardian spirits or demons—*alagad, gugurang, okot,* even *bathala,* of whom he wrote: "They say it was an anito that brought good luck to the one it accompanied" (Lisboa 1628a, 61). Thus, if a man was never hit by objects thrown at him, he was said to be *batalaan*. But Lisboa was also aware that Bikol religion was suffering attrition in his own day. *Alagad* was now being applied not to spirits but to any constant companion, and *lalala,* to

184

go out to check one's crops, had originally meant an anniversary pig sacrifice at the grave site of some departed relative.

However these supernatural forces were explained, they intervened in human affairs to sanction proper social behavior. If an upper-class lady, especially a real beauty, went out to the fields or into a strange community, she would become sick *(nadaay)*, and if a man was tattooed without having defeated an enemy in war, he would sicken or even die unless he performed a *sibong* cleansing rite. If one person's fields flourished ahead of other people's, it was considered a sign of impending disaster or bad crops. If a person showed hesitation or repugnance while enshrouding a parent's corpse, he would develop a facial tic or palsied limbs. *Dawat* was a destructive storm brought on by incest in the community. In addition, there were dangerous creatures such as the ghoulish *aswang* or *silagan,* and sorcerers *(agwahang)* who could cast spells. Even some chiefs might be so endowed with occult power *(pohon)* that any lower-class person who ate from plates or drank from cups that such a chief had used, would become ill.

Religious practitioners were female shamans called *baliyan,* or male transvestites called *asog.* They wore gold ornaments on their forehead, took ritual baths, spoke with the voice of departed spirits, and delivered prayers in song—though the people's response, "Ahom!" may have been derived from the Christian *amen.* Healing ceremonies included chicken sacrifices or smearing the patient's forehead with masticated betel nut. The precarious nature of infancy is reflected in the number of such rites performed for children—for example, *karinga,* the sacrifice of a pig carefully raised since the birth of the child. Serious illness required calling back the patient's wandering soul *(kalag),* which was then restored by shaking an *anahaw* sprout over the body. Shoots of the anahaw palm *(Palma brava)* were symbols of the life force itself: they were placed on the prow of cruisers departing on a raid, and brandished by returning victors, and might be stuck on the grave of the one whose death was avenged by the raid.

During a Bikol wake, the cadaver was exposed, fastened on a seat as if alive, while relatives donned mourning attire, began a fast, and cut their hair. There were two kinds of coffins—a wooden casket called *kabaong,* and a *longon* hollowed out of a whole log, and these were either buried or placed in a shed called *kalang.* The house in which an especially powerful chief died was abandoned, leaving his body in it. Gold ornaments which accompanied a body to the grave were often removed before interment, in which case they had to be disinfected by a sprinkling rite called *basbas.* After the grave was filled in, the *ayay* rite was performed in which the grave was covered with unhusked rice. In the case of a slave sacrifice *(hogot),* the double burial was called *lontog,* a word which meant the additional sum required by an underweight measure of gold.

The Alphabet

Missionary accounts make it clear that the Bikolanos were using an alphabet by the end of the sixteenth century. Juan Pobre de Zamora preserved the translation of a Bikol letter written by a chief in Gumaca *en letras tagalas,* and Father Ribadeneira (1601, 61) said that many Christian converts made little booklets "in their characters or letters" of lessons they learned in church. Fray Juan said the same thing, but added, "Never in their paganism did they ever use books" (Zamora 1595, 400). They called letters or any writing *guhit;* and the alphabet, *basahan.* They made the vowel signs—Tagalog *kudlit*—as little *V*-shaped marks called *kaholowan.* They distinguished three vowels and fifteen consonants, one more than the standard *baybayin* because of the addition of the letter *r.* Lisboa (1628a, 36) intended to illustrate these letters in his dictionary, but unfortunately the first edition (1754) has only blank spaces where the Bikol characters should be, presumably because of printing difficulties. The following is a typical entry:

> *Ba:* So they pronounce the B in their A B C's, and they write it with this character [ ] including B and A in the same character. And to say *Be* or *Bi,* they put a dot or comma on the left side like this [] and to say *Bo* or *Bu,* they put the comma or dot on the right side of the character like this [] because they read and write from the bottom up.

Warfare

Father Rada (1574, 181) referred to Bikol bravery unambiguously in 1574:

> They are the most valiant and best armed people of all these islands, because, although they never attacked the Spaniards, they defended themselves in all their towns, and were unwilling to give up unless they were conquered by force of arms.

Kota was any wall or fortification of a town, while *bantara* was a bamboo tower for archers armed with bows *(sikarom)* so long they had to be held under the foot to put the bowstring on. Bikolanos went into battle protected by carabao-hide armor and long wooden shields, and fought in

186

hand-to-hand combat with kris, *baladaw (garod* if mounted on a shaft like a spear), or a wide shortsword *(baed),* with a knife *(lagtip)* held in the shield hand. Any of these weapons might be decorated with locks of hair dyed red *(bangot)* if carried by chiefs. But the arquebuses, artillery, helmets, and full body armor of iron which were reported from the Salcedo expedition of 1573 were no doubt a confusion with Japanese weapons which that conquistador encountered the year before in a naval engagement on the Ilocos coast.

Bikol belligerence, however, was not limited to defense. *Gubat* was to conquer and raid, and *mangayaw* to do so by sea, either with a lone cruiser *(mongsad)* or ships in company *(abay).* Tarok (to transplant) was a rite in which a palm frond brought back from war was stuck on a relative's grave "as a sign that they had killed somebody to avenge his death" (Lisboa 1628a, 385). But raiding was usually a more businesslike venture—as evidenced by the word *hampil,* which was a contract for a joint raid where a shipowner and his partner split the outfitting costs between them but the owner received two-thirds of the booty.

Belligerence also had its place within the community. *Gagasod* was to swagger around boasting and threatening; *angat* was to challenge a man to come down from his house and fight; *rawal,* to enter the house for the same purpose; and *angag* was for two men to fight over one woman. *Natad* was feuding between clans, and *tokol* was a victim taken in revenge for a grievance committed by some other member of his family or community; but *bolaw* was a vendetta between two towns, and *budhi* was to kill an outsider.

The Lisboa dictionary contains one of the richest vocabularies of martial terminology in early Spanish lexicons of Philippine languages. It is worth sampling at some length.

Bonglo	For a ship's captain to buy or ransom a captive taken by one of his comrades
Bantolan	Reinforcements or substitutes
Dahog	To shout at the defeated
Dongas	An enemy attack on a town
Gaba	A surprise attack, or to take a victim by stealth
Hagbo	To finish off an enemy without leaving one alive or any goods after plundering
Laban	Foe, opponent; to fight
Labha or *dahas*	To take by violence
Libon	For a highwayman to kill on the road, or steal livestock
Limbaga	To exercise with arms in preparation for war
Limo	To kill by treachery

187

Maghat	Night raiders who enter houses to kill
Maray	Good fortune on a sea raid
Pogot	A head, hand, or foot cut from the body
Puti	For a captain to be the first to die
Rarong	To come out of battle wounded
Sabo	One about to fall into raiders' hands
Tangkas	To despoil captives or corpses of their clothes
Taop	A night attack on a sleeping target, or hunting before dawn
Tongol or *pogot*	To cut off a head
Tonob	To confront the enemy face to face, waiting for the signal to attack

188

CHAPTER 11

Tagalog Culture and Technology

Tagalog geographic terminology reflected their physical environment. It differed from that of the Visayans, most of whose islands were divided by north-south mountain ranges that produced an east-west dichotomy between upstream and downstream, *ilaya* and *ilawod*.

The Tagalog's World

The Luzon Sierra Madres to the east of the Tagalogs descended not to a seacoast but to the riverine plains of Bulacan, Laguna, and Manila Bay. Ilaya simply meant higher ground, with the highest being the mountains between Laguna de Bay and the Pacific—Kalaylayan—but it was not contrasted with *ilaot*. *Laot* meant the high seas, *dagat* being any salt sea, and *wala*, waters farthest from the land. Similarly, the Tagalogs were not obsessed with the Pacific monsoons and trade winds which struck the Visayas from the northeast, east, and southeast. They recognized *hilaga* as the north wind; *balas* as the northeast; *amihan*, the east; *timog*, the south; and *habagat*, the west. However, they gave special attention to the weather they encountered on the South China Sea which was their commercial highway to Borneo and Malacca: *balaklawot* was the northwest wind in general, but *aguyoy* was a gentle wind from the same bearing, and *dayaday*, a stormy one. They also distinguished among *bagyo* (typhoon); *sigwa*, a heavy rainstorm blowing from one direction only; and *hangin*, a squall at sea.

The word *taga* meant a native inhabitant, and *tagalog* was apparently a contraction of *taga ilog*, river dweller, presumably in distinction from *taga bundok*, the mountain dwellers between Nagcarlan (Laguna) and Lamon Bay, though they spoke the same language. Not all speakers of Tagalog called themselves by that name, however: Father Juan de Oliver, preaching to Batangueños on God's being Father of all people, distinguished Kumintang (Batangas) from Tagalog, Spanish, and Chinese. *Bundok* were high forested mountains; *gulod*, a lower cordillera; and *taluktok*, its upper slopes; the Spaniards called them all *tingues* from the Malay word for high, and coined the term *tinguianes* for their inhabitants. The plains of Lumban, Pila, and Santa Cruz below Mahayhay were real savannas called Parang from the word meaning any unforested grasslands suitable for agriculture. *Bakuwod* was high land that remained dry in time of flooding.

Tagalogs called themselves *tawo* (person, a term they did not apply to other tribes or nations: foreigners who spoke other languages were called *samot* or *samok*. Blacks living in the mountains were called *ayta*—or *dumagat* (sea people) if they lived on the east coast—but *agta* in Manila, or *ita* by the more sophisticated, presumably from Malay *itam* (black). Blacks from Africa introduced by Portuguese slave traders were called *pugot*. *Baluga* was the offspring of two different races—for example, an Ayta and a non-Negro, or a Spaniard and a Filipina. Chinese were called *sanglay* from two Chinese words—*chang* and *lai* in modern orthography—meaning "regularly come," that is, itinerants who could be trusted to keep commercial contracts from one trading season to the next. Old folks, however, called them *langlang*, which also meant pirate or corsair.[28]

A Tagalog's primary identity was with his *bayan* (town or community) and loyalty to his *kababayan* (townmates). (Father Oliver [1590a, 214] called heaven, "Bayan nang Dios" in contrast to this world, "Bayan nang luha [Land of tears]." Hospitality distinguished between inviting townmates *(patnugot)* and taking in travelers *(tuloy)*—for example, "Saan dito ang tinutuloyan nang manga ibangbayan [Where do strangers put up here]?"—though hospitality itself was so highly valued that the word *tawo* could also mean guest—*nagatatawo* was to invite guests (San Buenaventura 1613, 357). So, too, outsiders who settled in town *(salayo* or *salyo)* were distinguished from settlers who married in *(dugang)*. Bayan also meant the atmosphere—"Malinaw ang bayan [The weather's clear]"—but it did not

190

mean a people or language group (San Buenaventura 1613, 574). Indeed, even clear geographic regions were referred to by different names according to who was speaking; thus, Laguna de Bay was called Pulilan in Manila but Dagat by those who lived on its shores, while taga bundok neighbors called it Duungan, a place where boats tied up. And Lusong, what the Chinese and Malays called the Manila area, simply meant to come down from the heights.

Naturally, Tagalogs in the mountains had some customs different from those of the lowlanders. They fought wars with slings, carried babies hung from the shoulder in blankets, and communicated from mountain to mountain by beating resonant blocks of wood which could be heard long distances. In selling cotton thread, they counted eighty-four thread strands to the skein instead of seventy, and men still wore heavy shell bracelets which had disappeared from more "civilized" areas. Special vocabulary reflected their swidden farming techniques—*bakal* was a dibble stick; *gusamos*, to weed between rice plants; *gusad*, to pull up the roots of last year's straw; and any field under cultivation was *linang*. Old men counted *isa, alwa, atlo, pat*—one, two, three, four—instead of *isa, dalawa, tatlo, apat*. But many dialect variations were no more than those between any two Tagalog regions. Wild amaranth was called *bayangbang* in the hills, but *halom* in Pililla and Moron; *banlowag* (to water the wine) was *talas* in the bundok; and *suhol* (remuneration for a witness swearing in one's favor) in Laguna meant gifts a groom gave his bride's relatives, but was also called *talas* by highlanders.

The Borneo connection. The chiefdom of Manila, located in the present Intramuros district, was probably founded as a Bornean trading colony about 1500, with a royal prince marrying into the local ruling family. This was a common practice by which Islam spread throughout insular Southeast Asia: the first sultan of Sulu was the son-in-law of a Sumatran prince, and the sultanate of Maguindanao was founded by a scion of the Malaccan royal family. Chinese records list Mindoro (Ma-i) as a dependency of Brunei in the fourteenth century, and when Spanish Governor Francisco Sande invaded Borneo in 1578, Mindoro chiefs in his company acknowledged the Brunei sultan's uncle, Panguiran Salalila, as their overlord. The Manila ruler known to the Spaniards as Rajah Matanda was the grandson of Sultan Bulkeiah of Brunei, the Saripara whom Pigafetta had met there fifty years earlier. Brunei folk history identifies Bulkeiah as Nakhoda Ragam, the reputed conqueror of the Philippines, and tradition even names the cannon with which he was said to have taken Manila—Si-Gantar Alam, "Earthshaking Thunderer."

191

When the Spaniards arrived in 1570, the port of Manila had three recognized rulers—Ache, the old rajah (Ladyang Matanda), and his nephew, Soliman, the young rajah, and, in Tondo north of the Pasig River, Banaw Lakandula, Ache's cousin. Lakandula monopolized trade with two or three annual junks from China, but Manila vessels retailed the goods through the central Philippines, for which reason they were known to the Visayans as "Chinese." For the same reason, when Legazpi in Cebu wished to open trade relations with Manila, he sent Ladyang Matanda a diplomatic gift addressed to "the King of Luzon."

Ache's maternal grandfather was the Bornean sultan, and in 1521 he was in Brunei to command a naval task force for his grandfather and to marry a cousin, but was captured by the survivors of the Magellan expedition.[29] He was released on payment of a princely ransom. However, a Makassarese slave of Ache called Pazeculan was not freed, but he spoke enough Spanish to later conclude a peace pact between his Spanish captors and Tuan Maamud of Palawan.

Back in Manila, Ache experienced a deathbed conversion to Christianity in 1572, and named Rajah Soliman as his heir, his only son having predeceased him. Lakandula died three years later and was succeeded by his grandnephew, Soliman's adopted son Agustin Legazpi—evidently sponsored for baptism by Adelantado Miguel de Legazpi himself—who married the daughter of Sultan Bulkeiah's uncle Salalila.

When Governor Sande invaded Borneo in 1578, he took along two Balayan (Batangas) chiefs who had had long residence in that island, both of whom were captured by Panguiran Salalila during a naval engagement at the mouth of Brunei Bay. One of these Balayan chiefs was Martin Magadchina who had spent eight years in Borneo on trade, and who was killed following the battle; the other was Francisco Magat who was captured but ransomed off by a Bornean relative.

There were also resident Tagalogs who fought on the Bornean side. Matelin Magat Buxa Amat had lived in Borneo since childhood, and was related to both Martin and Francisco: his wife recovered Martin's body and buried him in her family grave, and Matelin himself ransomed off Francisco for a 175–kilo culverin. There was also Ami Gikon of Tondo, who had been there since 1565; he commanded an eighty-four-man warship mounting twelve guns during the action, but was not actually a chief: rather, he was a slave of Agustin Legazpi's. Following the Spanish victory, the governor demanded that Lakandula's and Soliman's property and slaves being held in Borneo be delivered to their heirs, and took twenty-seven vessels and an unspecified number of captives back to Manila, including Salalila and the daughter who became Agustin's bride.

However, in 1585 Agustin was deposed and jailed by the colonial government, together with his brothers and relatives, for having given his mother a Muslim burial. Not surprisingly, he headed an abortive uprising against the Spaniards the next year and was executed, the last Manila ruler to hold a royal office.

The town of Manila—or more correctly, Maynila—occupied what is now the Intramuros district, with a stockaded fortress on the site of Fort Santiago and a gun foundry in which the invaders found moulds for cannons and one large piece in the process of manufacture. Part of the present Intramuros, however, was then uninhabited swampland—the location of Letran College, for example. The present Ermita district was covered with sand dunes, and Bagumbayan ("New Town") was built by Filipinos displaced by the Spanish occupation of Manila. Upstream was another chiefdom in Namayan (Santa Ana) supposedly governed by a Rajah Kalamayin. To the south, Pasay was said to have been settled by a distant relative of his by that name, the child of a Bornean slave.

The Manila population was about six thousand, with forty Chinese and twenty Japanese, including two Christians.[30] The Chinese were actually political refugees who had fled to Japan before coming to the Philippines, and had been settled as fishermen and farmers by Lakandula in Longos (Tondo), where they promptly diked, drained, and reclaimed land along the waterfront, which was later known as Baybay.

The presence of Spanish customers willing to pay for merchandise in Mexican silver quickly attracted thousands more. There were only four junks anchored in Manila in 1570, but nine arrived in 1577, twenty-one in 1580, and forty-eight in 1588, with four thousand resident Chinese in 1586, and twenty-four thousand in 1598, even after thirteen thousand had been deported. This phenomenal growth of immigration profoundly affected the local economy by the introduction of new plants and fowls, horses and cows, and technology like the rice mill and two-roller sugarcane press, perhaps even the plow.

The Malay connection. Malay was the trade language from Malacca to the Moluccas in the sixteenth century. Indeed, it was in Malacca that Europeans first met Filipinos, ten years before Magellan died in Maktan. They called them Luzones—which the Portuguese spelled Luções—and who were no doubt Tagalogs since they were Muslims and were at first mistaken for Borneans. Tomé Pires (1515, 377) said in his *Summa Oriental* that Borneans and Tagalogs "were almost one people." There was also a colony of some five hundred Tagalogs at Minjam on the west coast of the

Malay Peninsula (where the Chinese had noted Mindoro cotton in the fourteenth century), and the Luzones community in Malacca had their own shops and included a number of prominent businessman. One of them, Regimo Diraja, was appointed *temenggong* (police commissioner or magistrate) by the Portuguese governor.

Luzon traders carried foodstuffs, wax, honey, and low-grade gold to Borneo, whence they proceeded to Malacca, but had only two or three ships on the run. But they ranged much farther afield than Malacca: Pigafetta noted a Luzon vessel loading sandalwood in Timor; Pires (1515, 362), describing the Chinese port of Canton before any Portuguese had seen it, commented, "This the Luções say who have been there," and Bras Bayao (1540), the Portuguese king's factor in Borneo, said there were many good pilots there, "mainly some called Luções, who are discoverers." It may be worth noting that Canton, Malacca, and Timor describe a triangle which included all of insular Southeast Asia. And since Magellan was one of the Portuguese who took Malacca in 1511, one wonders if he could have been unaware of the existence and location of Regimo Diraja's homeland. Perhaps the "discovery of the Philippines" was made in Malacca.

The fortunes of the Malacca Filipinos were not based on such petty commerce as the Philippines trade. Rather, they came from shipowning and the underwriting of large-scale export ventures in the China market, even letting out small shares which illiterate Portuguese sailors could afford. Regimo was the head of this community; he had migrated there from Luzon, married into a local family, and received the title of *diraja,* and then attracted his countrymen to follow him. A genuine tycoon who sent junks to Brunei, China, Pasai (Sumatra), Siam, and Sunda, he died in 1513, leaving his widow, sons, and father-in-law to continue his business. Another Filipino magnate was Surya Diraja who paid the Portuguese 9,000 cruzados in gold to retain his plantation and country estate, and annually sent 175 tons of pepper to China. One of his junks sailed in the first Portuguese fleet to pay an official visit to the Chinese empire.

But what impressed the Portuguese more than the Luzones' trade, was their participation in the local wars to control the Straits of Malacca. Luzon mercenaries took part in an unsuccessful attempt by the exiled sultan of Malacca to retake that port from the Portuguese in 1525, during which the "captain of the Luções" sailed in the flagship with warriors whom chronicler João de Barros considered "the most warlike and valiant of these parts" (Barros 1628; Teixera 1961, 166).

In 1529 Filipinos formed part of a Batak-Menangkabau army which besieged Atjeh, as well as of the Atjenese fleet which raised the siege under command of Turkish Heredim Mafamede. When this fleet later took Aru on the straits, Luzones were among four thousand Muslims aboard. Following his victory, Mafamede left a hand-picked garrison there under the command of a Filipino by the name of Sapetu Diraja. Luzones also fought on the mainland of Asia. They were in the ranks of the Burmese king when he took Martaban, and they faced the same king's war elephants during the defense of Ayuthia in 1547. And they also showed up as members of pirate crews—like those of Coja Achem's that Mendes Pinto encountered someplace off the Chinese coast north of Quanzhou in 1540.

By the time of Spanish advent, parts of Luzon with direct Bornean-Malay contact—Manila, Mindoro, the Batangas coast, and the Betis valley in Pampanga—had received Islam though Spaniards reported that the personal practice of the religion was limited to the proscription of pork flesh, if even that. The account of the taking of Manila comments,

> It is true that some who have been in Borneo know something [of the faith] and can read a little of the Koran, but these are few; and it is the opinion among them that those who have not been to Borneo may eat pork, and I have heard many of them say this (Anon. 1572, 94).

But in Balayan, Franciscan friars met Filipinos who were determined to make the pilgrimage to Mecca. Futhermore, the royal family of Manila obviously had a better understanding of the Islamic faith. Their hunters tried to reach the game before the dogs tore the flesh because of the ritual requirement that meat be bled before butchering. And, as said earlier, Agustin Legazpi's mother was given a proper Moro burial. Her body was wound with a white sheet and interred in a grave with a board on top to prevent contact with the soil, and two ornamental grave markers about 30 centimeters high. The mound was then sprinkled with water while prayers were offered by a *siyak* or *faqih* (expert in religious law)—"Allah ta ala [Allah be exalted]."

Malay loan words. The most lasting heritage of the Malay connection was the contribution of loan words to the Tagalog language. High on the list were trade terms such as *talaro* scales and *kaban* and *tsupa* measures, and many others which must have supplemented concepts already existing— for example, *lako* (peddle), *utang* (debt), *mamamayar* (slave dealer) from *bayar* (payment)—along with others which actually replaced native words— *karabaw* (buffalo) for *anowang*, *nila* (indigo) for *tayom*. Other words designated new pleasures of urban dining like *alak* (spirits), *atsara* pickles, and *puto* cakes; or new conveniences like *kalan* and *tungko* stoves, *kawa* cauldrons, *balanga* jars, and *sandok* ladles.

195

Intellectual and religious terms constituted another significant portion of the list—like *aral* (learning), *kawani* (clerk), and *pagsamba* (adoration). It is significant that the majority of these were already Malay borrowings from civilizations farther to the west at the time of their introduction into Tagalog. *Basa* (read), *guro* (teacher), and *diwa* (spirit) were ultimately of Sanskrit origin, while *hukom* (judgment), *asal* (custom), and *agimat* (amulet) came from Arabic. Indicative of the political changes which accompanied the new vocabulary were words pertaining to rule and social order—titles of royalty like *raja* and *hari*, expressions of deference like *tabi* (excuse me) and *po* (sir), and superior weapons like *balaraw* daggers, *baril* guns, and *lantaka* cannons.

The presence of Portuguese as an intermediary between Indian languages and Malay, and of Arabic-Malay terms which are Islamic, suggest that the major Malay impact on Tagalog occurred in the sixteenth century. The whole list of loan words reflects a process of urban sophistication which must have made it socially prestigious to speak the new language or at least to adopt some of its words. Well-bred ladies were now being called by the Malay word for female, *binibini*. *Gusali*, a blacksmith's shed, came to mean a large hall, and *biyaya* (disbursement) became "gracious gift" in Tagalog and thus the appropriate term for heavenly grace.

Because of this Malay influence, some Spaniards thought Tagalog was simply a Malay dialect, and Francisco de la Llave, who first served in Manila as a page boy to Governor Dasmariñas, concluded that the Tagalogs were themselves Malay immigrants. Thus, the Tagalog spoken in Manila in the late sixteenth century was a cosmopolitan dialect to whose speakers Malay was a second language.

It took years, however, for its novelties to reach the provinces. *Banyaga*, for instance, originally meant "tradesman who goes from town to town," but came to mean "foreigner" after it spread outside Manila. Experienced Spanish friars were well aware of the situation, and so always sent new missionaries out to the "boondocks" to learn the language from Filipinos who had not yet shifted from *bahag* to *pantalones*. The introduction to the famous Noceda and Sanlucar *Vocabulario* of 1753 *(prólogo)* says, "It is a common and true saying that to learn the Tagalog language requires almost one year of study and three of G-string."

Physical appearance. The most obvious physical feature which distinguished Tagalogs from "pintado" Visayans was their lack of tattoos. Nor did they reshape infants' skulls by head binding, though they filed and colored their teeth and pegged them with gold, had lips reddened by betel nut chewing, and distended their earlobes to the shoulder with heavy gold earrings—*malambing na talinga*. They cut their hair short and removed facial hair but grew mustaches to the extent they could, perhaps due to foreign influence. They did not wear penis pins, though Tagalog mountaineers east of Laguna inserted little pellets under the skin. They also practiced both circumcision and a Bornean custom called *sonat,* an incision in the clitoris sometimes called "female circumcision," a practice which survived into the eighteenth century in Pampanga, where it was called *gitang.* Tagalog ladies were well supplied with makeup—*tana* eyebrow paint, *pupol* face powder, red *kamuntigi* nail polish, and yellow *barak* root to rub on the body as a skin lotion. As a matter of fact, Father Blancas de San José inveighed against the vanity of their plucking their eyebrows every month.

The basic male garment was the G-string (bahag or *balabal*). This was large and wide enough to hang over the hips and thighs with a flap behind long enough to inspire facetious Spanish comments like, "Nababasa ang palawit mo [You're getting your tail wet]" (San Buenaventura 1613, 166). A silk one called *kalikot* came from Borneo, and so did a highly decorated one of silk and cotton called *kalikam,* which was restricted to upper-class chiefs. Both men and women wore a short-sleeved, collarless shirt or jacket *(baro),* and a cloak or long-sleeved gown on formal occasions—y*ambong* if ankle-length. A special piece of male finery was a scarf *(salampay)* thrown over the shoulders, intricately worked by their wives. There was also a mantle called *tapi* in which men wrapped up, but it was already considered old-fashioned in the colonial period and so then was only used by old men. The turbanlike *putong* was the normal male headdress, red in the case of those who had personally killed an enemy, or decorated with a plume of feathers, *sagisag* for chiefs, and *tambulok* for anyone sworn to avenge the death of a close relative.

The female dress was a rectangular wraparound skirt called *tapis*—or, more accurately, two tapis, an ankle-length white one, with a shorter, colored one over it, perhaps of *kayo* (Chinese cotton), *taluki* (silk), *kandaki* (fine black linen), or red *bangkuruhan* (named after the bark with which it was dyed). All fancy tapis worn for show were *talampukan,* among which the most prestigious were elegant silk-and-gold *kalumpata* from Borneo and *sinagitlong* patterned stuffs from Japan. *Sukob* was a tube skirt of colored abaca, not worn as a garment, however, but used as bedclothes, and *uwi* was an undergarment worn during menstruation. Above the tapis, women might wear a baro, an *anib* cloak, *talukbong* shawl, or loose smock called *kubong* or *kulubong* in Manila, *inuwak* in Laguna. An additional glossary suggests considerable clothing consciousness.

Basahan	Ordinary work clothes
Damit	Clothing of either sex
Giliw	Sackcloth or rough clothing
Gimay	Poor, worn clothes
Halos	Expensive clothes worn only for festive occasions
Panapin (from *sapin*, lining)	Underclothes worn by fastidious persons to protect new clothes from perspiration
Takdang	Any garments worn below the waist

The upper class, both male and female, fumigated their clothes with incense.

By the end of the sixteenth century, both styles and language had been affected by foreign influence. Dr. Antonio de Morga said Tagalog gentlemen were then adopting balloon pants *(calzones balones)* in place of the bahag, and he knew the baro as *chinanas* (Chinese). *Baro* itself was simply the Malay word for clothing *(baju)*. Malay *taryok* was a tuft of feathers or fragrant blossoms stuck in a man's putong, and Tagalog *paruka* (wooden shoes) were Malay *paduka*. (The Malay-Sanskrit honorific address for royalty, Sri Paduka—or Sarripada in the Visayas—actually meant "Your Highness' foot.") Spanish *zaragüelles* (trousers) appeared as *salawilis*, *zapatos* (shoes) as *patos kahuy* (wooden clogs), and ladies' tapis were now being called *saya* (skirt). Silk appeared not only as taluki, but as Malay *sutla* and Spanish *sedas;* Hokkien *husi* was a fine red silk woven only in Tondo. Indeed, clothing being a symbol of social status, it may not be surprising that the Malay word for wearing apparel, *pakayan,* came to mean all household possessions in Tagalog.

Technology

Tagalog technology, like that of Luzon in general, was much the same as Visayan. Blacksmiths used the two-cylinder Malay forge, and obtained raw iron from China in bars, ingots, or cast-iron pans; copper was reported in Lubang Island, but the Spaniards believed, rightly or wrongly, that Filipinos did not have the technical skill to extract it from the ore. Transportation was by water and there were no draft animals; heavy objects were moved on land with log rollers. Judging from the absence of the potter's wheel and the fact that pottery was fired in the open air with straw as fuel, Tagalog potters used the common Philippine paddle-and-anvil technique. Little is known about architecture beyond the names of such house parts like posts, beams, rafters, roofing, and a long list of cottages, huts, and shelters in the fields or forest. Nonetheless, there are some particular features worthy of description.

Agriculture. The staple food crop of the Tagalogs was rice, though millet was common enough for fine jeweler's work to be called "milletlike"—*dawa-dawa.* Twenty-two varieties of rice were recognized, among which *karataw* was both a quick-maturing type and the general term for dry rice grown without irrigation, and *kanin* (cooked food) was ordinarily taken to mean plain boiled rice—what the Spaniards called *morisqueta.*[31] The importance of rice is revealed by an extensive vocabulary of specialized terms connected with its growth, processing, and use—for example, there are four different words for a pile of unthreshed palay according to its size—*sipok, lampok, mandala,* and *salansan*—and one for any pile of rice whether threshed or not, *timbon.*

Root crops were also common but considered second choice as staples, however desired as vegetables. Spanish lexicographers listed six of them—*ubi, tugi, gabi, kamoti,* and two wild ones, *laksa* and *nami*—all of which they referred to as camotes, though they were aware that real camotes—that is, sweet potatoes—were introduced from the New World: as San Buenaventura (1613, 139) commented, "they did not have them before." All these crops were grown in swiddens.

Saka was the general term for fieldwork. *Tabtab* was to work fields in savannas; *gasak* was removing grasses and undergrowth, but not full-grown trees: that was *hapay.* *Lawag* was "to look for fields to farm every year as Tinguianes do" (San Buenaventura 1613, 127), and *salapsap* was to rework a swidden that had been fallowed. *Kaingin* meant to cut branches and small trees; *pagsisiga,* burning; *panting,* removing roots; and *dolok,* piling up for second burning. *Gusad* was to pull up the roots of harvested grain; *kuhit,* to uproot grass with a broad-pointed stick and scatter it so as not to take root again; *linlin,* an actual bundle of uprooted grass to spread out for the same purpose; and *halambat* was fencing the completed field with wood cut during its preparation. Swiddens planted to rice were *bukid*—as distinct from irrigated fields, *palayan.* *Budbud* was to drop the seeds into holes drilled with a *hasik* dibble stick. Root crops, however, were planted with large *baligway* or *balway* digging sticks, usually in mounds, while millet was planted by broadcasting *(sabog).*

Rice was also grown under irrigation by a sophisticated, labor-intensive method. Seasonal flooding of swampland, river plains, and lake shores often provided natural irrigation. For example, until Father Chirino persuaded its people to move to higher ground, Taytay (Laguna) was inundated from August to November; farmers harvested from boats in a meter and a half of water.

Opening a new pond field was called *bagbag*, and to channel water though canals was *alulod* or *salulo*, the latter term being the actual bamboo or palm-wood conduits. The preparation of a field already harvested began with *hapaw*, removing last year's stalks and roots by cutting the straw and throwing it down, and *himuno*, pulling up any roots still fixed, to be followed later by *kamkam*, removing newly sprouted weeds. Then came *timbunin*, piling up, followed by *palispis* and *pagi* cleaning, which left the field ready for planting after the soil had been soaked, without plowing. *Pinpin* and *bungton* were dividing mounds which served both as boundaries and pathways, and *pilapil* were ones made by piling up debris from the field itself. *Tarak* were stakes set out as boundary markers, but with the disadvantage that they could be moved surreptitiously, *ali*. Each of these divisions was one *luwang* or *habas*.

Seeding and transplanting was accomplished in five distinct stages. First, the seeds were soaked in a sack called *baluyot* until they germinated (*nagbabatad*), whereupon they were transferred to a basket to put out roots (*umuugat*). Next came *dapog*, placing them on inundated banana-leaf trays until the roots were long enough for transplanting. Third was *palan*, transplanting these seedlings (*bulubod*) "for the first time" into the field, matted together; and fourth was *punla* or *salip*, transplanting them the second time "by little handfuls." Fifth and last was *durol*, transplanting the third time by individual seedlings, inserting them into the muddy soil with a tool called *pandurol*. They might be spaced close together (*dasik*) with the intention of thinning them out later by further transplanting (*bugnos*). *Butikas* was the stage of growth when the head began to enlarge on the stalk; *turo*, when it broke out; *basag* or *baslay*, when it was just beginning to flower. When the plant had staminate blossoms, it was *maymuta, muta* being the mucous matter in the human eye; and while it was still green, it was called *mangagatas*, "milky."

Once the plants began to bear heads, placed in the fields were scarecrows, wickerwork or palm-leaf pendants kept moving by the wind, in a variety of different shapes—*pamanay, balian, palawit, salidangdang, bankiyaw,* or *pakanlog*. Even so, *bugawan* huts were constructed to shelter persons who stayed in the field to drive birds away. Finally, when the field of grain was *hinog na totoo* (fully ripe), harvesting was done stalk by stalk with a *pan-ani* knife or a blade of wood about 20 centimeters long called *gapas*. Day wages for such labor was called *nulang*.

Two presses were used to process agricultural products—the *alilisan* for sugarcane and the *hapitan* for coconut oil. The alilisan was made of two horizontal beams, the lower one fixed, the upper one pivoted at one end so as to move up and down and squeeze the cane near the fulcrum. The juice was boiled for wine, not sugar, though the syrup and solidified molasses were used as confections. The hapitan was a pressing bag pinched in a split beam tightened with cords; it was typically used in the hills where much coconut oil was produced. More common in the lowlands was to soak grated coconut meat before squeezing it, and then boil the juice.

The wheel was evidently unknown, even the potter's wheel. The Tagalog words, *biling, giling,* or *gulong,* were always illustrated in dictionaries by imported examples employing beasts—the Spanish cart and Chinese sugar press or rice mill. Native devices that rotated were limited to pulleys, reelers, rollers, and spindles. Nor was the carabao domesticated; rather, it was hunted wild for its flesh and hide. The Spaniards quickly provided a new market: by the end of the century, the Audiencia of Manila was providing arquebuses to licensed hunters under contract to supply at least one animal a day for butchering.

It is well known that Spanish missionaries introduced plows to Filipino farmers, a transfer of technology which is memorialized by the word for plow in modern Philippine languages—Spanish *arado.* But the plow they introduced was most probably Chinese. In the 1680s, Dominican Fray Domingo Pérez used to beg alms in Manila to buy plows for the Zambales natives he was trying to relocate: on one occasion he bought thirty plows (for 20 pesos), and on another was given fifty carabaos. It is unlikely that these plows were imports from Spain or Mexico warehoused in Manila when there were so many Chinese artisans ready and able to supply cheaper tools. Besides, the sixteenth-century European plow was much heavier than the Chinese implement: it required more than one beast to pull, and was characterized by a coulter, a knife-shaped "cutter" mounted in front of the blade. This was not the arado found in the Philippines in historic times.

Goldwork. Spanish accounts report of Tagalogs, as they do of other Filipinos, that everybody handled gold with dexterity, weighing and assessing it accurately, not only goldsmiths but even children. The Tagalog term was *ginto* (presumably Chinese 金子, *jinzî* or *kintoy*) though Blancas de San José also gave the northern Luzon term, *balitok,* as "a kind of gold." And to *ginto,* the San Buenaventura (1613, 456) dictionary adds the following curious entry under *balitok:*

Like the preceding, but since a chief is wont to be called Ginto, so as not to name him, they called gold *balitok*, [for example] *nag kakabalitok*—to have gold; after he died, *ginto* reverted to its meaning.

Pure gold was called *dalisay* or *urin buwo* ("absolute standard"), but also *lata* (soft) because gold is hard in proportion to the admixture of baser metals. Seven classifications were distinguished.

Dalisay	24 karats
Ginugulan	22 karats
Hilapo	20 karats
Panangbo	Somewhat less than 20 karats
Panika	18 karats
Linggingin	14 karats
Bislig	12 karats

Each of these categories was called "senior" or "junior" *(matanda* or *nabata)* in relation to the ones above and below it—for example, *ginugulang matanda* was *dalisay nabata,* and *ginugulang bata* was *hilapo matanda.* And below all these were *malubay* (weak), mixed with copper and reckoned as no karats at all, and *hutok* (bent over), mixed with silver and copper, hardly gold at all. Such adulterated gold was simply called copper *(tumbaga),* and so was any copper alloy like brass or bronze. Notary Hernando Riquel (1573, 240) commented, "They mix it with copper so skillfully they will deceive the best artisans of Spain." Cheap jewelry was made of panika, but no higher-grade gold was used in trade. Rather, it was reserved for expensive heirloom jewelry with which no Filipino would willingly part— although conditions of the Conquest often left them with no choice.

Some of these terms seem to reflect actual goldworking techniques: *ginugulan,* for instance, means "purified." Panika is a kind of hollow earring made by hammering a thin sheet of gold over a wax-resin mould, and it must be at least 18 karats to be soft enough to work. *Hilapo* (to wipe the face) may refer to the fact that 20–karat gold leaves a clear mark when rubbed on a touchstone, and *bislig* (hardened, petrified) suggests the stony hardness of the base mixture of 12–karat gold.

Gold dust was used as a form of currency, being weighed out when making purchases with little weights and scales carried by the customer. The basic weight was a little red seed called *saga,* probably Indian licorice *(Abrus precatorious),* known in English as jequirity beans, which are commonly used in the tropics as beads or weights. Thus, *sumasaga* was extended to mean buying any cheap items. Tagalogs reckoned them at three *palay,* from *sangpalay* or *kapalay,* a grain of rice. A larger bean was *bahay,* worth three saga; and a still larger one, *bulay,* was equal to three bahay.

Heavier weights were those standard to Southeast Asian commerce—the *kupang, mas,* and *tahil.* The tahil, *tael,* or *tae* was the Chinese ounce *(liang),* and the mas—*amas* in Tagalog from Malay *emas*—was reckoned at 16 to the tahil. The kupang was one-fourth of a mas, but which San Buenaventura recorded as 3 to the mas, and converts to the native scale at 3 bulay. Blancas de San José more plausibly gave the mas as 4 kupang, and as the equivalent of 16 saga. The Tagalogs also called half an amas, *balabato;* 4 mas, *sapaha;* and 8 mas—that is, half a tahil—*paningan.* If the sixteenth-century Philippine amas was the equivalent of the tenth-century Javanese gold *masa* coin stamped *ma,* it weighed 2.4 grams.

Hunting and fishing. Both coastal and inland waters were exploited by Tagalogs for their protein content in a variety of ways—an aspect of life for which they had an extensive vocabulary. To fish with a certain kind of small net was *sim;* with a long net at river mouths, *lambat;* while *salap* was a purse seine. Casting nets varied in the size of their mesh for different species— for example, *pamanak* for skates and *panamaw* for conger eels—with sinkers called *barundala* if they were made of lead. Basket traps included the *salakan*—"wide below with many prongs and narrow above with a hole for inserting the hand to get the fish"—or the Laguna *bubo,* for which channels *(bubohan)* were especially constructed. Fish-trap corrals were placed in mountain streams *(tain),* in canals *(bangkat* or the longer and larger *bankatan),* or along the seacoast *(pusod)* where fish were trapped when the tide went out. *Biwas* was to fish with hooks; *nilay,* with hook and line; and *pataw,* with hook-loaded rattan lines extended at sea or in rivers. Under favorable conditions, it was possible to spear fish with harpoons like the barbed *bulos* or three-pronged *salapang. Tangad* was to fish by moonlight to locate the schools before dropping the net; and *ilaw,* to fish by torchlight. *Tuba* was a tree whose fruit when rotten "makes fish drunk."

To go hunting with spears was *akar;* and if accompanied by hounds, *nangangaso.* If the dogs were used to drive game into nets, that was *bating,* and nets for wild boar might be as long as 60 meters. *Balaon* or *balon* pits were dug for large animals with bamboo spikes set in the bottom, but less laborious to construct were bamboo spring-powered automatic crossbows or arbalests set along runs frequented by game. *Balatik* and *balais* were the general terms, with *paraig* being designed for pigs and deer, or even dogs, and *pasulo* made for carabao. Small arbalests for rats were the *pasipit* and *paitbong,* while the *panloob* was an ordinary bamboo rattrap with no moving parts. Birds were caught in snares *(sagad)* or a sticky birdlime *(patda)* made of jackfruit juice, reeds, and a little clay, and were valued not merely as food but for their decorative plumage. So, too, civet cats were taken not so much for their flesh as for their perfume-fixing civet *(diris)*.

Weaving. The main Tagalog textile was cotton. Abaca was largely used for cordage, decorative fringe, and lightweight bedding. The cotton was received in the pod in exchange for rice from provinces like Bulacan—literally, "place of cotton" *(bulak)*—and as finished cloth from the Visayas. It was also imported from China where, ironically, it could be produced from Philippine cotton more cheaply with spinning and ginning machines and large frame looms than in the Philippines with distaff and backstrap loom. Cotton was quickly demanded as tribute by the Spaniards for sailcloth and export to Mexico both as thread and as piecegoods since, because of the limitations of the backstrap loom, it was marketed by the piece rather than as yardgoods in bolts. The first Spanish shipment to Acapulco included 11,300 such pieces collected as tribute and valued at 2 gold pesos each. Meanwhile, Governor Dasmariñas also notified the king that there was no need for shipping blankets from Mexico. Ordinary Tagalog blankets were called *kumot;* large red ones, *minalon;* those made in the Visayas, *lumpot;* and *tinalaban* was striped cloth in different colors, *sabasabat* if black, blue, and white.

Harvesting the pods from the tree was *bitin.* To remove the cotton inside was *baynos,* or *pipis* or *putpot* if done with a sort of rolling pin on a table. *Nutnot* was to untangle the wool with the fingers; and *pakpak,* to cudgel it to make it fluffy. Spinning with spindle and distaff was *sulid,* and one distaff-ful was *busugsodlan.* Cotton thread was simply called *sinulid*—that is, "spun"—and the general term for thread, *lubid,* always referred to cotton unless otherwise specified. *Galungang* and *labayan* were reels for winding thread, *tugas* was to wash it for dyeing, and *sapad* was to soak it in blue dye. Dyestuffs included *suga* (saffron or pomegranate), *tayom* (indigo), and red *agusip* or *talab* roots and *bangkuro* bark, while cotton husks themselves made a bright red dye. In preparation for weaving, doubling the threads was called *lambal;* to wax them, *hagod, higod,* or *pagkit;* and to starch them with cooked rice paste was *pangas.*

Weaving was accomplished with the backstrap loom. The whole paraphernalia was called *tandaya,* including the heddles, lease rods, *balila* batten, and loom bars. The warp was set up on a simple warping frame *(palatohat)* and once it was transferred to the two loom bars, with one loom bar suspended from a partition of the house, it was called *hanay.* The weft was *hilig;* the piece of bamboo which kept the shed open when the loom was at rest, *bahay-hilig* (weft-house); and the heddle for making the opposite shed, *anak-hilig* (weft-child) or *guyonan* (from *guyon,* the thread wound around the heddle to pick up alternate warp threads). Lease rods—that is, flat or round reeds inserted into the warp to prevent tangling and to preserve tension—included the *pugi* on the weaver's side of the shed and the *lilitan* coil rod on the far side. The shuttle, *sikwan,* was also called a weaving harpoon *(bulos sa paghabi),* and the bobbin inside was the *pingi* or *sinikwan.* Unlike the Visayan loom, there appears to have been no reed or comb, a feature the Tagalog loom shared with backstrap looms still in use in the mountains of northern Luzon.

Basketry. Baskets ranged from fine, split-bamboo weaving like the *bugsok* clothes hamper and tight-woven *bakay* for carrying rice—"wide above, narrow below"—to the rattan *alat* with openings as large as latticework. Tight weaving also appeared in the *bilawo* winnowing tray, *mitay* "mattress," *kupit* knapsack, and large or small *abubot* "suitcases," but not in the ordinary bamboo carrying basket, *bangkat.* Only one hat was actually woven—the *sawing;* the others were all plaited of leaves—for example, the ladies' *salip* or the large, wide *tankulok.* A container for carrying rice was also made of leaves sewn together, the *tuhog,* named after the palm from which the leaves were taken. *Papag* was a sort of ubiquitous frame or tray made of canes with their ends inserted into rectangular bamboo or wooden frames, and served a wide variety of uses—beds, tables, seats, rowing benches, house parts, trays for soaking rice seedlings or, in general, any light substitute for boards. Ships' sails were also woven of palm matting, though, ironically, the famous Manila galleons would carry sails of locally woven canvas.

Carpentry. Woodworking and carpentry for the Tagalogs were limited to—and they excelled in—hewing, joinery, and carving. That is to say, timber was squared *(pagpag)* and reduced to boards with an adze *(daras)* rather than with a saw, fitted together with mortise-and-tenon joints or rabbeting made with a chisel *(pait),* and given esthetic form by knifework— *liso* for carving in general, or *lilok* with a fine knifepoint. *Kuko* was mortising; *pasak* and *lapat* were wedges or tenons; and *pako* and *tilos* were bamboo pegs or nails. Benches and tables required such joinery, and so did the great *dalam* chief's houses with carved wooden walls. But by far the most highly developed skill was employed in the construction of boats and ships with long, curved strakes handhewn to shape all in one piece.

205

Unfortunately, all early descriptions of Philippine boat-building technology pertain to the Visayas and the Muslim south, though shipbuilding and seafaring were also Tagalog professions. Luzon ships were observed in Timor and Malacca early in the sixteenth century, and during the 1575 Limahon invasion, the Manila-Tondo royalty supplied ships, fully manned and armed, for the Spanish defense. Dictionary entries make it clear that Tagalog techniques differed from Visayan in only one important feature— the planks making up the hull were literally sewed, or laced together through holes drilled near the edges of adjoining strakes, caulked watertight afterwards.

Caulking was called *siksik* in general, with three specific stages which made use of coconut husk, bamboo, and resin—*balutbot, salugsog,* and *balibol*—or *galagala,* a pitch made of lime, oil, and coconut fiber. Nautical terminology included not only items to be expected like prow, poop, mast, sails, sheets, braces, outriggers, and rowing benches, but also *kamalig,* a shed for storage ashore, and such niceties as *kinsi-kinsi* railings on the stern, intricate *pimpin* carving, or *paminir* boards which "stop up and seal the sides of the boat where the gentlemen sit so they will not get wet" (San Buenaventura 1613, 565). Dictionary definitions are brief, but they at least provide an overview of the types of vessels which Tagalogs distinguished.

Balangay	A wooden vessel sewn with rattan
Balasian	A small but strong boat seating five persons
Banka	General term for all kinds of boats
Bawuto	A boat hewn of one piece of wood, larger than *bilog*
Bilog	A dugout canoe, a small boat hewn of one piece of wood, commonly used for fishing
Biray	A large vessel, also called a *fragata* (frigate), therefore probably includes the warships Spaniards called *karakoa,* that is, Indonesian *kora-kora*
Birok or *biruko*	A large, well-made vessel
Kupit	A large boat used for trade
Malo	A large boat ordinarily used for trade, more poorly made than the kupit, with washboards of rattan
Sata	A large, heavy, and very wide boat, used around Manila for carrying lime, rocks, etc.
Talangkas	A light vessel which can sail against the wind, swift and does not carry cargo
Tapak	A plank-built boat with a dugout keel, enlarged with nipa washboards, used for trade

Trade

At the time of Spanish advent, Manila was the main entrepot in the archipelago: here exports were accumulated and imports redistributed. A few of these goods were carried in Luzon bottoms to or from Borneo, Malacca, Atje, and the Moluccas, but most of them were handled by foreign merchants—Malay, Bornean, Chinese, Japanese, Siamese, or Cambodian, even Portuguese. (The first ship the Spaniards seized in Philippine waters was a Bornean vessel owned by a Portuguese but loaded with cargo that belonged to the sultan of Brunei.) The Chinese sent annual junks direct to the Philippines, but most Southeast Asian trade goods reached this remote region after being carried from island to island, often by petty traders who rented cargo space and bought and sold from port to port in response to local supply and demand. International commerce in Manila was therefore not limited to Philippine products but included the resale of exotic merchandise like Timor sandalwood, Bornean camphor, and rhinoceros horns from Siam. Slaves were also brought from Siam and Borneo; indeed, the Malay word for payment, *bayar,* became the root of the Tagalog word for slave dealer—*mamamayad.*

Nevertheless, Manila lay far to the north of the lucrative spice route. Native Philippine products were of limited variety and value, and handling them was not profitable enough to attract a resident Chinese colony. The few Chinese the Spaniards found married into Tondo in 1570 were political refugees and recent arrivals. Two or three seagoing junks a year were enough to supply what the local market could afford—and, indeed, to flood the archipelago with tens of thousands of pieces of porcelain.

But the situation changed dramatically with the arrival of Spanish customers willing to pay in coined silver. Thirty years after Legazpi occupied Manila, the Chinese quarter had four hundred shops and eight thousand residents, and it is estimated that almost 4 million Mexican pesos had been carried to China by that time. Chinese policy changes also facilitated the new trade: in 1567 licenses were issued to legalize what had been one hundred and fifty years of clandestine trade, two the first year and forty-four by 1587.

Political developments in Japan also favored increased trade. A century of civil war—and overseas piracy—ended with the establishment of a central regime in 1590 and the regulation of foreign trade in licensed "red seal" ships. By the turn of the century, friar missionaries bound for Japan could book direct passage in Manila.

207

Most Philippine exports were forest products—wax, honey, dyewoods, deerskins and leather, civet and live civet cats, and heavy timber for ballast in Chinese junks that had arrived heavy-laden with porcelain and hardware. Carabao horns and raw cotton also went to China, and palm wine, rice, and other foodstuffs to Borneo. Some commodities moved in both directions: gold, for instance, was traded by the Chinese for silver, and purchased by Japanese with their own silver. Cotton cloth went to Japan, Borneo, and Malacca, while expensive Indian printstuffs—the major eastbound tradeware in Southeast Asia—entered through Borneo, Cambodia, Java, Malacca, Siam, and Sumatra. The Japanese also purchased Chinese silks and porcelain in Manila, and supported a curious trade in little unglazed pots which had rough appeal for Zen tea ceremonies.

Philippine imports, on the other hand, were largely manufactured goods—silk and cotton textiles, porcelain and crockery, fine mats, hardware, gongs, kettles, and swords (Japanese *katana*). Other commodities included benzoin, camphor, copper, pepper, sago, sugar, and exotica like rubies, carnelians, sapphires, and—no doubt for the China trade—rhinoceros horns, hides, hoofs, and teeth. Many imports listed in Spanish accounts were probably for their own, not Filipino, consumption—biscuits, butter, cattle, ham, horses, and wheat flour—although many of the fruits they imported no doubt spread to local cultivation—chestnuts, figs, oranges, pears, pineapples, plums, and pomegranates. It is noteworthy, however, that Chinese foods which are common in modern Tagalog life like *bihon, hopiya, mami, pansit,* and *petsay* do not appear in seventeenth-century dictionaries.

In addition to retailing Chinese imports in the Visayas, Tagalogs also traded as far north as the Cagayan Valley. In 1572, Juan de Salcedo found a Manila vessel on the coast of Ilocos Norte whose crew provided him a Moro guide familiar with that region. Moreover, local business practices were well developed and specialized. *Kalakal* was the ordinary term for a merchant and *lako* was merchandise in general, though *maglalako* was taken to mean a dealer exclusively in clothes. *Dagangan* was bulk merchandise, especially expensive goods like silk. *Utay* was retailing; *baliwas* was hawking; and *tungo* was buying or selling one item at a time. *Banyaga* was an itinerant peddler of petty merchandise. *Bayad* was dealing in slaves; *tukal,* in textiles. *Dulhog* was selling foodstuffs in other localities, but this was called *sugat* if the producer simply carried vegetables to the marketplace for sale. *Apin* was to buy grain from the field. *Sama* was a business partnership (for example, "Nagsasama kamo nitong inyong lako [Are you partners in this merchandise]?), and *tapa* was the capital invested (for example,

"Mamolang salapi ang aming pinag tapa [We each put in ten *tostons*]") (San Buenaventura 1613, 175, 152).

Parian appears in the early dictionaries as the ordinary Tagalog word for marketplace, not only the Chinese Parian in Manila—for example, "Mamariang ka [Go to market]" or "Sumaga ka nang pinya sa parian [Buy some pineapples in the market]" (San Buenaventura 1613, 177). Here, customers often purchased cheap items like fish and fruit by weighing out bits of gold or silver in their own scales, a procedure called *sumaga* from the saga seeds which were the smallest weight for gold. (The scales and weights were carried in a purse called *karay*, but the gold itself was tied very tight in a kind of money belt called *unton*.) Here, too, marketing procedures might involve *tawad*, to beat the price down by haggling; *sahol*, to overprice; *mura*, to underprice; or *kagyot*, to misrepresent goods. *Angka* was to corner the market by buying out a particular item, *amam* was petty pilfering or shortweighting, and *daha* or *pig-it* was to detain merchandise en route to manipulate the market price—"as they do along the Pasig River and in Taguig," San Buenaventura said, "and then sell it much dearer in Manila."

Debt slavery and peonage being an important determinant in Tagalog social structure, interest rates were high. *Palaba* was a loan at 20 percent interest per month (*pahigit* if calculated daily) and *ganda*, 100 percent per annum; while *talinduwa* was any loan at 50 percent, *ibayiw*, at 100 percent, and *dalawa-lima*, 150 percent. Another word, *bintang*, as defined by San Buenaventura (1613, 59), was "to add more and more every day to the debt a person owes, as if it were *buwis* [tribute], by lending him more with the intention that he will not be able to repay it and so become a slave." Actual coins were called *pilak* (silver) and prior to the Spanish arrival were based on the Portuguese toston *(salapi)*, the equivalent of half a peso, or 4 *reales*. Thus, 2 reales or half a toston was *kahati* or *binting*; 1 real was *saikapat;* and half a real, *saikawalo*. Since all these denominations were too large for ordinary market purchases, they were chopped into pieces—*lamok* in general, *tatak-tatak* if silver. A few of the famous Chinese coppers with a square hole in the middle *(pitis)* were also in circulation.

The Alphabet

The Tagalogs had an indigenous script called *baybayin* when the Spaniards arrived.[32] The best description of their literacy is contained in the Boxer Codex (1590b, 371):

They have certain characters which serve them as letters with which they write whatever they wish. They are of very different shape from any others we have known until now. The women commonly know how to write with them, and when they write, it is on some tablets made of the bamboos which they have in those islands, on the bark. In using such a tablet, which is four fingers wide, they do not write with ink, but with some scribers with which they cut the surface and bark of the bamboo, and make the letters. They have neither books nor histories nor do they write anything of any length but only letters and reminders to one another. . . . [And lovers] carry written charms with them.

Father Chirino (1604, 39) rather fondly stated, "These islanders are so given to reading and writing that there is hardly a man, and much less a woman, who does not read and write in the letters of the island of Manila," and Dr. Morga (1609, 190) said, "There are very few who do not write it very well and correctly." Perhaps these exaggerated claims were occasioned by Spanish surprise that ordinary Filipinos could read and write when there were no professional scribes, archives, or libraries. But they are demonstrably incorrect. Among eight Ilocano chiefs who executed affidavits in May 1591, only one could sign his name—Juan Zamora of Narvacan—and of eleven in Pampanga, also only one—Nicolas Ramos of Lubao. During the 1599 plebiscite, 155 chiefs swore oaths in Lumban (Laguna) "and those who could do so signed their names" (Tello 1599, 287); and in Carigara (Leyte), "all those who knew how signed in their manner, since few knew ours" (Alcina 1668a, 4:66–67). As late as the 1620s, among title deeds with Tagalog signatures preserved in Dominican archives, there are some whose witnesses could not sign their names.

Nonetheless, whatever the Tagalog literacy rate may have been in the sixteenth century, it was high enough to induce the friars to publish Tagalog books in the baybayin. Father Plasencia's *Doctrina christiana en lengua Española y Tagala* was printed from wood blocks, one page to each, in 1593 (see fig. 8), and so, presumably, was Father Blancas de San José's 1602 *Libro de nuestra Señora del Rosario,* of which no copy is known to have survived. Actual types cast in the next century appeared in Fray Francisco López's Ilocano translation of the Bellarmine *Doctrina.* These were Tagalog types, "the most universal in these islands," despite their lack of a character for the letter *r* which is essential to Ilocano (López 1621, LXII). Thus Father López's substitution of *l* or *d* produced such Ilocano barbarisms as *sailo* for *sairo* (tempter) and *kadaduwa* for *kararua* (soul).

The Spaniards quickly learned that Tagalogs communicated in writing. Governor Sande took advantage of the fact to send Filipino ambassadors to Borneo in 1578 bearing letters in their own script—though they could not

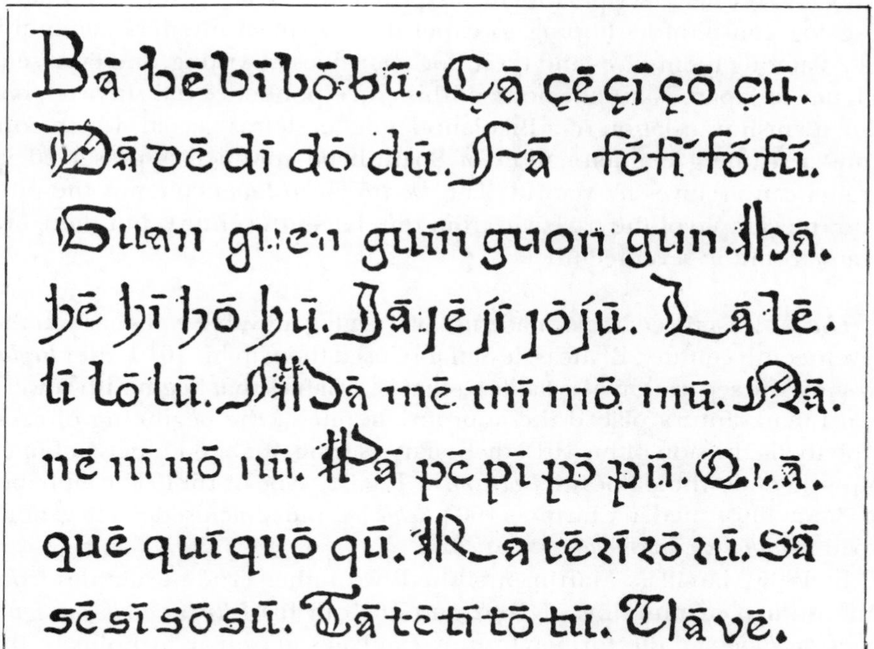

Bā bē bī bō bū. Çā çē çī çō çū.
Đā đē di đō đū. Ꞩā fē fī fō fū.
Ꞡuan guen guīn guon gun. Ꞩhā.
hē hī hō hū. Ꞽa je jī jō jū. Ꞥā lē.
li lō lū. ꞦꞩꞠā mē mī mō mū. ꞤꞠā.
nē nī nō nū. ꞤꞠā pē pī pō pū. Qꞡā.
quē quī quō qū. Ꞧꞧā rē rī rō rū. Ꞩā
sē sī sō sū. ꞦꞠā tē tī tō tū. Ꞩlā vē.
vī vō vu. Xꞗā xē xī xō xū. Yā yē.
yī yō yū. Zā zē zī zō zū. ⸻.

❧ El abc. en légua tagala.

❧ El pater nóster.

PADRE nueſtro que eſtas en

Fig. 8. A page from Plasencia's *Doctrina Christiana en lengua Español y Tagala*

read the Bornean script, which was probably Arabic. A few years later, Tagalog conspirators hoping to expel their Spanish invaders communicated among themselves and their Bornean allies in writing, and even sent a letter to Japan. Naturally none of this correspondence has survived, but the Spanish translation of a Bikolano letter "en letras tagala," which contains a scathing condemnation of Spanish misconduct, is preserved in Franciscan archives in Madrid. The *Doctrina christiana* contains the only known example of the baybayin from the sixteenth century, but there are many from the seventeenth.

Use. At least three books made use of Tagalog movable types early in the seventeenth century. Blancas de San José used them in his 1610 *Arte y Reglas* to show the separation of syllables—that is, syllables that begin with vowels; San Buenaventura placed the appropriate one at the beginning of each alphabetic division of his 1613 dictionary (see fig. 9); and Francisco López published his whole Ilocano *Doctrina* in Tagalog type in 1621. The alphabet itself was illustrated in Chirino's 1604 *Relación,* and Melchisedec Thevenot's 1646 *Relation de divers voyages curieux.*

In 1895 Marcilla y Martín published two rather crude examples from Augustinian manuscripts of 1602 and 1699 in his *Estudio de los antiguos alfabetos Filipinos,* the former from a Zambales grammar in Bolinao, the latter from a letter written in Bacolor, Pampanga. Between these dates, more than a hundred Filipino signatures appear in title deeds, donations, and petitions from provinces around Manila, usually written in Spanish and preserved in archives in Manila, Madrid, and Mexico.

With the exception of a few Tagalog deeds written in baybayin in full, none of the above examples are documents or texts—and even those few deeds in baybayin used Spanish form and dates. But Gaspar de San Agustín stated in his 1703 *Compendio* that the native script was still in use for poetry in Batangas at that time. Also, identifying letters were scratched, presumably by common sailors, on the surface of water jars recovered from the wreck of the eastbound galleon *Nuestra Señora de la Consolación* which went down off Guam in 1638. Moreover, the baybayin must have been in common use for chronicler Domingo Martínez (1756, 1:102) to have given credence to the following story about a plague of locusts:

> What happened was that on their inner wings, which were white, they had written in the Tagalog language and letters the following words: on the one wing, the word *galit,* which means to say "ire" or "anger," and on the other the phrase *nang Dios,* which means "of God," so all together, "the anger of God."

Thomas Ortiz described the "Tagalog characters" in his 1740 *Arte y Reglas*. However, his contemporary, Melchor de Oyanguren, said, "Nowadays these letters are being forgotten" (Oyanguren 1742; Lumbera 1968, 631), and the only known samples of Filipino penmanship from the eighteenth century are the signatures in a 1792 document from Mindoro. But these involve Mangyans, a people who, like the Tagbanwa of Palawan, have continued to use their script up until the present day. There are no other references to the use of the baybayin in the nineteenth century, although the memory clearly survived. In the absence of written records, Spanish observers often recorded alphabets, unaware that each character represented a separate syllable. Thus, a table of "Ancient characters with which these natives of the Tagalogs and Camarines used to write," dating from the time of Governor General Pascual Enrile (1830–1835), gives the following example: "Big man   ᜎᜎᜃᜒᜈᜄ ᜇᜃᜓᜎ
lalaquing dacola," but which actually reads *lalakinaga dakola* (Enrile 1835*)*.

In 1841, Spanish traveler Sinibaldo de Mas was able to collect five samples of the alphabet from Pangasinan, Pampanga, Tondo, and Bulacan, and one Ilocano example, though not as used in any texts (see fig. 10). He was himself aware that these were simply variants of a single alphabet; but they have come to be popularly regarded as distinct alphabets from different provinces, just as the Tagalog type font of the López Ilocano *Doctrina* has frequently been reproduced as an "Ilocano alphabet." Naturally, handwritten letters differ considerably from printed types, and from one another. But far from being different alphabets, these half-dozen anachronistic examples simply illustrate different hands, as evidenced by comparison with the many genuine specimens of Tagalog penmanship in the archives of the University of Santo Tomas. As Dominican Father Albert Santamaría (1938, 184) commented after an exhaustive study of all of them in 1938, "it has been most interesting, for, despite all having been written by Tagalogs, we found greater variations among them than, in general, among the different alphabets represented as coming from different regions."

Description. The baybayin is one of about a dozen indigenous alphabets from such Southeast Asian islands as Sumatra, Java, and Sulawesi, which are ultimately derived from ancient India, and share the Sanskrit characteristic that any consonant is pronounced with the vowel *a* following it, diacritical marks being added to express other vowels. It contained seventeen letters, three of which were the vowels *a, e-i,* and *o-u*—or rather, the vowels a, *e-i,* and *o-u* preceded by a glottal stop, since they were used in this way to begin syllables. The other fourteen were radical signs representing the conso-

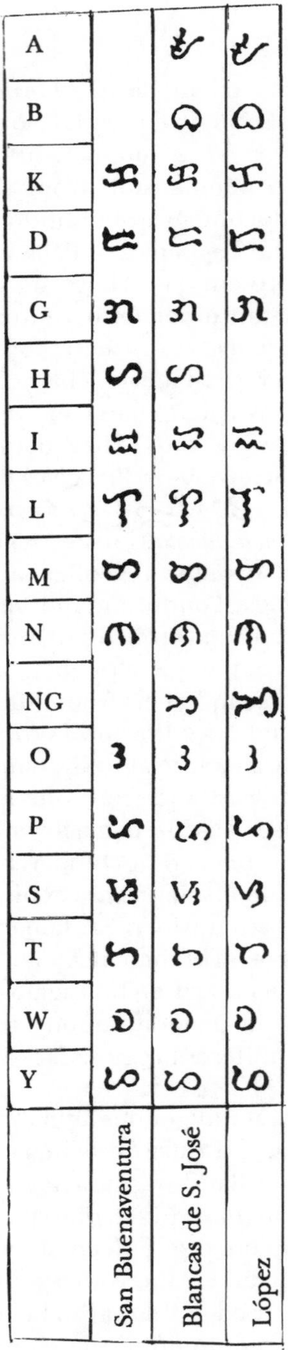

A			
B			
K			
D			
G			
H			
I			
L			
M			
N			
NG			
O			
P			
S			
T			
W			
Y			
	San Buenaventura	Blancas de S. José	López

Fig. 9. Tagalog alphabet in works of three authors

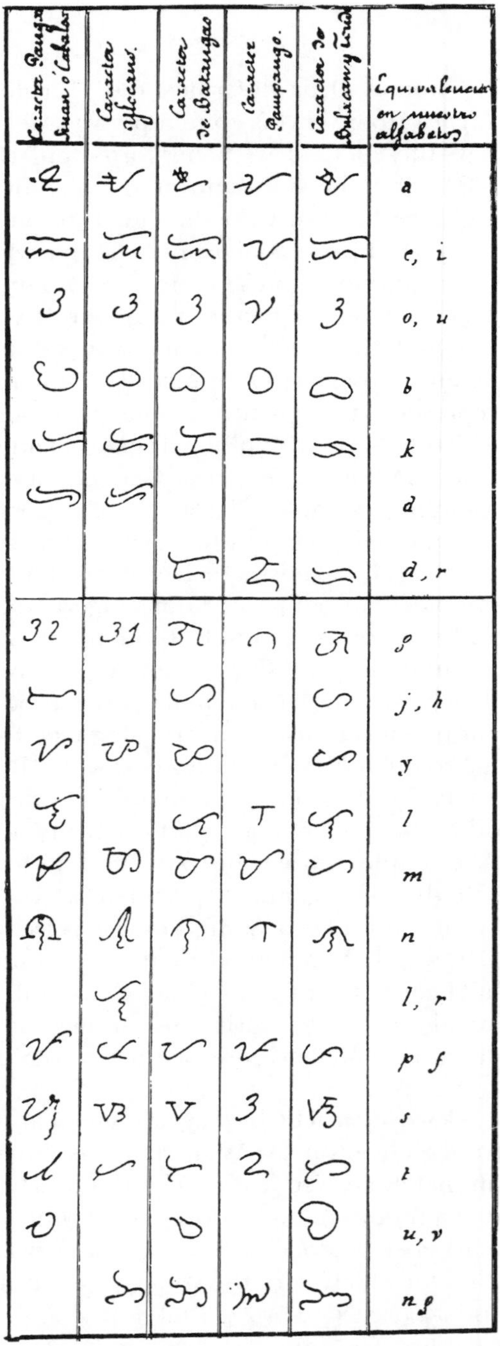

Carácter Pangasinan ó Caboloan	Carácter Ylocano	Carácter de Batangas	Carácter Pampango	Carácter de Bulacan y Tondo	Equivalencias en nuestro alfabeto
					a
					e, i
3	3	3		3	o, u
					b
					k
					d
					d, r
32	31				g
					j, h
					y
		T			l
			T		m
			T		n
					l, r
					p, f
	V3	V	3	V3	s
					t
					u, v
					ng

Fig. 10. Samples of the alphabet taken by Sinibaldo de Mas

nants *b, d, g, h, k, l, m, n, ng, p, s, t, w,* and *y,* which were pronounced *ba, da, ga, ha, ka, la, ma, na, nga, pa, sa, ta, wa,* and *ya* unless a mark called *kudlit* (which the Spaniards spelled *corlit*) was placed over them, in which case their value was modified to a front vowel like *e* or *i,* or under them, in which case they were pronounced with a back vowel like *o* or *u.* When writing vertically rather than horizontally, however, the kudlit were placed to the left or right of the letters rather than above or below them, and there was evidently no set rule for the direction of the writing. Completely wanting was any mark—like the Sanskrit *virama,* or what Dutch scholars call a *Klinkerdoder,* "vowel killer"—to cancel the vowel value of a letter and permit it to stand as a consonant alone. Consonants therefore could not be expressed at the end of a syllable, a considerable shortcoming, since *ba* and *ta,* for instance, could be read "batay" as well as "bata," depending on the context.

The baybayin was in common enough use to develop such orthographic conventions as the use of one letter with two kudlit to represent two different syllables. The bold and distinctive signature of Don Dionisio Kapolong, son of Lakandula, for example, places kudlit both under and over the letter *d* to represent the *do* of "Don" and *di* of "Dionisio," respectively, and a title deed of 1613 places two kudlit under the letter *t* to represent both the *to* and *tu* of "nitong tubigan [in this wet field]." When spelling aloud, Tagalogs called their letters *baba, dada, kaka,* etc. The inability of the baybayin to represent the *ng* of *nitong* illustrates its inadequacy for recording spoken Tagalog faithfully, probably a sufficient explanation for its limited use and the absence of Filipino documents, written records, or monumental inscriptions. Father Blancas de San José, after having published one book in Tagalog script, explained in the introduction to his 1605 *Memorial de la vida Christiana en lengua Tagala* that he now considered it impractical. And when Father López used it in his *Doctrina,* he introduced a kind of virama in the form of a little cross under the letters to cancel their vowel value, a reform which seems never to have been adopted by any Filipino. As he himself explained,

the reason for putting the text of the Doctrina in Tagalog type . . . has been to begin the correction of the said Tagalog script, which, as it is, is so defective and confused (because of not having any method until now for expressing final consonants—I mean, those without vowels) that the most learned reader has to stop and ponder over many words to decide on the pronunciation which the writer intended (López 1621, LXII).

215

Examination of all the native scripts of Southeast Asia suggests that they are local developments, share some common ancestor in southern India, but are not directly ancestral to one another. Perhaps the baybayin was derived—however imperfectly—from some intermediary script which no longer exists: Butuan, Borneo, Sulu, and Kumalarang (Mindanao) were once able to present memorials to the Chinese court engraved on gold tablets but have had no native script in modern times. It may be noted, however, that the Buginese-Makassarese alphabet of Sulawesi to the south share the Philippine characteristic of not using—indeed, not needing—any "vowel killer," a fact which recommends them as the intermediate source of the baybayin. In any event, whatever the form of the first Philippine alphabet and wherever it came from, there is no reason why Tagalog merchants should not have brought it back from their trading voyages themselves.

CHAPTER 12

Tagalog Society and Religion

The Tagalog father was *ama;* the mother, *ina;* and the two of them were *mangaama,* that is, parents. Children referred to their father as Bapa (Beloved), a term of respect and affection which elders also applied to youngsters, and which, indeed, was a general expression of admiration— for example, "Galing bapa [Oh, what a fine thing]!" Others addressed fathers with a derivative of *ama* which meant the father of so-and-so—for example, a-Maria, ami-Tiba, or ada-Lamba. Similarly, the mother of Francisco was addressed as i-Siko. A mother's own children addressed her with the honorific Bayi (Lady) if they had no surviving grandmother entitled to this name.

Kinship

Both husband and wife were *asawa,* with *inaasawa* being a secondary wife or concubine, usually of lesser rank than her husband. A slave concubine was called *pangapol,* however, and her children would not be heirs except in the case of a father's special affection. As for ranking wives, they commonly employed wet nurses for their offspring: because of

217

this, one of Father Blancas's sermons specifically praised the Virgin Mary for having nursed the infant Jesus with her own milk. The importance of both parents to the family unit was reflected in the term *kaanaktilik,* persons who married dead siblings' spouses even if both they and their new spouses already had children—for example, a widower with children who married his brother's widow, also with children.

Grandfather was *amba* and grandmother was *indo*—terms which meant father and mother on the east coast—and both were called Nono when they were old enough to be considered truly venerable, but not after their death. Grandparents and grandchildren were called by the same term, *apo,* and were reckoned to the third generation: great-grandparents were *apo sa tuhod,* literally, "grandparents at the knee"—or in the case of grandmothers, *apo sa sinapuponan,* "grandmothers in the lap"—and great-great-grandparents were *apo sa kalapakan,* "grandparents at the sole of the foot." If one was the head of an especially prolific lineage, he was called just that—lineage *(lalad).*

Children were *anak*—*anak sa inaasawa,* if born to a secondary wife, or *anak sa para,* if both parents were of equal rank—*panganay* being the first son, and *bungso,* the youngest. Siblings were *kapatid*—*kambal,* if twins; *dugtong,* if born to the same mother; *labot,* any babes suckled at the same breast, and they all called their eldest brother Kaka. Consanguinal cousins were *pinsan,* nephews and nieces were *pamangkin.* They addressed their aunts as Ali and their uncles as Mama—or Kaka, in the case of their parents' eldest brothers—but referred to aunts as *daga* and uncles as *amain.*

All these blood relatives were *hinlog,* or, more colorfully, *karugtong bituka* meaning "connected innards." Collateral relatives were *kabalayi:* father- or mother-in-law were *biyanan; hipag* being sister-in-law; *bayaw,* brother-in-law; and parents of a married couple called each other Baysan. A son-in-law was *manugang,* and was required to do a year's service in his father-in-law's residence before taking away his bride.

Adoption was common among upper-class Tagalogs. Rajah Soliman of Manila adopted a deceased brother's three children after his own son was executed by the Spaniards. One who was adopted by a childless parent was *inaanak naboo,* a sole heir, but more common were *kalansak,* joint heirs together with the adoptive parent's own children or brothers and sisters. This was a contractual investment on the part of either the person being adopted or his parents, for the mutual benefit of both parties—on the one hand, for the child to join a well-to-do family and, on the other, for the adoptive parents to enlarge their family. Adoption was done in one of three ways: *ibayiw* was an agreement for the adopted child to inherit twice the sum that was given at the time of adoption; *talinduwa* was to receive half as much as the adoption fee, also over and above that same fee; and *mulaying* was to receive a still larger share in case the family's fortunes increased.

Illegitimate children were called *anak sa kinaligawan* or *anak sa kaagulo*, from *ligaw* (passerby) and *agulo* (lover), respectively. Sexual mores were lax, and sanctioned a promiscuity which Father Chirino attributed to the belief that women could not enter the afterlife without the help of their lovers. *Kinadalagahan* was a man who deflowered a virgin, whether lover or husband, and Father San Buenaventura (1613, 510) explained, "They do not consider the easy, unstable women they call *handa na babayi*, harlots. . . . [It comes] from *handa*, which means prepared, because so they are." But those who were too ready and too frequent with their favors were scorned as *gibon* (wobbly) or *lagap* (common to all). *Abang* were the worst— lascivious, depraved, and completely profligate, "than whom no goat or hen gives herself more freely to all" (San Buenaventura 1613, 511). And *antol* was one with "body sickness."[33]

Social Structure

Like the Visayans, the Tagalogs had a three-class social structure. The ruling class was called *maginoo*, including datus, who were the heads of *barangay*s; and their supporters were *timawa* or *maharlika*. Everybody else was *alipin*—slaves, bondsmen, or debt peons. Moreover, the difference between the serflike householding slaves, *alipin sa namamahay*, and the more lowly domestic slaves, *alipin sa gigilid*, was so great that Father Plasencia described them as two separate classes. He also considered the *maharlika* a separate class.

Maginoo and datu. The Tagalog aristocracy or upper class were called "maginoo," those who could claim noble descent; one of the chiefs who surrendered the port of Manila in 1570 was Maginoo Marlanaway. *Ginoo* was a title of respect for both sexes, while Gat or Dayang preceding a proper name was the equivalent of Lord or Lady. *Panginoon* were those with lordship over many slaves and valuable property like houses or boats, more commonly called *may-ari* (one with plenty of possessions), or even *dalam*, which was actually a large, well-staffed house and household. *Poon* was an honorific contraction when addressing them—for example, "Oo poon [Yes sir]" or "Aba poon [Greetings, lord]" (San Buenaventura 1613, 551). But nouveaux riches were scornfully referred to as *maygintawo*, "fellow with a lot of gold"—or, as San Buenaventura (1613, 351) put it, "hidalgo by gold, not lineage, a 'dark knight,' as we would say." *Puno* (root) was the founder of a descent line (lalad), whose identity had to be established in reckoning precedence or settling dowries, with ritual boasting being a normal part of formal gatherings. (*Bansag* was boasting of lineage and wealth; *lingas,* of wealth and ferocity.) Careless claims to being *mahal*—well-born gentry— could evoke caustic comments like, "Sino ang nagpuno sa inyo di alipin din [Who founded your line if not a slave]?" (San Buenaventura 1613, 172).

Maginoo with personal followings were called datus; *nagdarato* meant "to rule a barrio or barangay," that is, a community or following (San Buenaventura 1613, 130).[34] They usually had a public lounging platform called *gulang-gulang* under their houses for the discussion of community affairs and the exchange of news and gossip. A datu's following or faction was called a *dulohan,* or more popularly, a barangay, literally a boat. Father Plasencia was told that the latter name came from the fact that Filipino settlers first arrived in the archipelago in boats each captained by a single datu with his whole family and retainers, though it is hardly likely that the entire Tagalog population could have maintained discrete boatload identities across centuries or millennia. But whatever its origin, this picturesque term was adopted by the colonial government to mean a tribute-collecting unit: right up until the end of the Spanish regime, baptismal registers listed parents not by their place of residence but as belonging to "the barangay of Don So-and-so."

Barangays ranged in size from a few households to as many as a hundred. Taytay (Rizal), for instance, had four hundred families under four datus when Father Chirino arrived there in 1591. A settlement which consisted of a single barangay was called *pook,* but usually from four to ten chiefs with their dulohan lived together in a *bayan* (town), giving precedence on the basis of wealth or military prowess. When they met together on mutual business, such a gathering was called *lipon, lupon,* or *pulong*—a municipal council, so to speak. Large bayan might be the seat of actual chiefdoms with paramount rulers called Lakan or Rajah, like the two at the mouth of the Pasig River, Tondo on the north and Manila on the south. The role of such a chief was revealed in a description of Si Banaw Lakan Dula by his great-grandson, Juan Macapagal, in 1665.

> Don Carlos Lacandola . . . was Lord and most principal of the town of Tondo, and of the other surrounding towns, whose natives paid him tribute and vassalage and other recognition as their natural lord, and when ships from China came to this bay, they similarly paid him duties and anchorage fees, he removing their sails and rudder for this purpose, and taking their merchandise by paying half its value at the time and

the other half the next year, without any other natives being able to buy anything from the Sanglayes [Chinese] but only from the said Lacandola, from which he had much profit (Macapagal 1665, 219).[35]

The datu's duties. A datu was expected to govern his people, lead them in war, protect them from their enemies, settle their disputes, and—as good administrator Dr. Morga (1609, 191) said—"succor them in their struggles and needs." His authority was reflected in his being called *basal,* the drumstick with which he beat a gong to summon his people. As captain either ashore or afloat—or pilot—he was called *tuway;* though as captain-owner of a large vessel he might take the more prestigious Bornean title of *anakora;* and when acting as guide for other datus, he was called *panugot* or *kanulo.*

But datus were not called kings *(hari),* not even paramount chiefs; that term was known only in reference to foreign monarchies *(kaharian)* and their viceroys *(halili).* It is significant that Spaniards called them *principales* (chiefs), not *régulos* (rulers). Plasencia likened them to *caballeros* (knights), that is, beneficiaries of a *caballería,* and a caballería was an encomienda, an assigned commission together with its duties, privileges, and income. This is precisely the role in which the colonial government would cast the Filipino *principalia* of later generations.

As a judge *(hukom),* a datu convoked the litigants, heard sworn testimony, and handed down a decision, all in the presence of his people, and sometimes with the assistance of older men. His decision could be appealed, however, to an arbiter of the contestant's choice from another community, even a non-datu. If he himself was sued by one of his peers, he appeared before a wise legalist acceptable to him and his accuser, but if such arbitration failed, the plaintiff initiated a blood feud which ran its violent course until mutual exhaustion satisfied honor and both parties agreed to a financial settlement. The law itself was handed down by tradition, but was liable to amendment by consensus among leading datus, and to circumvention by any among them powerful enough to do so.

Penalties varied with the social status of the parties (for example, alipin could be put to death for offending maginoo), and were usually fines heavy enough to result in debt slavery. Adultery was settled by indemnification of the offended husband, which sum was taken as future dowry and signified his adoption of any resulting child as his own. Capital punishment for offenders was prescribed only for witchcraft or infraction of religious tabus, in which case the presiding datu took possession of the condemned man's children, as he also did in the case of total enslavement, compensating the plaintiff himself.

Control over available arable land was vested in the datu, but only irrigated land was distributed among his barangay with right of usufruct; hillside swiddens could be worked freely by any resident, or even aliens. The datu also had the right to retain certain land use for himself—for example, the restriction of access to fisheries, or the collection of market fees at a strategic passage on a waterway. Indeed, upstream datus were known to manipulate Manila market prices by delaying the delivery of rice. He could also convert his rights into regular payments from his people, as the ruler of Pila (Laguna) did after he purchased that place in gold from its former chief, charging his maharlika a regular fee for use of the land. It is noteworthy that the rate was fixed at 4 cavans a year rather than at some percentage of the produce or size of the holding, making the holder his vassal, not his tenant.

The datu's privileges. A datu received services, agricultural produce, and respect from his people. The respect was shown by such deferential behavior as covering the mouth with the hand when addressing him, or contracting the body in a deep bow on entering his presence indoors and raising the hands alongside the cheeks, and he was never addressed as "Ohoy!" or "Oya!" the ordinary greeting among friends. The same deference was shown his family and descendants, in office or out—all maginoo, in short— and slander against any of them was severely punished. He received a share of harvests as tribute from the lower classes, and additional contributions such as a jar of sugarcane wine or *tuba* on such occasions as his feasts or funerals.

Personal services were of two kinds: seasonal field labor from which nobody was exempt of any class, participation in maritime and military expeditions, and unscheduled occasions like house construction or opening new land, for all of which labor the laborers were fed or feasted. Seafaring duties in service of a datu were especially demanding: to equip and supply the vessel and then to row it, either as slaves or as warriors, or to come, provisioned and armed, as soon as he called and as often, and to follow wherever he led.

Timawa and maharlika. A datu's nonslave followers were freemen called timawa and maharlika: they could not be legally bought and sold—for which reason the Boxer Codex and Plasencia called them "hidalgos"—and had the theoretical right to attach themselves to the datu of their choice. The earliest accounts called timawa "commoners" *(la gente común)* or "plebeians" *(plebeyos),* both terms suggesting in sixteenth-century Spain ineligibility to marry a person of noble or royal blood. They enjoyed agricultural rights to a portion of the barangay land, both to use and bequeath, and to harvest without paying tribute. Although contractual relations with their datus varied and even included tribute in some cases, their datus were basically their lords, not their landlords. Their normal obligation was agricultural labor worked off in groups when summoned for planting or harvesting; but they might also be liable to work fisheries, accompany expeditions, or row boats. Like members of the alipin class, they, too, could be called out for irregular services like supporting feasts or building houses.

Timawa were born into their class, but their ultimate origin lay in the maginoo class above them and the alipin below. From the former they absorbed the illegitimate offspring of maginoo with their unmarried slaves— or married serfs—and from the alipin, those who had successfully repaid debts, completed indenture, or literally purchased their freedom in gold. The definitions in the early dictionaries are unambiguous. San Buenaventura (1613, 389) defined *timawa* as "without servitude [*esclavonía*], the common people after the magnate," and illustrated with the example, "Titimawain kita [I'll set you free]." His contemporary, Blancas de San José (1614a, *timawa*), was even more illuminating:

> A free man who was formerly a slave, and from this they say *timawa* of one who escapes death by chance, like one in the hangman's noose and the rope breaks, or the bull that cannot be captured because of his bravery, and, changing the accent, *nagtitimawak* is a slave who has freed himself by running away from his master, and the same with animals.

The word *maharlika* is ultimately derived from Sanskrit *maharddhika*, a man of wealth, wisdom, or competence, which in precolonial Java meant members of religious orders exempt from tribute or taxation. In the sixteenth-century Philippines, they were apparently a kind of lower aristocracy who rendered military service to their lords. The maharlika accompanied their captain abroad, armed at their own expense, whenever he called and wherever he went, rowed his boat not as galley slaves but as comrades-at-arms, and received their share of the spoils afterwards.

Plasencia is the only sixteenth-century observer known to mention the maharlika, and he did not explain the origin of their status. They may well have been a sort of diluted maginoo blood, perhaps the descendants of mixed marriages between a ruling line and one out of power, or scions of a conquered line which struck this bargain to retain some of its privileges. At any event, they were subject to the same requirements of seasonal and

extraordinary community labor as everybody else in the barangay. Technically, they were less free than the ordinary timawa since, if they wanted to
transfer their allegiance once they were married, they had to host a public
feast and pay their datu from 6 to 18 pesos in gold—"otherwise," Father
Plasencia (1589a, 25) added, "it could be an occasion for war."

This maharlika profession was destined to disappear under colonial
pacification, of course, just as the raids in which it was practiced disappeared. Indeed, the effects of the change were already evident in Plasencia's
day: the lord of Pila had commuted his maharlika's services into feudal
dues. The process is reflected in seventeenth-century lexicons. Blancas de
San José (1614a, *maharlika*) defined *maharlika* as "freemen though with a
certain subjugation in that they may not leave the *barangay:* they are the
people called *villeins* [*la gente villano*]—meaning countryfolk living on
some nobleman's villa." But San Buenaventura (1613, 389) illustrated with
the example, "Sa ikapat ang kamaharlikaan ko [I'm one-quarter free]." At
the end of the century, Domingo de los Santos gave "For one who was a
slave to be freed," and in 1738 Juan Francisco de San Antonio (1738, 159)
cited as a common expression, "Minahadlika ako nang panginoon ko [My
master freed me]."

Alipin. *Alipin* was always translated as "slave," and their condition, both
men and women, was attributed to one of three causes—captivity, birthright, or debt. In a sense they were all debtors: that is, they had their price,
and their owner or creditor might recover it by resale or manumission.
Their subordination was therefore obligatory until their debt was redeemed,
and their masters were technically their creditors rather than their lords.
The alipin had birthright claim to work a piece of the barangay land which
could not be taken away from him or he from it, except in case of a
commuted death sentence by which he became a chattel slave. Alipin
might be born as such—in which case they were called *gintubo*—but what
they really inherited from their parents was their debt, indenture, or
sentence. Although they could not be legally seized and sold, their debt
could be transferred from one creditor to another for profit. For this
reason, a man who fell into debt sought to become alipin to his own
relatives if possible. As a matter of fact, men in extreme penury might
voluntarily seek the security of alipin status, that is, become *napaaalipin* as
opposed to *naaalipin*. Indeed, to take on a debt slave was even considered
a form of succor: Father Oliver (1590b, 26) said of a rich man with many
slaves, "Kaniyang inaalila [he took them in]." *Tubos, sakop,* and *ara* all
meant to underwrite a debt in exchange for bondage, occasions which no

224

doubt proliferated under colonial tribute demands—for example, "Paaraan mo ako nitong ambagan [Pay for me and cover this tax I owe]" (San Buenaventura 1613, 459).

Since the degree of alipin indebtedness could vary, when that debt was passed on to heirs it varied according to the debts of either parent or even those inherited from preceding generations. In the case of a mixed marriage between alipin and timawa, their offspring's condition was determined by their *saya,* and *saya* was defined as

> dependence of the children of slaves: if the father is free, so is the first child, and the second is slave like the mother, etc.; contrariwise, if the mother is free, the first is slave like the father and the second is free like the mother, and so on with all the rest, and if they are an odd number, the last one is half-slave and half-free (San Buenaventura 1613, 478).

Moreover, if alipin had three non-alipin grandparents, they were quarter-slaves. What all this meant in practical terms was that such alipin only worked off half their father's, or one-quarter their grandfather's, indebtedness during alternate months. Such partial alipin also had the right to enforce their manumission if they could afford the price.

The ordinary alipin with land rights was called *namamahay,* householder; and one who had lost that right, or never had it—for example, a gintubo, captive, or purchase—was called *alipin sa gigilid,* "hearth slave." In addition, the Boxer manuscript made the curious remark that there was a kind of slave of both namamahay and gigilid status called *tagalos.* If this was not a flat error, it may have been obtained from some informant of Bornean descent and thus reflected a perceived relationship between the two peoples.

Alipin namamahay. Spanish accounts consistently translated *alipin* as "slave," but their authors just as consistently deplored the illogic of including the namamahay in the same category as the gigilid, or even in the category of *esclavo* at all. It was obvious that the gigilid—or at least some gigilid—were chattel house slaves, "like those we have," as Morga (1609, 192) said, but it was just as obvious that the serflike namamahay were not. One of the longest entries in the San Buenaventura (1613, 299) dictionary belabors the point, and includes the following passage:

> These *namamahay* slaves in Silanga, which is on the way to Giling-giling from Lumban, make one field called *tungo* [contract], and it is to be noted that they have no further obligation to their master; in Pila, Bay, Pillila [Pililla] and Moron, they are

225

almost free for they serve their master no more than from time to time, and they say he almost has to beg them to go with him to other places or to help him with something, the same as he does with the freemen; in all the hills as far as Calaylayan, they serve their master from time to time if he calls them, but if he calls them too often it's considered an abuse.

Father Plasencia solved the problem directly and sensibly: he called them *pecheros* (tribute payers). The *pecho* they paid was called *handog* and amounted to half their crop, though the Visayan term *buwis* was in more common use; hence, *nunuwis*, tribute payer, and *pabuwisan*, encomienda. In addition, the namamahay was expected to present a measure of threshed rice or a jar of wine for his master's feasts, and generally a share of any special foodstuffs he might acquire for himself—like the leg of a deer taken in the hunt. Like everybody else, he came at his master's call to plant and harvest his fields, build his houses, carry his cargo, equip his boat, and row it when he went abroad—not as a warrior but as an oarsman, unless relieved of this status as an accolade for bravery—and in any emergency such as his master's being sick, captured, or flooded out. He owned his own house, personal belongings, and gold, and bequeathed them to his heirs, but his ownership of the land he used was restricted: he could not alienate it. If his master moved out of the settlement, he continued to serve him as a kind of absentee landlord, and if his master died, he was obligated to all his master's heirs and had to divide his services among them. Upon his own death, his creditor had the right to take one of his children for gigilid domestic service in the creditor's own house, but if such creditor took more, he was considered a tyrant.

Namamahay came into their condition in three ways: inheritance from namamahay parents, dropping down from timawa status, or rising up from gigilid. If one's debt arose from legal action or insolvency, he and his creditor agreed on the duration of the bondage and an equivalent cash value for its satisfaction. In Plasencia's day this never exceeded 10 taels in gold, or roughly the market value of 320 cavans of rice at Manila prices. Those who rose from the ranks of the gigilid hearth slaves might actually have purchased their freedom, but mainly they were transferred to namamahay householding status for their master's convenience when they married. For this reason, captives and purchased slaves may have been set up in namamahay housekeeping status from the beginning.

Alipin sa gigilid. *Gilid* was the "nethermost part of the house where the hearth is," but also where the family made their toilet and so was a deprecatory term in contrast to *duyo*, entrance or front. These lowly alipin were members of their master's household and ate out of their master's pot. They were as dependent on him as his own children, and from this circumstance arose his moral right to sell them. In actual practice, however, he rarely did so. He might transfer them to some other creditor, but raw material for the slave trade or human sacrifice was not procured from the household, or even from the alipin labor pool which implemented a datu's public and private projects. Quite the opposite, they might be rewarded at their master's pleasure, or his hope of motivating them, by being permitted to retain some of the fruits of their labor, even to the extent of eventually purchasing their liberty. Indeed, if they could accumulate enough gold—say, through the trade of goldsmith or by participating in raids—they could buy their way not only into namamahay status, but even timawa. Juan San Antonio (1738, 160), reporting the old 30–peso manumission price 130 years later, commented, "And if he gave 60 or more, he was free of everything and became a hidalgo."

The main source of alipin sa gigilid recruitment were the children born in their master's house, not infrequently natural children by his own alipin of either status, as well as those of men under such financial straits they could not afford to raise them. Once a hearth slave grew up and married, it was more practical and profitable to set him up in his own house instead of feeding and housing him and his new family. For namamahay, household status only fell to married alipin; domestic gigilid slaves were single. The author of the Boxer manuscript described the situation with some surprise:

> His master can sell him because none of these slaves who are in their master's house are married, but all maidens and bachelors, and in the case of a male who wishes to marry, the chief does not lose him, [for] such a one is called *namamahay* when married and then lives by himself, but rarely would they give the [female] slaves who were in the chief's house permission to marry, though they would hinder none of the men (Boxer Codex 1590b, 383).

The terms *gigilid* and *namamahay* therefore distinguished a man's place of residence and marital status, and were incidental to a sliding scale of downward social mobility occasioned by punitive disenfranchisement and economic reversal. The condemned man's debt to society and fiscal obligations could be underwritten by some other man motivated by kin loyalty or hope of gain. If both were alipin and neighbors and relatives, their new relationship might be no more evident than a redistribution of their labor. But the social stigma was considerable, for the gigilid of a namamahay was called by the insulting term *bulisik*, "vile, contemptible." Still worse, the poor wretch who became the gigilid of a gigilid was branded *bulislis,* "exposed"—like the private parts when one's dress is hitched up. The word *gilid* itself could also he derogatory, for that was the place where a household defecated—for example, "Mangigilid ako [I'm going down to the toilet *(hacer cámara)*]" (San Buenaventura 1613, 138).

Slaves purchased from outside the community and captives taken in war or raids could be real chattel without even the security of the parental affection of some master in whose house they grew up. If they were destined for resale or sacrifice, they would literally be nonpersons in society, but if they were brought into the community as functioning alipin, they would perforce enjoy the right of food, shelter, and work of other alipin. Their children would then be born into society not as aliens but as gintubo, "children of alipin," and as such be eligible for whatever social amelioration fortune might offer them.

In the absence of statistics, it is not possible to say what percentage of the Tagalog population belonged to which social class, or how much social mobility was upward and how much downward. Moreover, our sources were all written a generation after Spanish advent; and during that quarter century, historic changes had taken place which had profoundly affected Tagalog society. There were now more mouths to feed, and new tribute demands to meet; Chinese trade had increased tenfold; and colonial police power was preventing further procurement of captive slaves. These were all changes which would have inflated the value of local slaves, and provided incentive for reducing timawa to namamahay status, and namamahay to gigilid. That this was taking place in the 1590s is suggested by another passage in the Boxer Codex (1590b, 384):

> If they have many children, when many have been taken and he takes more, they consider it a tyrannical abuse, and once those who are leaving the chief's house to marry do leave, they do not return to render him any more service than the *namamahay* do, unless he uses force, and this they consider a worse tyranny in as much as they were given permission to leave his house and he makes them return to it; and these slaves inherited these customs from their ancestors.

A nice assessment of this kind of slavery is provided by Franciscan Father Juan de Oliver in a hortatory exposition on the Ten Commandments intended for the Tagalog faithful of Batangas in 1590. Addressing his listeners as Maginoo, he asked rhetorically: What rich man with alipin would not get angry if they did not obey him; and did that man not have the duty to order them what to do and teach them what is right? After all, it was he who "took them in"—*inalila,* meaning "to take care of something, like the sick, or some other thing, such as the shepherd his sheep" (San Buenaventura 1613, 211). But outright enslavement was inveighed against under the sin of usury: "How many maharlika had been thus enslaved *(inaalipin)* those days! That is why God likened men to the fishes of the sea, the larger gobbling up the smaller." But the householding alipin was mentioned under the commandment to keep the Sabbath holy: Just as the alipin namamahay and his master divided his working days alternately between them, so the infinitely more generous overlordship of God divided labor in man's favor, six to one.

Land and Property

Tagalog wealth was based on movable property like gold and jewelry, not real estate, and the possession of slaves, not the land which they worked. Dr. Morga (1609, 193), like many earlier observers, stated unambiguously, "These slaves are the major possessions and wealth the natives of these islands have." San Buenaventura gave *ari* and *pakayan* for "property" *(hacienda)* and equated them with Spanish *ajuar,* household possessions, furnishings, valuables, and ornaments. *Sadili* were the personal possessions brought into a marriage by either spouse, but *kasamahan* was conjugal property after the birth of children. Inheritance *(kamanahan)* was illustrated with examples like "Mag kano kaya ang gintong kamanahan mo sa daga mo [How much gold was your inheritance from your aunt]?" (San Buenaventura 1613, 350). Morga commented that inheritance might also include *bienes raices,* "goods with roots"—for example, coconut plantations and, presumably, irrigated rice fields—and Plasencia said that householding slaves inherited their parents' gold and enjoyed *(gozan)* their property and lands. But these were lands held in usufruct, not in fee simple—that is, to use but not to own or alienate.

Arable land, woodlands, and water sources occupied by a bayan were considered to be communal resources; and so were uninhabited forests, though these were only entered after asking the permission of sylvan deities for hunting, foraging, or timbering. Swidden rights were the same as in the rest of the archipelago: whoever opened a hillside plot had the right to the crops, but not to the land. Otherwise, Father Plasencia (1589a, 24) said, "the lands where they live they divide among the whole barangay, and thus each knows his own, especially what is irrigated." Since a community's land was perceived as unlimited, there was little incentive for alienation; rather, it was labor which was bought and sold or mortgaged—that is, through debt slavery. Such slaves may very well have continued to live in their own houses and work the same fields, giving their creditors a share of their crops, though they could also have been assigned elsewhere. Ruling datus, however, could dispose of untilled land for their own profit—by restricting fishing rights, for example, or taxing forest products. Rajah Lakandula permitted Chinese refugees to settle on the Tondo shore, a grant which became the basis of individual land claims in the next century.

These prerogatives enabled datus to take quick advantage of the Spanish concept of real estate introduced by the colonial government—alienable private property, registration of transactions and wills, and issuance of title deeds. By the 1590s, religious orders had need of land, private speculators were hungry for it, and datus were ready to supply it. A datu could logically claim and sell land his family, ancestors, and slaves had been working, and also—if less logically—all uncultivated land in his barangay domain. What happened to the land which had been divided so that "each knows his own" is not clear, but at least all early title deeds identify landowners as *principales*—that is, chiefs or maginoo. In most cases the land being sold or donated was not under rice cultivation, or even under cultivation at all. When Bartolome Alison and Andres Duarte made a donation to the Franciscan hospital in Los Baños in 1608, they stated that it was "to make use of and dispose the said land as the said Hospital most desires and considers most suitable for advantage from it" (Alison 1608). But when Rajah Matanda's granddaughter Catalina gave the Augustinians 200 pesos worth of land in 1621, this presumably represented the value of the crops grown on it. One wonders if this donation involved the dispossession of any timawa or namamahay tribute payers supporting Doña Catalina's family.

At the time of the conquest, the Spanish government only recognized land actually being farmed as alienable, and even then, in a vain attempt to protect Filipino property rights, the law required a specific justification for legal sale—for example, the owner was too old to farm, or the land was too hilly. But Tagalog sellers soon learned to collude with Spanish buyers to circumvent the law. On 13 January 1620, Dionisio Kapolong, son of Lakandula, obtained permission to sell a piece of land measuring 40 by 100 *brazas* (about 1 hectare) in Kinabayanan on the outskirts of Tondo to one Luis de Torres to cover debts amounting to 200 pesos. Dionisio presented witnesses who variously swore that the land was his, that it was inconveniently located, unsuitable for agriculture, or only had fruit trees growing on it; though one of them opposed the sale, and two others subsequently claimed payment for having planted the fruit trees. Torres promptly resold the land for the same price to Juan Pangiligan, who paid 100 pesos outright, bound himself to deliver the balance within three months, and took possession on the 5th of February as Torres's *inquilino* (tenant).

But on the 4th of February, Agustin Wika of Tondo had filed claim to the land, and so had his wife Monica Sayan the next day, and on the 8th they brought suit against both Torres and Don Dionisio. They testified that they had purchased part of the land at legal sale and inherited the rest from Wika's father, Ama ni Kalaw; that as soon as they learned of this sale, they had rushed to the Tondo court but found the records missing; that Luis de Torres was a Spanish bully who had threatened them, compromised the court, and had so intimidated other Filipinos that they were afraid to testify against him; and that Juan Pangiligan was his employee and being used as a dummy to circumvent Governor Juan de Silva's decree against Spaniards residing in Tondo or Binondo. They also swore that it was public knowledge that Don Dionisio was a ne'er-do-well who had squandered his patrimony in profligate living and had been selling off both his own and other people's property. They were therefore appealing to the Royal Audiencia in Manila for justice. Whatever the merits of the case or the decision of the court (the records have not survived), Luis de Torres seems to have prevailed in the end; the next year he sold the property to the Dominicans.

Warfare

Father Martín de Rada (1577, 484) said the Tagalogs were "more merchants than warlike," but this did not mean that they did not fight wars: the early accounts are unanimous in saying that one of a vassal's duties was to follow his datu to war. They made raids, avenged grievances, waged vendettas, seized captives, and took lives in mourning for prominent chiefs. Attacking forces taunted "those who were about to be defeated" with victory chants called *dayaw* or *tagumpay* (San Buenaventura 1613, 141). Real braves—*bayani*—were honored with special feasts in which they danced with a headdress made of gold-plated carabao horn, and were addressed as Bayani the rest of their lives. Indeed, one of the few Chinese words to enter Tagalog in the sixteenth century was *hukbo* (ambush), the Hokkien word for army. More than one observer equated male valor with the accumulation of wealth, and Rada (1577, 484), after saying the Tagalogs were less warlike, added, "But in robberies, thefts [and] tyrannies of property and persons . . . they exceed all others." By this he meant high interest rates, debt slavery even among relatives, dispossessing orphans, collecting from debtors' barangay-mates, and plundering vessels driven ashore. Nor did

Tagalog men suffer insults meekly: *balantogi* was defined as *lex talionis* (that is, an eye for an eye, a tooth for a tooth), and *sampal* was to split a man from top down. San Buenaventura (1613, 349) illustrated with the example, "Sa akoy lalaban niya'y sinampa ako nang aking katana [He defied me so I split him in half with my sword]." Unrequited enmity within the community often led to poisoning, especially in the case of those too powerful to be attacked openly.

Heads were brought back as trophies of war. When the Spaniards invaded Batangas towns, they often found enemy heads impaled on stakes, and *bayubay* meant "to hang the heads of the vanquished on long bars, as these natives used to do." *Pugot* and *sumbali* meant to cut a head off, and *tungol* or *bungol* was to grab someone from behind and cut his throat. Perhaps the *iwa*—a dagger wide and flat at the end—was a weapon designed for head taking. Father Plasencia, in his 1592 *Relación*, said, "When some chief dies, to avenge his death they had to cut off many heads, with which they would make many feasts and dances" (Plasencia 1592, 484), and the Boxer Codex (1590b, 383) said that when they brought back a head from war, "they would hold a drunken revel for two or three days." But the best known description came from Dr. Morga in 1609:

> They show great dexterity when they go after their opponent. Grabbing him by the hair with one hand, they cut off his head with the other with one stroke of their *balarao* . . . and carry it off since they keep them hanging in their houses afterwards where they can be seen; of these they make a display so they will be taken as braves and avengers of their enemies and their injuries (Morga 1609,175).

Tagalogs fought with the usual Philippine weapons—the single-edged *balaraw* dagger, the wavy kris *(kalis)*, spears with both metal and fire-hardened tips, padded armor and carabao-hide breastplates, and long narrow shields *(kalasag)*, or round bucklers *(palisay)*. The bow and arrow were used only in certain regions, and the blowgun nowhere. Those with access to foreign imports sometimes had Japanese swords *(katana)* or Chinese peaked helmets *(kupya* or *tangkulog);* but the Chinese evidently never shared their firearms, though Legazpi sent one to Spain which was taken from a Chinese junk in Mindoro. The Bornean arquebus *(astingal)* was also known, but the Spaniards seem never to have faced any in Luzon encounters as they did in Mindanao.

The usual defensework *(moog)* was a tower palisaded with logs and bamboo, but towns with Malay technology built more substantial fortifications *(kuta)* with the palisades standing on raised earthworks surrounded by a fosse or actual moat *(bangbang)*, and, at least in the case of one fort on

Lubang Island, a drawbridge. In the Moro region, these square stockades mounted small artillery—what the Spaniards called *falconetes* and *versos*— usually three pieces to a side. The Manila fort contained a gun foundry where the Spaniards found evidence of considerable industry after it was burned in 1570—clay and wax moulds and one 4–meter piece in the process of manufacture. They took twelve damaged pieces back to Panay, ten of bronze and two of iron, and recovered six from the river where they had been thrown to avoid capture, which were sent to Spain. The quantity and quality of Manila ordinance is indicated by Governor Sande's (1579, 147) collecting 18,000 kilos of bronze artillery from towns surrounding Manila, and his employment of Filipinos to cast him a 4,000–kilo cannon of which he reported, "There is not in the castle of Milan a piece so well made." Fortunately, one example of Filipino workmanship has survived: it is a swivel gun *(lantaka)* in the Museu Militar in Lisbon (see fig. 11).

Religion

Our earliest surviving account of Tagalog religion is a remarkable two-paragraph summary by encomendero Miguel de Loarca, remarkable in that it sounds much like what is nowadays called folk Catholicism. It presents a creator god who can only be approached through intercessors like deceased relatives or the patron deities of farmers, seafarers, or warriors, all of whom are worshiped in the form of idols which receive sacrifices and adornment. It stands in marked contrast to his lengthy description of Visayan religion with its origin myths, divine genealogies, pantheon of deities, and realms of the dead, a description obviously derived from personal observation and contact with worshipers themselves, rather than a native apologist. It must be said at the offset, however, that it is difficult to account for the actual practice of Tagalog religion within this theological framework. Missionaries in the field—and in the confessional—evinced no doubt that the multitude of deities, spirits, and ancestors being invoked by Tagalog shamans were objects of worship in their own right, not mere intercessors. A plausible explanation for the discrepancy might be that Spanish Christians like Loarca were predisposed to find concepts in other religions which were normative in their own.

Worship. Loarca and Chirino said that the Tagalogs recognized a creator god they called Bathala—though other informants named Molayri or Diwata—but Father Plasencia (1589b, 598) simply said,

"The one they principally adored among many other idols was one whom they called Badhala." The name itself is apparently derived from Sanskrit *bhattara* (noble lord), which appeared as the sixteenth-century title *batara* in the southern Philippines and Borneo. Bathala was described as "may kapal sa lahat [maker of everything]," *kapal* meaning to mould something between the hands like clay or wax. Dr. Antonio de Morga, among others, thought it meant an omen bird, but the author of the Boxer Codex (1590b, 379) was advised not to use it in this sense "because they did not consider it God, but only [his] messenger." He was also told that the first word of this god to reach the Philippines was brought by male prophets as "readers of the scriptures of God [taga pagbasa nang sulatan a (?) dios]" (Boxer Codex 1590b, 367). If the story is to be taken seriously, it may be worth noting that in Malay, *betara* means holy, and was a title applied to the greater Hindu gods in Java, and was also assumed by the ruler of Majapahit.

There was no single word in Tagalog for the other deities to whom Bathala was superior: when necessary, Spanish lexicographers referred to them all as *anito*. So Father San Buenaventura (1613, 255) commented of Bathala, "According to some he was considered to be the greatest of their anitos." Some of them had names descriptive of their functions. Lakan Bakod, the lord of fences *(bakod)*, was invoked to keep animals out of swiddens; and Aman Sinaya, father of Sinaya who became the inventor of fishing gear, was named when first wetting a net or fishhook. These were the kind of gods the Loarca summary explained as Bathala's agents. So, too, the early dictionaries used the word *abogado* (advocate) when defining their realms—for example, Lakambini, the abogado of the throat, invoked in case of throat ailments. But in actual prayers, they were petitioned directly, not as intermediaries. During sacrifices made in a new field to Lakapati, a major fertility deity, the farmer would hold up a child and say, "Lakapati, pakanin mo yaring alipin mo; huwag mong gutumin [Lakapati, feed this thy slave; let him not hunger]" (San Buenaventura 1613, 361).

Prominent among deities who received full-blown sacrifices were fertility gods. Lakapati, fittingly represented by a hermaphrodite image with both male and female parts, was worshiped in the fields at planting time; and Lakanbakod, who had gilded genitals as long as a rice stalk, was offered eels when fencing swiddens—because, they said, his were the strongest of all fences, "Linalakhan [*sic*] niya ang bakod nag bukid" (San Buenaventura 1613, 361).

Proprietary deities were appeased both for fruitful produce and protection from harm in their special domains—like Aman Ikabli, the patron of hunters, or Dian Masalanta, of lovers and childbirth. Tuba tappers who

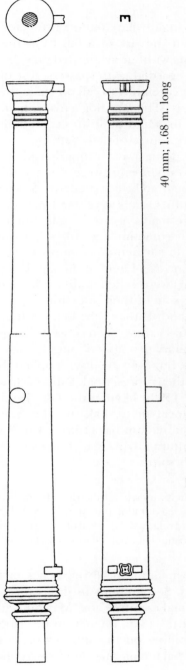

40 mm; 1.68 m. long

Fig. 11. Artist's rendering of the *lantaka* (swivel gun)
preserved in the Museu Militar in Lisboa

failed to make offering to Mankukutod, protector of coconut palms, before climbing a tree, ran the risk of a fall from the trunk. Nobody entered grasslands or forests without acknowledging the overlordship of Uwinan Sana lest they be regarded as trespassers, nor did seamen set sail before sponsoring a major ceremony to call on Haik, the sea god, for fair weather and favorable winds. The Tagalog environment was also peopled with lesser deities like Linga and Bibit who caused illness if not given recognition in the ordinary course of daily activities.

Images of these deities were properly called *likha*, but also *larawan*, a model or form. Wooden ones were often crudely anthropomorphic in form and large enough to be adorned with gold chains or have actual food placed in their mouth. Others were small enough to be carried around like talismans, and were made of stone, gold, shell, or clay—not necessarily always a figure but sometimes a crocodile tooth, a boar's tusk, or an unusual stone. Little earthenware figures in the shape of a man or cat, imported from China, were held in the hand to swear an oath. But images of deceased persons were called anito, which Father Blancas de San José defined as "idol or soul of their ancestors."

On the other hand, Father Ribadeneyra thought such anito were believed by the Tagalogs to have been conceived together with human beings, good ones for ordinary people, evil ones for slaves and the less fortunate. Other missionaries, however, regularly applied the term to all idols as well as the "false gods" they represented. Father Oliver (1590b, 32), preaching in Batangas in the 1590s, likened the Old Testament "great anito called Beelzebub" to a local deity, Lakan Balingasay—"malaking Anito ang pangalan si Belzebu, na kun baga dito Lakan Balingasay."

Father Buenaventura (1613, 361), however, insisted that the term really meant an act of worship:

> More appropriately would it be called an offering because *anito* does not signify any particular thing, such as an idol, but an offering and the prayer they would make to deceased friends and relatives... [or] an offering they made to anything they finished, like a boat, house, fishnet, etc., and it was mats, cooked food, gold, and other things.

Thus, *naga-anito* meant to perform such an act, and *pinagaanitohan* was the soul petitioned. So penitents in the confessional were asked, "Naga-anito ka [Did you make anito]?" or "May pinaga-anitohang ka [Have you invoked some soul]?" (San Buenaventura 1613, 361). Naga-anito also included any act calling on the supernatural—for example, *malimakan*, taking auguries by balancing one oiled cowry shell on top of another.

Celestial bodies were also venerated as deities—Tala, the Morning Star; Mapulon, the Pleiades; and Balatik, the Big Dipper—and the new moon was always invoked for material increase and wealth. Crocodiles were especially feared and venerated: offerings of food were set out for them, and the *salaksak* bird was considered sacred because it was permitted to pick a crocodile's teeth without harm. Some Tagalogs believed crocodiles had the souls of deceased human beings, and so anointed, shrouded, and buried them when dead. In Batangas, the same obsequies were given a flat-headed lizard called *tuko,* believed to be poisonous. The balete tree was reverenced as the abode of spirits: there the most solemn community sacrifices were made, and there prominent chiefs were sometimes given a secondary burial.

Omen birds and lizards were considered divine messengers, particularly the *tigmamanukan* bird, *manuk* being the general term for any bird, lizard, or snake that crossed the path as an omen. All such encounters were called *salubong.* If the tigmamanukan bird flew across from right to left when men were starting out on an expedition, it was giving the *labay* sign of successful plundering, but if from left to right, a sure warning that they would never return. If they happened to catch one in a trap, they would cut its beak and release it with the words, "Kita ay iwawala, kun akoy mey kakawnan, lalabay ka [You are free, so when I set forth, sing on the right]" (San Buenaventura 1613, 95).

The greatest religious attention was given to ancestor worship—that is, veneration of the spirits of the departed. These were generally parents or grandparents, but occasionally a popular hero known for his bravery, ferocity, and active love life. The former were considered the immediate cause of illness or misfortune, and had to be placated by sacrifices to likha kept in the house (those who could afford to do so set food aside for them at every meal), or the intervention of shamans called *katulunan.* Their memory was carefully kept alive by *himakas,* a personal garment or piece of jewelry preserved as a memorial, and *pahiyin* tabus against mentioning their name, eating from a plate they had used, or sitting in some spot they had frequented. At several points along the Pasig River, porcelain plates were set out with offerings by descendants who trafficked along that route.

The conviction that postmortal well-being depended on the religious ministrations of living descendants is reflected in the readiness of Christian Tagalogs to donate land to the church—for example, Rajah Ache Matanda's granddaughter Catalina, who donated 200 pesos worth to the Augustinians in 1621 for four masses a year for the repose of her soul. In a sense, the dead were considered merely absent: both himakas and *palok* (abstinence from a certain food) applied both to deceased loved ones and those only gone away on a trip. The same was true of a more serious kind of oath called *balata,* which might include not only abstinence but a promise to take vengeance or kill: the term also meant a deerhide or carabao collar which was worn until the oath had been fulfilled.

The mortal soul was called *kaluluwa* and the life spirit *diwa,* but the inner consciousness was *lagyo:* thus, two persons who took the same name were *kalagyo,* "soul mates." Each person also had an individual protecting spirit, a kind of guardian angel, called *katutubo* or *bathalang katutubo.* The kaluluwa could wander off or be seized or enticed to some strange place, thereby causing a fatal illness. After a death, therefore, a naga-anito was performed to determine where the soul had been afflicted, and the survivors would then go to that spot with an offering of gold and a live cock and request the soul not to come back to haunt. In the afterlife, souls went either to Maka, a place of rest, or Kasaanan, a place of anguish. Father Plasencia (1589b, 602) said that those who qualified for Maka were "the just, the brave, and those who had lived without doing harm and had other moral virtues."

The Boxer Codex (1590b, 374), however, probably more realistically attributed the division, not to morality, but to social condition—that is to say, the seamen "who are dressed in white," and the others "who are dressed in red for greater preeminence," a preeminence which, like their red clothes, no doubt arose from having taken a human life. Father Chirino, on the other hand, called the place of rest Kaluwalhatian, whence *luwalhati* entered Spanish lexicons as "glory" by analogy to the pious euphemism for the dead as being "in glory." Virgins, however, could not enter Kaluwalhatian because they had no lovers to help them cross a narrow plank over a raging torrent en route, and women who died in childbirth remained in this world as ghosts who could be heard moaning at night.

Death and burial. At the time of death, the cadaver was wrapped in a shroud and covered with a pall for a four-day wake or, in the case of the prominent, for many days during which the deceased was displayed dressed as in life. ("Though it smelled bad," San Buenaventura (1613, 254) remarked, "they suffered it for love.") The wake *(pulaw)* was characterized by extemporaneous dirges *(sambitan)* and heavy drinking *(tibaw): mapagtibaw* was a drunkard who frequented funerals for this reason. Exequies *(wakas)* held after the burial to assure the departed soul's safe arrival in the afterworld were full-scale feasts with a pig sacrifice and food contributed by guests, and so were Bangkay ceremonies for a secondary burial. But it was

238

the custom for close relatives to refrain from merrymaking for at least two years, until given a gift of gold or silver to end their despondency.

Graves were dug alongside houses or fields, and each mourner threw a handful of soil in, saying, "Dumamay sa iyo ang sakit ko [In thee, let my sorrows end]" (San Buenaventura 1613, 292), and on the way home they took a bath in running water. But the elite were entombed, together with gold and valuables, under their own dwelling in a coffin or boat with a shade above it, around which smoky fires were kept burning for days. Secondary burial was called Bangkay: the bones were exhumed, placed in a jar or other container, and either deposited at the foot of a balete tree or kept in the house. If a boat served as the bier, male-female pairs of chickens, goats, or deer served as oarsmen with a slave assigned to feeding them. If the deceased had been a great warrior, a slave was placed under his body. For that matter, all maginoo-class deaths, or those of people killed by violence, required the taking of additional human lives, few or many depending on the deceased's status or dowry stipulation. Male survivors carried out this requirement, sticking a *tambuyok* plume in their *putong* and donning a rawhide collar as warning they were on the warpath. Until this ended the mourning period, those under oath observed such dietary restrictions as not eating rice or hot food.

Shamans. Katulunan could be of either sex, or male transvestites *(bayugin)*, but were usually women of prominent families who were wealthy in their own right from the practice of their shamanic profession. Their remuneration ranged from foodstuffs to cotton and gold, depending on the means of their clients: one was said to have made 350 pesos in a two-year period. They came to their calling through training and kinship with other katulunan. As spirit mediums, they conducted seances during which they spoke with the voice of deities or spirits, assisted by an *alagar* (personal attendant) to carry on a dialogue with the supernatural, or sent their own kaluluwa to seek literally lost souls. They performed public ceremonies for community prosperity, fertility, or seasonable weather as well as private services to diagnose and cure ailments. They were respected for these functions and for producing charms *(saulupong* or *kabal)* which rendered men or fighting cocks invincible; but they were also feared as sorcerers able to work black magic. Their numbers, too, were large enough to put them in competition with one another: Father Chirino (1604, 112) said that in San Juan del Monte "there was scarcely a lane where there were not three or four, or more." Individual success was attributed to the power of the deities with whom they identified, and who took possession of them in their frenzied dancing.

There were no temples: family idols were kept in little spirit houses constructed at the corner of the dwelling or connected to it by a kind of catwalk. Community sacrifices were held in open fields, or, in the case of especially solemn rites—like one called *pandot*—under a balete tree. For such a festival, tabus on labor or travel were proclaimed *(pangilin)*. Further-more, the participants all contributed food and valuables for a feast, the katulunan's pay, and offerings called *galal*—a term missionary fathers would later adopt for their sacramental bread and wine. A rich datu might also sponsor a pandot, for which temporary roofs were constructed along both sides of his house, but in either case the feast included a fattened hog. By the end of the sixteenth century, if not before, some katulunan were using written incantations in these services, like "reading all night" by torchlight during wakas rites.

Curing ceremonies were performed in private homes, with the katulunan wearing a gold diadem *(basong-basong)* for first-class services, a simple one of palm leaves for the poor. She would begin by making her prognosis by augury, stating whether the case was serious or even fatal—by walking around the patient, for example, dangling a kind of rosary *(talihan)* with thick beads and observing their slight movements. During the healing rite itself, she would smear the patient's forehead with betel nut she had chewed, or with blood from a *padugo* sacrifice, such as two chickens mated before cutting their throats. The climax came when she fell into a trance and sent her kaluluwa to call the truant spirit of the patient, or that of the ancestor responsible for the affliction.

Katulunan presided over all "rites of passage"—for example, from the womb into the world, youth into marriage, or life into death. One of the most important was *dating*, the rite for a girl's first menstruation. The girl was blindfolded, secluded, and attended by the old woman for four days, and fed only a few mouthfuls of rice and two eggs morning and night, while her relatives feasted and celebrated. Then at dawn, she was led down to the river or a stream of flowing water for a ritual bath, without her feet touching dry ground, being either carried or guided across an elevated walkway of planks. Upon her return home, her body was rubbed with oil and civet or musk—traditional male scents—followed by two days and nights of exclu-sively female company and singing. She was then a marriageable damsel, no longer a girl.

Not only katulunan could make charms and cast spells, but also sorcer-ers—that is, ordinary mortals who could work both black magic and white without special appeal to deities. They themselves might disappear for two days at a time—"ilinalayas nang Dimonio [carried off by the Devil]," Father

240

Blancas de San José (1614a, *layas*) said. *Pamayinan* was a charm against harm by wild animals; *tagisama* was one to make a person hate; *tawak* was to be rendered invulnerable to harm, even snake venom; and *dapa* was to be killed by witchcraft. *Mantala* were exorcisms or magic formulas, considered most efficacious if in "the language of Borneo"—that is, Malay. If sorcery made life risky, the presence of a host of witches, ghouls, and monsters made it actually dangerous. The worst of these were the flesh eaters, those who ate away the liver of living persons or drew it out through the anus, doubly dangerous because they might reside in a Tagalog community as normal citizens. Spanish friars did not doubt their existence: a suspect might be asked in the confessional, "Nag-uuswang ka namang para nang ina mo [Do you become a witch like your mother]?" (San Buenaventura 1613, 122). Fray Juan de Mérida also reported burying a Spanish notary whose intestines had been extracted in this gruesome manner. A select roster of such creatures will illustrate their nature and variety.

Hukluban	The most powerful kind of witch, able to kill or cause unconsciousness simply by greeting a person
Matatangal	A liver-eating witch that travels through the air, leaving half its body behind, and which also appears at night without head or entrails, or carrying its head
Mangagaway	A sorcerer able to heal, cause harm, or kill
Mangisalat	A sorcerer able to prevent one from being loved
Mankukulam	A witch who appears at night as if burning, setting fires that cannot be extinguished, or wallows in the filth under houses, whereupon some householder will sicken and die
Patianak	A woman who died in childbirth and reappears as a hobgoblin, passing under houses calling people by name, and whoever replies, dies
Silagan	An earthbound liver eater
Tigbalang	A winged forest phantom that kidnaps men and either starves or releases them; appears as a tall, long-haired figure with very small feet and a beautiful G-string, and leaves a distinctive odor behind
Uswang	General term for liver eaters
Wiwit	Ghost

Foreign influence. By the time of Spanish advent, Tagalog had absorbed a number of religious terms from Borneo. *Binyag* was a kind ritual washing (*manga binyag* were those so purified); and *samba* (to worship) was Malay *sembah,* a worshipful prostration, the modern *simbahan* (church) being a corruption of *sambahan. Siyak,* a teacher or guide of youth, who San Buenaventura thought was a Moro "bishop," was actually the caretaker of a mosque. *Mantala* (exorcism or incantation) was Malay *mantera* from Sanskrit *mantra*. There were also jars *(suuban)* from Borneo in the shape of little figures with holes in the top to serve as a thurible. The psalters and prayer books of Christian worship quickly had their effect, too. A backsliding but repentant convert in 1590 handed over "a book of certain poems which they call *gulo,* very pernicious for including an express pact with the Devil" (Chirino 1604, 47). And Christian or Islamic influence seems apparent in the following description of Bathala:

> They say that this god of theirs was in the air before there was heaven or earth or anything else, that he was *ab eterno* [from eternity] and not made and created by anybody from anything, and that he alone made and created all that we have mentioned simply by his own volition because he wanted to make something so beautiful as the heaven and earth, and that he made and created one man and one woman out of the earth, from whom have come and descended all the men and their generations that are in the world (Boxer Codex 1590b, 367).

CHAPTER 13

Central Luzon

Sixteenth-century Pampanga was simply the basin of the great river system of that name from the Candaba Swamp to the Manila Bay delta. The rest of the modern province, and "Upper Pampanga" (Nueva Ecija), was the forest land with mountains on the west, north, and east inhabited by headhunting Alaguetes, Ilongots, Negritos, and Zambals.

Pampanga Culture

The valley itself produced a surplus of rice, and the forests unlimited deerskins, basic to an extensive trade and the wealth of communities with a high concentration of chiefs. (A 1616 report lists 60,000 deerskins a year collected as tribute for export to Japan.) In the low-lying western delta where counterflooding by salt water from the bay limited rice production, nipa wine was a commercial product.

All Kapampangans wore cotton—"chiefs, *timaguas* [*sic*] and slaves, without distinction of rank" (Dasmariñas 1591, 84)—though it was not grown locally: it was acquired raw from provinces to the south in exchange for rice and gold. The gold came down the river from its headwaters on the

243

Caraballo Sur: Dionisio Kapolong of Candaba regularly traveled that route to deal with Isinay chiefs in the upper Magat River valley (Nueva Vizcaya). He made good use of these connections when he accompanied four Spanish expeditions across the Caraballo and into the Cagayan Valley in the 1590s. The fact that Macabebe was able to attack Legazpi's fleet with forty *karakoa*s only two weeks after he landed in Manila also suggests that Kapampangans may have been among the "Luzones" who traded with Borneo, Malacca, Sumatra, and the Moluccas in pre-Hispanic times.

These vested interests gave Pampanga chiefs a special incentive for submitting to colonial authority once the superiority of Spanish arms had been demonstrated. Fortified Moro towns like Betis and Lubao with small bronze artillery, made initial resistance, and a Macabebe fleet actually challenged Spanish naval power in the disastrous Battle of Bankusay Channel on 3 June 1571. After they failed to inflict any damage on the Spanish ships—no doubt because Southeast Asian gunnery at the time was simply a matter of pointing guns at the enemy without taking aim—the Spaniards closed to arquebus range, and by nightfall had sunk all the Filipino vessels.

Four years later Pampanga was the granary of the colonial capital, and in 1586 while Tagalog chiefs were plotting a revolt, Pampanga chiefs were in Manila appealing for colonial courts not to enforce the manumission of their slaves. That same year, ten-year-old Martin Sancho was sent to Rome, where he eventually became a Jesuit, and in the seventeenth century, the only Filipino residents of San Jose College in Manila were the sons of Pampanga noble families—and their slaves—who were "paying generously for their sustenance" (De la Costa 1967, 505). By this time, the skill of Pampanga archers had made them regular auxiliaries in the consolidation and extension of Spanish conquest.

The Pampanga nobility were closely allied with the royal family of Tondo. The energetic Dionisio Kapolong of Candaba was Rajah Lakandula's son, and one of his brothers and two cousins were among the captives taken in the Bankusay battle. Lakandula himself mediated the peaceful submission of local chiefs, and persuaded them to support the Spaniards against Chinese invader Limahong.

Moreover, Pampanga and Tagalog cultures were very similar. As late as 1732, Diego Bergaño's *Vocabulario de la lengua Pampanga* provided many concepts Kapampangans and Tagalogs held in common, but with Kapampangan words—for example, *mangapia,* the nobility or well-to-do, and *pungapul,* a freedman who continues to serve his former owner—and a religious vocabulary which Christian converts were slow to give up. They would request masses for the repose of their *kaladduwa* (souls), and called the prophet Moses *siak ning Dios,* from Malay Muslim *siyak.* Missionary friars still had to contend with belief in the *batala* omen bird, and secret worship of *anito*s, "spirit of the Nono [grandfather]," and *diwata,* "idols or false gods." Considering these close Kapampangan-Tagalog connections, the limited spread of literacy is surprising: when eleven chiefs of Lubao, Guagua, Mexico, and Macabebe executed sworn statements in Bacolor in 1591, only one could sign his name.

Pampanga Law

We are fortunate to have an early Spanish treatise on Pampanga law. Following the aborted Tagalog conspiracy of 1586, the Spanish governor ordered pioneer missionary Juan de Plasencia to submit a report on local customs for the guidance of colonial magistrates trying native cases. Attached to Plasencia's account, written in Nagcarlan (Laguna) in 1589, was an appendix entitled "Information on the customs which the natives of Pampanga anciently held" *(Ynstrucción de las costumbres que antiguamente tenían los naturales de la Pan Panga).* These probably had wider application than Pampanga, however, since custom law was similar, though not identical, throughout the lowland Philippines. According to Plasencia's account, a distinctive feature of Pampanga law was the absence of any provision for commuting death sentences to debt slavery. If accurate, this is surprising, since labor must have been at a premium in the fields that were a major source of Manila rice.

Chiefs rendered justice to their barangay, settling disputes on appeal, and summoning, judging, and sentencing lawbreakers, but if they failed to take action against a known criminal, other datus intervened. They themselves were judged by their peers, who selected one among them with high status or a reputation for impartiality and good judgment, banding together to enforce his decision by arms if necessary. Such intervention was called for, too, in a conflict which was restricted to the chiefly class— arguments over planted fields.

In all cases, chiefs were compensated either as judges or enforcers, usually by half the fine or property involved. Laws were handed down by oral tradition and applied by precedent, and although a judge might interpret them in particular cases, there was no mention in Plasencia's account of any process for legislative amendment. Nor was there any reference to trial by ordeal, or arbitrary action by powerful chiefs for personal aggrandisement. Neither were slaves mentioned as having any rights under the law at all.

Lawsuits

Timawa could bring suit against one another before their chief, who would first try to arrange an amicable settlement between them. Failing this, he tried the case, examining both parties—"orally, since among them there is no writing in any suit" (Plasencia 1589c, 27)—and hearing their witnesses. The decision was given the one who produced the greater number of witnesses swearing by the crocodile, the sun, or the moon, who were then paid off, together with the chief, according to their rank. Those on the losing side received nothing, and if they had been paid in advance, it was taken away from them.

Murder. If a chief murdered a member of his own class, the aggrieved family immediately went to war, and the conflict continued violently until both sides were exhausted. The other chiefs would intervene to make a settlement and restore peace, requiring the guilty party to pay his victim's wergeld ("man-price"), which ranged from 70 to 100 taels in gold, or even more, depending on rank—at a time when a first-class slave was valued at 10 taels. Half the wergeld went to the victim's heirs, the other half to his timawa and the intervening chiefs.

If a chief was killed by a timawa, no wergeld was acceptable: the chief's relatives put the timawa to death, together with his wife and children, and seized all his property. If a timawa was murdered, his wergeld was from 10 to 20 taels, whether the murderer was a chief or another timawa, but if a convicted timawa could not pay, he was executed by spearing. If a man killed a first-degree kinsman—a brother, uncle, or nephew—all his property was given his victim's heirs. In the case of witchcraft, any chief could execute the alleged murderer, taking half his property and giving the other half to the dead man's relatives. The law was the same for women as for men, and in any case where there were no direct heirs, the judge or executioner took half the murderer's goods.

Insult. Insult was considered a serious crime, especially among chiefs. They could bring suit for satisfaction before one of their peers acceptable to both parties, and the penalty was a heavy fine depending on their relative social standing. If either refused to accept the decision, they would both

246

resort to a series of costly drinkfests to establish their prestige, a procedure which often resulted in war. But in the case of a chief insulting a timawa, the fine was very light, or there was no fine at all.

Theft. An apprehended thief, whether chief or timawa, was required to return the stolen goods and was fined; in the case of the former, he was fined by other chiefs. If a timawa could not pay, he was sold into slavery, and in the case of a slave, his master had to pay for him or deliver him to the one robbed for punishment. A thief caught in the act by the owner of the goods could be killed or whipped without trial.

Arson. In the case of fire breaking out in the village or fields, the one who set the fire was made to pay for the damage as assessed by the chiefs in the neighborhood. A chief might thus be reduced to penury; and a timawa was executed, and his property seized and wife and children sold into slavery, if necessary, to cover the damages.

Marriage and divorce. A man had only one wife, to whose parents he gave dowry—that is, bride-price—but if they separated, he could marry another, and a third or a fourth one besides, all of whom bore him legitimate children who figured in his inheritance. The one with whom he was actually living was considered his legitimate wife. Divorce was easy for either partner, but if the husband left the wife, he forfeited the bride-price, and if she left him, her parents had to return it double. And if she had borne him no children by the time of his death, it was also returned. It was this dowry, Plasencia (1589c, 28v) said, "which constituted their marriage, [together with] some gatherings in which they would drink."

Inheritance. All legitimate children inherited equally, though some favorite might receive 3 or 4 taels extra, or some strips of land. Children who were underage at the death of either parent were placed, together with their inheritance, in the custody of their grandparents and if they died as minors, that property went to those grandparents or other relatives of the deceased, not to the child's surviving parent. That is to say, property remained within a direct bloodline: a man's wife did not share his inheritance, nor he hers.

Slaves inherited their parents' condition, becoming the property of their parents' master. In the case of the parents belonging to different masters, the children were divided alternately, the first going to the father's owner, the second to the mother's, and so on; and if there were an odd

247

number of children, one of the owners paid the other one-half the child's value. Similarly, in the case of a mixed marriage between a slave and a nonslave, the first child inherited the father's status, the second the mother's, an odd-numbered last child becoming a half-slave.

Pangasinan Culture

Sixteenth-century Pangasinan was the coast of Lingayen Gulf from Bolinao (Zambales) to Balaoan (La Union), and the delta of the Agno River, where the largest settlement—Binalatongan (San Carlos) with some two thousand houses—was only 20 kilometers inland. Bolinao was a port of call for Chinese junks: when Chinese-speaking Father Bartolomé Martínez was shipwrecked on the coast nearby, he was able to baptize twenty Chinese traders he found there. This direct China trade was reflected in the Pangasinan use of porcelain jars for wine consecrated in religious ceremonies, and a Spanish complaint that not only chiefs but even ordinary people were wearing Chinese silks and cotton. It was presumably the proximity of the Zambales mountains which caused Miguel de Loarca to think the people of Pangasinan used the same language and costume as the Zambals, but were "more intelligent" due to their contact with Chinese, Japanese, and Bornean merchants. Agoo (La Union) was an emporium for the exchange of Igorot gold, which the Spaniards called "Port of Japan" because Salcedo found several Japanese ships there. Deerskins and civet were also objects of their trade. There was also an instance when a Dominican friar was captured by Japanese "pirates" upon returning from Manila.

Domestic trade included pigs, wild game, and carabaos, wax, pottery, and sugarcane wine called *kila* (that is, *kilang*). Farmers on the narrow coastal plain of La Union grew cotton and traded textiles for rice grown in the delta. Igorots brought down gold both to the coast and to the Agno River basin in exchange for pigs and carabaos which they took back to the mountains on the hoof. Traders went overland to Manila, crossing the forests to the tributaries of the Rio Chico of Pampanga. Salcedo was guided on his northern expedition by one he met in Manila trading gold for silver, while pioneer missionary Bernardo de Santa Catalina was befriended by another who had been baptized in Manila as Juan de Vera, brother of the chief of Calasiao. In early colonial days traders earned cash by escorting travelers through dangerous passages along this route.

But Pangasinans were also a warlike people who were long known for their resistance to Spanish conquest. Sixteenth-century accounts regularly

248

referred to them as either unconquered or rebellious, leading Bishop Diego Aduarte (1640, 2:53) to therefore boast that Dominican missionaries had won the hearts of those whom "Spanish arms could not dominate." One conquistador characterized them as a "rebellious and indomitable people . . . very warlike and free, and fond of human blood" (Baeza 1597, 128). Bishop Domingo de Salazar described them as "really the worst people—the fiercest and cruelest in the land—an unconquered tribe whose fiestas were cutting off one another's heads" (Aduarte 1640, 1:131).[36]

Tagam was a war dance—or cockfight—*dakep* meant to take captives, and *ngayaw* was "to go out looking for anybody they wanted to kill" (Cosgaya 1731, 225). Pangasinans themselves were subject to attack by Igorots, Zambals, and Negritos, but were able to defend their overland trade routes, and to take Zambal slaves for sale to Chinese.

Pangasinan culture appears to have been the same as that of Luzon groups to the south. Rice was grown in both swiddens and pond fields, where it was planted either by broadcasting or by transplanting seedlings from a seedbed. One manload of harvested palay—ten bundles (*betek*) of five smaller bundles (*tanay*)—was reckoned as one G-string (*san be-el*), presumably because it could be tied with one. Men practiced circumcision (*galsim*) or supercision (*segat*), wore G-strings, and blackened their teeth. They considered undecorated teeth ugly, and once told a friar that their war god, Apolaki, had scolded them for receiving "foreigners with white teeth" (Aduarte 1640, 1:130). Shamans were old women and the ceremonies they performed were *maganito,* but the practice of reserving a jar of vintage wine for their sacramental use, with small quantities being carried home by worshipers—"like holy water," Bishop Aduarte said—suggests missionary influence. Mourning rites required a human death, and there was an unusually strict sanction against adultery: both adulterers were buried alive. After colonial authority made this punishment impractical, a certain Chief Lomboy once killed his own sister for this crime. There was evidently the usual three-class social structure, with ruling chiefs being called *anakbanwa;* their supporters, *timawa.* And the fact that the chiefs were generally the most warlike moved Aduarte to cite a Spanish adage, *Viva quien vince*—"Let him live who wins."

The Zambals and Negritos

Zambals and Negritos living in Zambales mountains and forests in the Central Plain were known to farmers in Pampanga as head-taking raiders.

Early Spanish accounts described both groups in the same simplistic terms—hunter-foragers who wandered through the wilds like beasts with no fixed place of abode, and who took heads because rank among them depended on the number taken, and no woman would marry a man who had not taken any. Nothing is said about their agriculture, trade with other Filipinos, or the source of their gold, iron tools, and weapons. Seventeenth-century missionary accounts, however, made more detailed descriptions possible.

The Zambals. The Spaniards first met the Zambals when Juan de Salcedo rescued some who had been sold as slaves to a Chinese ship anchored in Bolinao. Four years later they appeared to repay the favor when the Spaniards were besieging a Chinese invader fortified at the mouth of the Agno River. As Father Rada (1577, 484) described the contact,

> when we were taking the field against the corsair Limahong, a chieftain of the Zambals came to us with 100 archers, saying he wanted to go to war with us, and that he wanted as his whole prize no more than simply the Chinese heads.

Similar contact continued into the next century. In 1610 during the Spanish-Dutch wars, Zambals presented the governor with the heads of six Dutchmen who had gone ashore near Iba. Fifty years later, when Chief Tumalang converted to Christianity, he returned the head of General Felipe de Ugalde he had taken along the coastal trail. By this time, the name *Zambal* had been extended to all head-taking tribes north of the Central Plain, including those around Gapan (Nueva Ecija) and the Igorots of Benguet.

Some Zambals grew rice, taro, and sugarcane in swiddens, but others lived off hunting, no doubt in an exchange that provided a healthy diet of starch and protein for both parties. The bolos and metal-tipped arrows they traded with Negritos may also have been for fresh meat. The significance of rice is indicated by the list of deities worshiped for good crops. Aniton Tawo ("Human Spirit") received the most important sacrifices; Dumagan was invoked to cause the rice to head, Kalaskas to cause it to ripen, and Damolag to prevent storms while it was in flower. But one called Kalasokos only needed to be placated in time of drought. In the early colonial period, Zambal fields were large enough to use Negrito labor, either as outright slaves or as vassals whose overlords paid their tribute for them. But as Spanish need for lumber increased, many Zambal farmers quit their fields and undertook to supply it, also with Negrito help.

Zambal society. Zambal communities were small, and both economically and politically undeveloped. Their clothing was limited to G-strings, short skirts, and jackets; men shaved the front half of their heads to leave long locks hanging behind, and nobody wore heavy gold jewelry (see fig. 12). Bride-price was paid in gold, and those who could afford it took gold with them to the grave, but not in large quantities. Men moved to their wives' residence, and marriages were strictly monogamous: both erring parties could be executed for adultery. They practiced infanticide if necessary to limit their offspring to one boy and one girl. Their houses were simple enough for Spaniards to call them huts, but permanent enough to permit the display of human heads taken—though surely not the hundred Martín de Rada claimed to have seen in one of them. Class structure was not obvious enough to attract friar attention. There were individuals reckoned in society as the descendants of slaves, but no chiefly class with inherited right to rule and receive tribute. Rather, chiefs were men respected or feared for the number of heads they had taken, but they exercised no authority outside their kin group and little within it. They could call on kin support, however, for vengeance or payment of debts, even to the extent of handing over a lesser member as wergeld. Many of them also had close ties with individual Negritos—like Chief Kalignaw who was accompanied by a Negrito archer by the name of Kibakar when he killed Dominican Fray Domingo Pérez in 1683.

Head taking was an expected part of Zambal male conduct, and men who did not comply with the custom were treated with scorn. Head taking was called *garro* or *mangaw* (that is, *mangayaw*), and skulls were fashioned into cups. Raids were thought to be made under the protection of a guardian spirit called Manalagar, and participants always afterwards addressed each other as *aroak*, "my comrade." Father Pérez estimated that not one in four died a natural death. Men carrying out a mourning duty for a deceased parent wore a headcloth called *balata* until they accomplished it. Reconciliation with the victim's relatives was attempted through sacrifices to Manglobar, a spirit who soothed angry hearts—compensation in gold or valuables, or a slave to kill. A brave credited with fifteen deaths was entitled to wear a *bantakan* legband of fruit seeds, adding more for seventeen, and bright-colored *siguey* shells for nineteen or more, and all of them would wrap an *anahaw* leaf around the haft of their *iwa* dagger. Fathers were known to kill a Negrito slave in front of a young son to instill a proper thirst for blood. Perhaps it was such childhood indoctrination that produced the following incident:

On one occasion, Father Fray Domingo Pérez was hiking with two Zambals, one in front and the other behind. The one in back said, "Look out, Father, I will go in front." He asked him if there were some enemies or danger, and the Zambal replied that there was nothing except his overpowering temptation to cut off his head, staring at the nape of his neck so well placed for it (Peguero 1691, 42).

Zambal religion. Zambal religion consisted mainly in the worship of ancestral spirits called anitos and individual deities with personal names. Malyari seems to have been the only one represented by an actual idol— a wooden head with straw body and arms constructed and clothed by a shaman for the occasion. Rice deities without such corporal representation escaped friar idol-smashing ministries and thus continued to be worshiped by Christian converts. Included among their deities, perhaps because of Tagalog influence, was Bathala Mey Kapal, "whose false genealogies and fabulous deeds they celebrated in certain tunes and verses like hymns" (San Nicolás 1664, 420). There were also fetishlike figures small enough to be held in the hand. Certain stands of bamboo were considered sacred and therefore dangerous to cut, and omen birds were called *salaksak* or *pasimanuken.*

Religious services *(maganito)* were conducted by shamans called *bayok,* male transvestites who nonetheless wore weapons at their waist like a man—a cutlass on the left, a head-taking iwa on the right. Each bayok was dedicated to a particular deity or spirit, and consecrated in an expensive ceremony attended by his relatives, in which he sacrificed a pig and anointed them with its blood, and then snipped off the ends of his long hair wound with gold ornaments to toss into the air for them to catch. A maganito was basically a seance during which the bayok would make three holes in the ground with a spear and fill them with wine before falling into a trembling trance to speak with the voice of the spirit that possessed him. Bayok were paid well enough for their services to recoup the costs of their initiation—for example, 10 taels for a funeral ritual in which the deceased was offered rice, buyo, wine, and tobacco so as not to return to haunt the living.

Negritos. Spaniards reported blacks or "little blacks"—*negros* or *negrillos*— in Mindanao, Palawan, Calamianes, Panglao, Negros, Panay, Mindoro, Pampanga, Zambales, Pangasinan, the modern provinces of Nueva Ecija and Rizal, and the Cagayan Valley. They were of smaller stature than other Filipinos, some of them described as robust, others as of delicate build, and not so dark as the natives of Guinea but with the same negroid features and *pasa* (raisin) hair—that is, crinkled like raisins (see fig. 13). They were

252

always referred to as inhabiting the interior mountains, though in fact the first one the Spaniards saw was along the seacoast of Negros—and he ran away so fast, "a horse could not have caught him" (Anon. 1565, 490). The island of Negros—Buglas before Spanish advent—was so called, not because it was mainly populated by blacks, but because there were more of them in the mountains than in other islands. Despite this presumed isolation, however, Negritos obviously had contact with lowland Filipinos. They possessed iron tools and weapons, and in many places were suppliers of wax, and probably other forest products valued in domestic and foreign trade, and certainly medicinal plants. Chirino told the story of a Negrito who had regular dealings with a lowlander of Tigbawan (Panay), whom the Negrito eventually killed by treachery, sparking a little tribal war after which the lowlanders celebrated their victory by displaying the losers' *pasa* scalps as trophies.

The Negritos' speed and accuracy with bow and arrow were proverbial, making unwary travelers or field workers easy targets. When the Zambal chief Kalignaw and his Negrito companion Kibakar killed Father Pérez, the Zambal missed his target by a hair, but the Negrito drove a shaft through the friar's chest to protrude a hand's breadth on the other side. When Magellan's survivors seized a Bornean overlord in southern Palawan, upon paying the ransom demanded, he begged for the return of his guns as protection against local blacks. But their small numbers, primitive economy, and lack of political organization also made them easy prey for better organized groups. Zambals seeking slaves took advantage of the internal feuds which resulted from their mourning customs: Negritos were said to bury their deceased upright in the ground with the head protruding, and then set out to take another head. In Panay they were captured both for domestic service and for sale to China and Borneo, and unlike Visayan debt slaves, had little chance of manumission. As Legazpi (1570, 51–52) wrote,

> these negroes are slaves among these pagans and will be for their whole life because the negroes do not ransom them, [so] they never expect to go free as indios do.

Some early accounts called Negritos "black Chichimecos," a Mexican word loosely applied to any unsubdued tribes. There were, indeed, non-negro tribes living in the same ranges inhabited by Negritos, and outsiders frequently confused them with each other because of their common dissimilarity to lowland Filipino cultures. The Mangyans of Mindoro, for example, were so called from a word which meant "savage or runaways [*cimarrones*], like blacks" in Hiligaynon, or "little blacks wilder than the

Fig. 12. Zambal folk attired in g-string; short jacket
(From the Boxer Codex)

Fig. 13. Negrillos with negroid features of the natives of Guinea
(From the Boxer Codex)

others" in Bikolano. Brief notices also referred to both groups as subsisting only on game, wild fruits, and roots, but Dr. Morga (1609, 172) wrote more perceptively of Luzon Negritos:

> They do not have houses or fixed settlements [but] wander through the mountains and crags in huts and campsites, moving from one place to another according to the season; living off a few clearings and planting of rice, which they make in swiddens, and the game which they bring down with their bows, at which they are very skillful and good marksmen, and the honey of the mountains, and roots which the land produces.

Spanish authors were persuaded that the Negritos were the original inhabitants of the islands where they lived, driven into the interior by usurping non-Negrito invaders. This may have been true, but it is also true that Negrito life-styles enabled them to exploit forests as sedentary agriculturists could not. They thus occupied an ecological niche which they were able to defend at least well enough to discourage further encroachment.

CHAPTER 14

Northern Luzon

The Spaniards heard reports of gold mines in the Ilocos even before they reached Manila, and Governor Legazpi's grandson, Juan Salcedo, died looking for them in 1576. Three months after Salcedo's death, these gold mines were discovered in the Benguet mountains near the present Baguio City, where they were being worked by Igorots—that is, *Igolot*, "people of the mountains," a word cognate with Tagalog *golod* (mountain range).

The Igorots

But neither in this expedition nor in four more which they mounted during the next fifty years were the Spaniards able to solve the logistic and military problems connected with occupying them. A report from the first attempt neatly summarizes their motivation and reaction:

> I was sent with 40 soldiers and 200 *indios* to discover the gold mines of the Ygolot province from which it is understood all the wealth comes which is known throughout the land, and I do not know by what chance it was that after such great fame and expectations, not even one grain of gold was obtained after discovering more than 200

mines, but only a lot of hardship and spear-thrusts, and the land was most rugged and almost uninhabitable for want of provisions and being 80 leagues from Manila (Ceballos 1576, 2).

Mining communities. Igorot mining communities occupied an ecological niche suited to their profession. They lived in mine fields at heights up to 1,000 meters above sea level, on some of the most precipitous terrain in the archipelago, where temperatures could drop to near freezing and forest cover was largely pines. They devoted little energy to either agriculture or animal husbandry, but obtained their food through trade—rice, cattle, and hogs from the lowlands, root crops and vegetables from highland neighbors. Nor did their women weave: miners dressed in bark G-strings—even women, according to one account—and purchased cotton blankets in the Ilocos. They built their villages on crests and open slopes that commanded all approaches from below, where they could release boulders and logs to roll down on invaders. It was a life-style very different from that of the Cordillera terrace builders whom the Spaniards would only discover two centuries later.

The mine fields drained into the Agno and Angalacan Rivers, carrying enough gold to make panning in riverbed placers profitable in the rainy season. Actual veins, however, were followed with tunnels provided with good drainage but so low that miners had to work sitting down, using pickaxes fitted with only small iron points because of the scarcity of that metal. The raw ore was pulverized on flat stones set in the ground, and then carried to running water to be sluiced three or more times to remove the particles, which were readily seen sparkling in the bright sunshine of the dry season. The crudely refined gold was then bartered with Pangasinan and Ilocano partners for rice, domestic animals, cloth, and crockery, with the Pangasinans and Ilocanos completing its refining and marketing the finished product at 20 or 22 karats. In this way, "it passes," Dr. Morga (1609, 183) said, "through the whole land through their hands."

Igorot houses were built on the ground and closed up tight against the cold climate. Windowless, with heavy thatched roofs that almost reached the ground, they had to be entered through low doors on all fours, and occupants slept in a kind of second floor made of planks. They were built on sites chosen for easy defense, and all approaches would be planted with sharp bamboo spikes in time of war. (The mining community of Boa was protected by a dry moat backed with solid planking.)

But Igorots who practiced agriculture periodically moved their houses when fallowing the swiddens in which they grew root crops like *games* (that is, *ñames*, yams) and camotes. They timed their planting season by the appearance of a star in the west called Gaganayan—presumably in the constellation of Orion—as they themselves were called by neighboring tribes.[37]

The people. Igorots had lighter skin than lowlanders and shoulder-length hair, and wore narrow bark G-strings only about 25 centimeters wide. They were also muscular and warlike. They fought with body-length wooden shields; and reed spears with sharpened bamboo points, or wooden ones with shafts almost 2 meters long and iron spearheads. They took heads in war—and sometimes captives for slave labor in the mines—and handed down the skulls as heirlooms. Victories were celebrated with feasting off sacrificial hogs and cattle, whose skulls and bones were hung on houses afterwards as displays of chiefly prestige. Their ferocity made them feared by both lowland and neighboring tribes, a reputation of which they were themselves well aware. Expeditionary commander García de Aldana reported in 1620 that when he told them that he had come to impose a 20 percent tax on their mineral production, "they laughed at what I said and asked when I would be leaving" (Aldana 1620).

The Igorots reacted vigorously to interference with their commerce by Spanish occupation of lowland communities, subjugation of their trading partners, and attempts to control their traffic in gold. It is noteworthy that while sixteenth-century reports by both friars and government officials concentrated on this lucrative highland-lowland trade, seventeenth-century accounts regularly inveighed against Igorot raiding, head taking, and kidnapping, and justified total war against them on the grounds that they impeded free passage along the coast to His Majesty's subjects, both Spanish and Filipino. Indeed, the 35–kilometer stretch from Pangasinan-speaking Magaldan to Ilocano-speaking Agoo had to be crossed by colonial travelers at forced march for fear of attack. Yet the profits of the gold trade to both highland producers and their lowland customers were such that Igorot raiding never put a stop to them. Father Juan de Medina's 1630 assessment would remain valid for the next two centuries:

> When peaceful they bring down gold which they extract there from their mines . . . but when the Igorots are on the warpath . . . then these mountaineers come down to hunt heads, in which they take great pleasure (Medina 1630, 150).

Government and religion. Igorot chiefs were family heads of eight or ten households, whose main duties were to settle local disputes and make peace with enemy villages. They were distinguished by gold plating on their teeth and their use of expensive Ilocano blankets, and were ranked accord-

259

ing to the number of animals they had butchered during a lifetime of prestige feasts. Such rank was given terminal validation by wakes that could last up to one month, during which the cadaver was repeatedly pricked to drain off putrefied matter. The valiant were buried seated against their shields in caves or rock ledges stopped up with stones afterwards, or in trees—though whether in hollow trunks or on branches is not clear. But age and wisdom were highly respected in both sexes, and real leadership in public affairs could only be exercised by those who enjoyed a reputation for such virtues.

Commander Alonso Martín Quirante, who spent four months examining the gold mines in 1624, commented of Igorot religion, "They say that their god is in the sky, whom they call Cabunian and to whom they make offerings and sacrifice pigs and carabaos at their banquets and feasts" (Quirante 1624). But from this it cannot be concluded that they did not worship other spirits and their own ancestors, like other Filipinos and like their descendants in more modern times. Don Alonso also said they were idolatrous, and that their old men and women held conversations with the devil—that is, performed seances.

Religious ceremonies were prestige feasts with the sacrificial victims tethered around the house of the person wealthy enough to feed participants and guests lavishly for two or three days, following which the skulls and bones picked clean would be mounted on the house walls as permanent escutcheons of high social status. Ancestor worship is indicated by the expensive obsequies such aristocrats received at the time of death, the food offerings made at their grave sites, and the fact that heads were taken as part of their mourning requirements.

Ifugao epic culture. The Ifugao—whom the Spaniards also called Igorots— lived on the southeastern face of the Cordillera Central, where their streams all drain into the Magat River. *Ifugao* is actually a lowland mispronunciation of Ipugaw, the people of Pugaw, the earth world—that is, mortals. To the east is Lagod, "downstream," and to the west, Daya, "upstream," to which theological cosmography adds the supernatural regions of Dalom, the underworld, and Kabunyan, the sky world. All five of these regions are peopled with a host of deities, spirits, ancestors, ghosts, and demons, all of which must be regularly placated with the odor of sacrificed pigs, chickens, and rice beer.

The Ifugao epic cycle is called Hudhud, and individual episodes are often called harvest songs because they are most commonly chanted to relieve the tedium of this labor by a female soloist, echoed by the other harvesters in chorus. Like other Filipino epics, it is an aristocratic form of literature: its protagonists are all members of an elite class. But unlike other Philippine epics, they are not nobility or royalty with individual titles like "Datu" or "Rajah"; they are all *kadangyan,* wealthy aristocrats who have qualified for their status by the performance of a requisite number of extravagant prestige feasts. They dominate non-kadangyan by feeding them during public feasts and by usurious loans of foodstuffs, but do not rule them in a political sense. It is a casual form of government which might be called a plutocracy. And their wealth lends Hudhud heroes and heroines an almost mystical nature. When Bugan goes out looking for a suitable mate, she carries her brother's prestigious sword belt, which will only fit a man of acceptable class. Just so, when it fits Daulayan, who is a poor man, everybody knows he will turn out to be the scion of some wealthy lineage though he does not know it himself.

The base of this wealth is the possession of irrigated rice terraces, a form of land which is private property par excellence: like houses, textile, basketry, or pottery, it is the product of human labor. They may be owned by either men or women, and do not become conjugal property unless acquired jointly by husband and wife. They produce the rice—*page,* as distinct from *bakan,* swidden rice—which is essential to religious ceremonies, both to attract supernatural imbibers and to inebriate guests and the priests performing the rituals. Indeed, the Hudhud hero often sways with a staggering gait which reveals his ability to afford such intoxication. The beverage is called *bayah,* and for large feasts, sugarcane juice is added—*bahi;* only the lower classes would think of adding water.

Ifugao religious practitioners are male priests, not female shamans—that is, they learn their profession by mastering a specialized field of knowledge, and do not fall into trances or speak with disembodied supernatural voices. Female shamans there are, but they are only called on for healing rites. Priests must be familiar with a bewildering number and variety of deities, and memorize long myths which are recited during religious ceremonies. It is they who interpret omens and set the time for rice planting. There is constant demand for their services, not only for funerals, weddings, or harvest rites, but household rituals like activating the wooden *bulol* figures which guard the granaries, sanctifying newly polished heirloom jewelry and restrung beads for status display, or conducting bone-washing ceremonies for secondary burials.

Ifugao material culture. Hudhud Ifugao appear to share a common technology with sixteenth-century lowland Filipinos—backstrap looms, one-lever sugarcane presses, two-cylinder Malay forges, nailless carpentry for house construction, rice reaped panicle by panicle and stored unmilled in bundles, G-strings and rectangular wraparound skirts, and an addiction to betel nut. But there are significant differences. Most obvious is the construction of stonewalled rice terraces tier on tier up the most inhospitable slopes of mountains, irrigated by an intricate hydraulic system. Furthermore, Ifugao houses display a style unique to their culture area—one-room wooden cubicles standing on four posts with cylindrical rat guards, and a pyramidal thatched roof which descends to the level of the floor outside. So standardized is this style that not even the most wealthy deviate from it to build a larger dwelling, though the greatest kadangyan are distinguished by a heavy, animal-headed lounging bench underneath.

The Hudhud hero's finery is only displayed during the rare Uya-uy feast in which he and his wife regale the whole community with the meat of pigs and chickens sacrificed to the deities and carabao sacrificed to their ancestral spirits. (These *nowang* are kept only for this purpose; they are not used as draft animals.) He wears a G-string of an elaborate design restricted to his class, a fancy hip bag with long tassels, and a sword belt decorated with large shell disks, and in his ears, kidney-shaped gold earrings and around his neck five or six more, together with a necklace of glass-encased gold leaf beads. And on his head, the ultimate kadangyan symbol—a big-beaked *kalaw* bird's skull painted red, set off by a kind of crescent of carabao horn, and a G-string worn like a turban. His wife wears an elegant skirt, lady's handbag, heavy tasseled belt, gold earrings, and three or four strands of amber beads, and in her long hair secured with strings of red and white beads, a little brass statuette.

The shell disks originally come from the seacoast and the glass beads from abroad, but the gold earrings are made locally by the lost wax process. The G-strings are also local products, and may display a white-on-black lizard design dyed into the warp threads before weaving, a technique known in Southeast Asia as *ikat,* but not mentioned in lowland Spanish accounts. The Ifugao weaver is held in high esteem, and in the Hudhud her *baliga* batten is actually magical: one mythic hero uses his wife's baliga to dig a hole which gains him entrance to the spirit underworld.

The Hudhud weapons are: spears, both elegant metal ones and plain sharpened reeds; a double-edged sword with hilt forged from the same steel; and long, narrow shields. In real life, the Ifugao were renowned for *mangayaw* raids and ambushes in which they took heads, whose skulls they displayed on their houses afterwards, either to avenge the loss of some relative's or neighbor's head, or to gain a warlike reputation attractive to the opposite sex. But in the epics, the battles are rather ritualized spear-throwing contests between individual champions, to win a bride or to rescue a kidnapped beauty. Like traditional head takers, they sleep outside their houses the night before a raid, examine the gall bladder of sacrificed chickens before starting out, and turn back if the omen bird flies across their path. On the field of battle, the best fighters catch enemy spears in their bare hands rather than on their shields, and throw them back, including even Bugan when, in one episode, she fights alongside her brother Dinulawan and displays just as great skill and courage as his. But when she pursues and catches her humiliated, fleeing enemy, she cuts off, not his head, but the end of his G-string.

Cagayan Culture

The Cagayan Valley in northern Luzon was one of the most fertile regions of the Philippines in the sixteenth century. Protected by the Sierra Madre mountains on the east, the Cordillera Central on the west, it enjoyed a mild climate. Its soil was deep and rich, and the Cagayan River, fed by the Chico and Magat Rivers rising on the Cordillera, carried a volume of water greater than any other river system in the archipelago. It produced rice that was considered the best in the land, millet, tubers, sugarcane, cotton, and hemp, wax, palm wine, hogs, goats, and fowl. Its forests abounded in timber, deer, wild boar, birds, and carabaos, and its upper tributaries gave access to Igorot gold mines. All this wealth quickly attracted Spanish attention, despite its distance from the colonial capital. A 1586 memorial reported that 2,000 casks of meat could be collected in a few days, and recommended the construction of a granary to hold 100,000 cavans of rice. Five years later, Governor Gómez Pérez Dasmariñas sent out an expedition from Pampanga, headed by his son Luis and guided by the prominent Dionisio Kapolong and a native woman of Tuy (Nueva Vizcaya).

Don Luis followed the Pampanga River up to its source on the Caraballo Sur, crossed over into the Magat headwaters through Balete (Dalton) Pass, and then followed a trade route down the Magat to its junction with the Cagayan River at Gamu (Isabela). Settlements averaged sixty to eighty households loyal to a single chief—Tuy itself had seventy-two houses and forty-two granaries—though there was a community of some five hundred houses near the present site of Aritao with two chiefs, one of whom, Ibarat, was Kapolong's friend. Blood compacts were made, or a ceremony in which each party threw an egg to the ground and swore that "just as those eggs

263

were broken, so might they be broken if they did not keep their word"
(Anon. 1591, 467). Well-made wooden houses with four large images as the
corners, three of them in human form, were surrounded by earthen fences,
and some communities were protected by bamboo-backed trenches. Hillside swiddens were planted to rice, vegetables, and root crops the Spaniards called *camotes* or *batatas*—probably yams. Tribute was collected in gold
chains, earrings, and bracelets, necklaces of blue-and-white or various
colored beads, or carnelians that had been handed down as heirlooms, in
exchange for cheap trade goods and what the Filipinos called Chinese
blankets.

The Ibanags. The Cagayan River below Gattaran was called the Bannag,
and the people living along its banks and their language were accordingly
Ibanag. Non-Ibanag enemies were called Kalinga, a term which later came
to mean non-Christian. There were also Negritos in the hills and hinter-
land, and the Ibanag attitude toward them is revealed by a belief connected
with the *dalaw* bird, or golden oriole. Only real braves could take omens
from this bird because, it was said, just as the dalaw defeats the crows, so the
braves defeated the Negritos "and drove them from the land." Nonetheless,
they had trade with them: *pagujjinan* was a patron or partner of Negritos,
and *amayat* was a love potion which could only be obtained from them. The
Chinese were called Daddal, and trade contacts with them, either direct or
through the Ilocos, are reflected in the elegant black textiles with gold-
embroidered lions which were placed on the stomach and chest of deceased chiefs and buried with them.

Cagayan men wore G-strings *(bag)* and headbands of bark or cotton, a
smock that reached to the thighs, and on gala occasions a sash large
enough to be wrapped around food to serve as a knapsack. They wore
shoulder-length hair cut in bangs across the forehead, filed their teeth level
and blackened them with a coating of boiled vitriol and *pili* sprouts, a
process referred to as "firing," like clay pots. They practiced circumcision
(kogit) and supercision *(gutub)*, and considered slender waists an essential
feature of male beauty, often restricting their diet or suffering a tight
waistband to achieve such a figure.

Tattooing applied with hog bile and ink was restricted to the back of the
hands, which were then called *appaku* because of the similarity of the
design to the *paku* fern. It was evidently also applied to warriors' wives since
the souls of women who were not so decorated could not enter the land of
the dead. Such ladies also wore red overskirts with white lining as a sign of
their station, and both men and women wore earrings. A child whose ears

264

were being pierced was called *inakawan* after the rice straw *(akaw)* which was placed in the holes to keep them open while healing; while *gitang* or *gilay* was an earlobe torn out by heavy earrings or abuse.

Technology. Cagayan settlements were bounded on one side by forest, on the other by water, either the sea or the river. The importance of the forest is indicated by its many uses. Besides providing timber for buildings and boats, rattan and bamboo for tools and utensils, it was a source of food, medicine, and even clothing, served as a refuge from enemies, and contained sacred spots for worship and healing. Deer, carabaos, hogs, and wild fowl were taken with hounds, traps, nets, and a crossbow *ballista* called *balet*.

Ibanags had an impressive inventory of woods distinguished for their specialized uses—ships' masts, planks, and thwarts; house beams, rafters, and pillars; dyewoods in black, red, and yellow; bark fibers for cordage; and bark removed in whole sheets to be pounded and bleached into cloth— *abutag* G-strings so named from the species of tree from which they were made, or *sinitu* for a fine white bark cloth.

Pharmaceuticals included a broth boiled from bark to remove the congealed blood from bruises, a sap to heal sores and wounds, a plant chewed to a poultice with saliva to cure boils, leaves rubbed on the body to relieve itches, and the juice of the wild jasmine (*makabbuling*, literally, to make blind) as an antidote for poison and an abortifacient for dead fetus.

The Cagayan River system and the waters of the Babuyan Channel provided the Ibanags with fish as well as avenues of trade as far as the Ilocos coast, so that boats were an ordinary part of daily life. The common word for boat was *barangay*, a term sometimes extended to the crew. Boats were plank-built and sewn, fitted with outriggers, oars, or paddles, and steering oars rather than center rudders. Large vessels were *biray* or *biwong*. *Takuli* were canoes hewn from a single tree trunk; *dalakit* was a raft; and *gakit*, any bundle of bamboo temporarily tied together to serve as one. There are no references to full-scale *karakoa* men-o'-war, or to naval engagements and sea raiding.

Rather, river traffic was not intended for the open sea. It was often characterized by sluggish vessels overloaded to the gunwales, with leaf washboards added to increase freeboard, and bamboo lashed to the hull of the outriggers to increase buoyancy. The intimate place of all this boating in riverine Cagayan society is reflected in special terms like *apayag*, to carry passengers on the shoulder to or from vessels anchored in shallow water. A woman dancing opposite a male partner with evasive movements from side to side was called *ayaw*, which meant the yawing of a boat. And whereas

265

European languages like Spanish and English speak of the male of a species mounting a female, the Ibanag expression was *takay,* to board.

Cagayan industries may be considered pan-Philippine. Blacksmiths worked with a two-piston Malay forge and stone mauls, using cast-iron Chinese *karahay* cauldrons as raw material. Goldsmiths adulterated gold *(bulawan)* with baser metals *(tubbaga),* and gave it a good color with an ochrelike earth called *fula.* Potters used the paddle-and-anvil technique: the process itself was *jun;* the potter, *manun;* and the paddle, *anajjun.* Cotton was important both for local consumption and trade: it was called *kapot,* and *kapok* pillow stuffing was *kapot nad daddal*—"Chinese cotton." The bolls removed from the pods were cudgeled and the seeds removed by hand, fluffed up with a bow, and spun into thread with distaff and spindle, then starched and burnished with coconut husk. Weaving *(tannun)* was done on a backstrap loom which included a reed, after warping on a simple two-stake warping frame. Traders from China and Japan were regular customers for these textile.

Agriculture. Tilling the soil, as distinct from cutting down trees for swiddens, was done without metal tools. Weeding and rooting up grasses or harvested rice stalks were done with a length of bamboo sharpened to a flat blade; and soil was leveled with a kind of rake called *aragaw*—probably from Spanish *arado* (plow). Dibble sticks were called *ibitu* from the *bitu* holes for seeds, which were distinguished from *balu* holes for planting sugarcane; *bikang* was to spread the holes far apart. To broadcast seed was called *sikkop,* or *batabat* if the seeds were scattered wide and sparse. *Koman* was the ordinary word for field; *ugad,* hillside swiddens—*binituwan* when planted by dibbling; and pond fields were sometimes specified as *payaw.* These irrigated fields were worked in the swamps or lagoons along the edges of the Cagayan River or its many tributaries, with dams and dikes of pounded earth, though these were often destroyed in seasonal flooding. Noisemaking scarecrows were placed in ripening grain fields, and fires were lighted at night in swiddens planted to root crops.

Staple foods were rice *(ammay),* taro *(gabit),* millet *(nanna),* and by the middle of the seventeenth century, two American crops—corn *(mangwit)* and sweet potatoes *(kamosi).* (The earliest Ibanag dictionary defines *gabit,* taro, as "native potato.") There were also two edible wild grasses—*marammay,* "ricelike," and *ammae na aran* "goblin's rice." Mushrooms were also called *pinayunganna aran,* "what goblins use for parasols." The *kusipa* tree also yielded a nut like filberts or hazelnuts which could be pounded into flour. But the crop that received the most attention and esteem was rice, especially a short-stemmed variety called *kuritay*, which yielded abundantly but had to be grown in standing water.

Rice was the only crop that had a special word for planting—*patok*, whence *appapatok* was planting season, and *tattok*, sowing a seedbed for transplanting. Planting other grains simply used a verb form of their names. *Mula*, on the other hand, meant to plant something other than cereals. *Gatab* was harvesting; *tabbag*, early harvesting of rice that had matured too soon; and *igub* was roasting before storage if the grains were too damp. Granaries in the house were called *agubuwan*, but those in the fields standing on posts with disk-shaped rat guards were called *alang*. After milling in a mortar, rice was called *baggat;* soft rice was *balugo*, and glutinous rice cakes boiled wrapped in leaves were *atatan*. But despite Cagayan's rich harvests, the uncertainties of cultivation are reflected in a special vocabulary—*dappok:* knocked over because of dry stalks; *kupot:* a head with few grains, or *bukaw*, with none at all; and *payakan:* stunted—"as if frostbitten," a Spanish dictionary says.

Salt was boiled from seawater on stoves dug out of coastal banks, and the same device was used for distilling alcoholic beverages in a wooden still, *barayang*, whence liquor was called *binarayang*. The ordinary Cagayan drink was sugarcane *bassi:* properly aged, it was called *pinalitaw* and likened to claret by the Spaniards, but when still not settled, it was *pangajo*. If it was distilled to a high alcoholic content, it was called *umafuafuy*, "inflammable," and was said to sting—like a merciless flogging. The production and marketing of nipa wine was only introduced in 1581 by Visayan, Tagalog, and Pampanga auxiliaries settled in the wild palm groves as compensation for their participation in a Spanish expedition to drive out a Japanese pirate.

Man and society. Leadership was exercised by chiefs whose authority depended on their reputation as *maengel* (braves), not on claims to noble lineage. They revalidated their positions by leading warriors on head-taking *ngayaw* raids, but also by feeding their followers in times of hunger. Non-maengel members of society were simply called *kaelian*, member of the same *ili*, settlement. Thus, to liberate a slave was *pakaelian*—literally, make him a townmate. The earliest surviving Ibanag dictionary—Father José Bugarín's, who died in 1676—lists neither *datu* nor *timawa*, but gives *kammaranan* for chief (that is, *principal*) and *buwit* for tribute. Such kammaranan had to be wealthy enough to afford the hospitality and display of gold ornaments required of their class during ritual occasions like harvest feasts, but the claim of the people of Camalaniugan that they had a chief who weighed out his gold with steelyard no doubt expressed the ideal rather than the fact.

Maengel raiders set out with the plumes of the dalaw bird on their heads and the hair of defeated foes on their spears, to which they added gold ornaments during victory dances around their trophies. An illustration in the Boxer Codex shows a Cagayan warrior with two little human figures and two birds on his headband (see fig. 14). If the *battay* bird sang on the left side of their trail, they turned back no matter how far they had gone, and if they were traveling by boat they cast food offerings into the water. They carried shields large enough to cover the whole body, and went into battle clad only in G-strings, with bodies well oiled in case of hand-to-hand grappling (although quilted armor was known upstream in Gaddang territory—that is, modern Isabela). Their weapons were leaf-shaped daggers 20 to 30 centimeters long *(inalag),* spears *(suppil* if plain, *saffuring* if barbed), and one which in modern times would be called a head ax—*bunang,* "machete of the natives," Father Bugarín (1676, 80) said, "like a crescent moon with a long point." Unlike the inalag, the bunang could not be put in a scabbard *(alag).* Maengel made little use of the bow and arrow, which was a weapon the Negritos wielded with great skill and deadly effect. Any sort of fortification was called *kuta; amata* was a watchtower or guard post; and *kagakuwan* were special places of refuge when a village was expecting an attack. Trails would be blocked up with underbrush, stakes, and ditches, and those left open were planted with sharpened bamboo spikes, and waterfronts were defended by stakes offshore.

The frequency of ngayaw raiding made intervillage feuds endemic. Peace could only be restored between warring communities by the shedding of blood: *poyud* was a person handed over to be beheaded for this purpose. Warriors' young sons would be taken along to participate in the kill to instill a thirst for blood at an early age. The fact that the object of ngayaw raids was the taking of human heads suggests that slave labor was not a significant part of Cagayan economy. It also earned Ibanags the reputation of sparing no victims—man, woman, or child. In fact, however, they did take captives *(biyag)* and hold slaves *(aripan),* and *taliw* meant to market slaves or livestock. Labor was also supplied by *kobung,* relatives or servants taken into the household, whose social status was ranked in between servant and slave, and by *mangalu,* hired hands who worked for their food.

Sometimes one maengel could dominate others until he was recognized as a kind of king *(patul). Inangnguwa* was the ordinary Ibanag word for customs, but *negagangay* were traditions handed down from the time of a legendary King Wamba. Such warlords were respected for both their ferocity and their magnanimity, Bishop Diego Aduarte (1640, 1:229) described one of them in the following terms:

268

Fig. 14. Cagayan warrior
(From the Boxer Codex)

On that great river a valiant indio named Guiab had risen up over the others and, with only 300 indios—inasmuch as he did not wish to lead more—was making himself lord of that province, and would soon have done so had the Spaniards not arrived. He was an indio so determined that nothing was too difficult for him to overcome with those few brave indios who accompanied him, and so wrathful that when he wished to address them, at first he could not speak for sheer wrath until little by little he would calm down and go on with his speech. He ruled his men like a great captain, rewarding them with great largesse at others' cost from the much he had looted, and punished any liberty or disrespect they showed him with great rigor or for not obeying the orders he gave them.

Marriage was characterized by bride-price and public feasting, but separation was easy: divorce could be initiated by either partner, and a person who had been married only once was the exception rather than the rule. But an adulterer caught *flagrante delictu* was killed by the offended husband. A newborn infant was bathed in the river, and the father cut the umbilical cord and preserved it in a pouch containing bits of gold.

Wedding feasts sponsored by those who could afford it might last twenty or thirty days, and were judged a success by the amount of wine consumed. Inebriated men were carried off by their slaves or womenfolk to recuperate enough to return for more, but women themselves did not imbibe: they were known to Spanish observers as sober and hardworking. Dancing was accompanied by the beat of gongs called *gassa*, with men and women in opposed lines engaging in poetic debate.

Music for more intimate gatherings, however, was provided by the *kuritang*, a bamboo lyre with strings cut and raised from the skin of the bamboo itself. Father Bugarín (1676, 58) commented admiringly, "Not even Orpheus could invent a musical instrument with all its strings and frets made from a single piece of bamboo."

Religion. Friar accounts use *anito* as a catchall term for any object of Ibanag worship. These included deities that possessed shamans or spoke to them during seances, spirits that inhabited sacred groves, personified forces of nature, and any supernatural apparition. (Starfish were called *kugita na anitu*—anito's squid.) Offerings were made to benevolent anito for fertility, good health, and prosperity, fair weather, and success in war. Evil anito were propitiated to avoid illness, crop failure, storms, accident, and death, or defeat at enemy hands. Insanity or grave illness was attributed to the soul being enticed away from the body. Just as the Ibanag world was filled with potential head-taking enemies, so it was filled with soul-snatching evil spirits. *Aran* and *anani* were goblins, and *ngata* were devils so terrifying that the first person to see one would become *nginata*—sick or moribund. The prudent therefore conducted cleansing rituals before bringing any purchase or object into the house from another settlement, and wore magic beads on the wrist when venturing outside home territory themselves. So, too, they observed all omens carefully on leaving the house—a sneeze or a bird, snake, or lizard—and if an omen bird alighted on the roof, appropriate ceremonies were conducted to forestall its portent; if it returned, the house would be abandoned.

Shamans were generally old women, occasionally male transvestites, who sang, danced, and fell into trances during both public and private worship. Public ceremonies like a three-day preharvest rite required the display of gold jewelry by those who had it, and victory dances included ritual boasting by maengel participants. Private healing services were followed by neighbors begging for leftover ritual food and drink for their supernatural effects. Dishes used in especially solemn ceremonies were never used again, but broken and discarded; porcelain plates in which offerings were made to forest spirits were left there—even gold—safe from all pilferage. To cut wood or foliage from sacred groves or hills was a sacrilege which invited public calamity like typhoons or plague. When Luis Dasmariñas ordered such branches gathered for making camp one night along the Babuyan Channel, a sudden storm came up which drove heavy seas over the site, from which the Spaniards only escaped with the loss of all possessions. It was just what the Ibanags had predicted.

Mourning restrictions included fasting which, in the case of the loss of an especially beloved and respected wife or child, might last for years. The bereaved would eat no rice nor drink any wine, and his companions would restrict their own consumption of alcohol as a sign of sympathy—"which must have been a real hardship," Aduarte (1640, 1:243) rather snidely remarked, "for a people so fond of it." If a chief's fasting took too obvious a toll on his physical strength, his community would provide him a slave to behead to end the mourning period, preferably an enemy captive. One early Christian convert confessed that he had dispatched twelve slaves in this manner on different occasions. The deceased was provided with food, clothes, and body oil for use in the other world, and gold for expenses en route—for example, payment to the old boatman who ferried souls across a river or lake, although he would not perform this service for any woman whose hands were not tattooed. Maengel expected to go to the grave accompanied by one or two slaves to serve them in a future life of feasting, drinking, and dancing. Bishop Aduarte also said they believed they would eventually return to this world after enjoying that paradise, but whether this is correct or not, it is a belief which was reported nowhere else.

271

Afterword

This survey of sixteenth-century Philippine culture and society may well elicit some surprise among modern readers. The nose flute is nowadays beloved of Filipino tourists who are unaware that their ancestors played the same instrument, and slavery is abhorred as a Moro aberration by the Christian descendants of Filipinos who regularly conducted slave raids. A few comments to explain this phenomenon will therefore not be out of place.

The Spaniards were shocked when they first saw Filipinos wearing both gold and G-strings. In their view, nakedness—including men in G-strings—was the final degradation of Adam's children, while gold jewelry in Spain was associated with a well-clothed Christian elite. Yet here they were combined in the same persons. So, too, modern Filipinos would be shocked to meet their sixteenth-century ancestors. In the sharp distinction they make between civilized and uncivilized, G-strings are characteristic of the latter. Yet their forefathers were proudly wearing the *bahag* from Sarangani to Aparri, slaves and datus alike. Worse, Rajah Humabon's tattooed body, decorated teeth, shoulder-length hair, and distended earlobes would now be regarded as marks of sheer savagery. This disparity is to be accounted for by the profound changes which have occurred in Philippine society and culture during the past four centuries, changes which affected not only clothing styles but value judgments.

It was these changes that produced the Philippine past which is recalled today with nostalgia and depicted in Christmas cards and romantic novels: Farmers in short pants follow the plow across irrigated rice fields, and carabaos drag their produce to market and turn sugarcane presses. Cloth is woven on upright treadle looms, and pots are thrown on wheels and fired in kilns. Men do not wear earrings or long hair, and nobody tattoos or files his teeth. The deceased are buried in Christian cemeteries, and no cadavers are left in houses to be abandoned, or disinterred for secondary burial.

Yet these changes did not reach the interior hinterlands, and many pre-Hispanic customs have survived up to the present time among Filipinos whose ancestors were never assimilated into the life of the Spanish colony.

The late archaeologist and social anthropologist Robert B. Fox once planned a book to be called *The continuity of Philippine culture.* The book was never written, but it would have examined the cultures of the ethnic minorities for clues to ancient Philippine practices which have disappeared among the Christian majority. This afterword will attempt to do the opposite—that is, look at those minority cultures today for surviving features of the sixteenth-century ethnography already presented. And because modern changes have affected even these cultures, some will be examined as they existed with their traditions still flourishing earlier in the century.

Dr. Fox meant to write about minority cultures like that of the Mangyans of Mindoro: The Mangyans are sedentary agriculturists who farm without plow or carabao, growing rice, root crops, and vegetables in hillside swiddens cleared on such carefully integrated schedules that the surrounding forest cover is not destroyed. Rice is planted by communal labor, with a line of men punching holes with a dibble stick, a line of women following to drop the seeds in. Game is taken with spears forged with an upright two-cylinder bellows, and bows shooting poisoned arrows. Salt is made by pouring seawater over burning logs, washing out the ashes, and boiling the resulting brine. Cotton is spun with distaff and spindle, and woven on backstrap looms for G-strings, skirts, and jackets dyed blue with indigo and elaborately embroidered. It is, in short, a genuine sixteenth-century Visayan technology.

As a matter of fact, this sixteenth-century technology survived into the twentieth century from one end of the archipelago to the other. It is almost standard practice among rice swiddeners for men to precede women across the fields, punching holes for them to seed: the Kalingas do so in the Mabaca and Saltan valleys and the Itnegs in Apayao subprovince, and so, too, do the Bagobo in the mountains of Davao. The two-piston forge is used by the Tugaya brass casters in Lanao del Sur, and by the T'boli of South Cotabato to forge blades unexcelled in temper and keenness, as well as by the blacksmiths of the Cordillera Central of northern Luzon, where anthropologist Alfred E. Jenks photographed a miniature version in Bontoc in 1905 used exclusively for making gold earrings. And like their sixteenth-century predecessors, all these metal workers use raw materials procured through trade, even breaking up cast-iron vats for this purpose. Cotton and abaca cloth are still woven on backstrap looms among the Mindanao Lumad from Davao to Agusan, and so are the elegant textiles and decorative edgings reserved for the elite and royalty in Marawi and Cotabato, while backstrap weaving has almost become a cottage industry in Ifugao and the Mountain Province to supply a tourist market.

The G-string remained the preferred male garment on the Luzon Cordillera up until the Second World War, and the rectangular wraparound skirt for women. Among the Bontoc and Ifugao, elaborately decorated G-string flaps were indications of high economic status, and expensive blankets worn as mantles or burial shrouds were strictly prescribed by social class and lineage. Warrior status was indicated in the Mountain Province and Kalinga not by clothing but by extravagant tattoos, and a man who tattooed without qualifying feats of valor could expect such divine retribution as illness or misfortune. So, too, the Bagobo believed that a man who participated in communal ritual boasting without having killed an enemy would be struck down by some terrible malady.

The T'boli also tattoo, and, in a further show of manliness, burn scars on their forearms with hot coals. Manobo braves called *bagani* were until recently set off by red garments—a red turban for those who had taken seven lives, a red shirt for twice that number, and completely red attire for fifteen or more.

If Father Alcina could return to the Philippines today and attend a Taosug marriage, he would recognize most of its elements. The arrangements are made in a series of ritual visits to the bride's parents by the suitor's go-betweens and relatives: to seek permission to open negotiations, to ask for the girl's hand, to fix the engagement, to settle the bride-price and later to deliver it, to set the wedding date, and finally for the wedding itself—following which, the bride's shyness must be overcome by repeated personal gifts before she unites with her husband. Among the Agusan Manobo, such visits and bargaining could go on for months and even years. John Garvan recorded a case in Pilar begun in 1898 in which the bride-price was only settled in 1904 at ten slaves, haggled down four months later to four slaves and the equivalent of six others in goods and valuables, and delivered the next year lacking one slave, for which deficiency the man was still working for his prospective father-in-law in 1910. In Apayao, a proud father may demand that his son-in-law join his household, or at least settle in his village, a demand that can lead to heated exchanges. In 1968, a young American anthropologist, John Smart, accompanied a suitor's party that was so intimidated during negotiations that they jumped through a window and fled.

Pre-Hispanic burial practices also continued up into the American regime. Traditional burials in Sagada, Mountain Province, are made in coffins with lids carved from the same tree, placed at the mouth of limestone caves or on almost inaccessible cliffs. The Kalinga bury below or between houses, and so do the Bukidnon, who may also abandon a house in which a death has occurred, as the Manobo also do, while the Mandaya burn such a building. The Mangyan, Suban-on, and Panay Sulod practice secondary burial, sometimes in ceramic jars, and so do the Ifugao. The late H. Otley Beyer's remains were interred in Banaue in 1967 and later disinterred for a traditional bone-washing ceremony. The Bagobo and Suban-on used to sacrifice a slave as a mourning requirement, and a Tagakaolo widower could not remarry without performing such a ritual. And the belief that those who die by the sword or in childbirth go to a separate afterworld is held by old folks in societies as far apart as the Bagobo in southern Mindanao and the Ifugao in northern Luzon.

These similarities give impressive testimony to the continuity of Philippine culture across three centuries. But even more impressive than its endurance is the extent of its distribution—from the mouth of the Cagayan River in the north to Saragani and Sulu in the south, from the seacoasts of Samar and Manila Bay to the heights of the Cordillera Central and Mount Apo. This does not mean, however, that all sixteenth-century Filipinos shared one and the same culture. After all, they spoke many different languages and had adjusted to many different environments; and communities stimulated by overseas trade, supplies, and ideas had developed more sophisticated societies than mountain villages. Igorot blacksmiths may have used the same tools as their Tagalog contemporaries but they did not have the same access to raw materials, and their chiefs certainly did not operate gun foundries or collect harbor fees. But the similarities do indicate pre-Hispanic culture contacts from one end of the archipelago to the other. They also suggest that lowland Filipinos in the sixteenth century had more in common with highland minorities in the twentieth than with their own Christian descendants.

Naturally, this common heritage did not survive intact the imposition of colonial authority. Subjugated Filipinos responded to military and moral suasion by abandoning customs which were offensive to their foreign conqueror—not only slave raiding and human sacrifices, but even G-strings and decorated teeth. As Father San Buenaventura (1613, 390) said, "Whoever files his teeth, I will certainly punish." So profound were these changes that by the beginning of the twentieth century, Filipinos who had grown up under Spanish domination considered themselves a different people from those who had not. The final triumph of this acculturative process can be seen in the fact that those whose ancestors experienced it are unaware that it took place. It is precisely this social amnesia which today stigmatizes as cultural minorities those Filipinos who resisted colonial acculturation.

A Select Bibliography on Twentieth-Century Minority Cultures

Barton, Roy Franklin. 1946. *The religion of the Ifugaos.* Menasha (Wis.).

Casal, Gabriel. 1977a. "The legacy of Ginton," *Filipino heritage* 2:455–60. Manila.

_____. 1977b. "The high-fashion world of the T'boli," *Filipino heritage* 3:729–37. Manila

Cole, Fay-Cooper. 1913. *The wild tribes of Davao District, Mindanao.* Chicago.

Conklin, Harold C. 1957. *Hanunoo agriculture.* Northford (Conn.), 1975.

Finley, John Park. 1913. *The Subanu: Studies of a sub-Visayan mountain folk of Mindanao.* Washington.

Garvan, John M. 1929. *The Manobos of Mindanao.* Washington, 1931.

Jenks, Albert E. *The Bontoc Igorot.* Manila

Jocano, F. Landa. 1964. "Notes on the Sulod concept of death, the soul, and the region of the dead," *Philippine studies* 12:51–62.

Manuel, E. Arsenio. 1973. *Manuvú social organization.* Quezon City.

_____. 1975. "The wake and last rites over H. Otley Beyer in Ifugaoland," *Philippine studies* 23:120–89.

Postma, Antoon. 1977a. "Please pass the salt," *Filipino heritage* 2:487–89. Manila.

_____. 1977b. "The unchanging Mangyan," *Filipino heritage* 2:554–60.

Scott, William Henry. 1958. "A preliminary report on upland rice in northern Luzon," *Southwestern journal of anthropology* 14:87–105.

Smart, John E. 1967. "The flight from Agiwan: A case study in the sociocultural dynamics of an Isneg marriage negotiation," *Philippine quarterly of culture and society.*

Notes

1. *La isla de Negros y las costumbres de los Visayas y Negritos,* attributed to sixteenth-century encomendero Diego Lopé Povedano, and *Las antiguas leyendas de la isla de Negros* and *Los cuentos de los indios de esta isla,* attributed to nineteenth-century Spanish clergyman José María Pavón, were donated to the Philippine National Library in 1913 by Jose E. Marco of Pontevedra (Occidental Negros). They have since been shown by internal contradictions and anachronisms to be deliberate forgeries, but the fantastic "Code of Kalantiaw," which is part of the forgeries, has been incorporated into standard Philippine history texts. *Maragtas* is a copyrighted 1907 local history of Panay by Pedro Alcantara Monteclaro, which contains a legend which has carelessly been considered a pre-Hispanic document. *See* Scott 1984.

2. It will be noted that the word *boat* does not appear in this text translated from the original in the Archives of the Indies. But the text given by Santa Inés (1676, 2–3:592) has an additional clause which BR (7:174) translate as "which is a boat, thus called."

3. *See,* for example, Eric San Juan's (1987, 112) statement, "When the term 'Filipino' later came into use, it was reserved for Spaniards on the archipelago."

4. *See* "The population of the archipelago, 1565–1898" in Corpus 1989, 1:515–70.

5. The theory was first published in 1918, updated in a historical introduction to Manuel's 1948 *Chinese elements in the Tagalog language,* and popularized in a 1947 newspaper supplement, *Philippine saga,* and in *Pictorial history of the Philippines* (Reyes, et al. 1953).

6. *See* Bennet Bronson's (1977) devastating "Against migration: A negative perspective on population movements in Southeast Asia."

277

7. What are regarded as the definitive study of population movements into Southeast Asia and the Pacific are Bellwood 1978 and 1985. The northern-vs-southern argument over the Austronesian migration route into the Philippines was joined at the Twelfth Congress of the Indo-Pacific Prehistory Association in Peñablanca (Cagayan) in 1985; *see* Bellwood, Meacham, and Solheim 1988.

8. Anthropologists call this unnatural formation a "casco foot" from the barges *(cascos)* which these men poled.

9. The best summary for the nonlinguist is Zorc's (1984) "The Philippine language scene."

10. Visayan terms are taken mainly from the Mateo Sánchez *Leyte-Samareño (Waray) dictionary,* and the Alonso Méntrida *Panay dictionary* (Hiligaynon with Aklanon and Kiniray-a variants notes). No early Cebuano lexicon is known.

11. *Cakra* is the Spanish word for wheel or disk, and a variety of penis inserts are mentioned from southern India in the erotic classic, Kama Sutra. Penis pins called *palang,* with or without knobby finials, are still known in Borneo, but the penis wheel secured with a crossbar has only been reported from the Philippines. For a modern survey, *see* Brown, Edwards, and Moore 1988. None of these actual implants, however, are to be confused with the condomlike devices nowadays called ticklers or exciters.

12. Splendid illustrations in full color of all this goldwork can be found in Villegas 1983. It is possible that such jewelry was exported. The royal regalia of the Makassar Gowa dynasty on display in Sungguminasa (Sulawesi) includes a gold chain necklace said to have come from Manila.

13. Taro was evidently farmed in huge quantities, even if Father Alcina (1668a, 1:103) was exaggerating when he wrote, "An indio may ordinarily plant ten or twelve thousand, and some good workers more, to eat and sell; they give 100 for a real if they are medium-sized, and if they're very large, 60 or 80 proportionately."

14. BR (5:44) misread as part of the sentence, "Tienen . . . unas raices como batatas de sancto domingo que llaman camotes," the beginning of the next sentence, "En esta isla y en todas las que se han descubrierto," etc. giving the misleading translation, "a kind of root resembling the potatoes of Sancto Domingo, called by the [Philippine] natives *camotes.*"

15. Like cows, horses were imported into the archipelago by the Spaniards from Mexico and China. But the presence of the Malay word for horse, *kuda,* in Mindanao and Sulu languages suggests an introduction from the south unknown to the Spaniards.

16. For a more detailed description, see "Boat building and seamanship in classic Philippine society," in Scott 1982a, 60–95, and Horridge's Alcina translation in National Maritime Museum Monograph no. 5.

17. The conversion of sixteenth-century measurements to modern equivalents must be undertaken with some reservation since Spanish units of measure have varied considerably over the centuries. The *braza* ("embrace"), for example, now reckoned at 1.67 meters, was probably somewhat shorter.

18. The fact that Magellan's Sumatran slave, Enrique de Malacca, was also understood by the Limasawa ruler, persuaded Magellan biographer Stefan Zweig that he must have been a native Visayan, now returned to the land of his birth. "What an amazing moment, one of the most remarkable in the history of mankind! For the first time since our planet had begun to spin on its axis and to circle in its orbit, a living man himself circling the planet, had got back to his homeland" (Zweig 1938, 234). Though this fantasy is

unsupported by any historical evidence, the idea that it was a Filipino who first circumnavigated the globe has had irresistible appeal in the Philippines, most recently to F. Sionil Jose in his novel, *Viajero*.

19. San Buenaventura (1613, 509), however, defines the *codyapi* as "Rabel or violon which they play with a bow." Perhaps this was the Chinese two-stringed *er-hu*.

20. The most famous was at Los Baños in Luzon, whose thermal springs had attracted Filipinos to their medicinal qualities in pre-Hispanic times.

21. Because the sun never appears directly overhead in European latitudes, it is due south of the observer at high noon. Mediterranean sailors therefore used midday (*mediodía*) for the compass bearing of due south.

22. Alcina (1668a, 4:60) gave a similar expression: "Akon ka ginoo; akun ka gintubo [I set you free; I held you as a slave]."

23. I use *money* to mean gold, goods, or any other medium of exchange.

24. This island was called Mazaua or Mazagua in the Spanish accounts, and there has recently been some controversy over its location. I see no reason to doubt its identification with Limasawa. Pigafetta placed it at 9 2/3 degrees north latitude, 25 *leguas* (150 kilometers) from Humunu (Homonhon), and Albo gave the same latitude but estimated the Homonhon-Masawa distance as 20 leguas (120 kilometers). In 1565, Legazpi pilot Esteban Rodríguez logged the distance from Cabalian (Leyte) at 8 or 9 leguas, and when Captain Ortiz de Rueda visited the island in 1543, he thought it was about 60 kilometers from Butuan. Considering the fact that these observers thought that Panaon Island was a continuation of Leyte, Limasawa is the only island found in this position. Its exact latitude is 9°54'58", but sun-sight readings were known to be a bit low in the early sixteenth century; Rodríguez (1565, 398) himself noted, "I always add a quarter of a degree to the sun sight according to the Mexican tables and not the Spanish." It may also be worth noting that the names Masawa and Limasawa have the same root—*sawa* (python); perhaps they mean Python Place and Five Pythons respectively.

25. Tolula is presumably Turang (Ibran) on the southeast coast, which was confused in the Villalobos account with Patuko and its fine harbor on the northwest.

26. I am indebted to linguist Ken Maryott for the following explanations of these names: "Candigar (i.e., Balut I.) looks very much like it might be Sandigang in Sangir and Sangil [languages], which means 'located nearby (Mindanao).' To this day, both languages use a synonym of Sandigang to refer to Balut" (personal communication 13 April 1993).

27. Members of Salcedo's expeditionary force of 1572 also reported one town that "seemed to have more than three thousand houses" (Ortega 1573, 135), a rather unlikely figure.

28. The Chinese characters 常 來 appear on an illustration of a "Sangley" couple in the Boxer Codex (1590a, pl.V). Langlang is probably *lan-nang*, a colloquial term by which Fujianese in the Philippines distinguish themselves from other Chinese immigrants.

29. Pigafetta (1624b, 222) said of him, "This captain was much feared in those parts, but more so by the pagans because they were enemies of that Moro king." Ginés de Mafra said he was in Borneo to marry the sultan's daughter, but I here follow the Aganduru Móriz account of 1623. This account, despite Móriz's own embellishments, preserves a Manila tradition that was current at the beginning of the seventeenth century, and is therefore worth quoting at length:

What had happened was that this Prince had been left without a father because he had died when he was newborn, and the government fell to the Queen mother whom the King of Tongdo, her nephew, challenged because she was a woman; he did not pay her much heed nor did the principal lords of Manila since each of them was trying to be king and lord of what he could.

The Prince grew up, and as he was raised with his own cousin, the King of Tongdo, who kept slyly encroaching on his land, when he was older he had a quarrel with him, for which reason he returned to Manila, offended that the King his cousin had no respect for him and presumed to bully him like an elder brother. He complained to his mother, who tried to soothe him and patch the thing up, but as the Prince was now a young man of high spirits, and understood how the King of Tongdo after his father's death had been encroaching on the kingdom of Manila, he discussed with some principal lords, relatives of his who looked on him as on themselves, that he wanted to go to Borneo and ask help from his grandfather, who was King Saripada, to return and recover his lands. He told this to his mother, who would like to have kept him with her and dissuade him from the voyage, but on seeing his determination, she gave him permission and a quantity of gold, and taking ships accompanied by some lords, he went to Borneo with them, where he was very well received by his grandfather, Saripada, in whose court and palace he was treated like a royal person so that he was able to put almost 200 ships under sail, both junks and galleys, and as many as 6,000 spirited Bornean soldiers. With this he set out shortly before General Juan Sebastián del Cano made port in Borneo and, since the Prince found himself with so fine a fleet, he wanted to take some prizes in order to return to Manila more powerful, giving pleasure in this to the Bornean soldiers who were dead set on robbery. This fleet, then, was the one that turned on our two galleons.

The General took the flagship and captured the Prince aboard her; he learned his plans and where he was going with his fleet, about which he had also had word in Borneo, and having learned that he was King Saripada's grandson, graciously gave him his liberty. Declining a sum of gold which he had first been offered for her, he returned the ship to him and what he had taken from him, telling him how much he owed the King of Borneo, since when he reached his port in need of food, he had succored him with great generosity, for which he was so obligated that, if it would not go against his King's orders who had commanded him to go out to the Malucos islands, he would interrupt his voyage to go and serve him until he restored him to his kingdoms, but that he could not delay. He asked him for a guide and pilot for Maluco [and] the Prince of Manila, grateful for the General's good treatment, gave him a good pilot, a slave of his and his freedom so he could guide them. The pilot was from Makassar, who after having been captured and passed from one master to another, had wound up in the service of the Prince of Luzon—or Manila, which is the same.

The island is called Luzon, where the kings had their court; the Ladyas [Rajahs] were called Kings of Manila. Great formalities having passed between the General and the Prince, Juan Sebastián del Cano asked him that, so the liberty he had given him should not go unrepaid, if perchance some Spaniards sometime made port in his lands and reigns, he should remember the nobleness with which he had been treated by His Highness in the present occasion and therefore treat them well; to this the

Prince swore according to his custom and he kept his word very well as we will see in the conquest of Manila, for this is the King Ladya Matanda who received Maestre-de-Campo Martín de Goiti hospitably (Móriz 1623, 78:59–60).

30. Our earliest population figure for Manila is two thousand in 1572, excluding the women and children—though BR translate *dexado* as "including." This figure I have increased to ten thousand, by reckoning five women and children to each man, but then arbitrarily lowered to six thousand to exclude the environs. The passage in question reads:

> The natives were many and of different classes, although not so many as has been said in Nueva España [Mexico], where they said that there were eighty thousand Moros gathered in this town of Manila when this [occupation] took place; because from the eighty thousand, seventy-eight thousand had best be removed, leaving two thousand which there could have been in the said town and the other towns around, besides the children and the women, who would have been many (Anon. 1572, 79).

Nonetheless, the tendency to exaggerate the size of Manila at the time of Spanish advent continued into the next century. In 1664, Andrés de San Nicolás (who was never in the Philippines) wrote: "When Adenlantado Miguel López de Legazpi took it by force of arms on 19 May 1570 [*sic*], ten thousand houses adorned it" (San Nicolás 1664, 415).

31. In an earlier work, I mistakenly thought these twenty-two varieties were all swidden rice—that is, unirrigated (Scott 1992a, 75). I regret the error.

32. Like Sanskrit, Arabic, and Hebrew, the Philippine script has separate characters for the consonants but represents vowels with diacritical marks; I therefore call it, like them, an alphabet rather than a "syllabary."

33. Kinship terms of Chinese origin which appear in certain Tagalog dialects today—like *ate* (eldest sister), *kuya* (eldest brother), *diko* (second eldest brother), or *sangse* (third eldest sister)—do not appear in early dictionaries.

34. San Buenaventura here curiously spelled *balangay* as "barangay," perhaps reflecting a contemporary sound shift. I have regularly used *barangay* in this work to accord with modern usage.

35. The fact that these chiefs were not kings was cited by Rajah Soliman as an excuse for having betrayed his peace pact with Legazpi:

> You know that in this land there is no king nor single head but each one holds his own views and opinion and so they do what seems best to them . . . and were I king of this land rather than only lord of my own estate, the word which I gave would not have been broken (Riquel 1573, 234).

36. I regret that in several earlier works I incorrectly attributed this quotation to Archbishop Miguel de Benavides (*see* Scott 1974, 49; 1992a, 9).

37. In 1974, I speculated that Gaganayan was Kankanaey, a Cordillera ethnolinguistic group (Scott 1974, 43n4), but have since learned that Ilocano *gagan-ayan* (warping frame) also means the constellation "commonly called the Three Marías" (Carro 1790, 116).

Bibliographic Essay

A major font of sources for this book is five collections of published historical documents. The Spanish government published three *colecciones de documentos inéditos* (collections of unpublished documents), beginning in 1825 with Martín Fernández Navarrete's five volumes, and totaling sixty volumes by 1932. These are indicated in the present bibliography as CDIA, CDIU, and CVD. A fourth collection is Blair and Robertson's *The Philippine Islands 1493–1898,* fifty-five volumes of translations into English between 1903 and 1907 (BR), which include the original texts of several of earlier more important documents. The fifth collection is the ongoing *Historia de la provincia Agustiniana del Smo. Nombre de Jesús de Filipinas* (HPAF) by Isacio Rodríguez which has reached volume 20 to date. The Augustinians were the pioneer missionaries in the colony, so their presence and activities figure not only in their own correspondence but in official records. Father Rodríguez presents an exhaustive, carefully edited, and extensively annotated selection.

When Portuguese invaders—including Ferdinand Magellan—occupied Malacca in 1511, they found a community of Luzon merchants engaged in business there. Correspondence with the Portuguese king referring to them was summarized by Manuel Teixera and Luis Felipe Thomaz, while Tomé Pires's 1515 *Suma Oriental* provides a more accurate description. References to both Luzones and Maguindanaons in the early sixteenth century are scattered all through Fernão Mendes Pinto's picturesque *Peregrinação,* a travel account which incorporates all his sources as personal experiences. Ternate Governor Antonio Galvao and historian João de Barros mentioned Portuguese excursions to Mindanao in the 1530s, and a letter from Bras Bayao, the king's factor in Borneo, gives a brief description of Sulu in 1540.

Spanish accounts begin with the Magellan expedition of 1521. Magellan was a Portuguese adventurer under contract to the Spanish king to find a westward passage to the spice islands, but he was killed in Maktan and most of his men were massacred in Cebu. The survivors escaped in two vessels, one of which was captured by the Portuguese together with all of Magellan's papers, which were subsequently lost in a Lisbon fire. The other ship managed to continue westward and finally reached Spain: five firsthand accounts have survived from this inadvertent circumnavigation of the world.

The best of the five is Antonio Pifagetta's justly celebrated *Primo viaggio intorno al mondo* of 1524, one of the most observant travel documents of the sixteenth century. Pigafetta's original manuscript has not survived, but four copies are known, two of them identical enough to be regarded as faithful to the original, one in Italian and the other in French. The so-called Ambrosian text was published by Blair and Robertson in Italian, and the beautiful Nancy (or Beinecke) text in facsimile by R. A. Skelton in French. The former contains a few careless non sequiturs, the latter a number of mistranslated words but is nonetheless considered the preferred text. Unfortunately, these manuscripts remained unknown to scholars until the nineteenth century, so Spanish historians in the Philippines had to rely on garbled paraphrase in French printed in 1525 as *Le voyage et navigation faict par les Espaignols,* and then translated into Italian and given wide circulation in Giovanni Battista Ramusio's 1550 *Della navigationi et viaggi*. It is this mutilated text which has given rise to the modern Philippine controversy over a supposed Magellan visit to Butuan, an event nowhere mentioned in the primary texts.

Pilot Francisco Albo's navigational log has also survived, as well as a running account by Ginés de Mafra (who would visit the Philippines again twenty-two years later with Villalobos), along with two anonymous undated Portuguese accounts. These provide a number of gossipy details like the fact that the rulers of Butuan, Limasawa, and Cebu—Awi, Kolambu, and Humabon—were all related, and that Lapulapu of Maktan was the uncle of Humabon's wife. They also regard Magellan's death as having been caused by an act of foolhardy aggression on his part, an opinion evidently shared by the Spanish court since the viceroy of Mexico, Hernán Cortés, tried to send the "King of Cebu" an apology.

Three more Spanish expeditions made landfalls on the east coast of Mindanao but could not reach Cebu because of adverse winds and currents, and wound up in Portuguese hands in the Moluccas. Two accounts are extant from the 1526 Juan García Jofre de Loaysa voyage, one by Hernando de la Torre, who assumed command following the deaths of Loaysa and three of his successors, the other by a daring Basque seaman by the name of Andrés de Urdaneta, who was to return to the Philippines forty years later as an Augustinian friar. The little *Santa María del Parral* got separated from Loaysa's fleet, and her crew mutinied, killed their officers, ran aground on Sangir Island, and were all seized and sold into slavery. From the 1528 expedition of Álvaro de Saavedra Cerón there are three accounts—two by Vicente de Nápoles and one by Francisco Granado. On the Davao coast, Saavedra recovered four of the Spanish slaves but hanged three of them as mutineers.

The 1543 Ruy López de Villalobos expedition was the first to attempt an actual settlement in the Philippines and therefore carried a contingent of friar missionaries, but during eighteen tragic months lost more than two hundred men to hunger, disease, or hostility. Father Gerónimo Santisteban has left one account, and senior officer García

283

Descalante Alvarado another, while an anonymous undated and incomplete account, recently discovered in the Biblioteca Nacional in Madrid and published by Consuelo Varela, runs to more than a hundred pages of detailed activities and local customs. It must also be the most frustrating document in Philippine historiography because the dozens of diagrams and maps it originally contained are all missing from the present manuscript. An even more detailed account written in the next century by Rodrigo Aganduru Móriz is evidently based on some original source now unknown, but is larded with imaginary conversations between parleying Filipinos and Spaniards.

Finally, in 1565 Miguel López de Legazpi successfully duplicated Magellan's Samar landfall, entered the archipelago through Surigao Strait, and established a permanent Spanish settlement in Cebu to begin 333 years of colonial occupation. There is a fine journal of the events—anonymous but probably written by royal notary Hernando Riquel—which includes careful observations of the islands and people contacted. Its first six months appear in HPAF, the next twenty-five months in CDIU, the former being profusely annotated with references to other documents, such as financial accounts with specific names, dates, and goods handed out to ingratiate Filipino chiefs. There are more than a dozen reports of local resources and products—and conquistador abuses— written by both civil officials and friar clergy, and Legazpi himself, of which the most useful for our purposes are those of Juan Martínez and Juan de la Isla, the latter also being incorporated into a later report by Diego de Artieda. BR also give the text of an anonymous report, *Copia de una carta venida de Sevilla,* printed in Barcelona in 1566.

In 1571 Legazpi shifted to Manila for greater access to provisions and trade, and three accounts of the voyage and conquest contain our only descriptions of that emporium at the time of Spanish advent: one anonymous, one by Legazpi, and the third by Riquel. Biographical details of its three rulers can be gleaned from these, together with two of the Magellan accounts, reports from the 1578–79 attacks on Borneo, letters to the king from royal auditor Melchor de Ávalos, a tale recorded in the early 1600s by Aganduru Móriz, and eighteenth-century genealogies preserved in the Philippine National Archives, all of which data have been skillfully exploited by Luciano Santiago (1990) in his "The houses of Lakandula, Matanda, and Soliman." Regular reports by the governors general for the rest of the century translated in BR add to increasing knowledge of Luzon conditions, and so do passing details in sworn testimonies to the role of the Augustinians in the Conquest. (*See,* for example, Baeza, Marín, Román, and Sotomayor.) Of special value among early sources is the correspondence of pioneer missionary Martín de Rada, an energetic, well-educated friar with close contacts with both colonial authorities and Filipino elite, but shocked by the social mores of a culture so different from his own.

The first-generation descriptions were written in response to a royal order to make reports on native conditions and customs. Miguel de Loarca's 1582 *Relación* was never published but its full text appears in BR. It reviews the whole archipelago but, inasmuch as Loarca operated a Spanish shipyard with Filipino labor in Oton (Iloilo), it is much better informed about the Visayas than Luzon. Franciscan Father Juan de Plasencia wrote succinct treatises on Tagalog religion in 1589; I have used the Archivo General de Indias (AGI) originals for the first two but an appendix in Santa Inés's *Crónicas* for the third. Plasencia also wrote a *Relación* published in 1592, whose only known copy is in the British Library.

Perhaps the richest source of Filipino detail is the "Boxer Codex," named for its scholar-owner, C. R. Boxer, because its title page is missing, though it can be dated to 1590 on internal evidence. It includes separate sections on Cagayan, Zambales, the Tagalogs, and the Visayans, as well as treatises on other regions of Indonesia and southern China, and is profusely illuminated with gold leaf—our only illustrations of sixteenth-century Filipinos. Readers should be aware, however, that, like other early Spanish documents, it regularly refers to Tagalogs as Moros, although their culture is clearly described as non-Muslim and animist.

The two best books for our period are Dr. Antonio de Morga's 1609 *Sucesos de las Islas Filipinas,* and Father Pedro Chirino's 1604 *Relación de las Islas Filipinas.* Morga was a highly placed colonial officer—once acting governor—with access to documentation of the "events" (that is, *sucesos*) about which he wrote. His work includes the most thorough and objective account of the archipelago and its inhabitants written in the sixteenth century. (He referred to Filipinos as *naturales*—natives—rather than *indios,* a term suggesting cultural inferiority.) Chirino's work is a history of the early Jesuit missions, and portrays Filipinos sympathetically for a European audience. He reported them as ready and faithful converts, lauded their cleanliness and ability to carry their liquor, and exaggerated their modesty of dress and extent of literacy. The Jesuit story was continued by Francisco Colín in his 1663 *Labor evangélica* from Chirino's own notes and a longer version of the *Relación,* which is happily reproduced almost in full in the annotations to Pablo Pastells's 1900 edition of Colín.

Since the Dominicans were given charge of missionary work in northern Luzon, Bishop Diego de Aduarte's 1640 *Historia de la provincia del Santo Rosario* is the best source for Pangasinan and Cagayan culture. Early Franciscan writers like Marcelo de Ribadeneira and Juan Pobre de Zamora, however, gave much less detail about the Bikolanos, devoting most of their space to glowing reports of native responses to their proselytizing efforts. Our earliest accounts of life in northeastern Mindanao are Recollect Fathers Andrés de San Nicolás's 1664 *Historia general de los religiosos descalzos del orden de los Ermitaños* and Luis de Jesús's 1681 continuation. Jesuit Francisco Combés's 1667 *Historia de las islas de Mindanao, Iolo y sus adyacentes* ranks as a classic of Spanish reporting of Philippine culture, being characterized by careful personal observations and rich recording of oral histories. And a curious little 1673 book by Pedro Mercado called *Vida de un mancebo indio llamado Miguel Ayatumo, natural de Bohollo* (Life of an indio youth called Miguel Ayatumo, a native of Bohol) contains a few unique references to religious practices on that island.

There are two books written in later centuries which are also valuable for information about the sixteenth—Gaspar de San Agustín's 1698 *Conquistas de las Islas Filipinas* and Juan Francisco de San Antonio's 1738 *Crónicas de la apostólica provincia de S. Gregorio.* San Agustín made use of contemporary documents of the Conquest, and preserved many details otherwise unknown, even a description of native culture by Legazpi himself (complete with date of dispatch to Mexico) whose original is not catalogued in the AGI. And San Antonio made a careful study of the work of earlier writers before producing his own descriptions of Philippine culture and society.

Special insight into Tagalog language and culture is provided by the sermons and hortatory expositions written by Spanish friars who were masters of the idiom. Unlike dictionary definitions, these specimens of prose illustrate how the language was actually spoken: their examples, common expressions, turns of phrase, and elegant metaphors must have been meaningful to a particular audience in a particular time and place. Juan de Oliver's exposition of the Christian faith—*Declaración de la doctrina Christiana en idioma Tagalog*—is found in a manuscript collection (now in the University of Indiana) which was looted by British officers during the 1762 occupation of Manila. A collection of sermons by Father Francisco Blancas de San José in the Rare Books and Manuscripts Section of the Philippine National Library (PNL) contains one for every Sunday of the church year from Advent to Easter. An *Explicación de los siete sacramentos de la Santa Iglesia* by the same author is also found in the PNL. It had been carried away from the church in Meycauayan during the Fil-American War by an enemy soldier who returned it in his presumably conscience-stricken old age.

The most important single work for this study has been Francisco Ignacio Alcina's unpublished 1668 *Historia de las islas e indios de Bisayas,* which indeed is one of the most remarkable literary products of the whole Spanish period. It is an ethnographic study which remained the most extensive work of its kind until the twentieth century, and a unique testimony to a missionary's intimate knowledge of his parishioners and their culture. It has been frequently quoted in this work. Part 1 contains four books on flora, fauna, and ethnography, totaling 1,485 pages; but part 2 on history only exists in fragments. A transcription of part 1 was made available in 1962 by the Philippine Studies Program of the University of Chicago, and the surviving books of part 2 were published by Kobak and Fernández in *Philippiniana sacra* 14–20 (1979–1986). The first two books of part 1 were also published in facsimile by Martín-Meras and Higueras in Madrid in 1974.

All these sources of information can be made more useful by recourse to early Spanish lexicons of Philippine languages, not only from the definitions themselves but, more revealingly, from the grammatical examples which illustrate their use. (The same may be said of the early Spanish grammars—*artes* or *compendios*.) Pedro de San Buenaventura's *Vocabulario de lengua Tagala* was printed in Pila (Laguna) in 1613, but the one by his contemporary, Francisco Blancas de San José, was never published, though there are three known manuscript copies—one each in the University of Santo Tomas, the Biblioteque Nationale in Paris, and the National Archives in Vienna. The Tagalog dictionary of Miguel Ruiz (d. 1630) is known only from a manuscript in King's College, London, which institution also preserves the manuscript of the Ilocano dictionary of Francisco López who died in 1631. Mateo Sánchez's *Bocabulario de la lengua Bisaya* was completed in Dagami (Leyte) in 1617 and printed in 1711, while the Hiligaynon dictionary of Alonso de Méntrida (d. 1637) and the Bikolano dictionary of Marcos de Lisboa (d. 1628) were reissued in the nineteenth century. José Bugarín's Ibanag dictionary dates from later in the century, and the Pampanga and Pangasinan dictionaries of Diego Bergaño and Lorenzo Fernández Cosgaya come from the eighteenth. They must therefore be used critically, since lexicons written so long after Spanish advent will have perforce incorporated semantic changes produced by colonial domination, especially in matters of religion, government, and warfare.

A word of explanation may be offered about the use of these dictionaries. In the first place, they have been used in conjunction with one another and with all other sources of information. The variation in the number of technical terms in different dictionaries, for example, no doubt reflects the interests of their lexicographers rather than different levels of technology in the language groups involved. San Buenaventura mentioned neither potter's wheels nor any other implements for pot making, though there were obviously Tagalog potters, but Visayan and Bikol dictionaries give the terms for the paddle-and-anvil technique. On the other hand, the fact that Tagalog and Bikol dictionaries contain extensive vocabularies for wet–rice farming but that Visayan dictionaries do not, certainly point to different agricultural technologies in these areas. Again, the absence of any Philippine terms for cart, sledge, yoke, or plow from a particular lexicon may not be significant, but that these terms are missing from all the early dictionaries, as well as from other accounts, persuasively argues that the carabao was not being used as a draft animal in pre-Hispanic times.

In addition to these historical sources, recourse has been made to the oral literature of Filipino groups occupying the interior mountains of Mindanao, Panay, and Luzon, where they were less exposed to colonial acculturation. It is not possible to date these epics, but they preserve the idealized memory of an earlier way of life in compositions of truly epic scope and style. Whenever they were composed, they depict an un-Hispanized Philippine culture and society with obvious parallels to the Philippine culture and society described in this work.

From the Cordillera of northern Luzon, Francis Lambrecht and Francis Billiet have published the Ifugao Hudhud and Kalinga Ullalim; and from Panay, F. Landa Jocano has published part of the Hinilawod; while Gina Barte has kindly made available her unpublished translation of part of the Humadapnon. Musicologist Elena G. Maquiso has produced a book-length study, *Ulahingan: An epic of the southern Philippines,* from the Manobo of South Cotabato; while their Manuvu neighbors' Agyu cycle has been the subject of studies and recordings by E. Arsenio Manuel. From Bukidnon comes Ludivina R. Opeña's recording of the Olaging; and from the Suban-on, Esterlinda Mendoza Malagar, Gaudiosa Martinez Ochoterena, and Virgilio Resma have published three epics in *Kinaadman.* In a class by itself for epic grandeur and literary sophistication is the Darangan of Marawi, which was first brought to public attention by Frank Laubach's "An Odyssey from Lanao" in 1930. The whole cycle is now being published by the Folklore Division of the Mindanao State University Research Center under the direction of Sister Ma. Delia Coronel; six luxurious volumes have been published to date, totaling 80,225 lines of elegant Maranao verse.

The Ilocano epic of Lam-ang—which might better be called a metrical romance—strangely does not depict an un-Hispanized culture: its hero performs his magical feats in a setting which might easily be that of a nineteenth-century Spanish colony. Similarly, a nineteenth-century Spanish poem which incorporates Bikol folklore has been passionately believed by Bikolano scholars to be a translation from a lost epic called Handiong of Ibalon. But whether translation or not, the poem is not written in the literary style of other Philippine epics: it lacks the rich repetitions of petty details which would permit the reconstruction of an archaic Philippine society. Neither of these works have therefore served the purposes of the present study.

Bibliography

Common Abbreviations

AFIO   Archivo Franciscano Ibero-Oriental, Madrid.

AGI   Archivo General de Indias, Seville.

AHHA   Archivo Histórico Hispano-Agustiniano.

BR   Emma Helen Blair and James Alexander Robertson. *The Philippine islands 1493–1898*, 55 vols. Cleveland 1903–1907.

CDIA   *Colección de documentos inéditos relativos al descubrimiento, conquista y colonización de las posesiones en América y Oceania, sacada en su mayor parte del Real Archivo de Indias,* 42 vols. Madrid 1864–1886.

CDIU   *Colección de documentos inéditos relativos al descubrimiento, conquista y organización de las antiguas posesiones Españoles de ultramar,* 13 vols. Madrid 1885–1932.

CVD   Martín Fernández Navarrete, *Colección de los viages y descubrimientos que hicieron por mar los Españoles desde fines del siglo XV,* 5 vols. Madrid 1825–1837.

HPAF   Isacio Rodríguez, *Historia de la provincia Agustiniana de Smo. Nombre de Jesús de Filipinas,* 19 vols.

Note: Sixteenth-century Spaniards are listed under the name by which they are commonly known today. Miguel López de Legazpi, for example, is listed under Legazpi rather than his surname, López de Legazpi. Modern authors, however, are listed under their first *apellido*—for example, Cayetano Sánchez Fuertes under Sánchez. Documents are listed under their date of writing and published works under their first edition, but where these dates are unknown, an estimated date has been supplied, or the date of the author's death.

Abella, Domingo. 1971. "From to indio to Filipino," *Philippine historical review* 4 (1971): 1–34.

Aduarte, Diego de. 1640. *Historia de la Provincia del Santo Rosario de la Orden de Predicadores en Filipinas, Japón y China*. Ed. Manuel Ferrero, 2 vols. Madrid 1962.

Albo, Francsco. 1522. "Diario o derrotero del viage de Magallanes desde el cabo de San Agustín en el Brasil, hasta el regreso a España de la não Victoria." CVD 4: 209–47.

Alburquerque, Agustín de. 1575. "Carte del P. Agustin . . . comunicando el suceso del corsario Limahon." Campo de Pangasinan 5 June 1575. HPAF 14: 234–61.

Alcina, Francisco Ignacio. 1668a. *Historia de las islas e indios de Bisayas*. Part 1, books 1–4. Victor Baltazar transcription. University of Chicago Philippine Studies Program 1962.

_____. 1668b. *Historia de las islas e indios de Bisayas* selected by Cantius Kobak and Pablo Fernández. *Philippiniana sacra* 14–20 (1978–1985).

_____. 1668c. *La historia de las islas e indios de Bisayas del Padre Alcina 1668*. Ed. Ma. Luisa Martín-Meras and Ma. Dolores Higueras. Madrid 1974.

Aldana Cabrera, García de. 1620. "Relación." Aringay 20 May 1620. AGI Filipinas 7.

Alisón, Bartolomé. 1608. "Recaudo y donación de tierras al Hospital de Los Baños." Tabuco 4 April 1608. AFIO MS.

Alonso, Carlos. 1989. *Primer viaje misional alrededor del mundo (1542–1549): Una gesta Agustiniana*. Valladolid.

Alva, Juan de. 1570. "Carta del P. Juan de Alva al Virrey de la Nueva España dándole cuenta de las islas." Panay 28 July 1570. HPAF 14: 59–62.

Alvarado, García Descalante. 1548. "Relación del viage que hizo desde la Nueva España a las islas del poniente Ruy López de Villalobos." Lisbon 1 August 1548. CDIA 5: 117–45.

Anon. n.d.a. *Um roteiro inédito de circumnavegação de Fernão de Magalhães*. Ed. M. De Jong, Coimbra 1937.

Anon. n.d.b. *El viage de Don Ruy López de Villalobos a las islas del poniente*. Ed. Consuelo Varela. Milan 1983.

Anon. 1524. "Navegacam e vyagem que fez Fernando de Magalhães de Sevilha para Maluco no anno de 1519 annos," *Collecçao de noticias para a historia e geografía das nacões ultramarinas, que vivem nos dominios Portuguezes* 4 (1): 147–76. Lisbon 1826.

Anon. 1565. "Relación del viaje y jornada de su magestad hizo en el descubrimiento de las islas del poniente . . . que fue por general el muy ilustre señor Miguel López de Legazpi." HPAF 13: 406–511.

Anon. 1566. *Copia de una carta venida de Sevilla a Miguel Salvador de Valencia*. Barcelona. BR 2: 220–30.

Anon. 1567. "Relación de lo que occurrido en el real y campo de la isla de Zubu de las Islas Philipinas desde 10 de Junio de 1565 . . . hasta el mes de Julio de 1567." CDIU 3: 91–225.

Anon. 1570. "Relation of the voyage to Luzon." BR 3: 73–104.

Anon. 1572. "Relación anónime de la conquista de la isla de Luzón." Manila 20 April 1572. HPAF 14: 73–99.

Anon. 1574a. "Relación de lo sucedido en las Islas Felipinas desde primero de julio del año de 1573." Manila 16 July 1574. HPAF 14: 217–22.

Anon. 1574b. "Relación del orden que la gente Española . . . a tenido y tiene en pacificar la tierra y sustentarse en ella." 17 September 1574. HPAF 14: 222–32.

Anon. 1578. "Relación de la Isla de Burney y jornada que allá hizo el Doctor Francisco de Sande." Manila 29 July 1578. HPAF 14: 511–25.

Anon. 1591. "Relación de la jornada que hizo don Luys Dasmariñas . . . al descubrimiento de la Nueva Tuy y sus provincias." Manila 7 July 1591. HPAF 15: 447–98.

Antolín, Francisco. 1789. *Notices of the pagan Igorots in the interior of the island of Manila.* Trans. William Henry Scott. Manila 1988.

Ávalos, Melchor de. 1585. "Dos cartas al rey contra los moros de las Filipinas, 20 de junio de 1585." In Lewis Hanke, *Cuerpo de documentos del siglo XVI sobre los derechos de España en las Indias y las Filipinas.* Mexico 1977.

Baeza, Melchor de. 1597. "Información hecha en Manila . . . acerca de los servicios prestados en Filipinas por los religiosos Agustinos." Manila 10 March 1597. HPAF 16: 114–220.

Barros, João de. 1628. *Decada terçiera de Asia de Ioão de Barros dos feitos que os Portugueses fezarão no descobrimiento e conquista dos mares e terras de Oriente.* Lisbon 1777.

Barte, Gina. 1987. Humadapnon. Unpublished ms. Manila.

Bayão, Bras. 1540. Letter to the king dated Goa 1 November 1540. Arquivo Nacional de Torre de Tombo: Corpo Cronológico, parte 1, maco 68, doc. 63.

Bellwood, Peter. 1978. *Man's conquest of the Pacific.* Auckland.

_____. 1985. *Prehistory of the Indo-Malaysian archipelago.* Sidney, New York, London.

_____. 1988. "A hypothesis for Austronesian origins," *Asian Perspectives* 26 (1984–1985): 107–18.

Beltrán, Alonso, et al. 1578–1579. "Expeditions to Borneo, Jolo, and Mindanao." *Borneo and Manila.* BR 4: 148–303.

Bergano, Diego. 1729. *Vocabulario de la lengua Pampanga en romance.* Manila 1860.

Bertuccioli, Giuliano. 1979. *A Florentine in Manila.* Manila.

Beyer, H. Otley. 1918. "The non-Christian people of the Philippines," Census of the Philippine Islands (Manila 1919) 2: 209–957.

_____. 1948. "Historical introduction" to E. Arsenio Manuel, *Chinese elements in the Tagalog language* (Manila 1948): ix–xxv.

Beyer, H. Otley and Jaime C. de Veyra. 1947. *Philippine saga: A pictorial history of the archipelago.* Manila.

Billiet, Francis and Francis Lambrecht. 1979. *Studies on Kalinga ullalim and Ifugaw orthography.* Baguio.

Blancas de San José, Francisco. 1605. *Postrimerías; o libro de los cuatro novíssimos en lengua tagala.* Binondo.

_____. 1608. *Librong pinagpinalamnan yto nang tavong Christiano sa pagcoconfesar, at sa pagcocomulgar ("Tratado de la Comunión").* Binondo.

_____. 1610. *Arte y reglas de la lengua Tagala.* Bataan.

_____. 1614a. Vocabulario de la lengua Tagala. Ms. Archives, University of Santo Tomas. Manila.

_____. 1614b. Sérmones. Ms. Philippine National Library. Manila.

_____. 1614c. Explicación de los siete sacramentos de la Santa Iglesia. Ms. Philippine National Library. Manila.

Blumentritt, Ferdinand. 1882. *Versuch einer ethnographie der Philippinen.* Gotha.

Boxer Codex. 1590a. C. R. Boxer, "A late sixteenth-century Manila ms.," *Journal of the Royal Asiatic Society* (1950): 37–49.

_____. 1590b. Carlos Quirino and Mauro Garcia, "The manners, customs, and beliefs of the Philippine inhabitants of long ago; being chapters of 'A late sixteenth-century Manila manuscript,' transcribed, translated, and annotated," *The Philippine journal of science* 87 (1958): 325–453.

Bronson, Bennet. 1977. "Against migration: A negative perspective on population movements in Southeast Asia," *Philippine quarterly of culture and society* 20 (1992): 341–57.

Brown, Donald E. 1970. *The structure and history of a Bornean Malay sultante. Brunei Museum journal* monograph 2: 2.

_____. 1984. "Brunei through the Sha'er and the Silsilah," *Solidarity* 99 (1984): 10–15.

Brown, Donald E., James W. Edwards, and Ruth P. Moore. *The penis inserts of Southeast Asia: An annotated bibliography with an overview and comparative perspectives.* Berkeley.

Bugarín, José. 1676. *Diccionario Ibanag-Español compuesto en lo antiguo por el R. P. Fr. José Bugarín.* Manila 1854.

Calleja-Reyes, Jose. 1968. "Ibalon: An ancient Bicol epic," *Philippine studies* 16: 318–47.

Carro, Andrés. 1790. *Vocabulario Iloco-Español.* Manila 1849.

Castaño, Jose. 1895. "Breve noticia acerca del origen, religión, creenccias y supersticiones de los antiguos indios del Bicol." In W. E. Retana, *Archivo del Bibliofilo Filipino* 1 (1895). Pp. 1–77.

Castro, Jovita Ventura, et al., ed. 1984. *Anthology of ASEAN literatures: Epics of the Philippines.* Manila.

Ceballos, Sancho Díaz de. 1576. Letter to the viceroy of Nueva España dated Manila 4 June 1576. AGI Filipinas 34.

Charles V. 1519. "Instrucción que dío el Rey a Magallanes y a Falero para el viage al descubrimiento de las islas de Maluco." CVD 4: 121–41.

Chen, Shao-hsing. 1962. "The migration of the Chinese from Fukien to the Philippines under the Spanish colonization and to Taiwan under the Dutch colonization: An analysis of their pattern of development and their correspondences," *Proceedings of the 2d biennial conference, International Association of Historians of Asia.* Taipei.

Chirino, Pedro. 1604. *Relación de las Islas Filipinas i de lo que en ellas an trabajado los padres de la Compañía de Jesús.* Rome.

Colín, Francisco. 1663. *Labor evangélica ministerios apostólicos de los obreros de la Compañía de Jesús, fundación y progresos de Islas Filipinas.* Ed. Pablo Pastells, 3 vols. Barcelona 1900.

Combés, Francisco. 1667. *Historia de las islas de Mindanao, Iolo y sus adyacentes.* Ed. W. E. Retana. Madrid 1897.

Coronel, Ma. Delia. 1983. "Stories from the Darangen," *Mindanao art and culture* 5.

_____. 1986–1990. *Darangen,* 6 vols. Marawi City.

Corpuz, Onofre D. 1989. *The roots of the Filipino nation.* Quezon City.

Cortés, Hernando. 1527. "Carta que escribió Hernán Cortés al rey de Cebú, manifestándole el objeto de la expedición que iba al Maluco mandada por Álvaro de Saavedra." 28 May 1527. CVD 5: 426–27.

Cosgaya, Lorenzo Fernández. 1731. *Diccionario Pangasinan-Español.* Manila 1865.

Cushner, Nicholas P. 1976. *Landed estates in the colonial Philippines.* New Haven.

Daguio, Amado. 1952. "Hudhud hi Aliguyon (The harvest song of Aliguyon)." M.A. thesis, Stanford University. In Castro, et al. 1984. Pp. 7–56.

Dasmariñas, Gómez Pérez. 1591. "Ordinance forbidding the Indians to wear Chinese stuffs" dated Manila 9 April 1591. BR 8: 78–95.

Dávalos. See Ávalos.

De la Costa, Horacio. 1967. *The Jesuits in the Philippines 1581–1768*. Cambridge (Mass.).

Delgado, Juan J. 1751. "Historia general sacro-profana, política y natural de las islas del poniente llamadas Filipinas." In *Biblioteca histórica Filipina* 1. Manila 1892.

Díaz, Casimiro. 1745. *Conquistas de las Islas Filipinas . . . Parte Segunda*. Valladolid 1890.

Díaz-Trechuelo, Lourdes. 1978. "Evolución urbana de Manila," *Cuadernos del Centro Cultural* no. 5. Manila.

Dingwall, Eric John. 1925. *Male infibulation*. London.

_____. 1931. *Artificial cranial deformation: A contribution to the study of ethnic mutilations*. London.

Eggan, Fred and E. D. Hester. 1957. *The Robertson translations of the Pavón manuscripts of 1838–1839*. University of Chicago Philippine Studies Program transcript nos. 5–a, 5–b, 5–c, 5–d. Chicago.

Encina, Francisco. 1760. *Arte de la lengua Zebuana, sacada del que escribió [Julián Bermejo]*. Manila 1836.

Enrile, Pascual. 1835. "Carácteres antiguos con los que escribían estos naturales del Tagalog y Camarines." Biblioteca del Museo Naval: Colección Enrile 18, ms. 2287, doc. 32: 214–214v. Madrid.

Espallargas, Joseph C. 1974. "A study of the ancient Philippine syllabary with particular attention to its Tagalog version." M.A. thesis, Ateneo de Manila University. Quezon City.

Espinas, Merito B. 1968. "A critical study of Ibalong: The Bikol folk epic fragment," *Unitas* 41: 177–239.

Espíritu Santo, Andrés de. 1645. "Relación de la fundación y progresos de esta Santa Provincia de S. Nicolás de Tolentino," *Boletín de la Provincia de S.N. de Tolentino de Filipinas* 54 (600: 1965): 67–179.

Ezguerra, Domingo. 1663. *Arte de la lengua Bisaya en la provincia de Leyte*. Manila 1747.

Francisco, Juan R. 1964. *Indian influences in the Philippines with special reference to language and literature*. Quezon City.

Galvão, Antonio. 1544. *A treaty on the Moluccas (c. 1544), probably the preliminary version of Antonio Galvão's lost* Historia das Moluccas. Ed. Hubert Jacobs. Rome 1971.

_____. 1563. *Tratado das descobrimentos antigos e modernos*. 3d ed. 1731, reprint 1944. Porto.

Granado, Francisco. 1529. "Relación del viage que hizo Álvaro de Saavedra, 1527–1528." CVD 5: 427–74.

Grijalva, Juan de. 1624. *Crónica de la Orden de N. P. S. Agustín en los provincias de la Nueva España*. Mexico.

Harrison, Tom and Stanley J. O'Conner. 1969. "Excavations of the prehistoric iron industry in West Borneo," *Cornell data paper* no. 72, Southeast Asia Program. Ithaca.

Herrera, Antonio de. 1601. *Historia general de los hechos de los Castellanos en las islas y terrafirme del mar Oceano: Decada terzera*. Madrid.

Hester, Evett D. 1954. *The Robertson text and translation of the Povedano manuscript of 1572*. University of Chicago Philippine Studies Program. Chicago.

_____. 1962. "Alzina's *Historia de Visayas*: A bibliographical note," *Philippine studies* 10: 331–65.

Horridge, G. Adrian. 1982. "The lashed-lug boat of the Eastern archipelagoes, the Alcina ms., and the Lomblen whaling boats." National Maritime Museum (Greenwich UK) monograph no. 5.

Huerta, Félix de. 1855. *Estado geográfico, topográfico, estadístico, histórico, religioso de la Santa y Apostólica Provincia de San Gregorio Magno.* Manila.

Isla, Juan de la. 1565. "Relación de las islas del poniente." CDIU 3: 226–43.

Jesús, Luis de. 1681. *Historia general de los religiosos descalzos del orden de los Ermitaños.* Madrid.

Jocano, F. Landa. 1957. "Hinilawod—epic of Panay," *Sunday Times Magazine* (9 June 1957). Reprinted in Castro, et al. 1984. Pp. 107–83.

_____. 1964. "Notes on the Sulod concept of death, the soul, and the region of the dead," *Philippine studies* 12 (1964): 51–62.

Keith, Agnes Newton. 1955. *Bare feet in the palace.* Boston, Toronto.

Kern, Hendrik. 1897. "Een Spanisch schrijver over den godsdienst der heidensche Bikollers" and "Een mythologisch gedicht uit de Filippijnen," *Bijdragen tot den taal-land-en volkenkunde van Nederlandsch-Indie* 47 (1897): 224–38, 498–507.

Kleiweg de Zwann, J.P. 1917. "Kunstmatige schedelvorming bij de inlanders van den Indischen Archipel," *Nederlandsch-Indie Oud & Nieuw* 2: 279–302.

Laarhoven, Ruurdje. 1989. *Triumph of Moro diplomacy: The Maguindanao sultanate in the seventeenth century.* Quezon City.

Lambrecht, Francis. 1960. "Hudhud of Aliguyun who was bored by the rustle of the palm tree at Aladugen," *Folklore studies* 19: 1–173.

_____. 1967. *The Hudhud of Dinulawan and Bugan at Gunhadan: A critical study.* (Baguio 1967). Reprinted from *Saint Louis quarterly* 5: 267–713.

Laubach, Frank. 1930. "An Odyssey from Lanao," *Philippine public schools* 3: 8. Reprinted as "How Bantugan died below the mountain by the sea" in Asuncion David-Madamba, ed., *Early Philippine literature.* Manila 1971.

Lavezares, Guido de. 1574. "Carta del Governador General de Filipinas . . . a S. M. dándole relación del estado de dichas islas." Manila 30 July 1574. HPAF 14: 193–205.

Legazpi, Miguel López de. 1565. "Bando sobre los que hubiesen abierto sepulchros y extraido de ellos oro, joyas y otras preseas." Cebu 16 May 1565. CDIU 2: 355–57.

_____. 1569a. "Carta . . . al Virrey de México, Marqués de Falces." Cebu 7 July 1569. HPAF 14: 17–24.

_____. 1569b. "Relación de las yslas Felipinas y de la calidad y condiciones de la gente della para su magestad," 7 July 1569. HPAF 14: 22n63, n65.

_____. 1570. "Copia de algunas capítulos de carta de Legazpi al Virrey de Nueva España." Panay 25 July 1570. HPAF 14: 49–53.

_____. 1572. "Copia de carta que el general . . . scrive al Virrey de la Nueva España." Manila 11 August 1572. HPAF 14: 117–31.

Lietz, Paul S. 1962. "More about Alzina's *Historia de Visayas*," *Philippine studies* 10: 366–75.

Lisboa, Marcos de. 1628a. *Vocabulario de la lengua Bicol.* Manila 1865.

_____. 1628b. *Diccionario y vocabulario de el idioma Español y Bicol.* Bound together with Lisboa 1628a. Manila 1865.

Llave, Antonio de la. 1622. *Chrónica primitiva de esta provincia de S. Gregorio . . . fecha en Manila en 4 de Mayo de 1622.* AFIO.

Loarca, Miguel de. 1582. *Relación de las Yslas Filipinas.* BR 5: 34–187.

López, Francisco. 1621. *Libro a naisurátan ámin ti bagás ti Doctrina Cristiana nga naisúrat iti libro ti Cardenal a agnagan Belarmino.* Manila 1895.
_____. 1627. *Arte de la lengua Iloca.* Ed. Andrés Carro, *Gramática Ilocana compuesta por el P. Predicador Fr. Francisco López.* Malabon 1895.
_____. 1631. *Vocabulario de la lengua Iloca.* Ms. King's College London.
Low, Hugh. 1880. "Salesilah (Book of the descent of the rajas of Brunei)," *Journal of the Straits Branch of the Royal Asiatic Society* 5: 1–31.
Lucarelli, Juan Bautista. 1592. "Viaggio," *Sinica Franciscana* 2 (1933): 3–47.
Lumbera, Bienvenido. 1968. "Assimilation and synthesis (1700–1800): Tagalog poetry in the eighteenth century," *Philippine studies* 16: 622–62.
Macapagal, Juan. 1660. Petition dated 24 November 1660. In Isabelo de los Reyes, *El folklore Filipino* 1. Manila 1887. Pp. 219–21.
Maceda, Marcelino N. 1972. "Artificial skull deformation: Its practice in the past in some Bisayan islands in the Philippines." Paper read at the Seminar on Southeast Asian Prehistory and Archaeology, National Museum mimeo. Manila.
_____. 1973. "Some remarks on artificial cranial deformation," *Philippine quarterly of culture and society* 1: 58–59.
Mafra, Ginés de. 1549. "Libro que trata del descubrimiento y principio del estrecho que se llama de Magallanes." In Antonio Blázquez y Delgado Aguilera, *Tres Relaciones.* Madrid 1920. Pp. 179–212.
Magdalena, Agustín de la. 1679. *Arte de la lengua Tagala sacada de diversas artes.* Mexico.
Malagar, Esterlinda Mendoza. 1980. "The Guman of Dumalinao: A Suban–on folk epic," *Kinaadman* 2: 253–380.
Maldonado, Juan de. 1572. "Carta en relación . . . tocante al viage y población de la Isla de Luzón en Filipinas." Rio de Panay 6 May 1572. HPAF 14: 100–109.
Manila, Cabildo de. 1576. "Copia de una carta que escrive la Ciudad de Manila al Virrey de la Nueva España." Manila 2 June 1576. HPAF 14: 365–78.
Manuel, E. Arsenio. 1958a. *The maiden of the Buhong sky.* Quezon City.
_____. 1958b. *Tuwaang attends a wedding: The second song of the Manuvu' ethnoepic Tuwaang.* Quezon City: Ateneo de Manila University Press.
_____. 1969. "Agyu: Epic of Mindanao," *Unitas* 42 (2): 1–104.
Maquiso, Elena G. 1977. *Ulahingan: An epic of the southern Philippines.* Dumaguete City.
Marcilla y Martín, Cipriano. 1895. *Estudio de los antiguos alfabetos Filipinos.* Malabon.
Marín, Esteban, et al. 1591. "El fruto de los Agustinos en Ilocos," AHHA 15 (1921): 207–19.
Marín y Morales, Valentín. 1901. *Ensayo de una síntesis de los trabajos realizados por las corporaciones religiosos en Filipinas,* 2 vols. Manila 1911.
Martínez, Domingo. 1756. *Compendio histórico de la Apostólica Provincia de San Gregorio de Philipinas de Religiosos Menores Descalzós de N. P. San Francisco.* Madrid.
Martínez, Juan. 1567. "Relación detallada de los sucesos durante el viaje de la nao San Jerónimo." CDIU 3: 371–475.
[Mas y Sans, Sinibaldo de.] 1843. *Informe sobre el estado de las Islas Filipinas en 1842.* Vol. 1. Madrid.
Mastura, Michael O. 1977. "The Maguindanao core lineage and the Dumatos," *Notre Dame journal* 7 (2): 9–24.
Meacham, William. 1988. "On the improbability of Austronesian origins in South China," *Asian perspectives* 26 (1984–1985): 89–106.

Medina, Juan de. 1630. "Historia de los sucesos de la Orden de N. Gran P. S. Agustín de estas Islas Filipinas." In *Biblioteca histórica Filipina* 4. Manila 1893.

Méndez, Martín. 1521. "El libro que trajo la nao Vitoria de las amistades que hicieron con los reyes de Maluco." In Mauricio Obregón, *La primera vuelta al mundo*. Bogotá 1984.

Méntrida, Alonso de. 1637a. *Bocabulario de la lengua Bisaya–Hiligueyna y Haría de las islas de Panay y Sugbu, y para las demás islas*. Manila 1841.

_____. 1637b. *Arte de la lengua Bisaya-Hiligayna de la isla de Panay*. Tambobong 1894.

Mercado, Pedro de. 1673. *Vida de un mancebo indio llamado Miguel Ayatumo natural de Bohollo en Filipinas*. Madrid.

Monteclaro, Pedro Alcántara. 1907. *Maragtas kon (historia) sg pulo nga Panay kutub sg iya una nga pamuluyö tobtob sg pag-abut sg mga taga Borneo nga amó ang ginhalinan sg mga Bisaya, kag sg pag-abut sg mga Kastila*. Iloilo.

Morga, Antonio de. 1609. *Sucesos de las Islas Filipinas*. Mexico. Ed. W. E. Retana. Madrid 1910.

Móriz, Rodrigo de Aganduru. 1623. "Historia general de las islas occidentales a la Asia adyacentes llammadas Philipinas," *Colección de documentos inéditos para la historia de España* 77: 1–546, 79: 1–230. Madrid 1882.

Murillo Velarde, Pedro. 1743. *Cursus Juris Canonici*.

Nápoles, Vicente de. 1534A. "Relación que presentó en Madrid el ceño 1534 Vicente de Nápoles sobre los sucesos de la armada Saavedra." CVD 5: 438–48.

_____. 1543b. "Relación de todo lo que descubrió el capitán Álvaro de Sayavedra." CDIA 5: 68–96.

Noceda, Juan José and Pedro de Sanlucar. 1753. *Vocabulario de la lengua Tagala*. Manila 1860.

Ochotorena, Gaudiosa Martinez. 1981. "Ag Tobig nog Keboklagan: A Suban-on folk epic," *Kinaadman* 3: 343–543.

Oliver, Juan de. 1590a. Declaración de la doctrina Christiana en idioma Tagalog. Ms. 21537, lot 527, Lilly Library, Bloomington (Indiana).

_____. 1590b. "Declaración de los mandamientos de la Ley de Dios." In Rosales 1984.

Opeña, Laudivina R. 1979. "Olaging: The battle of Nalandangan: A Bukidnon folk epic," *Kinaadman* 1: 151–227.

Ortega, Francisco de. 1573. "Carta al Virrey de Nueva España." Manila 6 June 1573. HPAF 14: 133–48.

Ortiz, Thomas. 1729. *Arte y reglas de la lengua Tagala*. Samloc 1740.

Oviedo y Valdes, Gonzalo Fernández de. 1557. *Historia general y natural de las Indias, islas y tierre-firme de mar oceano*, 14 vols. Asunción del Paraguay 1945.

Oyanguren, Melchor de. 1742. *Tagalysmo elucidado y reducido (en lo posible) a la Latinidad de Nebrija*. Mexico.

Pastrana Riol, Apolinar. 1982. "Fr. Bernardino Melendreras, OFM. (1815–1867), y su obra poética sobre la región del Bicol (Filipinas)," *Missionalia Hispanica* 39: 85–181.

Pavón. *See* Eggan and Hester 1957.

Peguero, Juan. 1691. "Vida del Ven P. Fr. Domingo Pérez." In Honorio Muñoz, *Un héroe dominicano montañés en Filipinas*, part 1. Santander 1951.

Pérez, Domingo. 1680. "Relación de los indios Zambales de la Playa Honda: su sitio, sus costumbres." In Honorio Muñoz, *Un héroe dominicano montañés en Filipinas*, part 2. Santander 1951.

Pérez, P. Lorenzo. 1933. "Un códice desconocido, relativo a las Islas Filipinas," *Erudición Ibero-Ultramarina* 4 (15–16): 501–29; 5 (17: 1934): 76–108.

Picornell, Pedro M. 1986. "Two early sixteenth-century Spanish landfalls on Mindanao," *Kinaadman* 8: 9–17.

_____. 1990. "The voyage of the patache 'San Lucas' 1564–1565," *Kinaadman* 12: 1–13.

Pigafetta, Antonio. 1524a.

_____. 1524b. *Primo Viaggio intorno al mondo.* BR 33: 26–366; 34: 38–180.

_____. 1524c. R. A. Skelton, "Magellan's voyage: A narrative account of the first circumnavigation . . . from the ms. in the Beinecke Rare Books and ms. Library of Yale University." New Haven 1969.

_____. 1525. "Le voyage et navigation faict par les Espaignols." Paris. In Paula Spurlin Paige, *The voyage of Antonio Pigafetta.* Englewood Cliffs (N.J.) 1969.

_____. 1550. "La Detta navigatione per messer Antonio Pigafetta Vicentino." In Giovanni Battista Ramusio, *Della navigationi et viaggi.* Venice. Pp. 380–98.

Pinto, Fernão Mendes. 1614. *Peregrinação.* New York, London 1891.

Pires, Tomé. 1515. *A suma oriental de Tomé Pires e o livro de Francisco Rodríguez: Leitura e notas de Armando Cortesão.* Coimbra 1978.

Plasencia, Juan de. 1589a. "Relación de las costumbres que los yndios solían tener en estas yslas." AGI Filipinas 18–b.

_____. 1589b. "Relación del culto que los Tagalogs tenían." In Santa Inés 1676. Pp. 598–603.

_____. 1589c. "Instrucción de las costumbres que antiguamente tenían los naturales de la Pan Panga en sus pleytos." AGI Filipinas 18–b.

[Plasencia, Juan de. 1592.] *Relación de las Islas Philipinas.* Madrid. In Cayetano Sánchez, "The first printed report on the Philippine Islands," *Philippiniana sacra* 26 (78: 1991): 473–500.

Povedano. *See* Hester 1954.

Pretty, Francis. 1588. "The admirable and prosperous voyage of the Worshiful Master Thomas Cavendish." In Richard Hakluyt, *The principal navigations, voyages, traffiques, and discoveries of the English nation,* vol. 16. Edinburgh 1890.

Quirante, Alonso Martín. 1624. "Relación del descubrimiento de las minas y pacificación de los Ygolotes en la provincia de Pangasinan." AGI Filipinas 30.

Quirino, Carlos and Mauro Garcia. 1958. "Narrative of Mr. Juan Masolong, first Christian of Lilio, Laguna, and the founding of the town in 1572,' an eighteenth-century manuscript translated and annotated, with a complete transcription of the original Tagalog text," *Bulletin of the Philippine Historical Association* 4: 13–49.

Rada, Martín de. 1569. "Copia de carta . . . al Virrey de México, dándole importante noticias sobre Filipinas." Cebu 8 July 1569. HPAF 14: 24–32.

_____. 1572. "Copia de una carta . . . al Virrey de la Nueva España." Manila 10 August 1572. HPAF 14: 110–17.

_____. 1574. "Carta al Virrey de México . . . dándole cuenta de como Juan de Salcedo fué a la conquista de Vicor e Ilocos." Manila 30 June 1574. HPAF 14: 181–86.

_____. 1577. "Carta al P. Alonso de la Veracruz . . . dándole noticias de las costumbres, ritos y clases de esclavitud que hay en Filipinas." HPAF 14: 476–94.

Resma, Virgilio. 1982. "Keg Sumba neg Sandayo: A Suban-on folk epic," *Kinaadman* 4: 259–426.

Reyes, Pedrito, Mercedes Grau-Santamaria, H. Otley Beyer, and Jaime C. de Veyra. 1953. *Pictorial history of the Philippines.* Manila.

Ribadeneira, Marcelo de. 1601. *Historia de las islas del archipiélago Filipino y reinos de la Gran China, Tartaría, Cochinchina, Malaca, Siam, Camboge y Japón.* Ed. Juan R. Legisma. Madrid 1947.

Riquel, Fernando. 1565. "Información del daño y fuerzas que los Portugueses de Maluco hizieron en las Yslas Philipinas." Bohol 25 March 1565. CDIU 2: 284–305.

_____. 1571. Act of taking possession of Manila, incorrectly dated 18 May 1572. AGI Patronato, Leg. 24, No. 24.

_____. 1573. "Las Nuevas quescriben de las yslas del poniente Hernando Riquel y otros." Manila 1 July 1573. BR 3: 230–48.

Rizal y Mercado, Jose. 1887. Letter to Ferdinand Blumentritt dated Berlin 13 April 1887. *Epistolario Rizalino* 5 (Manila: 1938): 110–13.

Rodríguez, Estevan. 1565. "Relación muy circunstanciada de la navegación que hizo el armada de S. M. a cargo del General Miguel López de Legazpi." CDIU 2: 373–427.

Román, Phelipe. 1591. "El fruto de los Agustinos en la Pampanga." AHHA 16 (1921): 257–79.

Rosales, Antonio Ma. 1984. *A study of a sixteenth-century Tagalog manuscript on the Ten Commandments: Its significance and implications.* Quezon City.

Ruiz, Miguel de. 1630. *Bocabulario Tagalog.* Ms. King's College London.

San Agustín, Andrés de. 1647. *Arte de la lengua Bicol por la ensanza de idioma en la provincia de Camarines.* Sampaloc 1795.

San Agustín, Gaspar. 1698. *Conquistas de las Islas Filipinas.* Ed. Manuel Merino. Madrid 1975.

_____. 1703. *Compendio de la lengua Tagala.* Sampaloc 1787.

San Antonio, Juan Francisco de. 1738. *Crónicas de la Apostólica Provincia de S. Gregorio de Religioso Descalzós de N. S. P. S. Francisco en las Islas Philipinas, China, Japón etc.* Parte Primera. Sampaloc.

San Buenaventura, Pedro de. 1613. *Vocabulario de lengua Tagala.* Pila.

San José, San Joseph. *See* Blancas de San José.

San Juan, Eric A. 1987. "Philippine ethnohistory: Anthropology, history, and the conception of the human as political agent," *Philippine development forum* 4 (2–3: 1987): 105ff.

Sánchez, Mateo. 1617. *Bocabulario de la lengua Bisaya.* Manila 1711.

Sánchez Fuertes, Cayetano. 1984. "Moros y Cristianos en Filipinas: Incursiones Musulmanas contra comunidades Cristianas del sur de la isla de Luzón, s. XVII," *Missionalia Hispanica* 41: 209–47.

Sande, Francisco de. 1575. "Informe de Gobernador Sande a Felipe II." Manila 6 April 1575. In Rafael Lopez, *The Christianization of the Philippines.* Manila 1965. Pp. 182–224.

_____. 1576. "Carta a Felipe II del Gobernador de Filipinas . . . da cuenta de su llegada y accidentes de su viaje." Manila 7 June 1576. HPAF 14: 387–441.

_____. 1577. "Relation and description of the Philippine Islands." Manila 8 June 1577. BR 4: 98–118.

_____. 1579. Letter to the king dated Manila 30 May 1579. BR 4: 144–47.

Santa Inés, Francisco de. 1676. "Crónica de la provincia de S. Gregorio Magno." In *Biblioteca Histórica Filipina* 2, 3. Manila 1892.

Santamaria, Alberto. 1938. "El 'Baybayin' en el Archivo de Santo Tomas," *Unitas* 14: 154–94.

_____. 1949. "Notas históricas y filológicas," *Unitas* 20: 193–95.

Santiago, Luciano P. R. 1990. "The houses of Lakandula, Matanda, and Soliman (1571–1898): Genealogy and group identity," *Philippine quarterly of culture and society* 18: 39–73.

Santisteban, Gerónimo. 1547. "Carta escrita a Don Antonio Mendoza . . . relacionando la pérdida de la armada que salió . . . al cargo de Ruy López de Villalobos." Cochin 22 January 1547. CDIA 15 (1870): 151–65.

Santos, Domingo de los. 1703. *Vocabulario de la lengua Tagala*. Sampaloc 1794.

Scott, William Henry. 1974. *The discovery of the Igorots: Spanish contacts with the pagans of northern Luzon*. Quezon City.

_____. 1982a. *Cracks in the parchment curtain and other essays in Philippine history*. Quezon City.

_____. 1982b. "Why then the Butuan tradition?" *Kinaadman* 4: 163–65.

_____. 1984. *Pre-Hispanic source materials for the study of Philippine history*. 2d ed. Quezon City.

_____. 1986. "Why did Tupas betray Dagami?" *Philippine quarterly of culture and society* 14: 12–31.

_____. 1990a. "Sixteenth-century Visayan food and farming," *Philippine quarterly of culture and society* 18: 291–311.

_____. 1990b. "Visayan religion at the time of Spanish advent," *Philippiniana sacra* 25 (75): 397–415.

_____. 1992a. *Looking for the pre-Hispanic Filipino and other essays in Philippine history*. Quezon City.

_____. 1992b. "Lost Visayan literature," *Kinaadman* 14: 19–30.

Shaariffuddin, P. M. 1969. "Brunei cannon," *Brunei Museum journal* 1 (1): 72–93.

Solheim, Wilhelm G. II. 1988. "The Nusantao hypothesis: The origin and spread of Austronesian speakers," *Asian perspectives* 26 (1984–1985): 77–88.

Sotomayor, Juan Paes de, et al. 1597. "Información hecha en Manila . . . acerca de los servicios prestados en Filipinas por los religiosos Agustinos." [Madrid] HPAF 16: 114–220.

Teixera, Manuel. 1961. *The Portuguese missions in Malacca and Singapore (1511–1958)*. Lisbon.

Tello, Francisco. 1599. Letter to the king dated Manila 14 July 1599. BR 10: 245–92.

Thomaz, Luis Filipe F. R. 1979. "Les Portugais dans les mers de l'archipel au XVIe siecle," *Archipel* 18: 105–25.

_____. 1986. "Malacca's society on the eve of the Portuguese conquest." Paper presented at the International Conference on Malay Civilization. Kuala Lumpur.

Torre, Hernando de la. 1528. "Derretero del viage y navigación de la armada de Loaisa." CVD 5: 241–313.

Totanes, Sebastián de. 1748a. *Arte de la lengua Tagala*. Binondo 1865.

_____. 1748b. *Manual Tagalog por auxilio de los religiosos de esta provincia de S. Gregorio Magno*. Binondo 1865.

Urdaneta, Andrés de. 1536. "Relación del viaje de la armada del Comendador García de Loaisa a las islas de la especiera o Moluccas en 1525." HPAF 13: 3–187.

_____. 1537. "La relación que Andrés de Urdaneta aze a V. S. M. de la armada que V. M. mandó para la especería con el comandador Loaysa . . . es lo siguiente." Valladolid 26 February 1537. HPAF 13: 218–72.

Urdaneta, Andrés de, et al. 1536. "Relación de lo que dixeron ciertos testigos con juramento que se les tomó por los del consejo de las yndias sobre el viaje del Comandador Loaisa a los Molucos." HPAF 13: 187–218.

Van Dijk, L. C. D. 1862. *Neerland's vroegste betrekkingen met Borneo, den Solo-Archipel, Cambodja, Siam en Cochin-China.* Amsterdam. Selections translated in J. Heuschen, "Relations of the East Indies Company with Borneo (Brunei), the Sulu Archipelago, Mindanao, etc.," *Brunei Museum journal* 5 (1984): 6–34.

Van Leur, J. C. 1955. *Indonesian trade and society: Essays in Asian social and economic history.* Dordrecht 1983.

Van Noort, Olivier. 1601. *De reis om wereld door Olivier Van Noort 1599–1601.* 's Gravenhage 1926.

Vera, Santiago de. 1587. "Carta del Governador de Filipinas . . . al Virrey de México, dándole cuenta del estado de las Islas Filipinas." Manila 25 June 1587. HPAF 15: 265–85.

_____. 1589. "Carta . . . refiere la rebelión que intentaron algunos principales de Filipinas." Manila 13 July 1589. HPAF 15: 370–87.

Villegas, Ramon N. 1983. *Kayamanan: The Philippine jewelry tradition.* Manila.

Wernstedt, Frederick L. and J. E. Spencer. 1967. *The Philippine island world: A physical, cultural, and regional geography.* Berkeley, Los Angeles.

Wicks, Robert S. 1992. *Money, markets, and trade in early Southeast Asia.* Ithaca.

Yabes, Leopoldo Y. 1935. *The Ilocano epic.* Manila 1935. Reprinted in *Philippine social sciences and humanities review* 23 (1958): 283–337.

Zamora, Juan Pobre de. 1595. "Historia de la pérdida y descubrimiento del galeón *San Felipe*," chapters 15–16. In Fidel de Lejarza, "Los indios de Camarines en el siglo XVI," *Missionalia Hispanica* 9 (1952): 394–403.

Zorc, R. David. 1984. "The Philippine language scene—the sociololinguistic contributions of historical linguistics," *Philippine journal of linguistics* 14–15: 135–48.

Zuñiga, Joaquín Martínez de. 1798. *Estadismo de las Islas Filipinas, o mis viajes por este país.* Ed. W. E. Retana. Madrid 1893.

Zweig, Stefan. 1938. *Conqueror of the seas: The story of Magellan.* New York.

Index